THE REVELS PLAYS

Former general editors
Clifford Leech
F. David Hoeniger
E. A. J. Honigmann
Eugene M. Waith

General editors
David Bevington, Richard Dutton, Alison Findlay,
J. R. Mulryne and Helen Ostovich

THE FIRST AND SECOND PARTS
OF KING EDWARD IV

MANCHESTER
1824

Manchester University Press

THE REVELS PLAYS

THE REVELS PLAYS

THE FIRST AND SECOND PARTS OF KING EDWARD IV

THOMAS HEYWOOD

edited by Richard Rowland

MANCHESTER
UNIVERSITY PRESS

Manchester and New York

Distributed exclusively in the USA by Palgrave

Published by Manchester University Press
Oxford Road, Manchester M13 9NR, UK
and Room 400, 175 Fifth Avenue, New York, NY 10010, USA
www.manchesteruniversitypress.co.uk

Distributed exclusively in the USA by
Palgrave, 175 Fifth Avenue, New York NY 10010, USA

Distributed exclusively in Canada by
UBC Press, University of British Columbia, 2029 West Mall,
Vancouver, BC, Canada V6T 1Z2

British Library Cataloguing-in-Publication Data
A catalogue record for this book is available from the British Library

Library of Congress Cataloging-in-Publication Data
A catalog record for this book is available from the Library of Congress

ISBN 13: 978-0-7190-8064-7

First published in hardback 2005 by Manchester University Press
This paperback edition first published 2009

Printed by Lightning Source

Contents

General Editors' Preface

Clifford Leech conceived of the Revels Plays as a series in the mid-1950s, modelling the project on the New Arden Shakespeare. The aim, as he wrote in 1958, was 'to apply to Shakespeare's predecessors, contemporaries and successors the methods that are now used in Shakespeare's editing'. The plays chosen were to include well-known works from the early Tudor period to about 1700, as well as others less familiar but of literary and theatrical merit: 'the plays included', Leech wrote, 'should be such as to deserve and indeed demand performance'. We owe it to Clifford Leech that the idea became reality. He set the high standards of the series, ensuring that editors of individual volumes produced work of lasting merit, equally useful for teachers and students, theatre directors and actors. Clifford Leech remained General Editor until 1971, and was succeeded by F. David Hoeniger, who retired in 1985.

Since 1985 the Revels Plays have been under the direction of four General Editors: initially David Bevington, E. A. J. Honigmann, J. R. Mulryne and E. M. Waith. E. A. J. Honigmann retired in 2000 and was succeeded by Richard Dutton. E. M. Waith retired in 2003. Published originally by Methuen, the series is now published by Manchester University Press, embodying essentially the same format, scholarly character and high editorial standards of the series as first conceived. The series concentrates on plays from the period 1558–1642, and includes a small number of non-dramatic works of interest to students of drama. Some slight changes have been made: for example, in editions from 1978 onward, notes to the introduction are placed together at the end, not at the foot of the page. Collation and commentary notes continue, however, to appear on the relevant pages.

The text of each Revels play, in accordance with established practice in the series, is edited afresh from the original text of best authority (in a few instances, texts), but spelling and punctuation are modernised and speech headings are silently made consistent. Elisions in the original are also silently regularised, except where metre would be affected by the change; since 1968 the '-ed' form is used for non-syllabic terminations in past tenses and past participles ('-'d' earlier), and '-èd' for syllabic ('-ed' earlier). The editor emends, as distinct from modernises, the original only in instances where error is patent, or at least very probable, and correction persuasive. Act divisions are given only if they appear in the original or if the structure of the play clearly points to them. Those act and scene divisions not in the original are provided in small type. Square brackets are also used for any other additions to or changes in the stage directions of the original.

Revels Plays do not provide a variorum collation, but only those variants which require the critical attention of serious textual students. All departures of substance from 'copy-text' are listed, including any relineation and those changes in punctuation which involve to any degree a decision between alternative interpretations; but not such accidentals as turned letters, nor necessary additions to stage directions whose editorial nature is already made clear by the use of brackets. Press corrections in the 'copy-text' are likewise collated. Of later emendations of the text, only those are given which as alternative readings still deserve attention.

One of the hallmarks of the Revels Plays is the thoroughness of their annotations. Besides explaining the meaning of difficult words and passages, the editor provides comments on customs or usage, text or stage-business—indeed, on anything judged pertinent and helpful. Each volume contains an Index to the Commentary, in which particular attention is drawn to meanings for words not listed in *OED*, and (starting in 1996) an indexing of proper names and topics in the Introduction and Commentary.

The introduction to a Revels play assesses the authority of the 'copy-text' on which it is based, and discusses the editorial methods employed in dealing with it; the editor also considers the play's date and (where relevant) sources, together with its place in the work of the author and in the theatre of its time. Stage history is offered, and in the case of a play by an author not previously represented in the series a brief biography is given.

It is our hope that plays edited in this fashion will promote further scholarly and theatrical investigation of one of the richest periods in theatrical history.

Acknowledgements

I've taken so long to complete this edition that some of those who deserve mention are sadly no longer around to receive their due; nevertheless, I would like to thank Don Fowler, Don McKenzie and Jeremy Maule for help in the early stages. I am grateful to Caroline Barron and Vanessa Harding, both of whom invited me more than once to talk to the informed and informative audience at the Institute for Historical Research in London, and both of whom solved awkward problems too. I would also like to thank Mary Bly, Sos Eltis, Roger Holdsworth, Richard Proudfoot and David Womersley for invaluable assistance. Anne Barton first introduced me to Thomas Heywood, and she has been endlessly encouraging ever since. Out of an unholy mess of black-letter type, my constant alterations and technological incompetence, Fiona Tweedie produced not only a legible text but a measure of calm; to her and to Mandy, thanks a lot. Gemma Varnom helped me greatly with the preparation of the index. Richard Dutton has been an exemplary General Editor, responding to queries with speed and enthusiasm; the painstaking work of John Banks as copyeditor has saved me from countless errors and has made the edition much better than it would otherwise have been. It has been a real pleasure to complete the project in the English Department at York, where my colleagues— especially the Writing and Performance team of Mike Cordner, Mary Luckhurst, Judith Buchanan and John David Rhodes—have provided such a convivial and stimulating environment. Isabel Davis suggested numerous improvements while I was working on the Introduction, and delightful distractions when I wasn't.

I probably first read *Edward IV* about the year Joe was born, so it's been a presence all his life, and probably not always a comfortable one. But he's never complained about it (only about other bits of bad parenting!), and since the project would never have been finished without his amazing patience and support, the book is dedicated to him.

Abbreviations

EDITIONS (IN CHRONOLOGICAL ORDER)

Q1 The First and Second partes of King Edward *the Fourth*. Containing His mery pastime with the Tanner of Tamwoorth, as also his loue to fayre Mistresse Shoare, her great promotion, fall and mi*sery*, *and lastly the lamentable death of both her and her husband*. Likewise the beseidging of London, by the bastarde Falconbridge, and the valiant defence of the same by the Lord Maior and the Cittizens[.] As it has diuers times beene publiquely played by the Right Honorable the Earle of Derby his seruants. Imprinted at London by *I. W. for Iohn Oxenbridge*, dwelling in Paules Churchyard at the signe of the Parrat. 1599. [The unique copy is in the Newberry Library, Chicago.]

Q2 Printed by F[elix] K[ingston] for Humfrey Lownes and John Oxenbridge, London, 1600. Copy consulted: British Library, C.71 d.4.

Q3 Printed by H[umfrey L[ownes] for Nathaniel Fosbrooke, London, 1605. Copies consulted: Victoria and Albert Museum, Dyce Collection 26, Box 18, 1 and 2.

Q4 Printed by Humfrey Lownes, London 1613. Copies consulted: British Library, C.12 f.11 (1); Bodleian Library, 8° T 27 (1) Art.Seld.

Q5 Printed by Humfrey Lownes, London, 1619. Copy consulted: Victoria and Albert Museum, Dyce Collection, Box 18, 3.

Q6 Printed by Humfrey Lownes, London, 1626. Copies consulted: Bodleian Library, Mal. 248 (3); Worcester College, Oxford.

F Barron Field (ed.), *The First and Second Parts of King Edward IV: Histories by Thomas Heywood*; Reprinted from the unique black letter first edition [*sic*] of 1600, collated with one other in black letter, and with those of 1619 and 1626 (London: Shakespeare Society, 1842).

P R. H. Shepherd (ed.), *The Dramatic Works of Thomas Heywood*, 6 vols (London: John Pearson, 1874), vol. 1.

OTHER WORKS

Arber E. Arber, *A Transcript of the Registers of the Company of Stationers of London*, 5 vols (London, 1875–94).

Archer I. A. Archer, *The Pursuit of Stability: Social Relations in Elizabethan London* (Cambridge, 1991).

Berry H. Berry, 'The Playhouse in the Boar's Head Inn, Whitechapel', in D. Galloway (ed.), *The Elizabethan Theatre* (London, 1969).

Carson N. Carson, *A Companion to Henslowe's Diary* (Cambridge, 1988).

Chambers E. K. Chambers, *The Elizabethan Stage*, 4 vols (Oxford, 1923).

Child F. J. Child (ed.), *The English and Scottish Popular Ballads*, 5 vols (1882–98; rpt New York, 1965).

Commines   *The History of Comines, Englished by Thomas Danett, 1596,* The Tudor Translations, 2 vols 17 and 18 (1896; rpt New York, 1967).

CSPD   *Calendar of State Papers Domestic.*

Dekker   F. Bowers (ed.), *The Dramatic Works of Thomas Dekker,* 4 vols (Cambridge, 1953–61).

Deloney   F. O. Mann (ed.), *The Works of Thomas Deloney* (Oxford, 1912).

Dent   R. W. Dent, *Proverbial Language in English Drama Exclusive of Shakespeare* (Berkeley, 1984).

Drayton   J. W. Hebel (ed.), *The Works of Michael Drayton,* 5 vols (Oxford, 1931–41).

Fabyan   H. Ellis (ed.), *The New Chronicle of Robert Fabyan* (London, 1811).

Grafton   H. Ellis (ed.), *Grafton's Chronicle,* 2 vols (London, 1809).

Gransden   A. Gransden, *Historical Writing in England, II, c.1307 to the Early Sixteenth Century* (London, 1982).

Great Chronicle   A. H. Thomas, I. D. Thornley (eds), *The Great Chronicle of London* (London, 1938).

Greg   W. W. Greg, *A Bibliography of the English Printed Drama to the Restoration,* 4 vols (rpt London, 1970).

Grosart   A. B. Grosart (ed.), *The Non-Dramatic Works of Thomas Dekker,* 5 vols (rpt New York, 1963).

Hall   H. Ellis (ed.), *The Union of the Two Noble and Illustre Families of York and Lancaster* (London, 1809).

Halliwell   J. O. Halliwell (ed.), *A Chronicle of the First Thirteen Years of the Reign of Edward the Fourth* (Camden Society, original series, X, 1839).

Henslowe   R. A. Foakes, R. T. Rickert (eds), *Henslowe's Diary* (Cambridge, 1961).

HMC   Historical Manuscripts Commission.

Holinshed   Henry Ellis (ed.), *Holinshed's Chronicles,* 6 vols (London, 1807–8).

Itinerary   L. T. Smith (ed.), *The Itinerary of John Leland,* 5 vols (Carbondale, 1964).

Jonson   C. H. Herford, P. and E. Simpson (eds), *The Works of Ben Jonson,* 11 vols (Oxford, 1925–53).

Lyly   R. W. Bond (ed.), *The Complete Works of John Lyly,* 3 vols (Oxford, 1902).

Mancini   Dominic Mancini, *The Usurpation of Richard III,* ed. and trans. C. A. J. Armstrong (Oxford, 1969).

Massinger   P. Edwards, C. Gibson (eds), *The Plays and Poems of Philip Massinger,* 5 vols (Oxford, 1976).

Middleton   A. H. Bullen (ed.), *The Works of Thomas Middleton,* 8 vols (Boston, 1885).

More   R. S. Sylvester (ed.), *The History of King Richard III,* Yale edition of *The Complete Works of Sir Thomas More,* vol. 2 (New Haven, 1963).

MSR   Malone Society Reprints.

Murray   John Tucker Murray, *English Dramatic Companies, 1558–1642,* 2 vols (London, 1910).

Myers   A. R. Myers, *The Household of Edward IV* (Manchester, 1959).

Nashe   R. B. McKerrow (ed.), *The Works of Thomas Nashe,* 5 vols (rev. ed. F. P. Wilson, Oxford, 1966).

Nichols J. Nichols, *The Progresses and Public Processions of Queen Elizabeth*, 3 vols (London, 1823).
Peele C. T. Prouty (ed.), *The Life and Works of George Peele*, 3 vols (New Haven, 1952–70).
Percy J. W. Hales, F. J. Furnivall (eds), *Bishop Percy's Folio MS*, 3 vols (London, 1868).
REED Records of Early English Drama.
Ross C. Ross, *Edward IV* (London, 1974).
Scofield C. L. Scofield, *The Life and Reign of Edward the Fourth*, 2 vols (London, 1923).
Sharpe R. R. Sharpe, *London and the Kingdom*, 3 vols (London, 1894–95).
Sisson C. J. Sisson, *The Boar's Head Theatre: An Inn-yard Theatre of the Elizabethan Age*, ed. and introduced S. Wells (London, 1972).
Survey C. L. Kingsford (ed.), *John Stow: A Survey of London*, 2 vols (Oxford, 1908).
Virgil H. Ellis (ed.), *Three Books of Polydore Virgil's English History* (London, Camden Society, 1844).
Webster F. L. Lucas (ed.), *The Complete Works of John Webster*, 4 vols (London, 1927).
MALONE SOCIETY EDITIONS
Anon., *A Knack to Know a Knave*, ed. R. Proudfoot (Oxford, 1965).
Anon., *Clyomon and Clamydes*, ed. W. W. Greg (Oxford, 1913).
Anon., *Edmund Ironside*, ed. E. Boswell (Oxford, 1929).
Anon., *George a Green*, ed. F. W. Clarke (Oxford, 1911).
Anon., *The Life and Death of Jack Straw*, ed. K. Muir (Oxford, 1957).
Anon., *The Rare Triumphs of Love and Fortune*, ed. W. W. Greg (Oxford, 1931).
Anon., *The True Tragedy of Richard the Third*, ed. W. W. Greg (Oxford, 1929).
Anon., *Thomas of Woodstock*, ed. W. P. Frijlinck (Oxford, 1929).
Anon., *Tom a Lincoln*, ed. R. Proudfoot (Oxford, 1992).
Heywood, T., *If You Know Not Me You Know No Body*, Parts 1 and 2, ed. M. Doran (Oxford, 1935).
Heywood, T., *The Captives*, ed. A. Brown (Oxford, 1953).
Heywood, T., *The Escapes of Jupiter*, ed. H. D. Janzen (Oxford, 1978).
Munday, A., *John a Kent and John a Cumber*, ed. M. St Clare Byrne (Oxford, 1923).
Munday, A., *The Downfall of Robert Earl of Huntingdon*, ed. J. C. Meagher (Oxford, 1965).
Munday, A., *The Death of Robert Earl of Huntingdon*, ed. J. C. Meagher (Oxford, 1967).
Munday, A., *The Book of Sir Thomas More*, ed. W. W. Greg (rpt Oxford, 1990).
Shakespeare, W., *The First Part of the Contention*, ed. W. Montgomery (Oxford, 1985).

References to Shakespeare are to the latest Arden editions, series 3 or series 2.

Introduction

THE PLAYERS AND THEIR PATRON

The assertion that *Edward IV* belonged in the repertoire of a company under the patronage of Sir William Stanley, the sixth Earl of Derby, is stated on the title pages of the first five editions of the play. The sixth and final early edition of the play, issued in 1626, omits all reference to any company of players. As a guide to the play's theatrical provenance, this link with Derby raises as many questions as it answers, because hard evidence concerning the character, personnel, repertoire and even playing spaces associated with 'Derby's Men', particularly as a London operation in the last decade of the Queen's reign, is scattered and inconclusive.

The Stanley family had connections with drama almost from the inception of commercial theatre in England. Sir Henry Stanley, eventually the fourth Earl, lent his patronage (in his capacity as Lord Strange) to a company which is found touring the southern counties as early as 1563.[1] The confusion surrounding what Sir Edmund Chambers referred to as a 'history perhaps more complicated than that of any other group' begins when a company of players bearing the title of Lord Strange's Men, under the patronage of the flamboyant Ferdinando Stanley, the eldest son of the Earl, are discovered touring throughout the 1580s, finally emerging in London in 1589 as the objects of—and defiers of—an attempt to suppress them by the Lord Mayor.[2] Strange's company survived this fracas with the civic authorities and went on to make several prestigious appearances at court in the early 1590s, and to enjoy a highly successful season in 1592 at the Rose theatre under the management of Philip Henslowe, where their performances included Kyd's *The Spanish Tragedy* and Marlowe's *The Jew of Malta*. In September 1593 Henry Stanley died and Ferdinando succeeded him as the fifth Earl of Derby; his company, for the six months he lived to enjoy the title, briefly became known as the Earl of Derby's Players, but under this appellation their only recorded performances were in Coventry and Leicester, although they also appeared as such on the title page of the 1594 quarto of *Titus Andronicus*.[3]

I

In April 1594 Ferdinando died and William became the sixth Earl of Derby. By the autumn of that year a company bearing his name made their first appearance—it was at Norwich—for which records have survived. This was presumably the nucleus of the company to which the first performances of *Edward IV* are accredited, but the identities and talents of its members are practically irrecoverable, not least because virtually every actor of distinction recorded as having been working in the earlier incarnation of Derby's/ Strange's Men—including Richard Burbage, William Sly, John Hemminges, Augustine Phillips, Will Kempe and probably William Shakespeare—accepted, on Ferdinando's death, the patronage of Henry Lord Hunsdon, and regrouped as the more prestigious—and far better documented—Lord Chamberlain's Men.

Evidence detailing the activities of Derby's Men over the next five years is widespread if perfunctory, and suggests that during this period they were almost exclusively a touring company. In 1599, however, the company appears to have extended its horizons, and there followed a brief period of more rewarding activities which included performances in the capital and at court, and which encouraged the production and printing of plays written specifically for them, of which the most important is *Edward IV*. For two years Derby's Men virtually disappear from the provincial registers—a visit to Leicester in October 1599 is their only recorded performance outside London between the autumn of that year and a stressful venture into East Anglia in the summer of 1602—and the evidence suggests that the company was now prepared to focus its efforts on performances in a newly acquired playhouse in the capital.

The emergence of Derby's Men as an established London-based company, however, was politically contentious, legally complex and indeed violent. The process was prefaced by either an amalgamation with, or large-scale defections from, another company, the Earl of Worcester's Men. A key figure in this scenario is Robert Browne, listed as far back as 1583 as a leading player and sharer in the Worcester company. In a letter (probably dating from 1597) written by the Earl of Derby's wife to her uncle, Sir Robert Cecil, Browne is now named as a player in her husband's service.[4] It is likely that Browne acted as an adviser to first Oliver Woodlif, and later to Richard Samwell, businessmen who had acquired a controlling interest in an inn-yard playing space, and who were now planning the extensive improvements and extensions which would turn that space into a permanent home for a newly enlarged company.[5] Their schemes soon met with opposition from the highest quarters. By February 1597 the Privy Council had clearly heard rumours of the emergence of a 'third' company in London, and they wrote sternly to both the Master of the Revels and the Justices of the Peace in Middlesex, insisting that this 'third company may be suppressed and none suffered heereafter to plaie but those two formerlie named belonging to us'.[6] In short, they acted to protect the exclusive rights of the Admiral's Men (playing at Henslowe's Rose) and the Chamberlain's Men (playing at the Curtain).

And yet, the prospects for the new operation must have seemed, for a while, rather favourable. The playhouse, the Boar's Head, stood approximately where the Petticoat Lane Market still operates, with its main entrance in Whitechapel Street. The playing space already existed—irregular performances had been taking place in the inn-yard for several years—but was now thoroughly modernized. With the provision of new galleries for spectators, not only could the Boar's Head boast a playgoing capacity to match their rivals, but also, since both the galleries and the stage would appear to have been covered, it could lay claim to being the first (and at that time only) all-weather playhouse offering performances by adult players. It is even possible that the inn's ample facilities for accommodation could have provided living-in quarters for the sharers and the core of the newly assembled company. Browne had eventually obtained a licence to play at the theatre from the Master of the Revels, and had attracted some impressive names to assist him in the launch of this new enterprise, including the prolific dramatist/actor Thomas Heywood, who arrived from Henslowe's Rose, and John Duke, the first player to transfer from the Chamberlain's Men. And so, with Browne holding bonds which theoretically secured for the Boar's Head the exclusive services of the six other principal sharers in the company, playing commenced in earnest in the Michaelmas season of 1599; and it is likely that *Edward IV*, licensed with the Stationers' Register on 28 August, was one of the first plays the new outfit offered, just as it is certain that it is the earliest (extant) play which was written especially for them.

But this opening season proved anything but peaceful. The entrepreneur Woodlif had effectively sold his rights to the inn twice over, first to Samwell and Browne, but then again, in a transaction dated 7 November 1599, to a maverick hustler called Francis Langley. Langley was in desperate financial trouble, not least because of his involvement in the demise of another theatrical venture, at the Swan playhouse—a collapse accelerated if not generated by a scandal in 1597 over the lost satirical play *The Isle of Dogs*, which landed Ben Jonson in prison, drove Thomas Nashe into hiding in Yarmouth and lost Langley his licence to put on plays. Rendered impatient by the enforced sale of his property in Paris Garden, Langley pre-empted the manoeuvres of the courts which had frustrated him, and, to lay claim to his stake in the Boar's Head, took the 'law' into his own hands. On 13 December, accompanied by an occupying force of seven men, Langley stormed into the inn-yard just as a performance was about to begin. This gang took possession of the stage, tiring house and galleries, and threatened Samwell's workmen and Browne's fellow actors alike. Browne himself still had vivid memories of the incident when he was asked to describe it in May 1603; in particular he recalled how Langley 'offered to disturbe the said Playes and Comodyes to be acted on the said Stage . . . and for feare thereof Extorted from the players there diuerse sommes of Money to permytt the said Comedyes there quietly to be acted . . .'.[7] But Langley had not done yet. He staged an apparently gratuitous show of strength at the theatre again three days later, and then, on 24 December, made an indelible mark on the fabric of the playhouse itself: he and his thugs broke down walls in the main gallery and opened up a new doorway which connected directly with Langley's parlour in the residential section of the inn. Now in control of the entrances and exits, on 26 December Langley turned this strategic advantage into instant profit: as the company played to a full house, Langley's agents collected, pocketed and departed with the gate receipts.

    It is impossible to be sure how much the writer of *Edward IV* could have known about Langley during the period of the play's composition, but, as we shall see, he was remarkably responsive to the most recent developments in political, economic and theatrical affairs, and there are striking correspondences between his portrayal of the extortionist Rufford—a character found neither in the chronicle sources nor in extant documents of the 1590s—and the racketeer who disrupted life at the Boar's Head. At the very least, the angry exchanges between the Shores and Rufford might have acquired a particular intensity when played by actors who were being intimidated by Langley, a 'barrator and common disturber of [her] majesty's subjects' who operated through 'prosecuting suits by sinister vexation of [her] subjects and upon buying of many other pretended rights and titles to lands and tenements and of divers debts', and against whom Sir Edward Coke had already given evidence in Star Chamber in July 1599, in a case examining the exaction of bribes from struggling East Anglian clothiers.[8]

Despite the turbulent atmosphere in their own playhouse, the company under Browne's stewardship did not collapse. Indeed, they made the first of their three most prestigious appearances of all only seven weeks after Langley's incursions; on 18 February they played at court. The only other evidence connected with the company surviving from 1600 is the transfer of the printing rights to *Edward IV* (from John Busbie to Humfrey Lownes), which occurred five days later. The next we hear of them is when they returned to play at court, on both 1 and 6 January (Twelfth Night), at the beginning of 1601.[9] There is, however, an unusual and significant feature in the entry in the court accounts recording the 1601 performances: in a ten-year span on either side of the entry, this is the only one which names the recipient of the payment (Browne) but which fails to add the name of the company he represents. This anomaly is surely indicative of the fluid, perhaps chaotic state of the company's affairs and identity. Whatever else Langley's violent interventions had achieved, it is certain that internal divisions amongst the players had been exacerbated in the process. A sequence of litigation and amalgamation was beginning, in which Browne would be the loser, and from which a larger and stronger company would emerge to carry *Edward IV* to popular success in playhouses less troubled than the Boar's Head. And the name of 'Derby's Men' would disappear from the theatrical life of London to return, rather ignominiously, to the provinces.

In March 1602 Thomas Heywood and John Duke were still playing at the Boar's Head, suing Browne, and declaring themselves, in both ventures, members of the Earl of Worcester's company. It seems as if this new, and powerfully backed conglomerate had absorbed not only those players in the 'Derby' operation who wished to join but also members of an even more nebulous group, the Earl of Oxford's players.[10] By September 1602 Worcester's Men had probably extricated themselves from the Boar's Head, and had begun a more stable if brief residency at Henslowe's Rose playhouse; in that month the impressario lent Thomas Heywood 2*s* 6*d* to buy himself silk garters, and the player Richard Perkins 15*s* to 'bye things for thomas hewode playe'.[11] It seems that around this time, *Edward IV*, the most successful product of the short-lived London operation mounted by Derby's Men, underwent substantial alterations in preparation for new performances by the company to which most of Derby's leading players had transferred; an undated entry in Henslowe's 'Diary' reads, 'Receiued of m^r Philip Hinchloes in earnest of the Booke of Shoare, now newly to be written for the Earle of worcesters players at the Rose of m^r Henchloes xl^s . . .'. There is some doubt as to whether this entry is in the hand of the playwright Henry Chettle, but by May of 1603 his involvement in the revamped *Edward IV* is clear: 'Lent at the apoyntment of Thomas hewode & Iohn ducke vnto harey chettell & Iohn daye in earneste of A playe wherin shores wiffe is writen the some of xxxx^s.[12]

In October 1603 the hapless Robert Browne died. His widow, Susan, married again rapidly, and her new husband, a comic player called Thomas Greene, soon emerged as a leading member of the company which owned *Edward IV*. Early in the reign of James this company changed patron and name yet again, and the King granted the newly titled Queen's Men a licence to perform at both the Curtain amphitheatre and the Boar's Head.[13] But this document may never have received the official sanction of the Great Seal, and it was not until April 1605 that the company received royal approval for its move to their new, and much more durable home. It was here, at the Red Bull playhouse, that the popularity and notoriety of *Edward IV* would be firmly established.[14]

THE PLAY ON THE EARLY MODERN STAGE

In its first five or six years of existence the play was performed by three linked but separate companies on the stages of at least three different playhouses. This would suggest that the play makes no exceptional demands in terms of either staging or personnel, and this is indeed the case. The play makes repeated and extensive use of a playing space which needs to be 'above'. This is unlikely to have posed insurmountable difficulties at the Boar's Head, and it would have been normal practice at both the Rose and the Red Bull.[15] Properties are similarly minimal: a ladder is specified for the scene in which Shore and Stranguidge are almost hanged (Part Two, Scene 12, l. 43.1), and the same arrangement is required for the actual execution of Aire (Scene 22, l. 45.1); drums and trumpets are needed for battle and ceremonial scenes, as are the customary array of swords and clubs. Costume is vitally important in the play, and the dramatist's instructions are detailed but not extravagant: neither the regalia of the London governors nor the multiple disguises adopted by the King and his courtiers would have stretched the resources of any playing company. Another easily achieved but noteworthy feature of the play's visual design is the repeated significance of food. A table should display the homely fare offered by Hobs (and ignored by Edward) in Part One, Scene 14, and the '*Banquet*' called for at Scene 17, l. 55.1 should be as elaborate as possible in order to register the King's even more shocking violation of the Lord Mayor's hospitality. The playwright is painstakingly precise in Part Two, Scene 20, in listing the ale, cheese and bread which Jockie secretly conveys to Jane (see ll. 255.1-2), but the audience should also be able to see that the 'relief' offered her earlier in the scene (see ll. 55.1 and 179.1) is in the form of food parcels. As we shall see, the distribution—or wastage—of vital foodstuffs was of crucial significance for spectators in the 1590s.

Casting is similarly unproblematic. What follows is a conjectural reconstruction of how actors may have been deployed in Part One, but similar strategies would work equally well in Part Two. Like most chronicle history plays, *1 Edward IV* has a formidable number of speaking roles: there are thirty-three individually named parts, not including the minor ones of the huntsmen in Scene 12, the apprentices of Scene 17, the watermen of Scene 22 or the various messengers which the text calls for. In addition, some scenes, such as those in which the King enters with a 'train', or in which the apprentices 'do great service' in combating the rebels, clearly demand a number of extra bodies. Three factors, however, would have helped the company manage this multiplicity of roles. First, the play has a tripartite structure. The insurrection which dominates the opening scenes is effectively over by the play's half-way point, and of the voluble rebels only Falconbridge himself, in the unusual scene (15) of his obduracy and execution, makes any further appearance. The second factor, linked to the first, is the episodic nature of the scenes' organization. Although the dramatist builds a remarkable series of conceptual, verbal and visual connections between the various sections of the play, it is clear that the scenes of banter with Hobs the tanner and the scenes of the Shores' domestic crisis possess a discrete coherence and are essentially self-contained. The third factor—and one which sets the play at some distance from most of its generic contemporaries—is the dearth of genuine 'starring' roles. Even the part of the eponymous protagonist himself is neither particularly long nor demanding; indeed, after the opening scene, Edward disappears completely from the stage until the close of the ninth, a conspicuous absence which lasts for more than a third of Part One's playing time. It is conceivable that the playwright was aware that the company did not have the services of an Alleyn or a Burbage to hand.

The company would have dealt with the large number of spoken roles by operating an extensive pattern of doubling. Detailed casting information which survives in the shape of 'plots' for the second part of *Seven Deadly Sins* (c.1592), *Frederick and Basilea* (1597) and *The Battle of Alcazar* (1589) reveals that some actors doubled as many as seven roles in a single production, but such radical allocation is not required for *Edward IV*.[16] The scheme offered here observes the practical necessities of staging, but also attempts to envisage ways in which idiosyncrasies of character or thematically connected situations might be imaginatively established by one player—perhaps conspicuously—adopting several parts.

Some roles, either because of their length or their juxtaposition with certain combinations of other characters, would need to be allocated individually: it would be difficult (although not impossible) for the actors playing King Edward, Falconbridge, the Lord Mayor, Hobs the tanner and either Matthew or Jane Shore to tackle other roles in the play. But the actors taking the roles of the Lord Howard and Sir Thomas Sellinger could also play, respectively, the parts of the Captain of the Isle of Wight and the Vice Admiral in the scene of Falconbridge's arraignment. One player could take the roles of the boisterous Ned Spicing in the rebellion scenes, the belligerent Harry Grudgen in the 'benevolence' scene (18), and the loquacious Scot, Jockie, in Scene 22; similarly, in the same scenes, one actor could play Smoke, Master Hadland, and the extortionist Rufford—and perhaps neatly turn the tables on his erstwhile comrade Spicing by playing the Miller who apprehends him.

Amongst the minor roles, an actor with an authoritative deportment could variously play the parts of Recoder Urswick, Master Aston, the petitioner Thomas Aire and the Master of St Katherine's; a player more gifted as a comic butt could take the parts of the bumbling Josselyn, the downtrodden Dudgeon and the hapless Robert Goodfellow. With the actor playing Chub doubling as Sir Humfrey Bowes and the petitioner Palmer, this scheme accounts for all the roles requiring adult players. The doubling of the boys' parts is equally straightforward. One player could be the constant recipient of the King's flirtatious overtures, combining the roles of Edward's queen, the tanner's daughter Nell and the Widow Norton in the play's final scene, while another doubles Edward's aggressive mother and the treacherous Mistress Blage. If the parts are apportioned this way the company's core would need to be fifteen strong, consisting of twelve adult and three boy players; this is exactly in accordance with the troupe sizes which theatre historians have calculated normally existed in the period.[17]

THE QUESTION OF AUTHORSHIP

Although none of the early quartos of *Edward IV* attributes the play to a named author, by the Restoration the earliest historians of the English theatre were designating the play unequivocally as the work of Thomas Heywood, and this attribution has gone more or less unquestioned ever since. The first writer to ascribe the play to Heywood was also one of his first detractors: Francis Kirkman, whose second *Catalogue* would ungraciously suggest that all Heywood's plays were 'written loosely in Taverns', named Heywood as the author in his first *Catalogue* of 1661.[18] Kirkman's immediate successors (and fellow-denigrators) followed suit;[19] and—a couple of notable doubters notwithstanding—the situation remains essentially unchanged.[20]

This introduction has the space to offer only a partial and qualified confirmation of Heywood's involvement in the play, and the possibility has still to be entertained that *Edward IV* is the sole surviving work of another dramatist who either chose not to repeat the experiment—improbable given the play's success—or who died before he was able to do so.

Two writers were delivering plays so relentlessly for the Henslowe operation during 1599 that they can be ruled out of contention. Besides producing *The Shoemakers' Holiday*, Thomas Dekker worked on no fever than eight plays in conjunction with other playwrights in that year alone.[21] His most frequent collaborator was Henry Chettle, a man who 'had a closer, possibly a more personal relationship with Henslowe' than any other writer.[22] Chettle worked on two plays apparently unaided, but also on seven more collaborations during 1599, and both the volume of his output and the extent of his financial indebtedness to Henslowe suggest that his first engagement with *Edward IV* is likely to have been when he was called upon to rework the play in 1602. Chettle's collaborator on that occasion, John Day, is one of several writers from the Henslowe stable whose involvement with the production of chronicle history plays is attested throughout the pages of the 'Diary'; others include Richard Hathway, Henry Porter and Robert Wilson, and any (or all) of these could, theoretically, have 'moonlighted' on a new play for a rival company.

The pages of the 'Diary', however, fall suddenly and conspicuously silent about three playwrights during the period of *Edward IV*'s composition. Michael Drayton had worked with Chettle and Dekker on a play called *The Welshman's Prize, or the Famous Wars of Henry I and the Prince of Wales* in 1598, and was receiving payments for the (unfinished) play *William Longsword* in January 1599. But then comes an unusual and protracted hiatus in Drayton's output for the company; he still had dealings with Henslowe—he acted as a witness for him in July—but he received no further remuneration until he and his collaborators were paid for the completion of *1 Oldcastle* and 'in earnest of the Second pte'.[23] Although he would later become heavily involved with the Children of the King's Revels it is probable that Drayton's uneasy relationship with the adult players was already in decline; after *Oldcastle* he made contributions to a play about Cardinal Wolsey in 1601 and to a play called *Caesar's Fall* in 1602, and then relinquished the amphitheatres for good. He was also heavily occupied at this period with non-dramatic work: he composed additional poems for *Englands Heroicall Epistles*, new sonnets for the reissue of *Idea*, he was recasting the *Mortimeriados* into the much longer *Barons Warres*, and had almost certainly begun work on *Poly-Olbion*. But it is still possible that Drayton could have temporarily departed the Henslowe stable and offered his services as a dramatist—on a subject with which, as will be shown, he was thoroughly familiar—to the emergent enterprise at the Boar's Head.

More noteworthy still is the inexplicable absence from Henslowe's records of one of Drayton's favoured collaborators: Anthony Munday. Munday had been a consistent contributor to productions at the Rose since the winter of 1597, but then, after receiving a payment on 19 August 1598 for a playbook called *Chance Medley*, he slips from sight completely for over a year, reappearing (again alongside Drayton) as a contributor to *Oldcastle* in October 1599. There is no evidence that this maverick but prolific author published anything else in the interim, and the chronicle history play, punctuated by scenes of comedy and sexual intrigue, was a format with which he was well acquainted. The external evidence certainly allows that Munday could have temporarily deserted the Henslowe outfit and defected to the new company.

And the same is true for Heywood himself. Although Heywood's exact status within Henslowe's company cannot be established with

any certainty, it is clear that the entrepreneur took pains to secure
his services as a *player*; in a contract dated 25 March 1598 Heywood
bound himself exclusively to Henslowe for two years. Yet after
two full payments for (lost) playbooks completed in January and
February of 1599 Heywood abruptly disappears entirely from the
'Diary' until his return as leading player, sharer and playwright with
Worcester's Men in the autumn of 1602.[24] The external evidence,
then, suggests that Heywood, Munday and Drayton suddenly and
simultaneously ceased to write for the Admiral's Men early in 1599;
Heywood and Munday might well have done so because they had
been tempted by the allure of London's new 'third' company. The
commentary will demonstrate frequent parallels between the techniques deployed in *Edward IV* and Heywood's habitual preferences
in matters of lexical choice, the composition of stage directions and
scribal practice; although final proof is lacking, there is a strong possibility that Heywood was at least a principal author of the play, and
this edition will assume hereafter that he was.[25]

Probably only a couple of years after *Edward IV* was first performed, Heywood certainly did write a play in which the vexed relationship between the Crown and its servants was interrogated. In
the Prologue (which he may well have added much later) to *The
Royal King and the Loyal Subject*, the dramatist claimed that

> no History
> We have left unrifled, our Pens have beene dipt
> As well in opening each hid Manuscript,
> As Tracts more vulgar, whether read, or sung
> In our domesticke, or more forraigne tongue.[26]

Whatever the extent of Heywood's involvement in *Edward IV*, there
could hardly be a better description of the resourcefulness with
which its author sought material for his play; the remainder of this
introduction will be, essentially, an attempt to uncover the remarkable range of his 'sources'.

THE FALCONBRIDGE REBELLION

Edward IV was written towards the culmination of the extraordinary
decade in which the tradition of the English chronicle play established itself and, in all probability, exhausted itself, and it is not
surprising that the play should be aware of, and responsive to that
tradition, nor, perhaps, that it should sometimes react against it.
But, besides ostentatiously offering itself for comparison with other

playtexts and non-dramatic historical literature, it also draws upon
a formidable array of other source materials, ranging from a contested (and in some cases irrecoverable) ballad tradition, through
manuscript and printed histories in both Latin and English, to works
of political philosophy then available only in French. This diversity,
together with the episodic structure of the play, requires an account
of the sources to be segmented—a necessary diffuseness which the
theatrical craftsmanship of the playwright ensures does not happen
within the play itself.

In the play's first movement London successfully resists an external threat, only to emerge with a tentative awareness that the monarchy on whose behalf it has struggled—and upon which it is
supposedly dependent for its authority and stability—poses a far
greater one. It is a movement which owes only the bare outlines of
its plot to (a broad range of) 'chronicles'; its political momentum
and its theatrical power derive, instead, from the debates, conducted
in speeches, sermons, pamphlets, proclamations, songs and other
plays, which anxiously addressed the social tensions of the capital
in the 1590s. In addition, it will be seen that the chorography of
John Stow, itself a reflection and a product of those tensions, was
a seminal influence on the play. *Edward IV*'s privileging of the
local, both urban and provincial, was an innovatory achievement
analagous to and almost exactly contemporaneous with the unprecedented contribution to cultural history that Stow's *Survey of London*
provided.

The fullest printed account of the rebellion, with which nine of
the first ten scenes of the play are concerned, is that found in the
second revised edition of Holinshed's *Chronicles* published in 1587,
and it is almost certain that Heywood used it; details which appear
elsewhere in the play, such as the King's kiss and the 'liberality'
it provokes in the widow in the final scene are missing from
Holinshed's first edition of 1577 and have been introduced by a
reviser (probably Abraham Fleming) after a rereading of Edward
Hall's quirkier but less comprehensive narration of the reign. Hall's
own report of the uprising is, however, perfunctory and it is surprising to find, given the political and symbolic importance of the
rebellion to London's sense of its historical identity, that the
accounts of it in the printed chronicles of its most civically aware
historians, Robert Fabyan and Stow, are similarly slim on detail;
Fabyan's *Chronicle*, despite being arranged according to the years of
London's mayorality, offers only a terse rendering of the episode's

central incidents, and neither Stow's *Chronicles* nor his generally more expansive *Annals* yield much more.[27]

But Fabyan and Stow left more detailed accounts of the rebellion in works that devote themselves wholly to the topographical, historical and political identity of the City. It is to Fabyan that the authorship of the most substantial extant London chronicle, the manuscript now known as *The Great Chronicle*, has been attributed.[28] The tonal shift from the closing moments of the opening scene, with the King's dismissive remarks on the futility of Falconbridge's aspirations, to the expansive and discursive style of the second scene in the rebels' camp itself, is analogous to the difference between Holinshed's account and that of *The Great Chronicle*. As the commentary to Scene 1, l. 146 makes clear, Edward's reductive characterization of Falconbridge as a modern Phaethon is, importantly, hackneyed by the multiplicity of its literary antecedents, but it is of a piece with the *sententia* interpolated near the opening of the revised account of the 1587 *Chronicles*, where Falconbridge provides an exemplary demonstration of how overweening ambition pulls upon its 'owne pate fatall destruction' (III, 322).

However, once the intensity of the play's focus on the vibrancy of the rebels' enterprise and the precision with which the citizens prepare to defend the city against it becomes apparent in the second and third scenes, the importance of accounts other than Holinshed's emerges. For instance, whereas Holinshed stresses the dynastic imperative of the Bastard's Neville connections and the related antagonism felt and fuelled by the disaffected Earl of Warwick— themes which the play relinquishes very early on—the civic preoccupations of *The Great Chronicle* elicit a colourful evocation of the rebels' strategies of social inversion much closer to the world of the play. Thus, when the Lord Mayor denies Falconbridge passage through the city, the London chronicler reports that the rebel leader 'was not a lytill myscontentid, But swore many grete othis that he wold passe that way mawgre the mayer & alle his powar, and that he wold Rule the Cyte by the space of a daye & a nygth at his pleasure'.[29] The vituperative energy of the Bastard and his 'lewd Counsayll' which is so central to the play's theatrical momentum is not only realized far more vividly in this manuscript chronicle than in any of its printed counterparts, but the articulation of its outspoken and acerbic political insights is achieved by the kind of ironic juxtaposition and echoes deployed by the dramatist. For, just as the play will stage the abrupt termination of the rebels' attempts to overturn the sexual and economic equilibrium of the city, only to provoke further tension by adding two consecutive scenes (17 and 18) which chart the King's successful predations in both spheres, so *The Great Chronicle* immediately follows its account of the Londoners' heroic—and unaided—defeat of the insurgents with a caustic analysis of how the King exploited a victory to which he had contributed nothing: 'Such as were Rych were hangid by the purs, and the othir that were nedy were hangid by the nekkis, By meane whereof [the] Cuntre was gretly enpoveryschid and the kyngys coffyrs somdele encreasyd'.[30]

It is not necessary to postulate that the dramatist had direct recourse to the unique extant MS of *The Great Chronicle* itself—although the playwright Drayton claimed to have access to the personal library of Stow, who, in 1599, owned that manuscript—because copies and distillations of it were clearly circulating throughout the sixteenth century, even if only a fraction of them have survived.[31] But it is also possible that Heywood, reputedly a former member of Cambridge University, could have explored historical manuscripts there; 'Warkworth's Chronicle', for instance, an account which not only uniquely concurs with the play's estimate of the numbers of Falconbridge's army, but which anticipates the play's temperate but insistent commentary on the King's derelictions of economic and political probity, was written by a Master of Peterhouse and deposited in its library.[32]

Yet it is the *Survey of London*, first published by Stow in 1598, to which the dramatist of *Edward IV* is most indebted. Until recently, historians have focused attention almost exclusively on the celebratory aspects of Stow's account of London; the corollary has been an obscuring of its admonitory urgency and intermittently caustic critique of *contemporary* civic government.[33] Stow himself contributed to this imbalance of response with his selection of 'framing devices': a judiciously nuanced 'Epistle Dedicatory' addressed to the lord mayor and the author's fellow citizens, and the polemical '*Apologie*' for the City's 'greatnesse', which is heralded on the title page and which concludes the volume. Yet, the *Survey* actually opens with Stow's deconstruction of London's long-cherished foundation myth, a legend—of the City's Trojan origins and reincarnation—of sufficiently residual credibility for even the iconoclast Falconbridge to deploy without irony (see Part One, Scene 9, l. 1). Moreover, Stow begins his meticulous description of London not at its centre but at its boundaries. This initial 'perambulation' takes in the City's walls, bridges and gates in a way that is paradigmatic for the *Survey*'s enterprise: the strategically pivotal locations of the City's defensive strength are also, inevitably, the sites of its enduring vulnerability, and, accordingly, the orderly and appreciative observation of physical features is punctuated unremittingly by lists of those who have attempted to obliterate them. And, just as the ominous figures of Wat Tyler, Jack Cade and Falconbridge himself impinge early on the *Survey*'s topographical landscape, so the same names erupt into the second scene of *Edward IV*.[34] Stow's dispassionate, indeed alphabetical approach to a material and observable present is disrupted by the spectres of a 'history' which cannot be forgotten, rather as Heywood shatters the discursive playfulness of a long resolved family tiff with the enactment of an 'historical' insurrection which, it transpires, has an exclusively Elizabethan dynamic.

Indeed, the meticulous care with which the Falconbridge rebellion is mapped on to particular London sites demands an even more precise chronological placing and reveals that the play's engagement with the internal tensions of the capital in the 1590s is an engagement which it not only shares with the *Survey* but which Stow's remarkable achievement may have made possible. For, if it has long been axiomatic in theatrical criticism to note the pervasive importance of locale—of the particularized semiotics of place—to English drama of the seventeenth century and beyond, neither the suddenness with which that topographical specificity achieved such prominence nor the agency of *Edward IV* in that emergence has been adequately acknowledged.

Given the phenomenally (and to some alarmingly) rapid growth of the metropolis in the latter half of the sixteenth century, it is not surprising to find that London exercised an almost obsessive fascination for writers of every genre in the period.[35] Yet, in spite of this momentous expansion—or perhaps because many saw it as a monstrous one—London was, before the late 1590s, invariably portrayed as a quasi-mythic, monolithic entity, significant in its entirety, but without the sharp differentiation of its constituent parts which, as Richard Helgerson has argued, characterizes the core of the chorographic enterprise.[36] It might be expected that the emergence of the commercial theatre in the last quarter of the century, and the eclipse of drama in the provinces as the capital surpassed and engulfed its competitors in this, as in virtually all financial enterprises, would instantly have generated work in which London anatomized its own evolving and sprawling self, but in fact this decisive and irreversible trend did not appear, fully formed, until more than two decades after the opening of The Theatre in 1576.

Even the early history plays, lent a chronological and spatial framework by the chronicles to which they could (but did not need to) adhere, did not significantly extend the deployment of topographical specificity. The pyrotechnics of Queen Elinor at Charing Cross in *Edward I* (c.1591) are remarkable not just because they are bizarre in themselves but because they occur at the only part of the city which Peele designates by name.[37] Similarly, Lawrence Costermonger and Robin Pewterer, representatives of the neighbourhood watch in *The Famous Victories* (c.1588), randomly mention 'Pudding lane end' and 'Billingsgate ward' in a desultory discussion of where their duty calls, but neither location appears to have any bearing on what they do or why they do it.[38]

The Shakespearean history plays brought to the genre a wealth of quotidian detail and an unprecedented concern with regional difference, in all of which the influence of London as an entity performs a necessarily central role. But, despite attempts to locate both the plays and the theatres in which they were acted within a network of conflicting localized areas,[39] the fact remains that Shakespeare's London does *not* emerge as a conglomeration of sharply differentiated parochial zones, but as an indivisible unit: a monolith, which may be protean, inflammable and a battleground for irreconcileable claims to control it, but no less a monolith for that. Allusions to particular London sites are invariably glancing, often lifted indiscriminately from the plays' chronicle sources, and are sometimes bunched together to form a cluster of images which would be recognizable to those with little or no knowledge of the places themselves. The tokenist grouping of London names to which adhere widely known social characteristics is exemplified in the juxtaposition of 'Paul's', 'Smithfield' and 'the stews' in *2 Henry IV* (1.2.39–40), although in this instance the sequence is, albeit with a Falstaffian twist, not merely familiar but proverbial. Intriguingly it is a proverb which had earlier been deployed in *The Book of Sir Thomas More*, the one play on which both Shakespeare and Heywood collaborated, and the one extant play written before 1599 in which the precise delineation of locale is of paramount importance.[40]

The distinctive approach to the sense of place is ubiquitous in *More*. Thus, as the 'Standard' was the setting for Lord Say's execution in *2 Henry VI*, so it is the setting for Lincoln's in *More* (573–4), but here it is also of political and theatrical significance that the street in which it stood, Cheapside, is realized as the site of the important food market that had been functioning long before the events of 1517 the play depicts, but which was still a vital and controversial operation during the period of the play's composition (see ll. 15–19). Using a technique which anticipates that of *Edward IV*, the *More* dramatist(s) re-create the Cheapside of the May Day Riots but simultaneously evoke the Cheapside in which a crowd of almost two thousand wrecked the pillories in the disturbances of the mid-1590s.[41]

This strategy is pervasive in *More*. Even when gleaned from the historical accounts, precise topographical references are carefully framed to elicit contemporary resonance. Lincoln and his allies, for instance, are anxious about the suitability of the 'Spittle Sermons' (67) given at St Mary's Hospital as a forum in which their grievances might be voiced; the fact that from the 1580s onwards the city vigorously disputed the Bishop of London's right to appoint the preachers there would have been one of several factors which prompted the Master of the Revels to mark this passage for deletion.[42] The entire manuscript is dense with the proper names of London's houses and streets, and, even if many of these are found in the various chronicles consulted by the playwrights, their inclusion involves a deliberate, and provocative, act of choice. Both the dramatists and the censor Edmund Tilney well knew that each time the play located a conflict precisely in Paternoster Row or Panyer Alley (Addition IV, 35–7), albeit the historical accounts of Holinshed, Harpsfield or, in this instance, Foxe had sanctioned them to do so, the (potential) audience was offered an interpretative possibility: they were invited to view the theatrical performance of acts of resistance to authority perpetrated in the past, and to reconstruct them imaginatively in the streets in which they still lived and worked.

The scenes of *More* for which Heywood was brought in as a reviser required (and elicited) considerable sophistication in creating a balanced tension between comedy, poignancy and violence, and they also demanded an unprecedentedly close attention to the social and political significance of London itself. It is Heywood who has Doll Williamson jest darkly about dragging the strangers into 'more feldes'—a suburb famous for, amongst other things, its laundries—and then beating them 'till they stinke a gaine' (Addition II, 33–4).[43] It is also Heywood who makes an acerbic joke, when, ignoring the chronicles, he has members of the Privy Council received 'at ludgate' (Addition II, 45)—a debtors' prison in such a parlous condition in the late 1580s that it required a substantial and unpopular citywide tax to fund its repair.[44]

Inevitably, one other circumstance surrounding the complicated enterprise of *Sir Thomas More* would have left a lasting impression on Heywood and the other dramatists who had contributed to it: it is almost certain that the intractability of the censor's disapproval ensured that the play was not realized in a professional London performance until the excellent Stage One production at the Shaw Theatre in September 1990. *More*'s experimental representation of a city, relentlessly familiar in its topographical detail and disturbingly so in its portrayal of the xenophobic intensity which was resurfacing in 1593/4, proved abortive. It seems that the fate of *More* provided dramatists with a salutary lesson, for during the ensuing five years of frenetic theatrical activity, the experiment was not repeated.[45] London in the mid-1590s was in turmoil, and yet its sharply differentiated streets and buildings receded from the pages of dramatic and other literature. It seems likely that governmental distrust of works which attempted to extrapolate social, economic and/or political significance from the close examination of geographical space extended beyond the confines of both the urban and the theatrical: the initial enthusiasm with which John Norden's projected county surveys were received had dwindled so abruptly that, although he had completed seven sections, the second part of his *Speculum Britanniae* (1598) was also the last to make it into print.[46]

But state interference in the printing and distribution of books would become both proactive and punitive in the months immediately preceding the registration of *Edward IV*. On 1 June 1599 John Whitgift, Archbishop of Canterbury, and Richard Bancroft, Bishop of London, instigated the most concentrated yet wide-ranging act of censorship of the Elizabethan era. They instructed the Stationers' Company to call in the works of Thomas Nashe and Gabriel Harvey, forbade the further printing of their books or any epigrams or satires, disallowed the printing of 'histories' which had not received the explicit sanction of the Privy Council and prohibited the publication of plays, 'excepte they bee allowed by suche as have aucthorytie'.[47] The enforcement of this order was both sporadic and inconsistent, but this directionless clampdown can be seen as a slightly delayed ricochet from the sustained assault, initiated by Whitgift in the preceding April, upon Sir John Hayward's *Life . . . of King Henrie IIII*.[48]

It seems certain that the brief but extravagant dedication to Essex which Hayward affixed to his book was the initial cause of the trouble; although subsequently withdrawn, that connection with the Earl, whose Irish campaign disintegrated into farce and whose relationship with the Queen deteriorated seriously during the late summer of 1599, would soon invite Attorney-General Coke's exhaustive and hostile scrutiny of the history itself. The substantial print-run of the first edition of *Henrie IIII* was a sell-out. The even larger one—1500 copies—prepared for the second edition, together with the author's alterations and an apology for misunderstandings arising from the first, never reached the public: all were burnt at Bancroft's house in Fulham.[49] This context makes the registration of *Edward IV* on 28 August 1599—albeit with the authorization of the Wardens only—all the more remarkable. It was a play, it was a history and parts of it could have been considered satirical, not least its terming of the King's financial demands as 'benevolences' (Part One, Scene 18, ll. 22–6 and commentary), for this was one of the 'anachronisms' upon which Coke would dwell during Hayward's examination the following summer. Yet by this time *Edward IV* had been registered again (23 February 1600) and printed without interference, proving just how selective the imposition of censorship could be, since the play tenaciously addresses tensions which had threatened to tear 1590s London apart.

If the urban crisis of the middle of the decade had receded by 1599, the arguments over its causes, its management and its repercussions had not. From the outset the play both reflects and participates in those debates, grounding the skirmishes of the Falconbridge uprising upon the issues which had troubled Londoners so recently, and precisely setting them against a network of sites which had been—and would continue to be—focal points in difficult times. The playwright's method in the opening lines of Scene 2 is one which will be deployed relentlessly throughout: the invocation of the familiar, immediately overlaid by techniques of displacement which render contestable the suppositions upon which that 'familiarity' is constructed. A noisy, quarrelsome, but quasi-military crew enter, '*marching*', and beating a drum. Within just four lines, an audience might have imagined that it saw an unruly group of apprentices, because, whether aping the activities of the trained bands or illicitly reproducing the regimentation sometimes required of institutionalized boys, this was certainly how gangs of them, 'beating upp the drum in a tumultuous manner in

Little Moorefields' and elsewhere, were regularly described in the period.[50] Even the ensuing misunderstanding over the correct terminology to describe their captain's manifesto could gesture towards the stereotypical—and probably inaccurate—representation of apprentices as linguistically deficient.[51]

But Falconbridge himself, after a brief flourish concerning his Neville ancestry—a dimension upon which the non-London chronicles were insistent but which the play promptly marginalizes—distances himself and his movement from objectives which had very recently provoked apprentice violence and with which all Londoners were vitally concerned in 1599: 'mending measures' and 'the price of corne' (l. 30). Four consecutive harvest failures (from 1594 to 1597) and the resultant dearth demanded the sustained vigilance of the royal, parliamentary and civic authorities. As early as 1574 Thomas Norton had reminded the incumbent lord mayor that he and his aldermen would be considered responsible for the purchase, distribution, pricing and—above all—the just and accurate measuring of supplies to the city, particularly food.[52] During the 1590s the burden of this responsibility was felt more acutely.[53] Even when the period of the most extreme shortages had passed, the Houses of Parliament were still struggling to agree on strategies for the storage and pricing of corn, and on the contentious issue of exportation which becomes prominent in the penultimate scene of *1 Edward IV* (see ll. 62–3 and commentary), and crops up in the further characterization of the extortionist Rufford in Part Two.[54] While the legislation faltered, the Queen was moved to distribute cash to the suffering inhabitants of each ward and the court of aldermen made ambitious attempts to restrict the price of meal sold in city markets to levels the poor could afford.[55]

Falconbridge and his fellow insurgents, approaching London through the suburbs (ll. 75ff), plan a wholesale yet detailed disruption of such schemes. The locations of their projected violations are minutely particularized. Besides abrogating monarchical prerogative in the administration of the coinage and the judicial system (ll. 49–50, 55–6 and commentary), they will

> shoe our neighing coursers with no worse
> Than the purest silver that is sold in Cheap.
> At Leadenhall we'll sell pearls by the peck,
> As now the mealmen use to sell their meal.
> (51–4)

Heywood's Cheapside is realized—both sociologically and chronologically—with far greater specificity than Jack Cade's had been. The
allusion to Bankes's horse (see commentary) deftly draws an audience into an explicitly Elizabethan Cheapside—the street in which
the centre of the trade in precious metals, as well as the hub of the
massive cloth industry (which Spicing promises to plunder, ll. 66-8),
was located. The punctuation of Falconbridge's inflated rhetoric
with the colloquial interjections of his refractory followers also
establishes the sense of a thronged concourse in which unremark-
able endearments, misunderstandings and insults are exchanged by
ordinary people.[56] But Falconbridge's later threat to humiliate the
Lord Mayor in Cheapside (Scene 4, ll. 52-6) serves as a sharp
reminder that such a vast confluence, in which conspicuous displays
of wealth coexist with, and possibly taunt, the poor and dispossessed, is also a site of potentially explosive class tensions.[57] So, the
play preserves a precarious balance: the rebels' schemes to usurp
both monarchical and civic authority in their imitation of established
routes of royal entries and mayoral inaugural processions are at once
flippant and dangerous.

Recent commentators have begun to realize that an important
aspect of the insurgents' agenda concerns their seizing control of the
city's commercial structures and spaces.[58] Falconbridge's vision of
selling pearls by the 'peck'—as the subsequent line makes clear, a
measure used invariably 'now' (i.e. in the 1590s) for the grain which
was in such short supply—is a calculated affront to the efforts the
civic authorities were making to ensure adequate provision of essential foodstuffs. As the weight of a one-penny loaf of bread drastically
declined in the years 1594-98 the aldermen made repeated attempts
both to standardize the product and to impose restraints on grain
exports; they also purchased annually large quantities of grain which
the livery companies then ground into meal and sold to the poor
at less than market rates.[59] The location the play envisages for
Falconbridge's violations is carefully chosen: twice in the 1590s the
London government gave instructions to facilitate meal-selling in
the market at Leadenhall. Similar nuances may attach to the 'hot
drinking' reported in 'Bishopsgate' at the opening of Scene 6, since
an audience—particularly an audience at the Boar's Head, separated
by only the few hundred yards of 'Houndsditch' (l. 4)—would know
that the Bishopsgate market erected in 1599, intended originally for
the sale of malt, had been almost immediately redesignated as a meal
market.[60]

This kind of topographical specificity is almost unprecedented in pre-1599 literature, although the dramatist might have recalled a stunning image from *Sir Thomas More*: on fol. 11a of the manuscript, in a passage to which Heywood had made an 'addition', Doll furiously suggests that, had she and her fellows anticipated the deception which led to John Lincoln's execution, they 'would first haue lockt vp in Leaden hall, / and there bin burnt to ashes with the roofe' (ll. 652–3). In the years intervening between *More* and *Edward IV* such desperate resentment had frequently threatened to spill over into violence. At first sight, the rebels' precisely directed challenges to municipal authority and its tenuous hold on the means of storage and distribution—and, by implication, social order—raise a spectre that haunted civic and national government alike: that poverty experienced in the capital might foster an alliance between the groups of discharged servicemen who (like Falconbridge) were gravitating towards London from the south-coast ports, and the discontented apprentices who were already living, working, and causing anxiety there.[61] As the rebels approach the Tower (ll. 14, 83), preparing to devour the best London can offer as if the city were a 'furnished feast' (l. 82), spectators might have recalled the crowd of apprentices, reputedly one thousand strong, which had marched on Tower Hill in 1595, allegedly planning to 'robbe, steale, pill and spoile the welthy and well disposed inhabitaunts of the saide cytye, and to take the sworde of aucthorytye from the magistrats and governours lawfully aucthorised'.[62]

But, almost as soon as these essentially conservative links are made they are complicated, not least by the insistence with which particular locations and resources are named. The most radical initiatives which brought apprentices on to the streets in the 1590s were not directed towards the flagrant violation of municipal regulations espoused by the rebels, but were rather aimed at the reinforcement of those measures. What the aldermen attempted by edict, the apprentices effected by force. In 1595 they seized supplies of butter and sold it at 3d per pound as opposed to the 5d demanded by its owners, and issued a proclamation insisting that sales be confined within the official markets, and not allowed in private inns or houses; in the same year they 'appropriated' fish at Billingsgate, refusing to pay more than the rates appointed by the lord mayor.[63] In contrast to the project of Chub and Smoke to secure limitless supplies of alcohol for themselves, wardmote petitions requesting beer of decent quality at prices affordable by all were granted by the building of a municipal brewhouse.[64] And, where the rebels propose the flouting of all exchange regulation and the indiscriminate seizure of commodities 'without control' (l. 93), 1598 saw London's governors meeting demands for more equitable distribution of resources by the provision of new scales in markets and the public burning of the unlawful measures Spicing covets—in Cheapside, the symbolic site where he would have them set up.[65]

The appetites and irreverence of the rebels have a compulsive energy which could seem especially attractive to apprentice (or indeed any youthful) spectators regularly disparaged by guardians of civic morality for similar predilections. But the dramatist undermines this putative alliance in several ways. It was a metropolitan phenomenon, by no means confined to London, that city governors defined the proper behaviour of young men in terms of militarized masculinity: the work ethic was to be supplemented by mustering and marching, and intense loyalty to neighbourhood and occupational fraternity was encouraged.[66] Gradually the play drives a crucial ideological wedge between the self-aggrandizing and indiscriminate violence of the rebels and the channelled aggression of the apprentices. For instance, if their euphemistic request to the aldermen, 'give us leave to work' (Scene 5, l. 62), neatly collapses the distinction between their occupational obligations and their pugnacity, it also opens a gap between themselves—who 'stick' to their officers and their city, demonstrating an identification with, and concern for a community—and the insurgents, manifestly devoid of either.[67]

It is in fact the apprentices themselves who fully effect the displacement proposed by the dramatist, for it is they who deflect the admonitory rhetoric so often directed towards them, on to the rebels:

> You are those desperate, idle, swaggering mates,
> That haunt the suburbs in the time of peace,
> And raise up alehouse brawls in the street;
> And when the rumour of the war begins,
> You hide your heads, and are not to be found.
>
> (Scene 5, 37–41)

It must be reiterated that this has nothing whatever to do with the 1470s, and everything to do with 1599; no war is imminent in the chronicle accounts of the period, nor is it—yet—even in the historical time-scheme of the play. Despite plentiful evidence that the apprentices of the 1590s were frequently accused of 'idle

swaggering', drunken brawling and haunting brothels in the suburbs
(and some evidence that such indictments were justified), the play
here, as elsewhere, takes risks; it teases with the possibility of an
alliance, but eventually posits an absolute distinction between the
youthful citizens and the rebels. However, as the apprentices go on
to speak of 'our shops' and 'our locks' (Scene 5, ll. 42, 45), eloquently
testifying to their investment in the economic machinery of the city,
their awareness of that machinery's vulnerability establishes—unwittingly on their part but not on the playwright's—affinities between
the insurgents' predations and other threats to the integrity and
security of London.

Scholars have at last begun to acknowledge the irony which
adheres to the fact that the Bastard's promise to have illicit sex with
Jane Shore (Scene 4, ll. 46–7)—and her husband's consequent
fear of such a violation (Scene 8, ll. 17–20)—are fulfilled not by
Falconbridge himself but by King Edward.[68] It should also be noted,
however, that the obstruction by corrupt courtiers of the city's
attempts to control licentiousness and prostitution was just one
of several areas of conflict between London's governors and
the Crown, but an important one: the complaints of Recorder
Fleetwood that in court circles 'twentie poundes for a reprieve is
nothing', and Elizabethan scandals about the inveterate whoring
of senior diplomats such as Sir Horatio Palavacino would echo
well into the Jacobean period.[69] But the resemblances between
Falconbridge and his entourage, and the King and his, extend far
beyond a shared appetite for sexual conquest.

In the study, it is relatively simple to detect instances when the
conduct of the rebels and the King coincide politically or militarily:
the insurgents' declared ambition to behave like kings is often
repeated and this general programme is supplemented by vignettes
such as their usurpation of the royal prerogative to cry 'havock' in
battle (see Scene 5, l. 69 and commentary). More complex, however,
is the flippant conversation between Falconbridge and Spicing
on their indiscriminate and wholesale distribution of knighthoods
(Scene 9, ll. 25–39). Not only is this minor skirmish juxtaposed later
in the scene with the King's conferring of the same honour on the
mayor and aldermen 'en masse'—a ceremony itself problematized
by Shore's refusal of the dignity and Edward's ironic promise to
'quittance' the goldsmith in other ways (see ll. 216–42)—but both
episodes remind the audience of troubling events taking place
beyond the confines of the stage: in spite of the total failure of the

Irish campaign, the Earl of Essex was using his military prerogative to reward his officers by conferring knighthoods with a profligacy his queen neither practised nor approved.[70]

At this, the mid-point of *1 Edward IV*, the military threat posed by the rebels has been averted, and the play is about to set off on a geographical (but not a theatrical) tangent. As it does so, we can observe which source materials have stayed the course so far, and which have been discarded—and why. Ever since the calculatedly jarring moment in Scene 4 when Recorder Urswick legitimizes the city's bearing of arms in the King's 'presence' (see l. 28 and commentary) the dramatist has taken every opportunity to emphasize Edward's inexplicable absence. In so doing the playwright elaborates upon the accounts offered by Fabyan (in both the printed chronicles and *The Great Chronicle*), in which the defeat of the insurgents is completed by the citizens entirely unaided, and Stow's *Survey*, in which a fleeting reference to a 'fresh companie' sent by 'the Earle *Riuers*' is the only contribution acknowledged from beyond the ranks of the Londoners themselves.[71] But this perspective, crucially, signals a fundamental departure from Holinshed, and Grafton and Hall upon whose foundations Holinshed built. The *Chronicles* of 1587 report that Edward 'sent to the succors of the maior and aldermen fifteene hundred of the choisest souldiers he had about him, that they might helpe to resist the enimies, till he had got such an armie togither as was thought necessarie, meaning with all conuenient speed to come therewith to the rescue of the citie'. Holinshed goes on to imply that without this show of royal strength the citizens' partiality to Warwick and their greed for plunder may have led them to side with Falconbridge; both the 1577 and 1587 editions reinforce this interpretation with a marginal note indicating 'Succours sent to the citie of London'.[72]

The dramatist's other and equally significant omission of material from Holinshed propels the play into the thick of the two related controversies which dominated affairs in 1599, the 'Bishops' ban' and the accelerating crisis over Essex. The *Chronicles* devoted considerable attention to the role played in the rebellion's defeat by the 'great lords of the realme', but particularly the *fifteenth*-century Earl of Essex. This peer, wrote Holinshed, together with 'manie knights, esquiers, and gentlemen, with their freends and seruants, came to aid the citizens, taking great paine to place them in order, for defense of the gates and walles . . . and suerlie', he added hopefully, 'by the intermingling of such gentlemen and lords seruants in

euerie part with the citizens, they were greatlie incouraged to withstand their enimies'.[73] The play carefully avoids any hint of such a
collusion. In eschewing explicit references to Essex, Heywood may
have been adopting the stance of judicious caution which would
shortly prompt the Chamberlain's Men (and/or the printer Thomas
Creede, and/or the publishers Thomas Millington and John Busby)
to leave out the allusion to Essex's return from Ireland from
the quarto text of *Henry V*. But the play's refusal to countenance
any correspondence of interests or activities between Essex and
London's governors also serves as an early illustration that the
Elizabethan Earl's long-affirmed belief in a 'special relationship'
between himself and the city was unfounded; that it was so would
be amply proved during the uprising of 1601, when it transpired that
Essex's faith in both the political leanings and the military capabil-
ities of Sheriff Thomas Smythe had been equally misplaced.[74]

The explicit failure of the King and the implicit failure of Essex
to assist the citizens in the defence of London have a significance
far beyond the revelation of the playwright's preference for one
chronicle rather than another; historically informed spectators
would have found both absences highly conspicuous. But if the
name of Essex doesn't sound in the play, even the most intermittently attentive listener could not have failed to hear, endlessly
repeated in banter and squabble alike, the Christian names of the
rebel leaders. And, as the play heads for Staffordshire, leaving behind
'Tom' Falconbridge temporarily and 'Ned' Spicing for good, those
names remain integral to the playwright's craft: the location may
change, but the sounds of 'Ned' and 'Tom', still attached to men
who appear to be outlaws and vagabonds, continue to resonate.
Alongside them, the shadowy presence of Robert Devereux, second
Earl of Essex, enters the text.

THE TANNER OF TAMWORTH

The play's first movement is a structure of remarkable complexity
for which chronicle histories provided only elementary foundations.
The relationship between *Edward IV*'s Tamworth scenes and the
ballad(s) of 'King Edward the IIIj[th] and a Tanner' is similarly proportioned, but the shift of location does not signify merely the aban-
donment of one set of source materials for another. The process
is rather one of an increasingly intricate enmeshing which links,
thematically and theatrically, the London confrontations with the
provincial skirmishes. A simple example is Hobs's claim to political

impartiality via kinship with a windmill that grinds 'which way so e'er the wind blow' (Scene 13, l. 46), and its allusion to the ballad 'Jack Miller's Song'; Miller was executed for his part in the 'Peasants' Revolt', the ballad first appeared in Stow's *Annals* and it actually belonged in the cultural milieu of the London apprentices.[75] A spectator imagining that leaving a tension-ridden London will bring relief in the form of a dramatized version of one well-known ballad, set in a reassuringly distant past, and amusingly illustrative of a time when social reconciliation was inevitable and effortless, will be disappointed within seconds of the Tanner opening his mouth.

As early as 1564 the Stationers had granted a licence for the printing of a book entitled *The story of Kynge Henry IIIJ*[th] *and the Tanner of Tamowthe*—the interchangeability of the king's name already indidcating the ballad form's customary lack of historical specificity (cf. note 84, below)—and again, in 1586, the Register has an entry for *A merie songe of the Kinge and the Tanner*.[76] The earliest extant printed text containing such material appeared in 1596 and no entry referring to it is found in the Register for that year, but its existence is acknowledged on 6 October 1600, when a double entry for both a 'delectable history' and a 'balad of the same matter' was recorded.[77] The 1596 text comprises just ten pages, contains only the fifty-six four-line stanzas of the 'history', and is adorned by a series of woodcuts.[78] The earliest surviving text of the ballad is considerably later (the title page offers no date but catalogues place it around 1660), and, amongst other relatively minor changes, it compresses the fifty-six stanzas of the 'history' into thirty-nine. With these texts it is impossible to establish with certainty questions of priority or transmission. The 'history', as Child pointed out, has an 'undoubted original' in the tale of 'The King and the Barker'; this text survives only in a badly mutilated manuscript of a much earlier date than any printed version of the Tanner story or its many generic cousins.[79] But the fact that the processes of transcription, cross-fertilization and adaptation in a sub-genre of this kind are largely irrecoverable means that even when incidents or phraseology found in one of these texts appear in *Edward IV*, the extent (or existence) of Heywood's indebtedness to that particular text cannot be proved. Nevertheless, whether inventions or borrowings, deviations from a probable source like the 1596 Danter 'history' are important, and there are a great many of them.

Not surprisingly, the most significant and thoroughgoing transformations to which the play subjects the ballad source material derive from the dramatist's insistent uprooting of virtually every exchange from a discrete historical past, and a corresponding relocation of these exchanges in a discernibly anxious present. At its simplest this means, for instance, that John Hobs—no tradesman in either the source ballad or its generic relations has a name—actually has a real job. As he enters, the audience encounters him returning from market, and the first thing they learn is that his business is a small-scale one, operating on the margins of legality. In Elizabethan England the leather industry was of massive national importance and inordinate complexity, and as such was subject to some of the strictest and most detailed legislation the Tudor regime ever attempted to impose. Reaction to the regulatory measures was extremely mixed. Hobs does rather well by the playwright's discarding of Holinshed here, since William Harrison's *Description of England*, with which the *Chronicles* opened, was unequivocal in its endorsement of the 'good lawes' which tried to halt the decline in the standards of tanning, and scathing about the fact that bribery of officials was none the less sufficiently widespread to have brought 'the tanner to so great libertie that his lether is much worse than before'.[80]

Harrison's 'good lawes' were incorporated in the 'Acte Touching Tanners, Couriours, Shooemakers, and other Artyficers occupyeng the cutting of Leather' (5 Eliz. I.c.8) of 1563, and one of its many provisions was a complete ban on the tanning of certain hides thought to be inferior; they included the 'bull's hide' (Scene 11, l. 5) Hobs is carrying back from a market which is presumably not one nominated by the Act, or supervised by the officials appointed to enforce it.[81] Although some sixteenth-century tanners became wealthy,[82] the tanner of the ballads is not. Nor is John Hobs, but the play conveys his social status in much greater detail. When, in both the ballad and the 'history', the tanner offers the King 'clouting leather for thy shon' ('History', st. 55) as a parting gift, the humble quality of the material contributes to the naive charm of the *rapprochement* between the two. In *Edward IV*, however, Hobs's reference to diminishing sales of even 'clout-leather' (l. 9) at the opening of his part in the play succinctly indicates the precariousness of his economic position, just as the 'liberal' Widow's contemptuous dismissal of his 'clouted shoes' (Scene 23, l. 147) at the end of it emphasizes the very class distinctions the ballads sought to obliterate.[83]

Hobs's insistence on assessing his profits and losses in pennies and groats signals a substantial financial gulf between himself and the balladic forebear who boasts of his self-sufficiency in a count of nobles (Ballad, st. 10; 'History', st. 13). Moreover, where the name-less tanner responds to the King's request for news by informing him that 'cow hides are deare' (Ballad, st. 14; 'History', st. 17), John Hobs's bad pun on 'deer' draws attention to what he adds to this formulaic exchange: 'what's dear? Marry, corn and cow hides' (ll. 25–6).[84] In the 'Tanner' ballads the protagonist's occupation is inci-dental: hides serve only as a narrative prop to make possible the swapping of saddles and horses, which in turn sets up the tanner's explosive fart, the ballads' climactic illustration of the artisan's uncouthness for which the play has no parallel. In *Edward IV*, by contrast, Hobs's participation in the leather industry permeates the (sometimes obscure) language he uses and, by extension, governs the rapport between himself and the audience.

Every member of that audience would have had some acquain-tance with the leather trade, if only as a consumer: apart from footwear, leather was used for all manner of clothing—it often served as a cheap substitute for cloth when the cloth industry was (not infrequently) in crisis—and for household implements, from pots to bellows. Many spectators, however, are likely to have had direct involvement with one of the many manufacturing outlets of the industry. At the beginning of the seventeenth century there were estimated to be about three thousand shoemakers around the city, and a similar number of workers in the lighter leather crafts.[85] The industry was particularly important in the areas in which *Edward IV* was first performed. Around the corner from the Boar's Head was the livery hall and headquarters of the Leathersellers' Company.[86] The tanning operation itself was concentrated in the streets of Southwark surrounding the Rose playhouse; by the end of the century some eighty tanneries were situated in this district alone.[87] It was in these areas, inevitably, that the precariousness of the trade was experienced most acutely, and here that resentment at the inconsistent but ruthless enforcement of the ill-conceived regula-tions governing it perenially simmered. Discontent with this legislation, and especially with the influence of the court upon its implementation, was particularly intense during the 1590s. In 1592 Edward Darcy's attempt to dominate a corner of the trade for which the 1563 statute failed to stipulate provoked a showdown between himself and a city-wide alliance: the Leathersellers resisted the scheme so resolutely that their warden was imprisoned, and when Darcy, in the ensuing argument, struck an alderman in the presence of the lord mayor, apprentices gathered to exact revenge.[88]

Of all the branches of a large and complex industry, Elizabethan tanners seem to have had the toughest deal. As *Hamlet*'s gravedigger reminds us, the roughness of the tanners' work rendered them proverbially durable, but the stink and water pollution occasioned by the tanning process ensured their social marginalization too: in most towns they were obliged to live and work in the outskirts.[89] In London, despite their numerical presence, tanners also remained the least organized sector of the leather labour market; they never managed to acquire the dignity or security of forming their own livery company, and, when the Bermondsey tanners (alone) finally achieved a charter of incorporation in 1703, such collectivization was of purely ceremonial significance.[90] When, during the meal at Hobs's home, the tanner talks of the 'horn' as 'a badge of our occupation' (Scene 14, l. 121), the allusion is a provocative one: in the wake of Hobs's scathing criticisms of the injustices bedevilling the trade in the previous scene, the word 'occupation', which was invariably used to denote a profession-based organization or company, serves as a reminder that, while provincial tanners could justifiably describe their collective associations as an 'occupation', their London counterparts could not.[91]

This speech may draw on older elements of the ballad tradition for aspects of social detail, but such political specificity is far removed from the earliest extant 'Tanner' sources. John Danter's black-letter text contains some archaisms, and even preserves the occasional dialect form, but these serve only to reinforce the comedy value of the tanner's rusticity. In terms of intellectual sophistication and social rank there is an unbridgeable gap between the King and the artisan, but Danter both interrupts and concludes the narrative with a series of woodcuts which cumulatively stamp the booklet as a document of amelioration. Stabilization is underlined by the framing of the text with two identical representations of the King, mounted on a plumed horse, armed, and alone (facing pp. 1 and 8).[92] And where the text closes with the tanner's generous but comic offer to mend the King's shoes in return for his sovereign's surprising largesse, the final visual image is unequivocally hierarchical: a throned monarch dispenses justice to a kneeling suppliant, before an audience of courtiers who appear to be applauding.

If the unresolved tensions of generic antecedents such as 'The King and the Barker' are textually cleansed in Danter's publication, the process is extended in the reissue of the 'History' in 1613; here the text is introduced as a 'Merrie and pleasant communication' between king and subject, and the five woodcuts of 1596 become six, including one which undermines the 'disguise' implicit in the narrative by stressing an obvious sartorial difference between the protagonists.[93] Sanitization is complete by the Restoration period, when the 'Ballad' is decisively located in an anodyne (and spurious) medieval past, and printed under the improbable rubric, 'To an excellent new tune'.[94]

Edward IV lifts some details from these 'sources' and then transparently distorts them. Where the king of the ballad extravagantly offers the tanner the estate of 'Plumton Parke . . . worth three hundred pounds by yeare' (in the 'History' three 'tenements' are thrown in too), the play's Edward repays the tanner for his 'sport' with—to use the king's phrase—'princely kindness' of a different kind: John Hobs receives a pardon for his condemned son (a character invented by the dramatist), £40 to cover his travelling expenses, and a marriage the tanner declines with evident relief.

Woodcut: 'A Merry, pleasant, and delectable Historie, betweene K. Edward the fourth, and a Tanner'. Originally printed by W. White (London 1613), courtesy of Corpus Christi College, Oxford. Shelfmark CORPUS delta 4.24 (4)

Other features which *may* derive from ballad tradition are complex
elaborations of the merest hints. In 'The King and the Barker', for
instance, there is a suggestion that the monarch is hunting not just
for deer but for information: enquiring for the local magnate, the
Lord Basset, the King asks, 'Thow hast harde hes servantes speke,
/ what wolde they saye?'[95] Heywood's Edward, by contrast, is
exhaustively inquisitive about the political leanings of the tanner and
his neighbours. And in the play, the King's gathering of intelligence
incognito is ominously recognized as an established strategy, practised nationwide, and one which—as the Londoner Emersley later
admits (Scene 20, ll. 7–9)—can be neither questioned nor resisted.

Ballads with the generic formula of the plain-speaking subject
encountering but not identifying his monarch provided, then, a
skeletal framework for the dramatist. The King, however, is by
no means the only imperfectly recognized character to be found
in Staffordshire, and when his courtiers, absent since the play's
opening scene, re-enter the drama, another distinct but related
ballad tradition enters with them. As Howard and Sellinger arrive
in Scene 11, l. 50, the stage direction requires that they do so dressed
'*in green*'. This simplest of visual gestures would instantly have
alerted a theatre audience to the emergence, in some form, of Robin
Hood and his followers: Henslowe's inventory of props and costumes included green garments for Robin and Marian, the same
characters had entered 'all in greene' in the first of Munday's Robin
Hood plays, and a group had adopted this outlaw mode of dress in
Peele's *Edward I*.[96] Spectators already attuned to picking up resonances of and deviations from the 'commoner and king' ballad tradition would now be prepared to do the same with a tradition much
larger and more diverse, and one which sometimes worked in a similarly ameliorative manner, but sometimes powerfully voiced ideas
of resistance to authority.

The 'king and the commoner' ballads and the Robin Hood ballads
share some distinguishing features. Most notable is the carniva-
lesque quality of the authority exercised by the monarch in his
kingdom, and by Robin in the forest, particularly evident in encounters with craftsmen or labourers. Affinities between playful king and
popular outlaw are carefully filtered into *Edward IV*. Disguise is virtually mandatory for ballad outlaw and king alike, and Robin is no
exception. This can effect an evanescent levelling fantasy, as when
the outlaw assumes the role of butcher, beggar or shepherd in order
to converse on 'equal' terms with men of the same social status; as

with ballad kings, the revelation of true rank produces temporary and comic trauma, followed by the reabsorption of the deceived into an unquestioned and benevolent hierarchy. But disguise can work in other, more problematic ways. There may be strategic or purely narrative motivations for the adoption of roles such as 'informant' (in 'Robin Hood and the Potter'), extortionist (in 'Guy of Gisborne') or keeper of the king's deer ('Robin Hood and the Tanner'), but the resultant reversals of authority pose questions about the hated and oppressive legal apparatus which subsequent revelations of identity cannot entirely silence.

There was a tradition, well established by the sixteenth century but quite possibly originating in the reign of Edward IV, in which real insurgents adopted 'Robin' as a *nom de guerre* and appropriated to themselves the dictatorial powers of kings, but *Edward IV* effectively reverses this process.[97] The play deliberately flirts with the notion of the *king* as slanderous rebel—it is Edward who speaks treasonably about himself in Scene 13, l. 49ff—and, resuming the colloquial frivolity of the opening scene, persists with the presentation of the monarch as the quasi-outlaw with raffish charm.[98] The King's 'rebelliousness' echoes, however, only the most anti-social elements of the Falconbridge uprising: the casual lechery, the pseudo-colloquial name-calling ('Ned' and 'Tom') and the insistence upon indulging his 'humour' (Scene 13, l. 117; cf. Scene 9, ll. 38–9).

But the strain of genuine resistance to unjust authority which inhered in the Robin Hood legend is not abandoned altogether, rather it is subtly realigned with the figure of John Hobs. This strain may have been much diminished by the latter part of the sixteenth century but it was not quite extinguished, and a reminder of it may have been published in the troubled 1590s. Scholars disagree about the date of composition of the *Gest of Robin Hood*, estimates varying from shortly before 1400 up to the reign of the 'comly kynge' Edward IV, but it was certainly reissued by the bookseller William Copland around 1560.[99] On 14 May 1594 a 'pastorall plesant commedie of Robin Hood and Little John' was entered in the Stationers' Register, and this may well have prompted Edward White to reprint Copland's edition of the 'Gest . . . wyth a newe playe for to be played in Maye games'.[100]

Just as the title page of *Edward IV* prioritizes its protagonist's 'mery pastime' with the tanner, so the title pages of both Copland's and White's editions had declared themselves 'very plesaunte and ful of pastyme', but the *Gest* and the play have more in common than (misleading) self-advertisement. Like the play, the long poem has often been read as a text in which social criticism is muted and the interrogatory energies of carnival are subordinated to, and ultimately snuffed out by, the irresistible but benevolent authority of the Crown. More recently, however, it has been acknowledged that the *Gest* gives voice to the radical discourses which arose from the 'Peasants' Revolt' in the late fourteenth century, in which resisters struggled to reconcile their opposition to the corrupt mechanisms of state with their allegiance to the Crown and the church.[101]

It is Heywood's tanner, rather than his king, who turns out to have genuine affinities with the hero of the *Gest*. Hobs's performance begins with generosity to the poor (Scene 11, l. 17) and Robin's ends with the same: he 'dyde pore men moch god' (stanza 456). For all the hospitality extended to them at court, both Robin and the Tanner find life there uncongenial and expensive: the outlaw returns to the forest, Hobs to his 'knobs of bark' and his 'tan-fat' (Scene 23, l. 144). The tanner's appearance at court might have been suggested by another ballad, 'The King and a Poore Northerne Man', in which a countryman refuses to enter the royal presence without his dog or his staff in case he is robbed by the courtiers, but although the balladeer's patronizing amusement at such rustic naivety may be reflected in King Edward's judgement of Hobs, such condescension is far from unchallenged in the play as a whole.[102] The tanner's attachment to his trade and his home offers not absurd parochialism but a sustained critique of the court's rural 'games': courtiers' hunting, durably emblematic of aristocratic prestige and privilege, was also a potential violation of the customary rights of commoners in the forests, including the right to gather the bark so essential—as the play repeatedly acknowledges—to the tanning process.[103]

It is the unremitting specificity of the play's handling of the tanner and both his industry and his habitat that reveals how the dramatist has moulded the material of his ballad sources and which demonstrates the distance between these sources and his achievement. Both sixteenth-century editions of the *Gest* included 'a newe playe for to be plaied in May-games', and David Wiles has written that 'in a may-game of Robin Hood the real world is incorporated into the mythical world and a measure of overt defiance becomes inescapably an ingredient in the genre'.[104] It is an observation perhaps more accurately made of *Edward IV*. Anti-clericalism provides one example. Robin Hood's frequent verbal and physical assaults on members of the church, although they did not endear him to the godly of Elizabethan England, were motivated by a distrust of corrupt individuals which became endemic: as the *Gest*'s companion piece, 'Robin Hood and the Friar', has it, 'He never loves fryar nor none of freiers kin'.[105] Hobs's attack on the church, by contrast, is impeccably Protestant in its doctrine—a denunciation of the traffic in indulgences—but he uses it merely as an analogy to supplement a more comprehensive protest against the Crown-sponsored corruption that is wrecking the livelihoods of himself and others (Scene 13, ll. 75–9). Neither Heywood nor Hobs will allow the play to linger in an arcane medieval past and the 'mery pastime' between king and tanner, far from subsuming the disputes of the 1590s, serves as a vehicle for their dramatization. And, as the playwright was well aware, the row about the tanning industry was one of the bitterest.

Hobs's maxim that "'tis pity that one subject should have in his hand, that might do good to many through the land' (Scene 13, ll. 82–3) was a sentiment which was supposed to be enshrined in the very laws of the kingdom, and especially in those laws addressing the availability of leather to workers dependant upon it. As early as 1554 it had been recognized that 'many poore Artificers . . . nowe being very poore Men and not able to buye twoo or three Hides or Backes of Leather at one tyme, nor to paye readye moneye for the same, arre enforced to gyve upp their Occupations in greate nomber, to their utter empoverishment and undooing'. It was further acknowledged that earlier legislation (5 & 6. Edward VI.c.15) had benefited only 'a fewe riche Shoomakers . . . that arre nowe, comon Rogratoures [i.e. 'regrators'] and Engrossers of Leather', men who respected neither good workmanship nor the commonwealth ('whiche is well perceyved both in mennes purses and also in their shoes'). This handful of rich men, it was conceded, now held 'thonelye trade of buieng of Leather Stuffe and Talowe in their handes'.[106]

The further measures passed in 1563 were conceived in ignorance, mutually contradictory, and, as was officially recognized when the regulations were drastically overhauled in 1604, 'impossible for [the tanners] to performe'.[107] The iniquities of legal provisions notwithstanding, the Elizabethan government received a steady income from penalties imposed on tanners who broke the laws, and they were enabled to do so by the granting of a patent in 1575 which empowered its holder either to enforce the regulations or to sell dispensations permitting tanners to infringe them.[108] John Hobs's principled objections to the King's detailed proposals for manipulating the leather market are precisely those voiced in acrimonious Commons debates on the issue. Francis Moore's passionate contribution was not unique:

> I cannot utter with my Tongue, or conceive with my Heart, the great Grievances that the Town and Country for which I serve, suffer by some of these Monopolies: It bringeth the General Profit into a Private Hand; and the End of all is Beggary and Bondage to the Subject. We have a Law for the True and Faithful Currying of Leather: There is a Patent that sets all at Liberty, notwithstanding the Statute.

The coda to his speech, however, was unusually bitter: 'to what purpose is it', he asked, 'to do anything by Act of Parliament, when the Queen will undo the same by Her Prerogative?'[109]

The tanners repeatedly complained that the operation of the patent prevented them from making 'any reasonable peneworthes of ther wares', and eventually a royal proclamation of 1601 conceded that the leather patent had been one of several in which 'there hath been abuse in the execution of them, to the hurt and prejudice of her loving subjects'.[110] Secretary Cecil, however, was anxious not only to remind Parliament that 'the Queen means not to be swept out of Her Prerogative' but to defend the integrity of the man entrusted with the leather patent: 'Sir Edward Dier, a Gentleman of good Desert, Honest, Religious and Wise'.[111] It is a character reference with which Hobs would have been unlikely to concur, since Dyer and his deputies had gained an evil reputation for extortions practised under the cover of his patent.[112] Dyer was, in fact, what Hobs would have called a 'courtnole': a courtier who enjoyed Elizabeth's favour more or less without interruption, and a man sufficiently trusted by the government to be asked to investigate the disappearance of Crown lands, through the setting up of a sophisticated network of informers.[113] Dyer also provides one of many links to the man who, in the autumn of 1599, could not be named in *Edward IV*, but whose presence—or conspicuous absence—impinges on the text so often and so elusively that he warrants discussion as a source in his own right: one of Dyer's closest, and most dangerous associates was Robert Devereux, Earl of Essex.[114]

When Henry VIII appropriated the identity of Robin Hood as a demonstration of his libidinal power back in 1510 (see note 98) he had been joined in the sport by the then Earl of Essex.[115] According to some observers, the second Elizabethan earl was equally 'to fleshly wantonnes . . . much inclined', but Devereux was of course unable to share the pleasures of masculine flirtation with his monarch; rather, his clandestine conquests produced in the Queen levels of rage similar to those experienced by the husbands Essex cuckolded—such as the patron of the company who premiered *Edward IV*.[116] The Earl of Derby's feelings of sexual betrayal may suggest one reason for the play's conspicuous omission of Essex's name from scenes dealing with the suppression of the Falconbridge rebellion (to which Holinshed insisted he had contributed so importantly). The disastrous news of the Irish campaign which was filtering back to London in the late summer of 1599, and the 'Bishops' ban' of a few months earlier, provide two more compelling ones. Yet, for the attentive spectator, there are constant reminders of Essex, and these allusions cluster in the play's Staffordshire scenes.

It has been shown that despite his fifteenth-century ballad origins Hobs is a definitively Elizabethan subject, and as such Essex would have been by far the most important figure in his locality. The Earl repeatedly referred to Staffordshire as 'my own countrey'; he was the keeper of the county's sessions rolls, steward of the town of Tamworth and, from 1590, effectively the lord lieutenant of the county as well.[117] Essex also controlled the election of MPs for both Tamworth and the town where Hobs's daughter has her schooling, Lichfield.[118] If, as seems likely, Grudgen's complaints about 'fifteen' and 'soldiers' in *Edward IV* refer to recruitment as well as taxation, Essex's military campaigns would have prompted them, since the Earl's authority over local musters ensured that his armies always included substantial numbers of Staffordshire men (see commentary to Scene 18, l. 73).[119] Essex's principal country estate was also in the county and Chartley, the house at its centre, was nationally known, particularly since 1586 when Elizabeth had commandeered it—to the Earl's considerable displeasure—for the incarceration of Mary, Queen of Scots.[120]

Chartley is not mentioned by name in *Edward IV*, but the name of the family with which it was most closely associated—and by

alliance with which the Devereux came to inherit the house—does
appear. When John Hobs first comes across the Queen and the
Duchess in their aristocratic hunting attire, he believes that he must
be addressing 'Mistress Ferris' (Scene 11, l. 20). As the 'Gentle-
women' depart Hobs is still not quite convinced of their regal status,
and he again explains to the audience: 'I took the Queen, as I am
true tanner, for Mistress Ferris' (ll. 49–50). Why this reiteration,
when neither the encounter nor the name appears in any of the
ballad 'sources'? The only plausible explanation is that this is a
cryptic and mischievous allusion to the dynasty which dominated
the area's affairs for more than three centuries: 'Ferris' (or 'Ferries')
was, in the Elizabethan period, a common spelling and pronunciation of 'Ferrers'.[121]

   Edmund, the fifth Baron Ferrers of Chartley, who would be celebrated by Drayton as one of the heroes of Agincourt, died in 1435,
and it was at the marriage of his granddaughter that the Chartley
estates passed into the Devereux family.[122] Thereafter, the two
names were intertwined and the honorific title of 'Lord Ferrers of
Chartley' was important to the Devereux, even after the creation of
Robert's father as the first Elizabethan earl of Essex; this is, for
instance, how Walter styled himself in his will.[123] It is, however,
the prominence in the text of *Edward IV* of the adjacent estate at
Drayton Basset that clinches the Essex connection. The name does
occur in the ballad sources where it has no other role than the provision of corroborative local detail. In the play, however, it is partly
as the country seat of Essex's mother (born Lettice Knollys) that
Drayton Basset has resonance; it was purchased in 1579 for his new
wife by her second husband, the Earl of Leicester, but it was a marriage which secured for Lettice Queen Elizabeth's unyielding hatred.
Essex's mother was a cousin of the Queen and, apparently, bore a
remarkable physical resemblance to her; indeed, her 'looks, temper
and taste for display were uncomfortably like a younger version of
the queen herself'.[124] So, Hobs's mistaking the identity of his queen
for that of Staffordshire's first lady (and his insistence on the old
dynastic name) has a neat comic propriety.

   But Drayton Basset had also acquired another, more problematic
significance in the spring of 1599. The Tamworth parish registers,
dominated throughout by the name of Ferrers, record births, marriages and deaths in the district; only once in a period spanning
thirty years (with 1599 at the mid-point) does the register acknowledge matters of national rather than purely local importance:

'Memor that the 30th day of this Aprill [1599] Robert Earle of Essex went from Drayton Bassett towardes Ireland with an Hoste of men to make warre gainste the Earle of Tyroone an Iryshman'.[125]

Edward IV contains nothing so straightforward as a single theatrical character who represents Essex. Rather, the play enfolds allusions to the disturbing presence of the Earl and the behaviour of his adherents throughout its episodic structure. The wilfulness and the indiscriminate distribution of knighthoods planned by the rebels in the opening scenes has already been noted, but no less significant is the scene in which the dispensing of such honours is actually realized. When the Lord Mayor expresses confidence that

> With the most happy conquest of proud rebels,
> Dispersed and fled, . . . now remains no doubt,
> Of ever making head to vex us more
> (Scene 9, ll. 193–5)

every spectator could have recognized the ironic contrast with Essex's utter failure to subdue the Irish rebellion. The more curious might also have observed that there was slender justification for the constant attendance of 'Sellinger'—a name either absent from or peripheral to the chronicle accounts of Edward's reign but whose presence is specified here (188, SD) and throughout the play— except that this was also the name of one of Essex's aides, one of only a handful of men who accompanied the Earl in the negotiation of the ignominious truce with Tyrone.[126]

Similarly, any Londoner would have recognized the play's demystification of the term 'benevolences' (see Scene 18, ll. 22–6 and commentary); such 'voluntary' contributions to the government coffers had been occasioned by the dearth of 1595–97, but a further one in 1599 coincided with the costly fiasco of the Irish campaign.[127] Moreover, detailed accounts of instructions given to collectors of such taxes in the late Elizabethan period suggest that the play's portrayal of their thinly veiled extortion is pointedly accurate.[128] This kind of coercion, succinctly suggested in the dark pun on 'stretched' in Scene 21 (see commentary to l. 13), is not the play's only example of where force is disguised as persuasion, and alongside all such instances is the unremitting sense of surveillance. It is clear throughout that all subjects/characters are under either the constant scrutiny of the King himself (Scene 20, *passim*) or that of his agents. Again, spectators might be expected to know that Essex supervised an intelligence network of an unrivalled range and complexity, although perhaps fewer would recognize in the names of the tax-collectors Aston and Bowes the identities of important figures within it.[129]

This section on the 'sources' for the Staffordshire scenes of *Edward IV* may seem to have veered a long way from ballads and Robin Hood. The play, however, does not. John Hobs, besides singing one ballad on stage, mentions another which explicitly connects the outlaw with the Earl. Back in 1569 Richard Grafton had argued that the 'real' Robin Hood had been 'for his manhoode and chiualry aduaunced to the noble dignitie of an Erle, excellyng principally in Archery, or shootyng', but that, having fallen into debt, he 'gathered together a companye of Roysters and Cutters, and practised robberyes and spoylyng of the kynges subiects'.[130] The ballad with which Hobs suggests he might demonstrate his entirely provisional loyalty to the regime of King Edward, 'York, York, for my money' (Scene 13, l. 48), also links expertise in shooting with a troubled and troublesome aristocrat, for it celebrates the patronage of archery contests by 'the noble earle of Essex'.[131] Both this ballad and Hobs's '*threemen's song*' (Scene 14, ll. 109ff) could imply a nostalgia, rather like John Stow's, for bygone days of martial prowess, and perhaps a wistful hope that Essex, beyond question the most powerful and charismatic soldier of the 1590s, might bring them back; plenty of ballads written from such a perspective were certainly in circulation.[132]

Expectations of Essex remained high in the year that *Edward IV* appeared. Francis Cordale observed that 'The common people still favour the Earl, hoping by his means to be freed from their intolerable exactions ... They would follow any who would be likely to procure them some immunities, for, never were they more oppressed, and subject to all servile conditions'.[133] *Edward IV* unquestionably invites an audience's consideration of 'intolerable exactions', but although these fleeting and refracted images cumulatively constitute an Essex 'presence' in the drama, the play refuses to endorse the validity of this (or any other) authority figure's claims to alleviate them. Hammer's fine study has done much to restore the picture of Essex as the precociously gifted politician and soldier, for long periods trusted and relied upon by a monarch whose feverish wilfulness he soothed, resented and emulated by turn. *Edward IV* does something similar: it offers a compelling, composite but ultimately puzzling triptych, part dangerous rebel (Falconbridge), part maverick king and part invisible but tangible power in Staffordshire.

The seventeenth-century antiquarian Abraham de la Prynne wrote that the famous philologist John Selden collected ballads because he believed 'there was more truth in them than there was in many of our historians'.[134] In fact, in the second (1631) edition of his massive *Titles of Honour*, Selden actually singled out the 'Tanner of Tamworth' ballad and quoted from it to illustrate a precise historical observation.[135] Heywood's handling of the ballad is at once less scientific and less deferential. He alters the story at will: the disguised King's visit to Hobs's home, for instance, occurs in no printed source and Heywood appears to include it to emphasize what might be expected to happen there but does not. Edward and Sellinger 'neither talk nor eat', and turn down the tanner's offer of 'clean sheets' in which to stay the night (Scene 14, ll. 76, 118–23). The 'courtnoles'' nonchalant disregard for Hobs's generosity—and their casual flirting with his daughter Nell—carefully anticipate the King's flagrant violations of hospitality and sexual morality in the home of the Lord Mayor a couple of hundred lines later. But in the very act of distorting these particular ballad 'sources', and refusing the easy reconciliation between king and commoner they disarmingly provide, the play paradoxically realizes the radical potential of the unlicensed Elizabethan ballad-singers; for, as D. R. Woolf has observed, 'oral tradition answered to no one: it was "masterless history"'.[136]

THE OPENING OF THE SHORES' STORY

For the plot which occupies the remainder of Part One, and which will dominate Part Two of *Edward IV*, the literary sources are the iconoclastic *History of King Richard the Third* by Sir Thomas More, and the diverse Elizabethan poems it inspired. The third and final 'movement' of the play then, dramatizes not a ballad but a 'complaint'. It is essential to the thematic continuity of the play that Heywood's treatment of the Jane Shore story, although sharing narrative and linguistic features with the corpus of poems that comprise the genre, is in one respect singular: where most 'complaints' are voiced in a sparsely populated rural or pastoral landscape—or echo in a literally deserted one—Jane tells her tale in London.[137] The play launches the Shore plot from the home of the Lord Mayor, and establishes its chronological and spatial locale by the incorporation of a detailed chorographical tour. This time, however, Heywood borrows from Stow's *Survey* his methodology—the blending of topographical description, social history and anecdote—but systematically distorts the data he finds there.

The playwright knew perfectly well that Sir John Crosby was not the lord mayor in the year of the Falconbridge rebellion, nor indeed

at any other time; he was, as Stow and Fabyan made clear, sheriff
during the mayorality of Sir John Stockton. Two factors concerning
Crosby attracted Heywood's attention. One was the idealized tale of
Crosby's foundling origins, dramatized in the opening soliloquy of
Scene 16; it is significant that Stow, whose version of the story in
the *Survey* (of Bishopsgate ward) provides the only 'source', dismisses it contemptuously as a mere 'fable'.[138] The second was the
'large and sumptuous building' Crosby erected for himself, which
Stow described as the most 'beautifull, and the highest at that time
in London'.[139] As every spectator in 1599 would have known, this
house was now the home of the most unpopular lord mayor of the
Elizabethan period.

Sir John Spencer purchased Crosby Place in 1594 and owned it
until 1601.[140] Described in the early Jacobean period as one of the
half-dozen richest men in the City, he was an early director of the
East India Company but above all a money-lender; indeed, with
clients including the Earl of Essex, he was perhaps 'the most prominent of all lenders to the courtly world of fashion of his day'.[141] But
serious and widespread hostility had marred Spencer's year in the
lord mayor's office. In the wake of the riots in 1595 he was accused
of corruption in the sale of offices, failing to consult with his colleagues, administrative incompetence and insatiable avarice. His
popular reputation could not have been lower—his conspicuous
failure to commiserate with or relieve the poor being arguably the
worst of his many offences—and the climactic illustration of the
hatred he aroused occurred in the late summer of 1595, when a
crowd erected a gallows outside his house.[142]

The banquet at Crosby's house is an invention of the dramatist
which is significant for two reasons. First, it effectively reverses any
relationship between host and guest he might have found in the
chronicle sources: King Edward was renowned, particularly in the
London chronicles, for assiduously courting London's governors
with lavish feasting.[143] Secondly, the orderliness and munificence of
London's hospitality establishes an absolute distinction between the
Lord Mayor of the play and the current owner of Crosby Place. The
domesticity of the scene is crucial, not only because it helps to shape
a cameo of urban social cohesion but also because it prepares for
the devastating theatrical impact of Edward's behaviour, from the
extraordinary tactlessness of the King's not bothering to ascertain
that the Mayor's wife has died (ll. 77–8) to his inexcusably abrupt
departure. In the early modern period any absence from a commu-

nal feast signalled a 'separation from fellowship', and a deliberate
refusal to share hospitality demonstrated the often irretrievable collapse of solidarity amongst the society assembled. That the implications of such a violation of social obligation were not merely secular
is attested to by the description of the 'great injury and wrong' occasioned by precisely this kind of ingratitude—analagous to the refusal
of the sacrament—in the Book of Common Prayer.[144] The scene
closes with the stunning tableau of the untouched banquet, and
Crosby's request to the Shores—'At night I pray ye both come sup
with me. How say ye? will ye?' (ll. 187–8)—is perfectly judged: for
an audience emerging from five years of food shortages, the Mayor's
hapless attempt to dispose of the untasted feast ensures that
Edward's insult is experienced by Londoners both on and off stage.
And this is where the London setting of the Shores' demise, peripheral to or absent from Heywood's literary antecedents but central to
his own enterprise, re-emerges with such distinctive emphasis.

From More's *Richard the Third*, the earliest detailed account of
Mistress Shore's rise and fall and one incorporated more or less verbatim into most subsequent national chronicles, Heywood could
have gleaned little of the landscape that shaped and witnessed her
remarkable life; that she was 'born in London', and put 'to open
penance' by the city's bishops are the only 'locations' the English
versions offer.[145] Of the abandoned husband, More divulges that
he too was a Londoner—'an honest citezen, yonge & goodly &
of good substance' (55/9–10)—but no more.[146] Until the publication
of Drayton's *Englands Heroicall Epistles* in 1597 poetic elaborations
of More's narrative abandoned even this notional placing of the
story.

One of the most important of these elaborations is *Shores Wife* by
Thomas Churchyard. The poem first appeared in the 1563 edition of
A Mirror for Magistrates, but Churchyard revised and substantially
expanded it for inclusion in his own volume, *Churchyards Challenge*,
in 1593. The poem also reappeared in the expanded 1587 edition of
A Mirror, where although the text remained unaltered, the tale
is announced, in a preface 'ascribed' to the 'eloquent wentch' herself,
as

> a matter scarce fit for womans shamefastnes to bewray. But since without
> blushing I haue so long beene a talkatiue wench, (whose words a world
> hath delighted in) I will now goe on boldly with my audacious manner:
> and so step I on the stage in my shrowdeing sheete as I was buried.[147]

The immediacy of this preface is Churchyard's tentative attempt to preserve something of the contemporaneity of More's account, which was composed, the humanist writes, while its protagonist 'yet . . . liueth' (55/27). The poem itself, however, slips at once into an irretrievable if recent past—the third line refers to Mistress Shore's career as 'a thing thus done so late'—and any sense of historical or topographical specificity is deliberately discarded. Not only is all mention of London jettisoned, but the 1593 revision translates the complaint to a generically appropriate woodland setting in which the 'princes vaine' is gratified by 'descant strange . . . / In quiet bower, when birds be all at rest'.[148]

Edward IV displays a thorough familiarity with Churchyard's poem, but where the poem uneasily (and unwittingly) vacillates between Jane's sexual attractiveness and the King's violence as alternative causes for ˙her catastrophe, Heywood presses home the contradiction: Churchyard's voyeuristic revelations of his heroine's jewel-like beauty—Mistress Shore is 'blasd', by Mistress Shore herself, at much greater length in the 1593 version as a 'piece of worke, should please a princes eie' (pp. 129–30)—become Edward's predatory and egotistical fantasies in the play. A similar process can be observed in Heywood's handling of another poem, published in the same year as (and probably intended to capitalize upon the success of) *Churchyards Challenge*: Anthony Chute's *Beawtie Dishonoured*.

The consistency, however, with which elements of Chute's work are uprooted, relocated and defamiliarized effectively constitutes an aggressive commentary upon the poem by the play. So, for instance, although the playwright ignores totally Chute's characterization of Mistress Shore's husband as a man 'crookt old, and cold', and one whose marriage arouses 'mallice' towards himself and 'pittie' towards his wife, he does seize on the one moment of remorse the poem allows its protagonist; but where Chute's narrator briefly perceives herself as the ostracized owl, 'wonderd at of all the byrdes who see', Heywood uses the analogy to express the anguished isolation Matthew Shore experiences as the King's cuckold (Scene 22, ll. 11–12).[149]

Unlike the play, *Beawtie Dishonoured* unfolds in a temporal and spatial vacuum. It occasionally manifests an anachronistic and incidental Protestant perspective, but even when the narrator speaks of the 'Monarke aspect of my recusant eye', what truly concerns Chute are the crude mechanics of a transference of power between man and woman, king and subject: the single line in which the poem concedes the altruism of the adulteress's dispensation of royal favour leads straight back to condemnation of her relish for command, the 'tribute dutie' she exacts from the King, and how she 'Made him my subiect, ere myne eyes had don'.[150] Whereas Churchyard's poem, particularly within its *Mirror for Magistrates* framework, preserved an intriguing tension between the self-styled 'talkatiue wench' of the prologue and the reticent victim of slander—'to speake alas I was affrayed'—of the narrative, Chute's 'heroine' is a glib and garrulous flirt, and whilst her urbane opportunism is inimical to Heywood's conception of Jane Shore, it could have prompted the creation of the unscrupulous (and otherwise 'sourceless') Mistress Blage.[151]

Chute's poem remains prurient to the last, even eroticizing the 'willing gaspes' (sig. A4r) of Mistress Shore's dying breath. The erotic, albeit masquerading as erudite antiquarianism, also features prominently in Heywood's other (and chronologically latest) non-dramatic source for this episode.[152] Michael Drayton's *Englands Heroicall Epistles* first appeared in 1597, was revised and reissued later in the same year, and was reprinted and expanded in each of the following two years.[153] Included from the outset was the pair of verse epistles between King Edward IV and Mistress Shore, and to each poem were appended prose 'Annotations of the Chronicle Historie'. In his 'annotation' of Mistress Shore's 'letter' Drayton proclaims More—'*that ornament of* England *and* Londons *more particular glorie*'—as the precursor whose celebration of her beauty legitimizes his own. More's account had indeed sustained a precarious balance between condemnation and a sexual fascination which the moralistic framework could not efface: 'she went in countenance & pace demure so womanly, & albeit she were out of al array saue her kyrtle only: yet went she so fair & louely . . . that her great shame wan her much praise, among those yᵗ were more amorous of her body then curious of her soule' (54–5/29–3). Drayton not only claims to reintroduce the historical specificity which Churchyard and Chute had evaded, he cites (untraceable) documentary evidence to validate a voyeurism which surpasses anything ventured by his acknowledged predecessors: in the '*picture which I have seene of hers*', Drayton asserts, '*shee rose out of her bed in the morning, having nothing on but a rich Mantle, cast under one arme over her shoulder, and sitting in a chaire, on which her naked arme did lie*' (12–15).

Despite enlisting, however, venerable historians—'*Master* Camden, *and Master* Lambert' (Lambarde)—to illuminate his poetic conceits, Drayton enriches his Ovidian epistles with little historical or topographical detail. The cuckolded Shore is identified (for the first time) as a goldsmith, but apart from his wife's reference to the 'golden Cheape' and the 'glitt'ring Change' (l. 12), the physical particularity of the city they inhabit is not evoked. But as the eroticism serves to intensify and complicate the dynamic between seducer and seduced, so the unmistakably urban setting of the poems does establish the social (and occupational) milieu of the Shores as a site of *economic* power which challenges the authority of the monarch. It is the symbiotic relationship between these two confrontations which emerges as the true focus of the 'epistles', and which, in turn, prompted Heywood to construct scenes which dramatize and act as an extended commentary upon Drayton's achievement.[154]

Tension between London and the Crown is announced early in the King's address—'O, why should Fortune make the Citie proud, / To give that more, then is the Court allow'd?' (ll. 7–8)—and some of Drayton's few revisions of the poem suggest that he wished to consolidate that emphasis. In 1597 (and subsequent Elizabethan reissues) the King, for example, had mused, 'When I envy that *Shore* should be so blest' (l. 18); but, in keeping with the poem's relentless objectification of Mistress Shore as a jewel, the Jacobean Drayton recast the line: 'When I maligne the Wealth wherewith hee's blest'. This sense of conflict over an economic resource, possessed by London's merchant class and desired by, but temporarily inaccessible to the Crown, remains central to the King's discourse of amorous persuasion: 'Nor is it fit, a Citie-shop should hide / The Worlds Delight, and Natures onely Pride'. Such a gem, he argues, should be reserved for 'a Princes sumptuous Gallerie' (ll. 153–5). This struggle, in which Drayton's Mistress Shore becomes the emblematic prize, provides the dramatic structure of Scene 17 of *1 Edward IV*, but in Heywood's hands this is but one skirmish in an on-going battle with which his drama as a whole is concerned.

The imagery, then, with which Drayton's king conducts his courtship is borrowed by Heywood, but, as if in acknowledgement of Drayton's nervous 'Annotation'—'George Bucanan (*that imperious* Scot) *chargeth* [Edward], *and other Princes of those Times, with affection of Tyrannie*' (ll. 27–9)—the dramatist deploys it to characterize his monarch's dealings with all his subjects. Thus, although there is no echo in the play's 'seduction' scene of the first epistle's exasperated complaint that the wealth the monarch covets is being hoarded by the citizens, who 'ingrosse it, as they doe their Ware' (l. 10), the play juxtaposes its dramatization of Edward's irresistible sexual greed with a scene of similarly inescapable tax demands; as Hobs the tanner observes with customary brevity (and acuity), 'the King wants money, and would have some of his commenty' (Scene 18, ll. 17–18). In addition, to corroborate the affinities between the King's hardworking subjects, rural and metropolitan alike, Heywood relegates his Mistress Shore to a rank beneath any she enjoyed in earlier literary treatments; when Drayton's adulteress, for instance, explains her capitulation to the King by referring to the boredom she (and other wives of her class) experience, with nothing to entertain them but 'Our Dogge, our Parrat, or our Marmuzet' (l. 148), in the play the King's courtship interrupts Jane Shore's methodical supervision of a family business she supplements with her own needlework (Scene 17, ll. 1–18.01).

It is worth pausing to note, however, that, when 'Mistress Shore' first made the transition from non-dramatic verse to the stage, continuity was observed (and announced) in the process. Shakespeare erased her voice altogether from his *Richard III*, which appeared in quartos of 1597 and 1598, but the anomaly of her modest origins and subsequent political influence was preserved: marginalized as only a subject for gossip she was none the less neatly caricatured by Richard as one of the 'mighty gossips in this monarchy' (1.1.83). Although appearing in print earlier, the anonymous *True Tragedie of Richard the Third* (entered in the Stationers' Register and published in 1594) was almost certainly composed later. Here Mistress Shore makes brief but important appearances. In most she is depicted as the unpitied victim of Richard's political (and sexual) vindictiveness, but before she is aware of her royal lover's death her evolution as an *arriviste*—she vows to 'feather my nest' from Edward's coffers 'were it halfe his reuenewes'—is less equivocal than either Chute or Drayton had suggested.[155] But the play also attests, in a darkly comic intertextual 'aside', to the contribution Mistress Shore's poetic personae had made to an anxiety generated by their representations of a woman whose sexual allure engulfed the King's economic and political power, and therefore governed its dispensation. Thus Lodwicke, an aristocratic functionary who acknowledges that he owes the restitution of his lands to Mistress Shore's intercession, resolves to 'shun her company and get me to my chamber, and there set downe in heroicall verse, the shameful end of a kings Concubin, which is no doubt as wonderfull as the desolation of a kingdome'

(1076–9). Paradoxes which emerge from troubling conflations of her erotic, economic and even altruistic authority accrue around this play's Mistress Shore. To some she is 'so noble a strumpet' (l. 1115), to others 'an holie whore' (l. 1173), and in her final destitution, even her own configuration—'tho he was King, yet Shores wife swayd the swoord' (ll. 1087–8)—sustains a disturbing sexual and political dynamic which emanates from the King's mistress herself.

In returning to Scene 17 of *1 Edward IV* it can be seen what a massive distance Heywood has put between his play and its poetic and theatrical antecedents and, furthermore, how much is achieved with extraordinary dramatic economy in the opening fifteen lines alone. As the two apprentices appear with 'weights and balance' (ll. 8–9) and Jane checks the exact weight of a cup just 'dispatched' to a 'gentleman' (ll. 12–15), the audience is visually and aurally reminded of the threat posed to such equitably regulated commerce in the play's first movement by the rebels who would 'sell pearls by the peck' (Scene 2, l. 53). But, as has been shown, the threat posed to the economic (and sexual) integrity of the London citizens is realized in this play not by the insurgents but by the Crown. And if a pervasive connection between women as vehicles of male sexual fantasy and women as visible participants in the purveyance of desirable commodities had been established before—Drayton's poem, for one, alludes to such a congruence—*Edward IV* marks a seminal moment in the *staging* of such a combination as the habitual stimulant to a predatory court and its satellites. For this scene offers a schematic miniature of a confrontation which would be re-enacted on London stages countless times in the ensuing decades. Ten years after the play's first performances, an anonymous writer attested to its enduring popularity, suggesting that *Edward IV* still attracted as many spectators (of different social rank) as more recently premiered entertainments:

> Amazde I stood to see a crowd
> Of *Ciuill Throats* stretch'd out so lowd:
> (As at a *New-play*) all the *Roomes*
> Did swarme with *Gentiles* [sic] mix'd with *Groomes*.
> So that I truly thought, all *These*
> Came to see *Shore*, or *Pericles*.[156]

During the decade that had elapsed between the play's premiere and this testimony to its durability, the clash it had staged between one citizen couple and the monarch himself spawned the central politi-

cal conflict in the genre of 'City Comedy'. It has been observed that
in these Jacobean plays 'Class antagonism mixed with sexual fantasies as the courtier-consumer sought to revenge himself upon the
city's bourgeoisie by sexually dominating women of their class';[157]
the ideological parameters of this scenario were pioneered in *Edward
IV*.

As might be expected of the mid-point in a two-part play, the
closing scene of *1 Edward IV* offers scarcely any sense of closure.
The eclectic expropriation of source materials continues unabated,
as various strands emerge, recede and converge. In terms of narrative, for example, 'The King and the Tanner' still provides a tragi-
comic structure for the plot, but the resources of the ballad itself are
quickly exhausted and its original ameliorative function is complicated, if not frustrated, at every step. This is achieved in part by a
remarkable swerve into metatheatre executed by the tanner himself.

When John Hobs arrives at court he is confronted by the King
and Sellinger who have adopted hastily improvised disguises, and
the Lord Mayor, who has not. Although, inevitably, the tanner is
unable to discern at once the identities behind the still-resounding
names of 'Ned' and 'Tom', he has, he assures his audience, some
experience in reading the theatricality of a court: certain conventions pertaining to the representation of kingship are 'always' main-
tained, he insists, whenever touring actors 'play an enterlout or a
commodity' in his neck of the woods (ll. 47–8). It seems possible
that the *play*'s audience is invited to recall the best-known tour of
the tanner's patch, the extended entertainments provided for the
Queen's visit to Killingworth in 1575: the published account of this
'pastime', Robert Laneham's famous '*Letter*', highlighted the star-
turn of Captain Cox, whose 'great ouersight . . . in matters of storie'
featured both 'The King & the Tanner' and 'Robinhood', and the
unpublished accounts, listing payments to the Lord Chamberlain's,
the Earl of Warwick's, and the Earl of Essex's players, provide some
explanation for the tanner's imprecise recollection of 'my Lord what-
ye-call's players' (44–5).[158]

The Tanner's awareness that the procedures of kingship are invariably and inextricably linked with masking and role-playing is typically shrewd, but he soon discovers that performances in the
metropolis have become more complex and difficult to interpret.
Hobs's naive belief that grandeur of costume signifies authority leads
to a mistake and, in theatrical terms, a poignant one. The regalia
of office are all that is left to the Lord Mayor who expressed such

confidence in the reciprocal relationships between citizens, monarch and himself in Scene 16; pained and confused by the King's betrayal, the Mayor's uneasy and muted presence in this final scene is only confirmed by another rejection—albeit the tanner's polite one—of the hospitality his one short speech offers (ll. 61–5). The splendour of Crosby's robes provides a reminder of the Mayor's soliloquy when, flushed with the Londoners' successful defence of their city, he had been preparing to meet his grateful king. But the Mayor's assurance in the cultural and political authority of his office had been at once ahistorical and unwarranted; his proud (yet loyal) conviction that he could bear the mayoral sword with impunity 'in court, in city' (Scene 16, ll. 1–7) was hopelessly at odds with the Tudor regime's increasingly prescriptive regulation of areas in which it allowed even the sword of office to be borne *before* London's mayor, and the visibility in this closing scene of the worried, ignored, and largely silent Crosby provides an uncomfortable but accurate reminder of the true axis of power relations the play has uncovered.[159]

There is a neat theatrical symmetry at work as Part One closes: as the play had begun with Edward's unassailable assertion of his sexual desire for one widow, so it ends with his casual flirtation with another, and this re-staging of the King's libidinal power is likely to have been emphasized visually by the assumption of the two female roles by the same boy player. The episode also provides the vehicle for a deft twist in the play's dramatization of the ballad's *rapprochement* between the King and the Tanner.[160] In the ballad the money with which the monarch defuses the Tanner's anxieties and rewards his integrity is a spontaneous and generous donation; in the play the sum Edward offers to defray Hobs's travelling expenses is precisely the sum he teases out of Widow Norton with his kisses. The King's final gesture towards these two figures who have contributed so lavishly to his entertainment and his coffers is to propose a match he knows will be socially and financially unacceptable to them, and which would have been risibly incongruous in the eyes of the audience. With a handkerchief—an emblematic product of a Midlands industry in terminal crisis—sent by the Tanner's impressionable daughter nonchalantly pocketed, and both his betrayed queen and his newly acquired mistress out of *his* sight and mind, Edward ends Part One as he began it, toying with his loyal subjects and preparing for battle.

THE FRENCH EXPEDITION

As the closing section of this introduction ('The Text(s)') will show, at least one seventeenth-century reader found the entire opening movement of Part Two expendable. Recent critical accounts of the play preserve an almost complete silence about the 'war' in France too, and this distaste is clearly shared by theatre practitioners in the twenty-first century.[161] Given that both early modern chroniclers and modern historians seem to agree that the whole episode was, while of some territorial and political significance for the French, a slightly embarrassing non-event for the English, it is indeed difficult to see exactly why the dramatist(s) chose to include it.[162]

The play's depiction of Edward's French expedition does, however, reveal some continuities with the theatrical strategies and complex appropriations of source materials adopted in Part One. The sequence begins with Edward's military posturings, bombastic and politically imprecise as many pre-battle speeches in Elizabethan plays are, and this formulaic rhetoric is then immediately interrupted by the urbane comedy offered by Scales in his accounts of the new English allies, Burgundy and St. Pol. The debt to the tavern scenes in *1 Henry IV* is clear, but Scales's sophisticated rendering of the indolent mimickry practised in the Constable's camp (ll. 45ff) may in turn have influenced Shakespeare's portrayal of the scurrilous 'imitations' which Achilles and Patroclus perform in *Troilus and Cressida* (1.3.141–83).

For the bare outlines of his narrative the dramatist again relied primarily upon the 1587 *Chronicles* of Holinshed; although the extraordinary *Historie of Philip de Commines*, a senior diplomat in the service of the play's French king, had appeared in a fine translation by Thomas Danett in 1596, it appears that the playwright used it only sparingly. Despite the fact, however, that both of these works include (rather different) accounts of bizarre events such as the duping by the two kings of the messengers from Burgundy and the Constable (dramatized in Scene 7), the dramatist could have found little in either to generate the play's turning of such incidents into desperate farce. But readings of the 1475 episodes which viewed the bewildering sequence of shifting alliances and betrayals in precisely this way were available to him, because historians and political analysts in late sixteenth-century *France* frequently went back one hundred years to search for foreshadowings of, and solutions to, the prolonged crises of their own age.

It seems plausible to surmise that Heywood, who would, within the next decade, produce a translation of the French political philosopher Jean Bodin, had begun to be interested in French *reportage* and historical writing by the turn of the century. Such a fascination would not have been singular; it has been estimated that translations of French political writing accounted for at least one-fifth of the total output of English printers in the late Elizabethan period.[163] Printers whose work the dramatist certainly knew were heavily involved in this process. John Wolfe, who printed the play's 'source' poems on Mistress Shore, was commissioned by the government to deliver French 'news' from around 1589 onwards;[164] John Windet, the printer of *Edward IV*, also produced some of the most distinguished of these translations.[165]

One of the earliest works of French historiography to appear from Wolfe's printshop was *A Politike Discourse most excellent for this time present* (1589). The book explicitly cites the Piquigny Treaty between Edward IV and Lewis XI as a precedent which the contemporary governments of France and England should remember in negotiations governing their current relationship. The anonymous author urges that France should regard England not as a traditional enemy but as a strong ally against the encroachments of Catholic powers. The attempts by the fifteenth-century Burgundian court to undermine the authority of the French monarchy are viewed as a fore-taste of the machinations of sixteenth-century Spain, and the lesson of the past should not be forgotten: 'then the gentlenesse of king *Edward* stood *France* in steede of a greate and strong bulwarke, against the violence and heady force of the Burgonians'.[166] This book also offers an example of the way in which early English readers habitually responded to the discussion of such pressing concerns. The copy in the Bodleian Library in Oxford has generous manuscript annotations, amongst them a comment written opposite this passage, which reads: 'Fauors of the Englisshe to the Frenche'. Not all the annotations, however, are as objective as this. Many anticipate the flippantly aggressive tone with which *Edward IV* will treat instances of political treachery, as when, against a passage in which Philip of Spain offers to assist his French 'brother' with fifty thousand troops but sends only two thousand, the marginal note reads: 'Great brags. Small performance.'[167]

Although opinions continued to differ as to Lewis's strengths and weaknesses as a ruler—some regarded him as the shrewdest of diplomats,[168] some as impressionable and eccentric—[169] the tone of amused condescension which the play adopts towards the political manoeuvring of England's neighbours was not confined to marginal commentaries, but was also to be found amongst the most sophisticated of the printed texts. It seems likely, for instance, that the dramatist may have consulted the compendious historical writings of Jean de Serres, whose vivid accounts of the French civil wars had begun to appear in English translations in the 1570s, and whose work was frequently revised and expanded right up to the close of the century. There he would have found not only the most detailed analysis of the English expedition of 1475—de Serres is strikingly precise in his cataloguing of the personnel involved, as well as the sums of money and kind of gifts that were exchanged—but a wry and dispassionate scrutiny of the self-interest and unprincipled behaviour of its protagonists.[170]

If de Serres reserves his most caustic observations for discussions of the duplicities practised by the Constable and Burgundy, no political figure is beyond the reach of his pervasive cynicism. Writing of Lewis's apparently odd choice of an unknown servant—the play's 'sourceless' Mugeroun—as a herald, de Serres argues that, had negotiations gone badly, the King 'might disavow him if need required, as intruding himselfe, or at the least adventuring without his privitie: and at all hazards', he concludes, 'the losse of a servant was not great' (p. 253). Again, like the playwright, de Serres is at pains to expose the casual pragmatism which, for all the inflated rhetoric of public diplomatic exchanges, is uncovered as the real agent of political causation. Having recorded dutifully the strenuous oratory concerning territorial rights from both the English and French delegations, his summary is a dry one: 'But the quietist course is the best, and both being willing to agree, an accorde is soone made' (p. 254).

Holinshed found the episode of Lewis's eavesdropping (Scene 7, ll. 41ff) bewildering and absurd; de Serres, noting the response of the Burgundian envoy Contay, who was 'no lesse amazed then the King was pleased', found it funny.[171] It is ironic, then, that it was actually upon *Burgundian* models that Edward IV modelled his own approach to more serious forms of surveillance and propaganda. Charles the Bold was an ardent self-publicist who flooded his dukedom with accounts of court festivities and letters justifying his policies to provincial authorities, a tireless composer of preambles to ordinances in which he expounded his views on princely powers and duties, and the patron of a court workshop in which clerks were encouraged to fashion favourable versions of recent history.[172] Edward began to institute similar practices after his return from exile, but in the play that bears his name it is his successor whose innovations in communication technology—anachronistically Tudor as they are—help to destroy both Matthew and Jane Shore.

THE END OF THE SHORES' STORY

In the closing moments of *1 Edward IV* John Hobs's normally astute powers of political analysis had let him down; his mistaken belief that the Mayor and the Recorder of London were in fact 'court-noles' had irreverently conflated the functions, identities and efficacy of the executive officers of the Crown and the city. The play, however, had continued to explore irreconcileable differences between London and the court, and, as a Chorus returns the audience to the city in Part Two, it is in the vignettes of the capital's social life—so like Stow's anecdotes which, for all their apparently random diversity, yet acquire a cumulative and collective power—that the dramatist demonstrates his radically innovative deployment of 'sources' and makes his most important contribution to a rapidly evolving theatrical tradition.

There is a contiguity between the achievements of Heywood and Stow, although the antiquarian might have disdained the connection. This is less a matter of the playwright's plundering of the historian's data than of projects which are different in kind but analogous in direction and accomplishment. When, in the decade following the composition of *Edward IV*, Heywood came to prepare his defence of the theatrical 'profession', he would define comedy as a 'discourse consisting of diuerse institutions, comprehending ciuill and domesticke things'.[173] The same phrase might have described the work of post-Reformation 'historians', not just in London but throughout the country. The keeping of local records, in late medieval England a haphazard business where it occurred at all, underwent a gradual but massive methodological change: compilers were employed, they recorded new observations in (and translated old ones into) English rather than Latin, gathered their documentation into paper books as opposed to disparate rolls of parchment, and were allocated rooms or repositories specifically for the preservation of their findings. The results ranged from the registers which each parish was required to keep in a purpose-built chest after 1538, through garnerings of oath and order books, breviaries, custumals and other records of legal and administrative procedures into codifiable collections, to the compendious urban histories of antiquarians such as Henry Manship (Yarmouth), David Rogers (Chester), John Hooker (Exeter) and of course Stow himself.[174]

It is clear to modern scholars that such endeavours were not merely landmarks in the emergence of a more rigorous and precise historiography, but that they possessed, with or without their compilers' conscious assent, an ideological momentum of their own. In charting simultaneous and analagous developments in the production of *county* 'histories', Richard Helgerson came to the conclusion that 'chorography defines itself by opposition to chronicle'.[175] Without losing sight of the fact that, as Annabel Patterson and others have shown, the Tudor chronicles were far from univocal and monolithic conveyors of absolutist ideology, Heywood's play stands in a similarly antithetical relationship to chronicle history.[176] Just as Hall, Grafton, Holinshed and even Stow himself used the monarchical reign as the unit of division and organizational principle in their national histories, so Heywood—with surely an eye on the healthy gate receipts of the Chamberlain's Men—launched his sprawling drama under the protective titular umbrella of a king's name. But the work he actually produced, with its unrelenting attention to the particularity of places and the customs associated with them, has more in common with the output of those writers who called their works 'survey', 'description' or 'chorography', or indeed with the achievements of some whose labours of retrieval and classification were not dignified in their lifetimes with any appellation at all.

In the 1580s the lawyer and archivist Robert Smith was instructed by the Court of Aldermen that 'Conferences in matters touching the Liberties of this City (the memory whereof may be profitable to posterity), [were] to be gathered in a book by themselves and so continued'. London's governors were reacting to a burgeoning awareness that not only did the city's rights and privileges command high market prices, but that they were an attractive target for powerful courtiers and their clients who sought lucrative patents in the wards and suburbs. Perhaps in response to the disastrous mayorality of Sir John Spencer, in 1596 the Aldermen required Smith's findings to be rendered more permanent and more visible: 'notes shall be set down in writing and hanged up in a table in the Inner Chamber of the Guildhall what things appertain either by charter, usage, Acts of Common Council or by custom to be yearly done and performed by the Lord Mayor for the time being.'[177] The 'posterity' invoked by the aldermen would see these activities as tentative steps towards the fashioning of an urban identity, in which the authority of the Crown was at least marginalized, and in some cases challenged. Perhaps in tacit acknowledgement of the innovatory nature of the enterprise, the aldermen occasionally expressed anxiety about the accessibility of these records of local custom and definition.[178]

Heywood's own attempts to record and shape the identity of urban spaces intersected with much of the archivists' (and aldermen's) agenda, but neither in 1599 nor in his long subsequent career did he share their unease concerning exposure. The connections the playwright makes between what is enacted and the experiences (including playgoing itself) of the audience compel a shared capacity and responsibility for such (self) fashioning; almost forty years later, when he was investing his theatrical energies in the street drama of the lord mayors' pageants, Heywood was still insisting that unrestricted access to shows was not 'to be vilefied by the most supercilious, and censorious, especially in such a confluence, where all Degrees, Ages, and Sexes are assembled'.[179]

Edward IV takes the people and spaces which the chronicles often overlooked and places them centre-stage. The subsistence industry of a Tamworth tanner, the bustle of buying and selling in the marketplace, and the domestic tribulations of an unexceptional London couple are played out against the issues of which national history was (and often still is) thought to consist—the power politics of an Essex, rebellion, the dynastic imperatives of royal marriages and foreign policy—and the rich evocation of the spectators' quotidian existence contextualizes, critiques and sometimes effaces the antics of not one but two kings. And it is in this respect that the projects of the chorographer and the playwright overlap, even when their strategies diverge.[180]

Part Two turns Richard's rise to power into a rather perfunctory black comedy. Heywood effectively picks up the most witheringly sarcastic of More's observations—Richard was 'a goodly continent prince clene & fautles of himself, sent oute of heauen into this vicious world for the amendment of mens maners'—and produces from them a pantomime villain.[181] But the play's handling of Richard as a very modern propagandist is at once more precise and more disturbing. This is a ruler acutely aware of the control which can be exercised by the written word—'This paper is the organ of our power' (Scene 21, l. 14)—or by the printed one; with his exact prescription of Jane Shore's penitential route through the city, and his blanket coverage of the capital with the 'proclamation' which denounces her (Scene 18, ll. 97–110), the King attempts to define the parameters of the capital's spaces and to impose his authority over those who live in them. Yet, the theatrical conclusion to the story of the Shores comes when ordinary Londoners are said to have named the district of Shoreditch after the squalid spot on which the wronged couple died (Scene 23, ll. 71–4). A year earlier Stow had, in a testy marginal note, dismissed the historical authenticity of this already current attempt at cultural memorialization: 'Soerditch so called more then 400. yeares since as I can proue by record'. But Stow's tone shifts from one of fastidiousness to one of rage when he moves to explore more recent inscriptions of authority in this depressed area. As if to demonstrate that his approval is conditional upon moral considerations rather than the narrow affiliations of class, the target of the antiquarian's scorn is one Russell, a draper, who rebuilt delapidated houses, 'and let them out for rent enough, taking also large Fines of the Tenantes, neare as much as the houses cost him purchase, and building: for hee made his bargaines so hardly with all men, that both Carpenter, Brickelayer, and Playsterer, were by that Worke vndone. And yet in honour of his name', Stow scathingly concludes, 'it is now called *Russels* Row'.[182]

Ultimately, for Stow and Heywood alike, it is the details of lives lived by ordinary people in ordinary places, their casual kindnesses, neighbourliness and sense of identification with a community, which are worth preserving, and which might withstand the predations of unscrupulous authority. Neither writer was complacent, but neither was acquiescent. And Heywood would almost certainly have endorsed the response of the alderman in the 'Apologie' Stow appended to the *Survey*, who, with less timidity than his brethren who employed Robert Smith, asked a courtier during Queen Mary's 'displeasure against London', whether, along with the Parliament, 'she meant also to diuert the Riuer of Thames from London, or no? and when the Gentleman had answered no, then, quoth the Alderman, by Gods grace wee shall do well enough at London.'[183]

THE TEXT(S)

Although the two parts of *Edward IV* are far too long to have been played in a single continuous performance there is no evidence to suggest that the plays were not planned and composed together, in the course of 1599, to provide a coherent theatrical event—perhaps

performed on consecutive afternoons—for the newly expanded playhouse at the Boar's Head. Unlike Marlowe's *Tamburlaine*, the two
parts of which were originally printed together in single quartos but
which were subsequently (in 1606 and 1605) issued separately, all
six early modern editions of *Edward IV* printed the two parts
together.[184] Both the title pages of these early issues, and the preambles with which each of them preface the opening scene of Part
One allude to the narrative thread which runs throughout both
parts—'Mistresse Shoare, her great promotion, fall and misery'—
and it would be the story of Jane Shore which would both dominate
the critical reception of *Edward IV* and which would elicit attempts,
early in the seventeenth century, to transform the two-part work into
a single five act play (see below).[185]

   Edward IV was entered in the Stationers' Register on 28 August
1599, as follows:

   Entred for their copyes vnder the handes of the Wardens: Twoo *playes*
   beinge *the ffirst and Second parte of* EDWARD *the IIIJth and the Tanner of
   Tamworth* With *the history of the life and deathe of master* SHORE *and* JANE
   SHORE *his wife as yt was lately acted by the Right honorable the* E[a]rle *of*
   DERBYE *his servantes*   xijd

   It was entrusted to two booksellers, John Oxonbridge and John
Busbie; the resulting book was sold from the premises of the former,
'in Paules Churchyard at the signe of the Parrat'. Greg suggested
that 'the printer appears from his initials and the ornaments used
to have been John Windet', and this identification is undoubtedly
correct.[186]

   Q1 is a genuine quarto and collates as follows: A–Y^4 Z^2, with all
signatures fully signed except P and Z; there are ninety unnumbered
leaves. The title, as in all six early editions, encompasses 'The First
and Second partes' of the play, and is situated on sig. A1r, with A1v
blank. A2r comprises an ornament (unidentified), the complete title
of both parts (verbatim from A1r, but with variant spellings and set
throughout in roman), with the text beginning half-way down. The
text, like its successors Qs 2, 3 and 4, is in black-letter, with roman
for incidentals: stage directions, speech prefixes and, with variable
consistency, proper names of persons and places.[187]

   Given that *Edward IV* was probably Windet's first attempt at a
playtext associated with the commercial theatre—his shop's involvement with the Countess of Pembroke's translation of Garnier's

Antonius in 1592, with its long verse speeches, centred speech prefixes serving for stage directions and obviously close relationship to
a fine scribal manuscript, would have offered little preparatory experience—the 1599 quarto is a competent piece of work, and one
which suggests copy presenting few serious difficulties. The complex
and descriptive stage directions strongly imply authorial presence in
the copy, but the almost unfailing accuracy of short directions indicating entrances, re-entrances and exits might also suggest the
supplementary attentions of a book-keeper. This is so even on the
rare occasions when the printed text introduces extraneous matter,
as it does in the opening lines of Part One, Scene 2 (sig. A4v). Here,
each of the four lines of text following Falconbridge's 'Hold
drumme' is prefaced in Q1 (and the five subsequent early editions)
by a number: 1, 2, 3, and then 1 again (reproduced in the textual
apparatus for this scene). It is possible that the playwright had not
yet designated names (Spicing, Smoke and Chub) to Falconbridge's
'troupes', and that the compositor has reproduced vestigial traces of
preliminary stages in the compositional process which the author
had failed to eradicate from the manuscript. Since, however, the
names are given in full in the stage direction which introduces the
scene, and the significance of the names forms part of the dialogue
less than sixty lines later—and especially the fact that the number
3 is not aligned with a new speech at all—it is perhaps more likely
that someone rapidly marking up the text for playhouse use had
merely indicated how many speaking parts are required immediately
after the stage has been cleared at the close of the opening
scene. Further evidence that suggests an authorial manuscript
rather than a tidy promptbook as the copy for the printed edition is
found in the almost incessant variations in speech prefixes; these
alterations cannot be attributed to the variable preferences of different compositors—they frequently occur on the same sheet—but
they are consistent with Thomas Heywood's habitual practice in his
extant theatrical manuscripts.

The punctuation of Q1 is light throughout, but it rarely renders
the text unintelligible. Speeches often end with commas or semi-
colons rather than a full stop, but it should be noted that this too is
a recurrent feature of Thomas Heywood's practice in the surviving
manuscript of *The Captives*. Similarly, the omission of words that
makes the sense of a passage difficult to recover is a rare feature.
It is significant that one such instance—one which eluded the
compositors of the first three editions—occurs in the same area of

the text as the aforementioned confusion over numbers: the lack of an 'and' in Part One, Scene 2, l. 57 perhaps suggests that the manuscript was particularly tricky to decipher at this point.

There are a few cases of speech misattribution, such as the awkward one (promptly rectified in Q2) at the opening of Part One, Scene 13, but the only sustained instance of this error is, again, readily explained: Q1's reversal of the prefixes 'Smoke' and 'Spicing' at Part One, Scene 5, ll. 74–87—perpetuated in all the early editions—was probably caused by the easily misread MS abbreviations of 'Sp' and 'Sm', abbreviations which often appear elsewhere in the printed text.

There are recurrent problems with verse lineation, but these occur primarily where half-lines have been misinterpreted as prose; examples can be seen in Part One, Scene 9, ll. 227–9 (sig. D3v), Scene 17, ll. 45–55 (sig. H3r), and Scene 19, ll. 1–7 (sig. I3r). Once more, the source of the problem might be illustrated by reference to the manuscript of *The Captives*, in which it is clear that Heywood never indented the second half of a verse line, and in which the playwright compounded the difficulty by the infrequency with which he capitalized the first letter in a line of verse. This habit might also account for other failures to replicate verse patterns. It is possible, for example, that the printer's copy for Scene 22, ll. 62–70 (sig. K4r) was a particularly crowded sheet, in which more than one line of verse was written into a single line of the manuscript, with line endings perhaps indicated by only a dash; Jane Shore's important speech is printed as prose in Q1, but with large gaps in the text which correspond exactly with the endings of lines 63, 65, 66, 69 and 70, and with upper case 'A' at the beginning of line 68 when preceeded only by a comma.[188]

One further difficulty in relation to lineation is worthy of note. On occasion Q1 wavers uneasily between verse and prose, sometimes within a single speech. There is a graphic instance at Part One, Scene 10, ll. 136–41, the Lord Mayor's penultimate speech in this scene. The first two and a half lines—'Bring him away . . . thousand marks'—form themselves into four reasonably regular pentameters, and all early editions print them as such; the remainder of this speech, however (and the Mayor's final contribution to the scene, ll. 147–8), cannot be so rendered, despite the fact that Crosby never speaks anything but verse throughout the rest of the play. Once more, both of Heywood's extant dramatic manuscripts offer analagous instances, particularly the rare excursions into prose made by the normally impeccably poetic Lady Averne in *The Captives*.

In short, the proximity between the printing of Q1 and the registration of *Edward IV* with the Stationers—and everything the
Introduction has to say concerning the 'provenance' of the play—
leaves little doubt that Q1 was its first realization in printed form.
This printed text bears clear signs that it was set from authorial
copy, and that such copy shared many of the idiosyncrasies revealed
in the extant theatrical manuscripts known to be by Heywood; given
that only a distinguished palaeographer like Richard Proudfoot
might be generous enough to say of Heywood's hand that it 'is
perfectly legible, with practice, but its extreme cursiveness can
cause great trouble until one becomes thoroughly familiar with it',
the printer of Q1 has produced a text of admirable clarity—
and clearly the text upon which any modern edition must be based,
especially since all the subsequent early issues of the play derive
from it too.[189]

On 23 February 1600 Busbie transferred his interest in the play
to Humfrey Lownes, and a second edition, printed by Felix
Kingston for Lownes and Oxonbridge, duly appeared. To simplify,
I have referred to this text as Q2, although it is in fact an octavo in
quarto size. The text has no independent authority since it clearly
has been set from Q1. It follows Q1's lineation with remarkable
precision—the letter 'I', for instance, is the only departure in the
setting of a prose speech of fifteen lines on A2v (Part One, Scene 1,
ll. 39–54)—and it reproduces pagination (including catchwords)
exactly until the beginning of sheet C (corresponding with Q1's
sheet E), when a drive towards compression in layout first manifests
itself; here, by closing spaces around the stage direction, two extra
lines are incorporated on to the page. This tendency intensified as
the printing of Q2 proceeded, until, for example, the lucidity of stage
action conveyed in Q1's isolation of stage directions on H4r (Scene
17, ll. 108–34) is almost entirely obliterated in the densely packed
sheets of Q2. Some attention is paid in the second edition to obvious
mistakes in the first: thus, turned letters are righted at Scene 4, l.
36, and Scene 9, l. 140, but the latter 'correction' is counterbalanced
by the omission of 'I' at the beginning of line 144, an error perpetuated in Q3. In short, whilst Q2 provides some intelligent minor
emendations which this edition has assimilated, it is demonstrably
one stage further removed from the playwright's manuscript, and
its occasional attempts at 'regularization' sometimes misfire
completely: at Part One, Scene 5, l. 65, Q1's '*Sm.* get thee vp . . .'
becomes Q2's '*Sm.* Get thee vp . . .', thus rendering '*Sm.*' as if it is

a speech prefix, a symptomatic loss of theatrical clarity which demands that this derivative text be treated with caution.

Lownes was the printer of the third and all subsequent early editions of the play. Q3 (1605) is an almost exact reprint of Q2, faithfully reproducing virtually all of its predecessor's typographical features, including its errors; its correction of 'Gat'es', the reading of Part One, Scene 5, l. 120, in both Q1 and Q2, to 'gates' is a rare exception. The bibliographical significance of Q3—actually another octavo in quarto form—inheres almost exclusively in the annotations which have been made to the two surviving copies, both housed in the Dyce Collection at the Victoria and Albert Museum in London. The annotations in the first and better preserved of the two copies (Dyce 25, Box 18, 1) have not been noticed before. These are mostly supplementary stage directions, written in a seventeenth-century hand (before the sheets were trimmed and now partially obscured), but several of them—an 'exeunt' scribbled at the end of Part One, Scene 9, l. 153, 'exeunt mayor' after l. 148 of the following scene, an 'aside' marked for the King at Scene 17, l. 140, and Matthew Shore's exit at Scene 22, l. 130—suggest interpretations of stage business absent from all the printed texts but sufficiently plausible to be incorporated into this edition.

The second copy (Dyce 26, Box 18, 2) is incomplete (lacking the leaf Y4) but a (different) seventeenth-century hand has made a coherent attempt to transform this text into a promptbook. The structural project of the annotator is the ambitious one of streamlining the two-part work into a single play consisting of five acts. The marginalia commence at Part One, Scene 11, l. 19—implying the omission of all the scenes relating to the Falconbridge uprising—and it transpires that the first intervention differs from most of those which follow in that it points to a (rare) error in the stage directions of the printed text, sensibly adding '& a huntsman' to the SD marking the entrance of the Queen and the Duchess (two huntsmen are in fact required).

Thereafter the annotations mark, with impressive consistency and approximately twenty lines before they are due to be executed, cues for the entrances of players and properties: thus at Part One, Scene 13, ll. 79–80, for instance, the prompter warns 'howard sellinger ready' (sig. F2r), and at l. 106 on the same page he anticipates the 'Messenger wth lett.'. This procedure is followed diligently until Scene 15, the scene of Falconbridge's irregular arraignment, where both ruled and unruled vertical lines are drawn in the margins to indicate the deletion of the entire scene; these lines terminate and action is signalled to recommence at line 35 of the Mayor's soliloquy in Scene 16. The trumpets the printed text requires for the accompaniment of the entry of the royal train are noted—'Cornets ready' appears against the SD at l. 60 and again at l. 142 (G3r, and G4r)—and the prompter interestingly suggests at l. 177 that they should also fanfare the King's abrupt and unceremonial departure.

The annotator has second thoughts in Part One, Scene 18: he writes 'Act: 2' against the opening stage direction, and at l. 10 prompts Howard's entry at l. 27, but then changes his mind, marks the scene for deletion, and writes 'Act: 2' again against the opening of Scene 19. In the prompter's scheme the remainder of Part One (Scenes 19–23) comprises the second act of the projected performance, and, with the entire French action which opens Part Two omitted, he envisages a resumption of the narrative—'Act: 3'—at the point where Jane Shore enters with Jockie and '*is met by Sir Robert Brakenburie*' (Part Two, Scene 9, 0.1–2; sig. P1v in Q1, O4v in Q3). 'Act: IIII' is then deemed to begin when Lord Lovell and Doctor Shaw '*meet on the Stage*' (Part Two, Scene 13, 0.1; R4v in Q1, R3r in Q3), although the annotator again has a change of heart and rather oddly deletes the exchange between the two, then giving them a new entry alongside Catesby's at l. 45. His 'Act: V' opens where Shaw enters '*pensiuely reading on his booke*' followed by the ghost of Friar Anselm (Part Two, Scene 19, 0.1–2; U2r in Q1, U1r in Q3). Although the copy bearing these annotations is lacking the final leaf, the prompter's interventions dry up well before the end of Part Two, but without the indication of further deletions. His last contribution coincides with Jane's entrance in penitential garb, but his attentions are not sustained as far as the Shores' tragic demise, ending rather with an anticipation of Brackenbury's poignant entrance 'wth a book, releife' (Scene 20, l. 55.01; U2r). Apart from the deletion of large blocks of text, on only one occasion is there any interference with the play's content: perhaps disturbed by its recidivist Catholicism, the prompter has drawn a box around Hobs's oath 'By my halidom' in Part One, Scene 18, l. 77. In sum, the commentator has given serious consideration to some of the play's visual and aural demands—he is particularly conscientious about the ceremonial qualities of the scene in Crosby's house, carefully specifying that the players should have 'wine & bowle ready' for the royal toast (G4r), and he also substitutes 'soft musick' for the 'solemn music' the printed text requires for the murder of the princes (Part Two, Scene

17, l. 21.01)—but, in his sidelining of the politics of urban unrest, territorial conflict in France and King Richard's manoeuvres in the field of dynastic marriage, he also adumbrates the prioritizing of the 'Jane Shore' story which would be fully realized by Nicholas Rowe early in the eighteenth century.[190]

There is little to be said of the ensuing issues of the play which emerged from the shop of Lownes. Q4 (1613), the last of the texts printed with the bulk of the text in black-letter, makes some important corrections—the addition of the 'and' required in Part One, Scene 2, l. 57 being perhaps the most important of them—but also introduces errors which were perpetuated in the subsequent quartos derived from it; thus Q4 incorrectly begins a new speech for the First Apprentice at Part One, Scene 5, l. 42, incidentally indicating in the same passage that it may have been set from Q2 rather than its immediate predecessor, since it fails to distinguish which Apprentice is speaking at l. 32, as Q1 and Q2 had also done but Q3 had not. Q5, the first issue to set the bulk of the text in roman type, derives from Q4 and differs from it in little more than this basic typographical feature. Q6, however, although set from its 1619 predecessor, undertakes an extensive revision of the play's punctuation, and a substantial number of its 'modernizations' have been incorporated into this edition in an attempt to make the text more approachable to the modern reader.

This edition is based on the first and only authoritative quarto of 1599, and, as far as possible, emendations have been introduced only where sanctioned by their deployment in subsequent editions dating from the early modern period. Speech prefixes have been silently expanded and regularized. Place and proper names, inconsistently italicized in the quartos, are silently and consistently rendered in standard type, and spellings are regularized; spellings are of course modernized throughout, in accordance with the policy of the Revels series. The first letters of all verse lines are capitalized. Letters which had slipped or which were poorly inked in Q1 are corrected without further comment. Stage directions not present in Q1 have occasionally been introduced; when these derive from Q2–6 (or manuscript additions to Q3) this is indicated only in the textual apparatus, but modern interpolations are enclosed in square brackets. The playwright frequently blurs the distinction between entrances and stage directions—a perennial feature in both the printed plays and the extant theatrical manuscripts of Heywood—and Q1 follows its copy in reproducing the sometimes unusual positioning of these directions. This edition, while it aims to ensure that all stage business is clarified for both reader and actor, also attempts to preserve as much as possible of this typographical and compositional singularity, and in doing so sometimes departs from the usual Revels conventions.[191] No early text of *Edward IV* has act or scene divisions; the scene divisions, invariably introduced to represent major exits and entrances and usually requiring a cleared stage, are original to this edition and are similarly enclosed in square brackets.

NOTES

1 Murray, I, 294.
2 Chambers, II, 119; Murray, I, 75–6. Despite having access to unpublished volumes of the *Records of Early English Drama* series, Andrew Gurr unearthed no new information about Derby's Men; see *The Shakespearian Playing Companies* (Oxford, 1996), 265–6. E. A. J. Honigmann has argued that Lord Strange was Shakespeare's patron as early as 1586, and that the dramatist was a long-standing member of Strange's company; *Shakespeare: The 'Lost' Years* (Manchester, 1985), chapter 6.
3 Murray, I, 90–1, 108.
4 *HMC, Hatfield House MSS*, XIII, 609.
5 Sisson, 35–6.
6 *Acts of the Privy Council, 1597–98* (London, 1904), xxviii, 326.
7 Berry, 67–8.
8 Lawsuit quoted in Sisson, 64. A colourful account of further extortions is given in W. Ingram, *A London Life in the Brazen Age: Francis Langley, 1548–1602* (Cambridge, Mass., 1978).
9 'Dramatic Records in the Declared Accounts of the Treasurer of the Chamber', *Malone Society Collections VI* (Oxford, 1962), 31–2.
10 See 'Dramatic Records of the City of London: The Remembrancia', *Malone Society Collections I.i* (Oxford, 1907), 85–6. Besides this letter from the Privy Council, the evidence for the activities of Oxford's Men is sparse. The title page of *The Weakest Goeth to the Wall* (1600) announces that it had been played by them, and a 1601 entry in the Stationers' Register for a lost play, *The History of George Scanderbarge*, makes a similar claim; Greg, I, 171–2, and Chambers, II, 102.
11 Henslowe, 213.
12 Henslowe, 225–6. In the first scholarly edition of Henslowe's papers Sir Walter Greg was certain that the first entry was in Chettle's hand (*Henslowe's Diary* (London, 1904), 232), but Foakes and Rickert were more cautious; see Henslowe, 194 n.3.
13 Chambers, II, 225–30.
14 The play, however, may have been taken further afield. On 19 November 1607 it was reported from the court at Graz in Germany that 'The English have today for their farewell play again given a comedy, about a king of England who is in love with a goldsmith's wife and has abducted her, it was nothing very special'; the translation is found in O.

Murad, *The English Comedians at the Hapsburg Court in Graz, 1607–1608* (Salzburg, 1978), 31. It is impossible to know whether this was the new version prepared by Chettle and Day, the 'original' preserved in the early quartos or a different rendition of the story altogether.

15 Berry (53) believed the Boar's Head galleries would have been exclusively for spectators, but Sisson (xix) was convinced that they could have been used as a performance space too. See also E. L. Rhodes, *Henslowe's Rose: The Stage and Staging* (Lexington, 1976), 79–83, 252–7, and G. F. Reynolds, *The Staging of Plays at the Red Bull Theatre, 1605–1625* (New York, 1940), *passim*.

16 The 'plots' are printed in W. W. Greg, *Dramatic Documents from the Elizabethan Playhouses* (Oxford, 1931); see also discussion in Carson, 36–7.

17 See W. A. Wringler, 'The Number of Actors in Shakespeare's Early Plays', in G. E. Bentley (ed.), *The Seventeenth-Century Stage* (Chicago, 1968), 110–34.

18 *A True, perfect, and exact Catalogue of all the Comedies, Tragedies, Tragi-Comedies, Pastorals, Masques and Interludes, that were ever yet printed and published, til this present year 1661* (London, 1661), 4. Kirkman's subsequent reissues of his *Catalogue* (1671, 1680) restated the attribution.

19 See Edward Phillips, *Theatrum Poetarum* (London, 1675), 176; William Winstanley, *The Lives of the most Famous English Poets* (London, 1687), 96; Gerard Langbaine, *Momus Triumphans* (London, 1688), 11; and Langbaine, *An Account of the English Dramatick Poets* (Oxford, 1691), 262.

20 For reservations see F. G. Fleay, *A Biographical Chronicle of the English Drama*, 2 vols (London, 1890), II, 288; and Chambers, IV, 10–11.

21 Chambers, IV, 103, 106–7, 119, 121–30.

22 Carson, 62–3; cf. C. Rutter, *Documents of the Rose Playhouse* (rev. edn, Manchester, 1999), 26–7.

23 Henslowe, 64, 88, 103, 125.

24 *Ibid.*, 241, 104.

25 Space does not allow discussion of the 'internal' evidence for Heywood's authorship here, but see R. Rowland, ' "Speaking some words, but of no importance"?: Stage Directions, Thomas Heywood and *Edward IV*', *Medieval and Renaissance Drama in England*, 18 (2005).

26 *The Royall King and the Loyall Subject* (London, 1637), sig. A3r.

27 Robert Fabyan, *The Chronicle of Fabyan* (London: Jhon [*sic*] Kyngston, 1559), fols Uuiir–iiv; John Stow, *The Annales of England* (London: Rafe Newbery, 1592), 698–9.

28 *Great Chronicle*, xli–xliii.

29 *Ibid.*, 219.

30 *Ibid.*, 221.

31 Drayton, I, 208. On the proliferation of manuscript histories, see, for instance, F. W. D. Brie (ed.), *The Brut, or Chronicles of England*, 2 vols (Early English Text Sciety, CXXXI, CXXXVI, 1906–8), I, x, and *Great Chronicle*, xxv.

32 In William Cartwright's reissue of Heywood's *Apology for Actors* it was claimed that Heywood had been a 'Fellow of *Peter*-house'; *The Actors Vindication* (London, 1658), sig. A2v. He was more probably the 'Thomas Haywood . . . pensioner' who entered Emmanuel College in 1591; see J. A. Venn, *Alumni Cantabrigiensis*, 4 vols (Cambridge, 1922),

II, 343. On the bibliography of Warkworth's MS, see L. M. Matheson, *Death and Dissent: The Dethe of the Kynge of Scotis and Warkworth's Chronicle* (Woodbridge, 1999), 61–92, and Gransden, 257–61. For connections with the play see Halliwell 4, 8, 12, and commentary to Part One, Scene 1, ll. 141–3.

33 Exceptions are I. Archer's 'The Nostalgia of John Stow', and L. Manley's 'Of Sites and Rites', both in D. L. Smith, R. Strier and D. Bevington (eds), *The Theatrical City: Culture, Theatre and Politics in London, 1576–1649* (Cambridge, 1995), pp. 17–34; 35–54; cf. P. Collinson, 'John Stow and Nostalgic Antiquarianism', in J. F. Merritt (ed.), *Imagining Early Modern London: Perceptions and Portrayals of the City from Stow to Strype, 1598–1720* (Cambridge, 2001), 27–51.

34 *Survey*, I, 25, 30.

35 For demographic analyses see, *inter alia*, S. Rappaport, *Worlds within Worlds: Structures of Life in Sixteenth-Century London* (Cambridge, 1989), 61–122; J. Boulton, *Neighbourhood and Society: A London Suburb in the Seventeenth Century* (Cambridge, 1987), 13–59; A. L. Beier, R. Finlay (eds), *London 1500–1700: The Making of the Metropolis* (London, 1986), passim. For the impact on literature see L. Manley, *Literature and Culture in Early Modern London* (Cambridge, 1995), 1–167.

36 R. Helgerson, *Forms of Nationhood: The Elizabethan Writing of England* (London, 1992), 135–6.

37 Peele, vol. II, Scene 18, ll. 2200–7; Scene 20, ll. 2273–81; Scene 23, ll. 2637–47.

38 *The Famous Victories of Henry the Fifth* (printed 1598), in G. Bullough (ed.), *Narrative and Dramatic Sources of Shakespeare*, 8 vols (London, 1957–75), IV, 302. *Arden of Faversham* (1592) is an unusual exception to the rule; actual features of the urban landscape do appear in it, and they are not in the sections dependent upon Holinshed's *Chronicles*. See, in M. L. Wine's edition (Manchester, 1973), scenes 3.39; 6.25; 2.99; and 14.11ff.

39 See, for instance, S. Mullaney, *The Place of the Stage: License, Play, and Power in Renaissance England* (Chicago, 1988); D. Bruster, *Drama and the Market in the Age of Shakespeare* (Cambridge, 1992).

40 *The Book of Sir Thomas More* (Malone Society Reprints, 1990), Additions V–VI, ll. 66–7; all further references are to this edition and are cited in the text.

41 *HMC, Hatfield House MSS*, VII, 249–50.

42 P. E. McCullough, *Sermons at Court: Politics and Religion in Elizabethan and Jacobean Preaching* (Cambridge, 1998), 46, 131; M. MacLure, *The Paul's Cross Lectures, 1534–1642* (Toronto, 1958), 11–12.

43 The mid-sixteenth-century 'Agas' map showing the laundering activities at Moorfields is reproduced in A. Prockter and R. Taylor, *The A to Z of Elizabethan London* (London, 1979), 10; for a discussion of this and other maps, and their social and literary significance, see R. L. Sanford, *Maps and Memory in Early Modern England: A Sense of Place* (Basingstoke, 2002), 105, 125–6.

44 B. R. Masters (ed.), *Chamber Accounts of the Sixteenth Century* (London Record Society, 20, 1984), 75–80; cf. V. Gabrieli, G. Melchiori (eds), *Sir Thomas More* (Manchester, 1990), 88.

45 If the lost collaborative work *The Isle of Dogs* ventured into similarly provocative territory, its reception would not have encouraged imitation either: Ben Jonson was imprisoned for it and Thomas Nashe fled the city.

46 Helgerson, *Forms of Nationhood* (note 36), 125–6. See also Norden's *Civitas Londini*, a remarkable city map printed in 1600, and the discussion of it by A. Gordon, 'Performing London: The Map and the City in Ceremony', in A. Gordon, B. Klein (eds), *Literature, Mapping, and the Politics of Space in Early Modern Britain* (Cambridge, 2001), 69–88.

47 Arber, III, 677–8.

48 J. J. Manning (ed.), *The First and Second Parts of John Hayward's The Life and Raigne of King Henrie IIII* (London: Royal Historical Society, 1991), 24–5.

49 See, for instance, C. S. Clegg, *Press Censorship in Elizabethan England* (Cambridge, 1997), 198–217.

50 P. Griffiths, *Youth and Authority: Formative Experiences in England, 1560–1640* (Oxford, 1996), 166–7.

51 In fact, according to David Cressy, London's apprentices were 'extraordinarily literate': *Literacy and the Social Order: Reading and Writing in Tudor and Stuart England* (Cambridge, 1980), 129.

52 *Instructions to the Lord Mayor of London* (1574), reprinted in J. P. Collier (ed.), *Illustrations of Old English Literature*, 3 vols (1866; New York, 1966), III, 11–12.

53 See, for example, B. R. Masters, 'The Mayor's Household before 1600', in A. E. J. Hollaender, W. Kellaway (eds), *Studies in London History presented to P. E. Jones* (London, 1969), 95–114.

54 For parliamentary attempts at legislation see, e.g., D. Dean, *Law-Making and Society in Late Elizabethan England: The Parliament of England, 1582–1601* (Cambridge, 1996), 158–9.

55 M. J. Power, 'London and the Control of the "Crisis" of the 1590s', *History*, 70 (1985), 371–85.

56 See, for instance, L. Gowing, *Domestic Dangers: Women, Words and Sex in Early Modern London* (Oxford, 1996), 175, 40, and her essay, ' "The freedom of the streets": Women and Social Space, 1560–1640', in P. Griffiths, M. S. R. Jenner (eds), *Londinopolis: Essays in the Cultural and Social History of Early Modern London* (Manchester, 2000), 130–51.

57 See, e.g., P. Griffiths, 'Politics Made Visible: Order, Residence and Uniformity in Cheapside, 1600–45', in Griffiths, Jenner (eds), *Londinopolis*, 176–96.

58 See, e.g., G. A. Sullivan Jr, *The Drama of Landscape: Land, Property and Social Relations on the Early Modern Stage* (Stanford, 1998), 199–225; J. Dillon, *Theatre, Court and City, 1595–1610: Drama and Social Space in London* (Cambridge, 2000), 43–58.

59 R. M. Benbow, 'The Court of Aldermen and the Assizes: The Policy of Price Control in Elizabethan London', *Guildhall Studies in London History*, 4 (1980), 93–118; J. Walter, 'The Social Economy of Dearth in Early Modern England', in R. Schofield, J. Walter (eds), *Famine, Disease, and the Social Order in Early Modern Society* (Cambridge, 1989), 118–19.

60 I. Archer, C. Barron, V. Harding (eds), *Hugh Alley's Caveat: The Markets of London in 1598* (London: Topographical Society, 1988), 15–17.

61 P. L. Hughes and J. F. Larkin, *Tudor Royal Proclamations*, 3 vols (New Haven, 1964–69), III, 134–6, 196–7; P. Williams, *The Tudor Regime* (Oxford, 1979), 128–30.

62 R. B. Manning, 'The Prosecution of Sir Michael Blount, Lieutenant of the Tower of London, 1595', *Bulletin of the Institute of Historical Research*, 57 (1984), 222; see also Archer, 1.

63 *Hugh Alley's Caveat* (note 60), 25.

64 Archer, 52.

65 William Jaggard, *A View of all the Lord Mayors of London* (London: W. Jaggard, 1601), *passim*; see also Rappaport, *Worlds Within Worlds*, 194. The significance of equitable market regulation is particularly clear in Jaggard's entry for 1598 (pagination is marked by year only), in which mayor 'Sir Stephen Some' is congratulated for organizing a large muster at Mile End 'to guard the Queenes person' and for addressing the 'great corruption . . . namely false weightes and measures', as if the two achievements were of equal importance.

66 See, for example, R. C. Davis, *The War of the Fists: Popular Culture and Public Violence in Late Renaissance Venice* (Oxford, 1994), 109–12; Archer, 83.

67 For evidence that ties of loyalty and affection did exist between apprentices and their governors see, e.g., M. Pelling, 'Apprenticeship, Health and Social Cohesion in Early Modern London', *History Workshop Journal*, 37 (1994), 33–56; see also *A Students Lamentation* (1595), in which the 'sometime . . . Apprentice' author writes that to the 'Citie . . . & the inhabitants therein [I] account my selfe bound' (sig. A4r).

68 See, e.g., L. C. Orlin, *Private Matters and Public Culture in Post-Reformation England* (New York, 1994), 119–25; C. W. Crupi, 'Ideological Contradiction in Part I of Heywood's *Edward IV*: "Our Musicke Runs . . . Much upon Discords" ', *Medieval and Renaissance Drama in England*, 7 (1995), 224–56 (235); Sullivan (note 58), *Drama of Landscape*, 215.

69 Thomas Wright (ed.), *Queen Elizabeth and Her Times*, 2 vols (London, 1838), II, 245; Archer, 232; L. L. Peck, *Court Patronage and Corruption in Early Stuart England* (London, 1990), 185–207.

70 M. James, *Society, Politics and Culture: Studies in Early Modern England* (Cambridge, 1986), 428.

71 *Survey*, I, 30.

72 Holinshed, III, 322.

73 *Ibid.*, 323.

74 See, e.g., *CSPD, 1598–1601*, 577–8; William Camden, *The Historie of the Princesse Elizabeth*, trans. R. Norton (London: Nicholas Okes, 1630), 174; see also D. H. Sacks, 'London's Dominion: The Metropolis, the Market Economy, and the State', in L. C. Orlin (ed.), *Material London, ca. 1600* (Philadelphia, 2000), 26–36.

75 See C. Mackay (ed.), *Songs and Ballads Relative to the London Prentices and Trades* (London: Percy Society, 1840), I, 3.

76 Arber, I, 264; II, 451.

77 The entry reads: 'William White. Entred for his copie by the consent of wydowe danter *A merye pleasant and delectable history betweene kinge EDWARD the IIIJ^{th} and a Tanner of Tamworthe*—

Item Entred for his copye by like consent of the Wydoe Danter the balad of the same matter that was printed by her husband John Danter' (Arber, III, 173).

78 *A merrie, pleasant and delectable Historie, betweene K. Edward the fourth and a Tanner of Tamworth* (London: John Danter, 1596). The sole surviving copy is in the Bodleian Library (shelfmark: S. Seld.d.45). Pages 2, 3, 4 and 9 are cropped, partially or entirely obscuring lines in stanzas 12 (2), 20 (4), 29 (2), and 52 (4). Citations will preserve the spelling and punctuation of this copy, but will be given (in the text) by reference to the stanza numbers of Child's edition: see vol. V, 81–3.

79 The MS of 'The King and the Barker' is in Cambridge University Library (MS.Ee.iv, 35.1). Child printed a version of it (III, 78–80), but one which he admitted was 'freely treated in the remodelling' (*ibid.*, 68); references are to this transcription.

80 Holinshed, I, 357.

81 See L. A. Clarkson, 'English Economic Policy in the Sixteenth and Seventeenth Centuries: The Case of the Leather Industry', *Bulletin of the Institute of Historical Research*, 38 (1965), 149–62 (150).

82 L. A. Clarkson, 'The Organization of the English Leather Industry in the Late Sixteenth and Seventeenth Centuries', *Economic History Review*, 2nd series, 13 (1960), 245–53.

83 More serious class tension is registered, however, in the 'source' ballad of 'The King and the Barker'; the barker claims to have 'lytyll to don' with the local dignitary, the Lord Basset, since 'wolde he neuer bey of me / clot-lether to clowt with schon' (st. 27).

84 Of all the generically similar ballads only one has a comparable complaint: in *John the Reeve*, a fifteenth-century ballad now extant only in the Percy MS but once widely known amongst sixteenth-century poets, Edward I is initially denied a warm fire on the grounds that fuel is beyond his host's means. This observation is neither historically specific nor accurate; see Percy, II, 565, ll. 191–8. Hobs's remark, by contrast, is true and crucially linked to both the exchanges on food distribution of Scene 2 and the argument about corn exportation in Scene 22.

85 Clarkson, 'Organization' (note 82), 246.

86 *The Parish of St. Helen's Bishopsgate*, ninth volume of *The Survey of London* (London County Council, 1924), 19, 24; W. H. Black, *History and Antiquities of the Worshipful Company of Leathersellers of the City of London* (London, 1871), 88.

87 Clarkson, 'English Economic Policy' (note 81), 150.

88 G. Unwin, *The Gilds and Companies of London* (London, 1908), 257; I. W. Archer, 'The London Lobbies in the Later Sixteenth Century', *Historical Journal*, 31 (1988), 17–44.

89 Clarkson, 'Organization', 253n.

90 J. W. Waterer, *Leather, in Life, Art and Industry* (London, 1943), 106–7.

91 See, e.g., C. F. Whiting (ed.), *The Book of the Tanners' Company, Durham, 1612–55* (Surtees Society, 1945), in which the term 'occupacion' signifies the Company throughout the records.

92 A smaller but otherwise identical woodcut occurs on p. 7, with the addition of another armed knight (with a lance) behind the king.

93 *A Merry, pleasant, and delectable Historie, betweene K. Edward the fourth,*

a[n]d a Tanner... (London: W. White, 1613), sigs A2v, A8r. The unique copy of this issue is in the library of Corpus Christi College, Oxford (shelfmark: CORPUS 4.24 (4)). Amongst dozens of insignificant variants there is one substantive one. In stanza 22 of 1596 (in Child's numbering) the tanner refuses the king's offer to become his apprentice on the grounds that a courtier 'wold spend me more than he would get / by fortie shillings a yere'; 1613 reads 'more than I should get'.

94 The unique copy is in the Bodleian Library; Douce Ballads, 1 (109).

95 Child, V, 79, st. 28. Neither the Danter 'History' nor the Ballad has an equivalent incident.

96 Henslowe, 317, ll. 20–1; *The Downfall*, l. 1260; Peele, *Edward I*, l. 1368.

97 See S. Billington, *Mock Kings in Medieval Society and Renaissance Drama* (Oxford, 1991), 9–29. Robin Hood's reputation as the antithesis of sovereign power which violated the lands and liberties of the common subject is neatly preserved in a libellous rhyme written against Robert Cecil early in the seventeenth century, in which the Earl is described as 'Not Robin Goodfellow nor Robin Hood / But Robin the encloser of Hatfield Wood'; quoted in A. Cecil, *The Life of Robert Cecil, First Earl of Salisbury* (London, 1915), 379.

98 See also Edward Hall's account of Henry VIII and his courtiers startling the Queen and her entourage by entering her chamber dressed as Robin Hood; *Union*, 515.

99 Stanzas 353, 365, in Child's text, III, 39–89. The earlier date is favoured by R. B. Dobson and J. Taylor, *Rymes of Robin Hood* (London, 1976), 8; the middle ground is held by J. C. Holt, *Robin Hood* (London, 1982), 15, 56, 188; S. Knight, *Robin Hood: A Complete Study of the English Outlaw* (Oxford, 1994), argues for the 1460s, 45–8.

100 Greg, I, 108; II, 966.

101 See, e.g., D. Gray, 'The Robin Hood Poems', *Poetica*, 18 (1984), 1–39; P. R. Coss, 'Aspects of Cultural Diffusion in Medieval England: The Early Romances, Local Society and Robin Hood', *Past and Present*, 108 (1985), 35–79.

102 'The King and a Poore Northerne Man', in W. Chappell, J. W. Ebsworth (eds), *The Roxburghe Ballads*, 10 vols (Hertford: The Ballad Society, 1871–99), I, 520–9.

103 See, for instance, B. Sharp, *In Contempt of All Authority: Rural Artisans and Riot in the West of England, 1586–1660* (Berkeley, 1980), 171–2. A representative image of aristocratic hunting culture (including the adoption of luxuriant green costumes) is Robert Peake's 1604 oil painting of Henry, Prince of Wales, reproduced in R. B. Manning, *Hunters and Poachers: A Social and Cultural History of Unlawful Hunting in England, 1485–1640* (Oxford, 1993), between pp. 148 and 149.

104 D. Wiles, *The Early Plays of Robin Hood* (Cambridge, 1981), 20.

105 Dobson and Taylor (note 99), *Rymes*, 211. For Elizabethan denunciations of Robin as a tool of the Pope and/or Satan see T. Watt, *Cheap Print and Popular Piety, 1550–1640* (Cambridge, 1991), 39–40.

106 1 Mary st.3.c.8 (1554); *The Statutes of the Realm* (Record Commission, 1819), vol. IV, part 1, 232.

107 Cited in Clarkson, 'English Economic Policy' (note 81), 155.

108 *Ibid.*, 154–5.

109 R. H. Tawney, E. Power (eds), *Tudor Economic Documents*, 3 vols (London, 1924), II, 274. In purely linguistic register, however, Hobs's response is closer to that of the Southwark plasterer who, chastised (a year before the play) for disregarding the terms of his company's letters patent, allegedly exclaimed: 'Letter me noe letters nor patent me noe pattentes. I care not a Turde for your letters nor patentes'; cited in Archer, 135–6.

110 Clarkson, 'English Economic Policy', 155; Larkin and Hughes, *Tudor Royal Proclamations* (note 61), III, 237.

111 *Tudor Economic Documents*, II, 291.

112 See, for instance, W. H. Price, *The English Patents of Monopoly* (Cambridge, Mass., 1906), 14.

113 S. W. May, *The Elizabethan Courtier Poets: The Poems and Their Contexts* (London, 1991), 89–105, 287–316; L. Stone, *The Crisis of the Aristocracy, 1558–1641* (Oxford, 1965), 415.

114 The relationship was a long-standing and intense one, which had certainly begun by 1587; a passionate letter of that year from Essex to Dyer is quoted in R. A. Sargent, *At the Court of Queen Elizabeth: The Life and Lyrics of Sir Edward Dyer* (London, 1935), 92–3, and the same source reveals that the two dined together on the night after Essex's return from Ireland, in September 1599 (146). Dyer was also part of Essex's formidable intelligence network, and was clearly still active in it in 1598; *HMC, Hatfield House MSS*, VIII, 253.

115 Hall, 515.

116 Cited in P. E. J. Hammer, *The Polarisation of Elizabethan Politics: The Political Career of Robet Devereux, 2nd Earl of Essex, 1585–1597* (Cambridge, 1999), 319 n.16. Elizabeth's fury, particularly at Essex's fathering an illegitimate child with Elizabeth Southwell, is discussed by Hammer, 95–6, 319–20.

117 Hammer, *Polorisation*, 270–2; James, *Society, Politics and Culture*, 426 n.36, 439 n.85. Essex's servant, Richard Broughton, was Tamworth's 'Recorder' until May 1598; H. Wood, *Tamworth Borough Records* (Tamworth, 1952), 16.

118 Hammer, *Polorisation*, 271–2; see also W. B. Devereux, *Lives and Letters of the Devereux Earls of Essex*, 2 vols (London, 1853), I, 280.

119 R. J. Stevenson (ed.), *Correspondence of Sir Henry Unton, Knt, Ambassador from Queen Elizabeth to Henry IV King of France, in the years MDXCI and MDXCII* (London, 1847), 250.

120 W. Beresford (ed.), *Memorials of Old Staffordshire* (London, 1909), 179–93.

121 The names were interchangeable even in official documents: see, for instance, T. E. Hartley (ed.), *Proceedings in the Parliaments of Elizabeth I*, 3 vols (Leicester, 1981–97), I, 490–1.

122 Drayton, II, 378; V. Gibbs, H. A. Doubleday (eds), *The Complete Peerage* (London, 1926), V, 317–29.

123 H. E. Malden (ed.), *Richard Broughton's Devereux Papers, 1575–1601*, Camden Society, third series, xiii (1924), 16.

124 Hammer, *Polarisation*, 34.

125 *Ibid.*, 168. The date is wrong; the correct one, 3 April, is given in Devereux, *Lives and Letters* (note 118), II, 18.

126 The names 'Sellinger' and 'St Leger' were entirely interchangeable; Devereux, *Lives and Letters*, notes that Sir Warham St Leger, son of Henry VIII's Deputy of Ireland, was a notable presence at the capitulation to Tyrone, II, 70–1. The name would also have been known from 'Sellinger's Round', a tune which probably got its title from Sir Warham's father, and so over-familiar that a student in Thomas Morley's *A Plaine and Easie Introduction to Practicall Musicke* (1597) finds the imitation of it a clear sign of cultural ineptitude; see C. M. Simpson, *The British Broadside Ballad and Its Music* (New Brunswick, NJ, 1966), 643–6. Heywood refers to the tune again in *A Woman Killed With Kindness* and *2 Fair Maid of the West*.

127 M. J. Braddick, *The Nerves of State: Taxation and the Financing of the English State, 1558–1714* (Manchester, 1996), 84–7.

128 See, e.g., A. H. Smith, G. M. Baker (eds), *The Papers of Nathaniel Bacon of Stiffkey III, 1586–1595* (Norfolk Record Society, LIII, 1987, 1988), *passim*, and cf. especially Scene 18, ll. 98–9. The play may have acquired a renewed urgency in later revivals; the sixth edition of 1626 coincided with the most controversial of such taxations; see R. Cust, *The Forced Loan and English Politics, 1626–8* (Oxford, 1987).

129 Hammer, *Polarisation* (note 116), 165, 170 n.109.

130 Richard Grafton, *A Chronicle at Large, to the first yere of Q. Elizabeth* (London: H. Denham, 1569), 84. Hobs describes the courtier-huntsmen as 'roysters', Scene 11, l. 79.

131 *Roxburghe Ballads* (note 102), I, 4–9.

132 See, e.g., *Survey*, I, 104. Several ballads celebrating Essex's military career were entered in the Stationers' Register: see Arber, II, 591, 594; III, 53, 71. Ballads relating to Essex are also collected in F. J. Furnivall, W. R. Morfill (eds), *Ballads from Manuscripts*, 2 vols (London: Ballad Society, 1868–73), II, 195–252.

133 Cited in C. Bright, *Surveillance, Militarism and Drama in the Elizabethan Era* (London, 1996), 226.

134 C. Jackson (ed.), *The Diary of Abraham de la Prynne, the Yorkshire Antiquary*, Surtees Society, liv (1869–70), 67.

135 Cited in Child, V, 68.

136 D. R. Woolf, 'The "Common Voice": History, Folklore and Oral Tradition in Early Modern England', *Past and Present*, 120 (1988), 26–52 (37).

137 See, for instance, J. Kerrigan's anthology, *The Motives of Woe: Shakespeare and 'Female Complaint'* (Oxford, 1991).

138 *Survey*, I, 173.

139 *Ibid.*, I, 172–3.

140 *Ibid.*, II, 300.

141 The estimate of R. Ashton, *The City and the Court, 1603–1643* (Cambridge, 1979), 40.

142 L. Stone, 'The Peer and the Alderman's Daughter', *History Today*, 11 (1961), 49–55; Archer, 56, 1. The importance which contemporaries attached to a lord mayor's care for the poor is shown throughout William Jaggard's *A View of All the Lord Mayors* (London, 1601); comparisons are inescapable, between the likes of 'Wilam Allin' (1571)—'he would buy wood from the carte and distribute it with his owne hands'—and 'Sir Iohn Allat' (1590), who failed to alleviate a 'hard yeare with the poore',

or 'Sir William Web' (1591), for whom Jaggard cannot 'yet find any notes of his bounty'. Of Spencer's generosity Jaggard ominously says nothing.

143 In addition to Fabyan (see headnote to Scene 16), see, for instance, '*Gregory's Chronicle*', in J. Gairdner (ed.), *The Historical Collections of a Citizen of London*, Camden Society, second series, V (1876), 232; *Great Chronicle*, 228. Edward's relationships with the City are usefully summarized in Ross, *Edward IV*, 352–6.

144 See F. Heal, *Hospitality in Early Modern England* (Oxford, 1990), 312, 336; *The First and Second Prayer Books of Edward VI* (London, 1910), 382–3.

145 More, 55 (ll. 7–8), 54 (l. 27); further references are cited, by page and line number, in the text. Both the printed Latin text of the *History* and the Latin 'Arundel MS' (but no subsequent English versions) note that the penance was publicly enacted at St Paul's (*ibid.*, 54, 132), an observation which may have suggested Jane's route—'from Temple Bar . . . to Aldgate' (Part Two, Scene 18, ll. 194–5)—in the play, since the cathedral was the half-way point. For Heywood's use of More's Latin text see commentary to Part One, Scene 1, ll. 12–15, 104–7.

146 Subsequent versions of More's *History* in the chronicles of Harding, Hall and Holinshed read 'godlie' for 'goodly'; see, for example, Holinshed, III, 384.

147 L. B. Campbell (ed.), *The Mirror for Magistrates* (Cambridge, 1938), 372.

148 References to *Shores Wife* are to Kerrigan's edition of the 1563 text, except in cases, such as this one, where material is found only in the 1593 text: *Churchyards Challenge* (London: J. Wolfe, 1593), 133.

149 Anthony Chute, *Beawtie Dishonoured written vnder the title of Shores Wife* (London: John Wolfe, 1593), sig. E2r.

150 *Ibid.*, sigs D4r, E2r.

151 *Mirror* (note 147), 372; *Shores Wife*, l. 49. *Beawtie Dishonoured* also alludes to a false friend, a 'bad seede of base sedition' (D1r), on to whom responsibility for inflaming both the adulteress's lust and the King's is momentarily displaced.

152 Although no text predating its inclusion in *The Garland of Good Will* (earliest extant edition, 1631) has survived, it is quite possible that the dramatist also knew Deloney's ballad, 'A New Sonnet, conteining the Lamentation of *Shores* wife, who was sometime Concubine to King *Edward* the fourth, setting forth her great fall, and withall her most miserable and wretched end . . . To the tune of, the hunt is vp', entered in the Stationers' Register in June 1593—the same year as *Beawtie Dishonoured*, and to the same printer, John Wolfe; see Mann (ed.), *The Works of Thomas Deloney*, 302, 565. It has been suggested, however, that the *Garland* was itself first published in 1596, and by Edward White rather than by Wolfe; see E.Y. Beith-Halahmi, '*Angell Fayre or Strumpet Lewd': Jane Shore as an Example of Erring Beauty in 16th Century Literature* (Salzburg, 1974), 197 n.36, which discusses the Shore ballads, all of which postdate the play, pp. 177–230; see also N. Wurzbach, *The Rise of the English Street Ballad, 1550–1650* (trans. G. Walls; Cambridge, 1990), 117–18, 132–4. Deloney's ballad is short (84 lines), but, in the seven (of twelve) stanzas that deal with Mistress Shore's humiliation, suggestive in its detail; see, e.g., the 'clacke and dish' of l. 62 (cf. Part Two, Scene 20, l. 132.01).

153 Drayton, 269–71. Citations of the *Heroicall Epistles* will be to this edition and will appear in the text; Hebel's base text is the 1619 edition of Drayton's *Works*, and variants (other than spelling and punctuation) are noted accordingly.

154 As the commentary to Scene 17 (in particular) makes clear, there can be little question concerning the priority of Drayton's text. Hebel's assertion that Drayton was the probable borrower is based on a number of mistaken assumptions, including ignorance of the first edition of *Edward IV*, and the unwarranted identification of the play with entries in Henslowe's *Diary* from the early 1590s. A similarly unconvincing attempt to date the play (as a reincarnation of the lost *Buckingham* of 1593) is by S. Longstaffe, 'The Date of *Edward IV*', *Notes and Queries*, new series, 44 (1997), 487–9. It is inconceivable that such close (and so many) verbal parallels could result from Drayton's recollection of a (still unpublished) play in performance.

155 *The True Tragedy of Richard the Third*, ll. 224, 217. It is probably this play to which Heywood referred (and to which he contributed a Prologue and an Epilogue), when many years later he reminisced about a 'young witty Lad playing the part of Richard the third: at the Red Bull'; *Pleasant Dialogues and Drammas*, 247.

156 Anon., *Pimlyco, or, Runne Red-Cap. Tis a mad world at Hogsdon* (London: J. Busbie and G. Loftis, 1609), sig. C1r.

157 J. Twyning, *London Dispossessed: Literature and Social Space in the Early Modern City* (London, 1998), 81.

158 Both Robert Laneham's *A letter: whearin part of the entertainment vntoo the Queen at Killingwoorth Castl* [*sic*] *is signified* (1575) and the Wardens' accounts are cited in Ingram (ed.), *REED: Coventry* (Toronto, 1981), 270–5.

159 See, for instance, the Letterbook which specifies that the sword of office may be borne by the swordbearer *before* the mayor, 'his grace [the monarch] . . . being present, unto the utter [outer] Court gate & no further And in his graces absence unto the churche of Westm[inster] & lykewyse in Suthwerke & suche other the Suburbes of the sayd Cytie . . . w[ith]out eny man[ner] of dyspleasure or offence of hys highnes . . .'; cited in L. Jewitt, W. H. St John Hope, *The Corporation Plate and Insignia of Office of the Cities and Corporate Towns of England and Wales*, 2 vols (London, 1895), II, 111.

160 Also recapitulated here are the most provocative observations of the chronicles concerning Edward's dangerous elision of political and erotic power. See, e.g., the 1587 edition of Holinshed, where Fleming glosses the King's defiance of maternal and ecclesiastical objections to his impending marriage: 'This spake he [Edward] as alluding to the libertie of princes, whose lust standeth oftentimes for law, and their opinion for reason' (III, 388).

161 Actors who participated in the dramatized readings of the play at Shakespeare's Globe in the summer of 2003 found it difficult to establish relationships and motivations for the characters, and experienced confusion with both the plot and the historical context. Barrie Rutter, director of the Northern Broadsides company, believes that the French scenes could be cut without any loss of narrative coherence.

162 Commines, for instance, writing in the immediate aftermath of the destruction of both Burgundy and the Constable (foretold at the end of Scene 7), observed that 'the King of France never found man afterward of his owne subjects that durst lift up his finger against him' (I, 290).

163 H. S. Bennett, *English Books and Readers, 1558–1603: Being a Study in the English Book Trade in the Reign of Elizabeth I* (Cambridge, 1965), 102–4, 245–6.

164 L. F. Parmelee, *Good Newes from Fraunce: French Anti-League Propaganda in Late Elizabethan England* (Rochester, NY, 1996), 33.

165 See, e.g., two translations by Sir Edward Hoby: M. Coignet, *Politique Discourses Upon Truth and Lying* (1586), and L. Voisin, *The Historie of France: The Foure First Bookes* (1595).

166 *A Politike Discourse most excellent for this time present* (London: John Woolfe, 1589), sig. C3r. Similar sentiments are found in John Fregeuille, *The Reformed Politicke* (London: Richard Field, 1589), sigs I4r–K1r.

167 *Politike Discourse*, sig. E3v. See also [M. Hurault], *A Discourse Upon the Present Estate of France* (n.p., 1588); on the closing page of the Bodleian copy, beside a letter in which the Duke of Guise describes his 'protection' of the French king, a marginal note reads, 'Ah Syrrha, might you so?'

168 See Jaques Hurault, *Politicke, Moral, and Martial Discourses* (trans. A. Golding, London: Adam Islip, 1595), sig. Bb3v.

169 Anon., *The Mutable and Wavering Estate of France, from the yeare of our Lord 1460, untill the yeare 1595 . . . collected out of sundry, both Latine, Italian, and French Historiographers* (London: Thomas Creede, 1597), sig. A1v.

170 The fullest translation is by Edward Grimeston, *A General Inventorie of the History of France, from the beginning of that Monarchie, vnto the Treatie of Vervins, in the yeare 1598* (London: George Eld, 1607); see, e.g., p. 254 for the pensions paid to Howard and Sellinger. The French edition consulted was the second volume of *Inventaire General De L'Histoire de France* (Paris: A. Saugrain, G. de Rues, 1600), where the 'invasion' is covered on sigs hh5v–kk2r.

171 *General Inventorie*, p. 255; cf. Holinshed, III, 337–8.

172 See R. Vaughan, *Charles the Bold* (London, 1973), 145, 186, 400–3; S. Gunn, 'State Development in England and the Burgundian Dominions, c.1460–c.1560', *Publication du Centre Européen d'Etudes Bourguignonnes*, 35 (1995), *passim*.

173 Thomas Heywood, *An Apology for Actors* (London: Nicholas Okes, 1612), sig. F1v.

174 B. Kumin, *The Shaping of a Community: The Rise and Reformation of the English Parish* (Aldershot, 1996), 243; R. Tittler, *The Reformation and the Towns in England: Politics and Political Culture, c.1540–1640* (Oxford, 1998), 287–93.

175 Helgerson, *Forms of Nationhood* (note 36), 132.

176 A. Patterson, *Reading Holinshed's Chronicles* (Chicago, 1994); see also W. Wall, 'Forgetting and Keeping: Jane Shore and the English Domestication of History', *Renaissance Drama*, new series, 27 (1998), 123–56.

177 Cited in P. Cain, 'Robert Smith and the Reform of the Archives of the City of London, 1580–1623', *London Journal*, 13 (1987–88), 3–16 (3, 11).

The resulting manuscript has not survived; Cain conjectures that the pamphlet *Generall matters . . . lord maior* of 1600 (STC. 16718.5) may be a printed redaction.

178 Sir Robert Cotton appears to have 'borrowed' some records which were then broken up and recovered only in fragments; Cain, 'Robert Smith', 6–7.

179 *Londini Speculum* (1637), in D. M. Bergeron (ed.), *Thomas Heywood's Pageants: A Critical Edition* (New York, 1986), ll. 260–2.

180 Andrew Gordon has argued similarly that both Norden's 1600 map (*Civitas Londini*) and the Lord Mayors' pageants enact this same challenge, intervening 'in a struggle to appropriate the civic sign, displacing the monarchic ceremonial city from the map, and relegating royal authority to an isolated compound [Westminster] from which all indication of the sovereign presence is. . . . absent'; 'Performing London' (see note 46), 83.

181 More, 54/24–6.

182 *Survey*, II, 74–5. For further discussion of cultural inscription see I. W. Archer, 'The Arts and Acts of Memorialization in Early Modern London', in Merritt (ed.), *Imagining Early Modern London* (note 33), 89–113.

183 *Ibid.*, II, 201.

184 Greg, I, 171–4.

185 For further discussion see R. Rowland, 'Two Plays in One: Annotations in the Third Quarto of *Edward IV* ', *TEXT* (*Transactions of the Society for Textual Scholarship*), 17 (2005, forthcoming).

186 Greg, I, 255. The initials are conclusive, but the ornaments less so; the latter appear in R. B. McKerrow, *Printers' & Publishers' Devices in England & Scotland, 1485–1640* (London: The Bibliographical Society, 1949), but are there identified with the Scottish printer Andro Hart; see no. 379.

187 One example of inconsistency may serve to illustrate the point. At Part One, Scene 4, ll. 65–6 (sig. B4r), the districts of '*Bowe*' and '*Mileend Greene*' are specified in two consecutive lines; in both Q1 and Q2 the first place-name is set in roman, but the second in undifferentiated black letter.

188 The same phenomenon occurs at Part One, Scene 23, ll. 50–4 (sig. L2r). Heywood was certainly capable of indicating important pauses by the insertion of a mere vertical stroke: see, for example, *The Captives*, l. 1319, where such a stroke appears to mark both an 'aside' and a shift— within a single speech—from prose to verse.

189 *Tom a Lincoln*, ed. Proudfoot, xix.

190 Although it fails to acknowledge the existence of the annotations in Q3 of *Edward IV*, Leslie Thomson's essay 'A Quarto "Marked for Performance": Evidence of What?', *Medieval and Renaissance Drama in England*, 8 (1996), provides a thorough and very valuable analysis of the theatrical implications of a similarly annotated playtext, *The Two Merry Milke-Maids* (1620).

191 See Rowland, ' "Speaking some words" ' (note 25), *passim*.

THE FIRST AND SECOND PARTS
OF KING EDWARD THE FOURTH

Containing his merry pastime with the Tanner of
Tamworth; as also his love to fair Mistress Shore,
her great promotion, fall, and misery, and lastly,
the lamentable death of both her and
her husband.

Characters in the Play (Part One)

KING EDWARD IV
QUEEN ELIZABETH, former wife of John Gray, new wife of
  Edward
THE DUCHESS OF YORK, the King's mother
JOHN, LORD HOWARD
SIR THOMAS SELLINGER
THOMAS NEVILLE, the Bastard Falconbridge

QUEEN ELIZABETH] Daughter to Sir Richard Woodville (later Lord Rivers) and Jacquetta, Duchess of Bedford. Widow of Sir John Gray, who was killed fighting against Edward at St Albans. See G. Smith, *The Coronation of Elizabeth Wydeville* (Cliftonville, 1975), 27–37, and D. Baldwin, *Elizabeth Woodville* (Stroud, 2002).

JOHN, LORD HOWARD] The last of only eight men ever raised by Edward from the gentry to the peerage, Howard was treasurer of the royal household from 1467 to 1471. He became England's leading envoy to France by the mid 1470s, and his unswerving devotion to the Yorkist dynasty earned him both the dukedom of Norfolk in the first moments of Richard's reign, and death at Bosworth in the last. Even hostile chroniclers acknowledged his courage and loyalty, Virgil calling him 'a man very politic and skilfull in wars' (187), and Hall conceding that 'as he had faithfully lived under [Richard], so he manfully died with him, to his greater honour and laud' (419).

SIR THOMAS SELLINGER] Variously known in chronicles and records as Salinger, St Leger, or Seintlegier. Listed as squire 'for the bodie' (Myers, 199) and clearly a boisterous favourite; in 1465 he was pardoned for striking a marshal within the Palace of Westminster, unlike the luckless John Davy who lost his hand for the same offence four years earlier (*Calender of Patent Rolls, 1461–1467*, 380; Stow, *Annals*, 682). He eventually became Edward's brother-in-law, marrying the widow of the only notable casualty of the French expedition, the Duke of Exeter, who, though 'comaunded to folow the kyng was put to death by drounyng & cast ouer a shyp by sir Thomas Sent Lyger, whiche after married his wyfe contrary to the promise made' (Grafton's 'Continuation' of *The Chronicle of John Hardyng*, 1543, fol. xxvii, v).

THOMAS . . . Falconbridge] Illegitimate son of William, Lord Fauconberg of Kent. A sometime naval commander in the pay of the Yorkist monarchy who defected with his fleet to the cause of his cousin, Warwick, some months before the rebellion with which the play begins.

NED SPICING
SMOKE
CHUB
JOHN CROSBY, Lord Mayor of London
THOMAS URSWICK, the Recorder of London

SMOKE] His name is suggestive of his manner rather than his occupation. *OED* (II.5.b.) offers the definition, to 'subject to smoke, so as to suffocate, stupefy'—which is the implication of Scene 2, 60–1—but then incorrectly cites Jonson's *Every Man in His Humour* (Quarto, 1601), 3.6.23: 'I was smookt soundly first', where Cob means that he was fooled. Biancha in the same play uses the term to suggest that she has exposed the fraudulent practices of Thorello; '(I am glad) I haue smokt you yet at last' (5.1.35) and this antedates *OED*'s earliest (1608) citation of this meaning. Smoke's speeches at Scene 5, 74–7 and 81–6 (misattributed to Spicing in Q1) hint at both Jonsonian senses. Smoke's sheer violence may further be illuminated by noting that throughout both *A notable discouery of coosenage* (1591) and *The second part of conny-catching* (1591) Robert Greene uses the words 'smoake' and 'smacke' interchangeably.

CHUB] Again, a name of probably composite derivation and significance. It is likely to mean rustic or dolt as in Thomas Phaer's 1558 translation of *Aeneid*, VII, 523–4: 'like frayes of contry chubbs' (*OED*) and also to anticipate Randle Cotgrave's translation of the French word 'Raccourci'—'compacted; chubbie, short and strong'—in the 1611 *Dictionarie*. The chandlers seem to have had a reputation for duplicity: a subordinate devil in Dekker's *If This be not a Good Play, the Diuel is in It* (1612) claims to have 'had a chandlers soule' for 'one halfe ounce' of cheese (4.2.105), and the hypocritical puritan of *The Atheist's Tragedy* (1611), Languebeau Snuffe, is forcibly returned to his 'candle-making' at the end of the play (5.2.64–6).

JOHN CROSBY] Crosby was not, as the dramatist must have known from his reading in Fabyan and Stow, Mayor at the time of the uprising or indeed at any other time. Crosby was in fact Sheriff and Sir John Stockton was Mayor. Clearly the playwright was attracted by the story of Crosby's origins (see Scene 16, ll. 1–33), which, though it may be apocryphal, can be found in Stow (*Survey*, I, 172–3); see Introduction, pp. 41–2.

THOMAS URSWICK] The Recorder, an official defined by Stow as 'a graue and learned Lawyer, skilfull in the Customes of this Citty, Also assistant to the Lord Maior: Hee taketh place in Counsels, and in Courts before any man that hath not beene Mayor: and learnedly deliuereth the sentences of the whole Court' (*Survey*, II, 187). Sir Henry Calthrop, writing in the turbulent atmosphere of 1642, adds that the Recorder shall 'record and certifie the Customs being traversed. And his certificate shall be as strong in the Law as the verdict of 22 men'; *The Liberties, usages, and customes of the city of London* (1642), 23. The constitutional centrality of the office is recognized by Shakespeare; see *Richard III*, 3.7.28–41. Most of the chronicles mention Urswick's contribution to the defence of the City; none of them mentions his twice being the recipient of royal pardons—for trespass and theft (*Calendar of Patent Rolls, 1467–1477*, 21, 202).

RALPH JOSSELYN
MATTHEW SHORE, a goldsmith
JANE SHORE, his wife, later mistress to the King
A MILLER
JOHN HOBS, the tanner of Tamworth
NELL, his daughter
DUDGEON, his man
SIR HARRY MORTON, the Vice Admiral
The CAPTAIN of the Isle of Wight
SIR HUMPHREY BOWES
MASTER ASTON
HARRY GRUDGEN
ROBERT GOODFELLOW
MASTER HADLAND
MISTRESS BLAGE
THE MASTER OF ST KATHERINE'S
WIDOW NORTON
THOMAS AIRE
MASTER PALMER

RALPH JOSSELYN] A draper; Sheriff of the City in 1458 and Lord Mayor in 1476 (*Survey*, II, 175, 177). Stow and the other chroniclers are unanimous in commending Josselyn for his 'diligence' and *The Great Chronicle* has him the active leader of the resistance to Falconbridge and a vigorous pursuer of the rebels (219–20). Quite unlike the dramatist Fabyan actually credits him with a 'sharpe and quycke mynde' (666).

MATTHEW SHORE] The historical Shore was called William and he was not a goldsmith but a mercer; he was, furthermore, one of sufficient wealth to have made a considerable loan to the King at the time of the French expedition (*Tellers' Rolls*, Easter 14, Edw. IV.; cited in Scofield, II, 162); see also A. Sutton's article in *Derbyshire Archaeological Journal*, 106 (1986). Though the dramatist almost certainly knew 'Shore's Wife' from *The Mirror for Magistrates* he does not follow Churchyard in declaring Shore a 'prentyse' (l. 108). This poem, particularly the section on Shore's forbearance (ll. 190–6), draws on More's *English History*, whereas the play's handling of this episode indicates a knowledge of the Latin version. Shore is designated a goldsmith in Drayton's 'Edward IV to Mistres Shore' (ll. 33–42); so he is in the anonymous ballad 'Jane Shore'—see H. B. Wheatley (ed.), *Reliques of Ancient English Poetry*, 3 vols (London, 1886), II, 269, l. 20—but the earliest surviving copy of this ballad is late seventeenth century and it probably derives from the play (see Introduction, p. 74, n. 152).

JANE SHORE] The most recent attempts to uncover the origins of this mysterious figure are the articles by Nicholas Barker in *Etoniana*, 125–6 (1972).

MASTER RUFFORD
JOCKIE
Apprentices, Huntsmen, Messenger, Watermen, Executioner

None of the six quartos has a list of characters.

The First Part of King Edward IV

[Scene 1]

> *Enter* KING EDWARD, *the* DUCHESS OF YORK, *the*
> QUEEN, [*the sons of the queen, including* DORSET,] *the*
> LORD HOWARD, *and* SIR THOMAS SELLINGER.

Duchess. Son, I tell ye, you have done—you know not what!
Edward. I have married a woman, else I am deceived, mother.
Duchess. Married a woman? Married indeed!
    Here is a marriage that befits a king!
    It is no marvel it was done in haste.   5
    Here is a bridal, and with hell to boot!
    You have made work!
Edward. Faith, mother, some we have indeed; but ere long
    you shall see us make work for an heir apparent, I doubt
    not. Nay, nay; come, come; God's will, what, chiding still?   10
Duchess. O God! That e'er I lived to see this day!
Edward. By my faith, mother, I hope you shall see the night
    too! And in the morning I will be bold to bid you to the

The skirmish between Edward, Queen Elizabeth and the Duchess of York
is based largely on material from More's *History*. The playwright may have
had access either to the 1565 Louvain edition of the Latin *Opera* or, (less
likely) to one of several MS versions in circulation, as well as to the many
printed 'appropriations' in the English chronicles; the commentary below
indicates some of the likely borrowings. The King speaks a robust prose,
larded with proverbs, for which there were numerous hints in the moralistic
interjections of historiographers such as Commines and Holinshed's revis-
ers, and he moves into blank verse and classical allusion only at the moment
in which the dramatist violates historical chronology by intruding the public
events of 1471 into the domestic squabbles of 1464.

12–15. *By . . . world!*] Cf. More, 64/12–17 (Quamobrem . . . conciliet):
'Therefore may you also, sweetest mother, approve this marriage which I
have contracted for myself with the blessings of the gods; and may you
support it with your auspicious prayers and that it may turn out happily
for us. For even if you are opposed to it at present, a little grandson will
shortly be born from it, who will win you over to our point of view with his
caresses.'

christening: grandmother, and godmother to a Prince of
Wales. Tut, mother, 'tis a stirring world!   15
Duchess. Have you sent Warwick into France, for this?
Edward. No, by my faith, mother. I sent Warwick into France
for another, but this by chance being nearer hand, and
coming in the way—I cannot tell how—we concluded;
and now, as you see, are going about to get a young king.   20
Duchess. But tell me, son, how will you answer this?
Is't possible your rash, unlawful act
Should not breed mortal hate betwixt the realms?
What may the French king think, when he shall hear
That whilst you send to entreat about his daughter,   25
Basely to take a subject of your own?
What may the Princess Bona think of this?
Our noble cousin Warwick, that great lord,
That centre-shaking thunderclap of war,
That like a column propped the house of York,   30
And bore our white rose bravely in his top;
When he shall hear his embassage abused,
In this but made an instrument by you,
I know his soul will blush within his bosom,
And shame will sit in scarlet on his brow,   35
To have his honour touched with this foul blemish.
Son, son! I tell you: that is done by you,
Which yet the child that is unborn shall rue.

---

25. *daughter*] Bona was actually sister-in-law to the French king though
both MS and printed chronicles offer bewilderingly divergent accounts of
her genealogy. For contemporary references to the marriage settlement see
J. R. Lander, 'Marriage and Politics in the 15th Century: The Nevilles and
the Wydevills', *BIHR*, 36 (1963).

28. *cousin*] Warwick was actually Edward's cousin and the King calls him
so in More's (English) *History*, 63/29.

31. *white rose*] The Yorkist emblem. There is an extended theatrical treatment of the initial 'roses' quarrel in *1 Henry VI* (2.4), and see also York's
vaunt in *The First Part of the Contention*: 'Then will I raise aloft the milke-
vwhite Rose' (266).

top] appears here to mean helmet rather than the more usual hair or head.

37–8. *that . . . rue*] Cf. *Richard II*: 'children yet unborn / Shall feel this day
as sharp to them as thorn' (4.1.322-3).

Edward. Tush, mother. You are deceived. All true subjects
shall have cause to thank God, to have their king born of   40
a true Englishwoman. I tell you, it was never well since
we matched with strangers; so our children have been still
like chickens of the half kind, but, where the cock and
the hen be both of one breed, there is like to be birds of
the game. Hear you, mother, hear you: had I gone to it   45
by fortune, I had made your sons—George, and Dick—
to have stood gaping after the crown. This wench,
mother, is a widow, and hath made proof of her valour,
and for anything I know, I am as like to do the deed as
John Gray, her husband, was. I had rather the people   50
prayed to bless mine heir, than send me an heir. Hold
your peace; if you can see, there was never mother had a
towarder son. Why, cousin Howard, and Tom Sellinger,
heard you ever such a coil about a wife?
Howard. My sovereign lord, with patience bear her spleen.   55
Your princely mother's zeal is like a river,
That from the free abundance of the waters
Breaks out into this inundation.

39–42. *All . . . strangers*] A remarkable display of xenophobia, with theatrical and political resonance; audiences might recall that Margaret of Anjou
was the villain of both the contemporary Yorkist chronicles and Shakespeare's
Henry VI plays, but also that the man most likely to be their next king was
the son of Mary Queen of Scots.

43–4. *the cock . . . breed*] This sounds proverbial but though Dent lists four
examples of the cock/hen conjunction this is not amongst them; see,
however, Rusticano's ill-judged pass in *Tom a Lincoln*: 'I showld be the Cocke
& yow the hen, & then wee should well agree together' (l. 1815).

50–1. *I had . . . an heir*] He would rather the commons blessed offspring
generated by natural desire rather than coerced him into a dynastic
marriage.

54. *coil*] squabble, uproar.

56–8. *Your . . . inundation*] Howard is possibly punning mischievously on
the Rivers family connection with which, for instance, *The True Tragedie of
Richard III* was much concerned. This is the essence of the Hobs-like episode
recorded in *The Great Chronicle of London*: 'Abowth thys tyme oon wood-
hows a Sage dyzour (jester, scoffer) beyng In good ffavour of the kyngys grace
ffor his manerly Raylyng & honest dysportys which he offtyn exercysid In
the Court, cam upon a daye of the hoot & drye Somyr Into the kyngys
Chambyr . . . when the Kyng hadd beholdyn his apparayll, he ffraynyd of
hym what was the cawse of his long botis & of his long staff, upon my ffayth
sir said he I have passyd thorwth many Cuntrees of your Realm, and In placys

From her abundant care, this rage proceeds,
O'er-swoll'n with the extremity of love.   60
Sellinger. My lord, my lord, avoid a woman's humour!
If you resist this tumour of her will,
Here you shall have her dwell upon this passion
Until she jade and dull our ears again.
Seem you but sorry for what you have done,   65
And straight she'll put the finger in the eye
With comfort now, since it cannot be helped;
But make you show to justify the act,
If ever other language in her lips
Than 'out upon it, it is abhominable', I dare be hanged.   70
Say anything, it makes no matter what,
Than thus be wearied with a woman's chat.
Duchess. Ay, ay, you are the spaniels of the court,
And thus you fawn and sooth your wanton king.

---

64. jade] *Q1–2*; lade *Q3–6*.

that I have passid the Ryvers been soo hie that I coude hardly scape thorw theym' (208).

inundation] For the juxtaposition of inundation (weeping) and rage see Lewis's commendation of Salisbury, *King John* (5.2.47–57).

61. *humour*] Sellinger refers to the theory, derived from the second century AD physiologist Galen, in which a person's temperament was composed of four elements or humours. If the elements were not proportionate—and he suggests here that in the Duchess the humour of choler (anger) predominates—the result would be an irrational obsession or personality disorder. Ironically, both the psychopathic rebel Spicing and King Edward will insist on the right to indulge their 'humour' later in the play; see Scene 9, l. 39, and Scene 13, l. 117.

62. *tumour*] haughtiness, arrogance.

64. *jade*] Weary or exhaust; although *OED* cites this meaning as early as 1606 it offers no examples which do not refer specifically to horses until much later. Q3's 'lade' also makes sense; meaning 'unload by the bucketful', it continues the water imagery from Howard's previous speech.

66. *finger in the eye*] Make herself weep. Proverbial (Dent, F229); Sellinger is suggesting that if Edward is apologetic the Duchess's tears will turn from the angry to the sentimentally maternal. See also Part Two, Scene 13, l. 56. Heywood employs the expression in *The Wise Woman of Hogsden* (c.1604), I1r.

73. *spaniels*] Cf. *Nobody and Somebody* (c.1606) where a character called Sicophant is reminded: 'Time was base spaniell thou didst fawne as much / On me, as now thou striuest to flatter her' (E2v).

But, Edward, hadst thou prized thy majesty,   75
Thou never would have stained thy princely state
With the base leavings of a subject's bed;
Nor borne the blemish of her bigamy.
A widow! Is't not a goodly thing?
Gray's children, come ask blessing of the King.   80
Queen. Nay, I beseech your grace, my lady York,
Even as you are a princess and a widow,
Think not so meanly of my widowhood.
A spotless virgin came I first to Gray;
With him I lived a true and faithful wife.   85
And since his high imperial majesty
Hath pleased to bless my poor, dejected state
With the high sovereign title of his queen,
I here protest, before the host of heav'n,
I came as chaste a widow to his bed,   90
As, when a virgin, I to Gray was wed.
Edward. Come, come, have done; now you have chid enough.
God's foot, we were as merry, ere she came, as any people
in Christendom, I with the mistress, and these with the
maids—only we had no fiddlers at our feast. But, mother,   95
you have made a fit of mirth. Welcome to Grafton,
mother; by my troth, you are even just come, as I wished
you here. Let us to supper; and, in charity, give us your
blessing ere we go to bed.

75–9. *But . . . thing?*] Cf. More: 'only [the] widowhed of Elizabeth Grey
. . . shold yet suffice as me semeth to refrain you from her mariage, sith it is
an vnsittingthing, & a very blemish, & highe disparagement, to the sacre
magesty of a prince, yt ought as nigh to approche priesthode in clenes as he
doth in dignitie, to be defouled wt bigamy in his first mariage' (62/23–9;
Latin, 21–7).

90. *chaste*] the Queen refers to sexual fidelity, not virginity.

96. *fit of mirth*] An interruption or pause. 'Fit' is a technical term to
describe the sections or pauses in a ballad. Puttenham uses it in his chapter
'The maner of Reioysings at Mariages and Weddings' and significantly
observes of the ritual of the 'Epithalamie' that the 'ceremony was omitted
when men maried widowes or such as had tasted the frutes of loue before';
G. D. Willcock, A. Walker (eds), *The Arte of English Poesie* (Cambridge, 1936),
I.xxvi.51, 53.

Grafton] The Woodville family home in Northamptonshire; the wedding
is located there by Fabyan (654) and Hall (264). It was still used as a royal
palace in Elizabethan times; see Nichols, II, 6.

Duchess. O, Edward, Edward, fly, and leave this place   100
Wherein—poor, silly king—thou art enchanted.
This is her dam of Bedford's work, her mother,
That hath bewitched thee, Edward, my poor child.
Dishonour not the princes of thy land,
To make them kneel with reverence at her feet,   105
That, ere thou didst empale with sovereignty,
They would have scorned to look upon.
There's no such difference 'twixt the greatest peer
And the poor, silliest kitchen maid that lives,
As is betwixt thy worthiness and hers.   110
Queen. I do confess it. Yet, my lady York,
My mother is a duchess as you are,
A princess born, the Duke of Bedford's wife,

102–3. *This . . . child*] Behind the witchcraft allegation may lie an old legend in which Melusine, the Serpent-witch, a water-witch of Lusignan, was the supposed ancestress of the House of Luxembourg, from which Elizabeth's mother was descended. Historically, Jacquetta was accused, by a henchman of Warwick, of making images of lead 'to use with witchcraft and sorcery'; she cleared her name in theatrical fashion in 1471 (see *Calendar of Patent Rolls, 1467–1477*, 190). Elizabeth herself would come to be similarly accused by Richard III. The allegation is recorded by Hall and Holinshed, and there is a particularly vivid account in Polydore Virgil (180); the charge had also been staged (*True Tragedy*, 943–6; *Richard III*, 3.4.68–71).

104–7. *Dishonour . . . upon*] Cf. More (Latin only): (Sustinere . . . generet?) 'Could you bear to have mongrel and degenerate princes rule this most flourishing kingdom of yours? Could you bear to have your blood producing brothers for the sons of a Grey?' This passage may also have influenced ll. 70–2.

106. *empale*] Variant form of 'impale'. May simply mean to adorn as in Greene's *Menaphon* (1589): 'he impalled the head of his yong nephew . . . with the crowne and diademe of Arcadie' (L4v) but may also, in this context, anticipate *OED*'s earliest (1611) example of a technical heraldic term, to 'combine (two coats of arms, as those of a husband and wife) by placing them side by side on one shield'. Camden scornfully alludes to Edward's innovations in this area; see R. D. Dunn (ed.), *Remaines Concerning Britain* (Toronto, 1984), 161.

108–110. *There's . . . hers*] The comparison is from More, 62/15–16: 'Forasmuch as there is betwene no merhant & his own maid so gret difference, as betwene ye king and this widowe', but also see Chaucer's *The Clerk's Tale* (814–26) for both this analogy and the Queen's Griselda-like response.

112–15. *My . . . Burgundy*] Not an entirely accurate claim, though less extravagant than that advanced in a 1474 Coventry pageant, which declared the Queen a descendant of the Magi; see M. D. Harris (ed.), *The Coventry Leet Book*, 2 vols (EETS, original series, 1907–13), II, 393. Her mother,

And, as you know, a daughter and a sister
Unto the royal blood of Burgundy.   115
But you cannot so basely think on me,
As I do think of these vain, worldly titles.
God from my soul my sin as far divide,
As I am far from boasting this in pride.
Sellinger. Madam, she is the mirror of her kind.   120
Had she but so much spleen as hath a gnat,
Her spirits would startle to abide your taunts.
She is a saint, and, madam, you blaspheme
To wrong so sweet a lady.
Duchess. Thou art a minion and a flatterer.   125
Sellinger. Madam, but that you are my sovereign's mother,
I would let you know, you wrong a gentleman.
Howard. Good cousin Sellinger, have patience.
Her grace's rage, by so much violence,
Hath spent itself already into air.   130
Dear madam, I beseech you on my knee,
Tender that loving kindness to the Queen
That, I dare swear, she doth in soul to you.
Edward. Well said, good coz; I pray thee, make them friends.
Why, how now, Bess? What, weep? Nay then, I'll chide
    you.   135
What sudden news comes by this messenger?

Enter a MESSENGER.

Messenger. My sovereign lord, the bastard Falconbridge
Of late hath stirred rebellion in the south,
Encouraging his forces to deliver

Jacquetta of Luxembourg, was daughter to the Count of St Pol, a powerful French magnate, and through him she could claim descent from
Charlemagne (Ross, 88–9); her brother Jacques represented the Duke of
Burgundy at Elizabeth's coronation but even the Burgundian chronicler
Jean de Waurin makes no mention of blood ties. The Queen did later
become a 'sister' to royalty by virtue of the marriage between Edward's
sister Margaret and Charles, Duke of Burgundy (1468). Elizabeth's father,
Richard, Lord Rivers, began as merely a son to the chamberlain of Jacquetta's
first husband, John, Duke of Bedford.

125. *minion*] servile favourite. The resonance of the word in Marlowe's
Edward II may have invoked sexual connotations thereafter; certainly the
author of *Tom a Lincoln* (1611) uses it unequivocally to mean the monarch's
whore (l. 27).

King Henry, late deposed, out of the Tower.   140
To him the malcontented commons flock
From every part of Sussex, Kent and Essex.
His army waxes twenty thousand strong,
And, as it is supposed by circumstance,
Mean to take London, if not well defended.   145
Edward. Well, let this Phaethon that is mounted thus,
Look he sit surely, or, by England's George,
I'll break his neck. This is no new evasion.
I surely thought that one day I should see
That bastard Falcon take his wings to mount   150
Into our eagle aery; methought I saw
Black discontent sit ever on his brow,
And now I see I calculated well.
Good cousin Howard, and Tom Sellinger,
This night we'll spend in feast and jollity   155
With our new queen, and our beloved mother.
Tomorrow you shall have commission
To raise up power against this haughty rebel.
[*To Messenger*] Sirrah, depart not 'till you know our pleasure;
You shall convey us letters back to London,   160
Unto the Mayor, Recorder, and our friends.
Is supper ready? Come by, my bonny Bess;
Welcome, mother! We are all your guests.   *Exeunt.*

---

142. every] *Q2*; everies *Q1*.

141–3. *To . . . strong*] Only Warkworth's MS chronicle gives this estimate
of numbers (p. 20). The dramatist makes no use of the intriguing piece of
social history found in Fabyan (666) and, more expansively, in *The Great
Chronicle* (218): the Essex men wore their wives' smocks and cheesecloths to
express their resentment of the low prices paid by London buyers for their
dairy produce.

146. *Phaethon*] Drayton compared the aspiring Mortimer with Phaethon,
the charioteer who lost control of the sun (*Mortimeriados* [1597], 2521–7);
Clifford taunts York with the same allusion in *3 Henry VI* (1.4.33–4). The
most familiar source of the story was Ovid's *Metamorphoses* (II, 1–237). The
most probable influence here is Tamburlaine's final speech, particularly in a
play in which the protagonist has been much concerned with the breaking
of necks, principally Callapine's: see 2 *Tamburlaine*, 3.2.155–8, 3.5.100–1.

147. *England's George*] Probably refers to the knightly order, whose chapel
Edward endowed richly in 1473 and 1478; see Scofield, II, 431–3.

148. *evasion*] A rare use of the Latin-derived sense of sallying forth, and in
this case deviation from obedience; antedates *OED*'s earliest example (1659).

[Scene 2]

> *Enter* FALCONBRIDGE *with his troops, marching;*
> SPICING, SMOKE, CHUB *and others.*

Falconbridge. Hold, drum.

Spicing. Hold drum, and be hanged!

Smoke. Hold, drum, hold! Peace then, ho! Silence to the
proclamation!

Spicing. You lie, you, rogue, 'tis to the oration.

Chub. Nay then, you all lie; it is to the coblication.   5

Falconbridge. True-hearted English, and our valiant friends—

All. Ho! Brave general, i' faith!

Spicing. Peace there, you rogues, or I will split your chaps!

Falconbridge. Dear countrymen, I publicly proclaim,
     If any wronged, discontented English,   10
     Touched with true feeling of King Henry's wrongs—
     Henry the Sixth, the lawful king of England,
     Who, by that tyrant, Edward the Usurper,
     Is held a wretched prisoner in the Tower—
     If any man that fain would be enfranchised   15
     From the sad yoke of Yorkish servitude,
     Under which we toil like naked galley-slaves,
     Know he that Thomas Neville, the Lord Falconbridge—

All. Ay, ay, a Faconbridge, a Faconbridge!

1–4.] *Qq read:* Fal. Hold drumme, / *1* Spi. Hold drumme and be hangde,
/ *2* Smoke Hold drumme hold, peace then ho, silence to the / *3* proclamation. / *1* Spi. You lie you rogue, tis to the oration.

---

5. *coblication*] A nonce word (not recorded in *OED*), which implies the
sense of something inexpertly cobbled together. There may also be an
oblique allusion to the story of the cobbler who attempted to train a crow
to repeat a phrase flattering to Augustus Caesar, but whose bird, when tested,
recited something quite different; the tale originated with Macrobius, and
had recently been invoked by Nashe in *Pierce Penilesse* (1592); see *Works*, I,
174.

8. *chaps*] jaws.

15. *enfranchised*] As the following line makes clear the primary sense is
simply 'liberated from subjection', but Falconbridge's attempt to disasso-
ciate this rebellion from the artisanal uprisings of the fifteenth century (ll.
27–41), particularly the stress on 'ancient liberty', 'lawful right' and 'warrant',
gestures—as Shakespeare was surely doing in *Julius Caesar* (1599), 3.2.81—
towards the more modern sense of being admitted to political privileges.

Spicing. Peace, ye clamorous rogues! On, General, on with   20
    your oration. Peace there!
Falconbridge. —Pitying King Henry's poor distressèd case,
    Armed with his title, and a subject's zeal,
    Takes up just arms against the House of York,
    And do proclaim our ancient liberty.   25
All. Liberty! Liberty! Liberty! General liberty!
Falconbridge. We do not rise like Tyler, Cade, and Straw,
    Bluebeard, and other of that rascal rout,
    Basely, like tinkers, or such muddy slaves,
    For mending measures, or the price of corn,   30
    Or for some common in the weald of Kent
    That's by some greedy cormorant enclosed;
    But in the true and ancient lawful right
    Of the redoubted house of Lancaster.
    Our blood is noble: by our birth a Neville,   35

---

27. *Tyler*] Wat Tyler, leader of the Peasants' Revolt of 1381.
Cade] John (Jack) Cade, leader of the Kent uprising of 1451.
Straw] Jack Straw, another of the 1381 rebels.
28. *Bluebeard*] leader of the 1448 rebellion against the influence of the
Duke of Suffolk (see Grafton, I, 639, and Hall, 219). Cade had featured
prominently in Shakespeare's *2 Henry VI* (and the 'reported' text of *The Contention*); Tyler and Straw were the revolutionary protagonists (with John Ball)
of *The Life and Death of Jack Straw* (printed 1593/4), the former meeting
his death in disturbingly obdurate fashion. These names consistently sur-
faced in sixteenth-century political discourse at all levels: a 1595 pamphlet
acknowledges Straw and Tyler as the ideological forerunners of recent urban
troublemakers (*A Students Lamentation*, B2v–B3r), and a holograph written
by Cecil which contemptuously links Tyler and Cade survives amongst
papers pertaining to the Essex rebellion in 1601 (*CSPD, 1598–1601*, 599).
29. *tinkers*] Falconbridge affects the kind of class hostility displayed by
Suffolk in *The Contention*, who denounces Salisbury as an 'Embassador / Sent
from a sort of Tinkers to the King' (1336–7).
30–2. *mending . . . enclosed*] the perennial grievances cited in justification
of rural insurrection from before 1381 through to the Midlands Rising of
1607 and beyond. Alexander Neville's Latin account of Kett's 1549 Norfolk
rebellion, *De furoribus Norfolkiensium* (1575), for instance, includes them all,
as does the English translation of the same, significantly published in the
wake of further serious food riots (see *Norfolkes Furies, or A View of Ketts
Campe* (London, 1615), esp. B1v–B2v). Hobson, the iconoclastic hero of
Heywood's *2 If You Know Not Me* (1605), is moved to tears by 'Inclosures'
and the consequent rural poverty, F3r–F4r.
mending measures] regulation of weights and prices.

And by our lawful line, Lord Falconbridge.
Who's here that's of so dull a leaden temper,
That is not fired with a Neville's name?
All. A Neville! A Neville! A Neville!
Falconbridge. Our quarrel, like our self, is honourable;   40
    The law, our warrant.
Smoke. Ay, ay, the law is on our sde.
Chub. Ay, the law is in our own hands.
Spicing. Peace, you rogues!
Falconbridge. And more: a blessing, by the word proposed,   45
    To those that aid a true annointed king.
    Courage, brave spirits, and cry, a Falconbridge!
All. A Falconbridge! A Falconbridge!
Falconbridge. We will be masters of the Mint ourselves,
    And set our own stamp on the golden coin.   50
    We'll shoe our neighing coursers with no worse
    Than the purest silver that is sold in Cheap.
    At Leadenhall we'll sell pearls by the peck,
    As now the mealmen use to sell their meal.

37–8. *Who's . . . name*] Salisbury in *The Contention* places similar confidence in the 'Neuels' name' (161–2) but *Edward IV* skirts the issue of the Warwick/Neville opposition upon which the chronicles were uniformly insistent.

51–2. *We'll . . . Cheap*] Amidst the catalogue of Cade-like projects, this could be a specific and topical reference; the racy biography *The Life and Death of Mary Frith* (1661) recalls that a Cheapside vintner named Bankes had his talking horse, Marrocco, shoed with silver. The horse was a topic of conversation for Londoners for decades: apart from the extraordinary dialogue *Maroccus Extaticus* (1595), the horse crops up in texts as diverse as Donne's *Satires*, *The Black Book* (1604), and William Rowley's *A Search for Money* (1609).

Cheap] Cheapside, the quarter for gold and silversmiths and thus invariably a target for insurgents.

53. *Leadenhall*] an imposing building which stood at the intersection of Gracechurch Street and Cornhill. It was erected in Edward IV's reign by Simon Eyre (an event celebrated at the conclusions of Deloney's *I The Gentle Craft* (1597), 169, and Dekker's *The Shoemakers' Holiday* (1599), 5.5.127–31, 151–60), and intended as a market for leather and grain. In the sixteenth century it also acquired considerable ceremonial and even military significance; see *Survey*, I, 157–60.

peck] a large measure of grain.

In Westminster we'll keep a solemn court,   55
And build it bigger to receive our men.
Cry Falconbridge, my hearts, and liberty!
All. Falconbridge! And liberty!
Smoke. Peace, ye slaves, or I will smoke ye else!
Chub. Peace, ye slaves, or I will chub your chaps; but indeed   60
   thou mayst well smoke them, because thy name is Smoke.
Smoke. Why, sirrah, I hope Smoke, the smith of Chepstead,
   is as good a man as Chub, the chandler of Sandwich.
Spicing. Peace, ye rogues! What, are you quarrelling? And
   now, list to Captain Spicing!   65
   You know Cheapside? There are the mercers' shops,
   Where we will measure velvet by our pikes,
   And silks and satins by the street's whole breadth!
   We'll take the tankards from the conduit cocks,
   To fill with Hippocras, and drink carouse!   70
   Where chains of gold and plate shall be as plenty
   As wooden dishes in the weald of Kent!
Smoke. O, bravely said, Ned Spicing: the honestest lad that
   ever pound spice in a mortar. Now speaks Captain
   Smoke.   75
   Look, lads; for from this hill ye may discern
   The lovely town which we are marching to.
   That same is London, lads, ye look upon.
   Range all arow, my hearts, and stand at gaze,

57. hearts, and liberty] *Q4*; harts liberty *Q1-3*.

---

55. *Westminster*] important administrative centre, site of coronations, courts of justice and exchequer, treason trials (Star Chamber) and a royal palace (see *Survey*, II, 108, 113-20). The progression that the rebels collectively describe, here and throughout the ensuing scenes, imitates and parodies both the coronation route and the mayoral investiture procession.

61-3. *smoke . . . chandler*] See notes on characters.

67. *pikes*] Spicing means their weapons but is also punning on the word 'pic', a measure of cloth. John Newberie wrote to Leonard Poore in 1584 about the sale of 19 'pikes of cloth, which cost in London twenty shillings the pike' (Hakluyt's *Voyages* (1599), II, 249).

70. *Hippocras*] a cordial of spiced wine. That it was highly prized is attested to by a poor servant's vowing to drink a pledge 'were it the best Hipocras' in *II Gentle Craft*, 187, and by Elizabeth's drinking it from a solid gold cup at her coronation; see Nichols, I, 61.

74. *pound*] pounded.

79. *arow*] in rank.

As do the herds of deer at some strange sight;   80
Or as a troop of hungry travellers,
That fix their eyes upon a furnished feast.
Look how the Tower doth 'tice us to come on,
To take out Henry the Sixth, there prisoner!
See how St Katherine's smokes! Wipe, slaves, your eyes,   85
And whet your stomachs for the good malt pies.
Chub. Why then, belike I am nobody! Room and avoidance,
for now speaks Captain Chub.
No sooner in London will we be,
But the bakers for you, the brewers for me.   90
Birchin Lane shall suit us, the Costermongers fruit us;
The poulters send us in fowl,
And butchers meat, without control;
And ever when we sup or dine,
The vintners freely bring us in wine.   95
If anybody ask who shall pay,
Cut off his head, and send him away.
This is Captain Chub's law, whosoever say nay.
Falconbridge. Bravely resolved. So, march we forward all;
And boldly say, good luck shall us befall.   *Exeunt.*   100

---

82. *furnished*] well supplied; cf. *Timon of Athens*, 3.4.110–11.

83. *'tice*] entice, beckon.

85. *St Katherine's*] a precinct by the Tower. As the following line suggests it was famous for its alehouses; see Iniquity's recommendation in Jonson's *The Devil Is an Ass* (1616) 1.1.59–62, and the 'character' of 'A drunken Dutch-man resident in England' in Overbury's *New and Choise Characters* (1615) (Webster, IV, 32, ll. 2–4). Stow says the rebels burnt the alehouses; *Survey*, I, 42.

86. *malt pies*] beer; Smoke's invitation is to a 'liquid lunch'.

91. *Birchin Lane*] A corruption, according to Stow, of Birchover Lane; he indicates that hosiers had fairly recently become prominent there, along with 'wealthie Drapers', but asserts that at the historical time of the play the usual occupants were 'Fripperers or Vpholders, that sold old apparell and housh-olde stuffe' (*Survey*, I, 81). The author of *The Black Book* (1604) recalls 'passing through Birchin-lane, amidst a camp-royal of hose and doublets . . . I took excellent occasion to slip into a captain's suit' (Middleton, VIII, 29). See also Dekker's description in *Lanthorn and Candlelight* (Grosart, III, 219), and *Nobody and Somebody* (c.1606), C2r.

98. *Chub's law*] Not just an assertion of anarchic individualism but probably a quibble on 'Club Law', a quasi-proverbial term for mob rule which was the title of a 1599 Cambridge play satirizing town bullies.

[Scene 3]

> *Enter the* LORD MAYOR, MASTER SHORE, MASTER
> JOSSELYN, *in their velvet coats, and gorgets,*
> *and leading staves.*

Mayor. This is well done. Thus should good citizens
    Fashion themselves, as well for war as peace.
    Have ye commanded that in every street
    They hang forth lights as soon as night comes on?
    Say, cousin Shore; that was referrred to you.   5
Shore. We have, my lord. Besides, from every hall
    There is at least two hundred men in arms.
Mayor. It cheers my heart to hear this readiness.
    Let never rebels put true subjects down:
    Come when they will, their welcome shall be such   10
    As they had better kept them further off.
    But where is Master Recorder? His advice
    Must not be wanting in these high affairs.
Shore. About an hour ago, and somewhat more,
    I left him fortifying the bridge, my lord;   15
    Which done, he purposèd to meet you here.

0.1–3. in . . . staves] There were elaborate procedures concerning which
kind of costume was to be worn by the civic governors on each ceremonial
occasion; see, for example, the pamphlet printed by Jaggard, *The order of my
Lord Maior, the Aldermen, and the Sheriffs for their meetings, and wearing of their
Apparrell throughout the yeere* (1621), *passim*.

   gorgets] armour for the throat. The Mayor is clearly self-conscious about
his appearance (as is Archidamus in his 'Gorgit' in Massinger's *The
Bondman*, 2.1.0.SD and 18) and Falconbridge picks up the incongruity at
Scene 4, l. 71.

   staves] Staves were a frequent feature of civic ritual including the pageants
which celebrated the inauguration of a new mayor; see, for instance, the MS
entitled '*A breffe description of the Royall Citie of London*', written by 'William
Smythe citizen and haberdasher of London 1575', cited in R. T. D. Sayle,
The Lord Mayors' Pageants of the Merchant Taylors' Company (London, 1931),
2–3.

   3–7. *Have . . . arms*] See Stow (*Survey*, I, 102) for the role played by the
livery companies—'halls'—in the lighting of streets and the arming of the
watch. Since the 1570s a permanent 'Committee for Martial Causes',
composed of aldermen and members of the Common Council, organized
the mustering of the City's trained bands; see F. F. Foster, *The Politics of
Stability* (London, 1977), 17 n.2.

Mayor. A discreet, painful gentleman he is;
  And we must, all of us, be so inclined,
  If we intend to have the city safe,
  Or look for thanks and credit with the King.   20
  I tell ye, masters, agèd though I be,
  I, for my part, will to no bed this night.
Josselyn. Why? Is it thought the Bastard is so near?
Mayor. How mean ye, Master Josselyn, by near?
  He neither comes from Italy, nor Spain,   25
  But out of Kent, and Essex; which, you know,
  Are both so near, as nearer cannot be.
Josselyn. Nay, by your patience; good my lord, a word.
  Simple though I am, yet I must confess,
  A mischief further off, would—and so forth.   30
  You know my meaning. Things not seen before
  Are—and so forth. Yet, in good sadness,
  I would that all were well, and, perchance,
  It may be so. What, were it not for hope,
  The heart—and so forth. But, to the matter: 35
  You mean, and purpose—ay, I am sure ye do?
Mayor. Well, Master Josselyn, we are sure ye mean well,
  Although somewhat defective in your utterance.
Josselyn. Ay, ay, my Lord Mayor. I am, you know,
  Willing, ready—and so forth. Tut, tut, for me—ha, ha! 40
  My mansion is at Ham, and thence, you know,
  I come to help you in this needful time.
  When rebels are so busy—and so forth.
  What, masters? Age must never be despised.
  You shall find me, my lord, still—and so forth.   45

    Enter URSWICK *the* RECORDER.

Shore. My lord, now here comes Master Recorder.
Recorder. Good even, my good Lord Mayor. The streets are
  chained,

---

 17. *painful*] careful, painstaking.
 32. *good sadness*] all seriousness.
 41. *Ham*] Josselyn is probably referring to the village near Richmond in Surrey, since already in this period the two rather closer villages of Ham which lay four or five miles to the east of the City were usually distinguished (as their inner-city counterparts are today) as either West or East Ham.
 47. *chained*] Heavy chains were occasionally used to defend crucial thoroughfares. In resisting Cade 'Malpas of London drewe the cheyne of London

The bridge well manned, and every place prepared.
Shall we now go together, and consult
What else there is to be determined of?   50
Mayor. Your coming, Master Recorder, was the thing
     We all desired; therefore, let us consult.
     And now, what say ye if, with half our power,
     We issue forth and give the rebels fight?
Recorder. Before they do provoke us nearer hand?   55
     There were no way to that, if all be pleased.
     What's your opinion, Master Josselyn?
Josselyn. Good sooth, my Lord Mayor, and Master Recorder,
     You may take your choice; but, in my conceit,
     Issue if you will—or else stay if you will.   60
     A man can never be too wary—and so forth.
     Yet, as to issue, will not be the worst—
     Even so, to tarry. Well, you may think more on't,
     But all is one; we shall be sure to fight,
     And you are wise enough to see your time;   65
     Ay, ay, a' God's name.
Recorder.   My lord,
     Accept his meaning better than his counsel.
Mayor. Ay, so we do, or else we were to blame.
     What if we stop the passage of the Thames
     With such provision, as we have, of ships?   70
Recorder. It's doubtful yet, my lord, whether the rebels
     Purpose that way to seek our detriment;
     Rather, me seemeth they will come by land,
     And either make assault at London Bridge,
     Or else at Aldgate—both which entrances,   75
     Were good they should be strongly fortified.
Josselyn. Well said, Master Recorder! You do, ay, ay—I
     warrant ye.
Recorder. As for the other, the whole companies
     Of Mercers, Grocers, Drapers, and the rest,
     Are drawn together for their best defence   80
     Beside the Tower, a neighbour to that place;

---

brygge'; J. G. Nichols (ed.), *Chronicle of the Grey Friars of London* (Camden
Society, original series, 1852), 19.
    56. *no way to that*] no way better than that.
    72. *Purpose*] intend.
    73. *me seemeth*] it seems to me that.

As on the one side it will clear the river,
So on the other with their ordnance,
It may repulse and beat them from the gate.
Mayor. What noise is this? Provide ye suddenly,   *A noise*   85
    And every man betake him to his charge.   *within.*

Enter a MESSENGER.

Shore. Soft, who is this? How now, my friend, what news?
Messenger. My master, the Lieutenant of the Tower,
    Gives ye to understand he hath descried
    The army of the rebels.
Recorder.   Which way come they?   90
Messenger. From Essexward; and therefore 'tis his mind
    You guard both Aldgate well, and Bishopsgate.
Mayor. St George, away! And let us all resolve,
    Either to vanquish this rebellious rout,
    Preserve our goods, our children, and our wives,   95
    Or seal our resolution with our lives.   *Exeunt.*

[Scene 4]

Enter FALCONBRIDGE, SPICING [*and* SMOKE],
with his troops.

Falconbridge. Summon the city, and command our entrance;
    Which, if we shall be stubbornly denied,
    Our power shall rush like thunder through the walls.
Spicing. Open your gates, slaves, when I command ye!

---

82. *As*] so that.
83. *ordinance*] Weaponry, by this date usually meaning guns; for the
controversy over exporting it see Scene 22, ll. 62–3 and commentary.
85. *suddenly*] immediately.

1.1.0.] Transcripts of the letters which passed between Falconbridge and
the Mayor and aldermen are in Sharpe, III, 387–91, and, with some variations, in *Archaeologia Cantiana*, 11 (1877), 359–63. The best modern account
is C. F. Richmond, 'Fauconberg's Kentish Rising of May 1471', *English
Historical Review*, 85 (1970). Amongst the printed chronicles available to the
dramatist Holinshed gives the fullest account; Stow mentions the rising
several times in the *Survey*, but is surprisingly thin on detail in both the
Annals and the *Chronicles*—as is Fabyan in his printed version. Spicing is

SPICING *beats on the gates, and then enters*
the LORD MAYOR *and his associates, with prentices.*

Mayor. What's he that beats thus at the city gates,   5
    Commanding entrance as he were a king?
Falconbridge. He that will have releasement for a king:
    I, Thomas Neville, the Lord Falconbridge.
Spicing. Ho, sirrah! You, clapperdudgeon! Unlock, unbolt, or
    I'll bolt you if I get in. Stand you preaching, with a pox?   10
Mayor. We have no warrant, Thomas Falconbridge,
    To let your armèd troops into our city,
    Considering you have taken up these arms
    Against our sovereign, and our country's peace.
Falconbridge. I tell thee, Mayor—and know he tells thee so   15
    That cometh armèd in a king's defence—
    That I crave entrance in King Henry's name,
    In right of the true line of Lancaster.
    Methinks that word, spoke from a Neville's mouth,
    Should like an earthquake rend your chainèd gates,   20
    And tear in pieces your portcullises.
    I thunder it again into your ears:
    You stout and brave, courageous Londoners,
    In Henry's name I crave my entrance in.
Recorder. Should Henry's name command thee entrance here,   25
    We should deny allegiance unto Edward,
    Whose true and faithful subjects we are sworn,

---

15. thee, Mayor] *Q2*; the maior *Q1*.

mentioned by most writers but Chub and Smoke appear to have been
created by the playwright from sparse references to a rebel captain (and
butcher) named Quintin. The heroic role credited to the alderman Robert
Basset by both Fabyan and Holinshed is displaced on to Matthew Shore.
For the significance of the dramatist's calculated omission of the aristocratic
and regal contributions to London's defence and for *The Great Chronicle* as
a possible source see Introduction, pp. 25–6, 13–14.
   9. *clapperdudgeon*] In *A Caveat for Common Cursetors* (1567) Thomas
Harman uses this term to identify beggars, usually Welsh, who are given to
inducing unsightly but harmless blisters on their bodies by the application
of ratsbane (C4r–C4v). In *George a Green* (1595), however, the word appears
to denote a cowardly assailant (ll. 1002–3); perhaps a characteristically
composite insult.

And in whose presence is our sword upborn.
Falconbridge. I tell thee, traitor, then thou bearst thy sword
    Against thy true, undoubted king.
Shore. Nay then, I tell thee, bastard Falconbridge,   30
    My Lord Mayor bears his sword in his defence,
    That put the sword into the Arms of London,

---

28. *presence*] A curious but important word in this context. Urswick
appears to imply 'right' or even 'defence' but *OED* records neither sense.
What *OED* does record, in almost every variation of meaning, is the fact that
the word invariably carries connotations of the space, physical or imagined,
around a monarch. The exercise of sovereign power in the absence of the
monarch's person was a contentious issue, the roots of the controversy lying
in the interpretation of the medieval theory designated, and exhaustively
scrutinized, by Ernst Kantorwitz in *The King's Two Bodies* (Princeton, 1957).
Bacon discussed the problem, weaving it into his defence of an extended
royal prerogative in the context of his dispute with Coke over the 'Post Nati'
case; J. Spedding *et al.* (eds), *Works*, 7 vols (London, 1857–74), VII, 655–9.
The chronicle plays had also investigated the implications of 'presence'. In
the 'Countess' scenes of *Edward III* the word appears frequently, though in
a conventional examination of the King's personal morality, B3r–B4r; the
issue reappears in a politically more sensitive context when Copland refuses
to surrender his prisoner to the King's deputy—in this case the Queen—but
a theatrically promising confrontation is defused tamely by the King's
sudden magnanimity. The titular 'hero' of *Jack Straw* provokes the climactic
stabbing by demanding of Mayor Newton, with the King standing by, 'the
sword thou bearest vp', defying the royal sword-bearer to wear the weapon
in his presence, and, at least in terms of royal dignity, Straw's death is an
orthodox and appropriate reward for a grotesque inversion of precedence.
The handling here, however, is strikingly different. The mayor himself can
justify wearing a sword in the king's 'presence' only after he has been
knighted (Scene 16, ll. 1–7)—but equally there is surely a gesture toward the
physical 'presence' of the monarch. That monarch is, of course, conspicuous
by his absence; perhaps the actor would have looked hopefully over over his
shoulder at this point.

32–4. *My . . . knights*] Shore is alluding to the legend that Richard II, in
gratitude for Mayor William Walworth's crushing of Wat Tyler's revolt,
awarded automatic knighthoods to all mayors thereafter, and had a red
dagger, representing Walworth's crucial stabbing of the rebel leader, incorporated into the City's Coat of Arms. The story long sustained the stamp of
authenticity; it was rehearsed as fact by Holinshed (II, 747), and dramatized
in *Jack Straw* (1179–84). Notwithstanding Stow's exasperated demonstration
that the Arms episode was a fiction (*Survey*, I, 220–1), Londoners were
clearly reluctant to relinquish it; see, for example, Munday's 1616 pageant
Chrysanaleia: The golden fishing, C3v. Walworth's action and subsequent
knighting 'in the field' are recounted also in Heywood's 2 *If You Know Not
Me*, C4v.

Made the lord mayors for ever after knights:
Richard—deposed by Henry Bullingbrook—   35
From whom the House of York doth claim their right.
Falconbridge. What's he that answers us thus saucily?
Smoke. Sirrah, your name, that we may know ye hereafter.
Shore. My name is Shore, a goldsmith by my trade.
Falconbridge. What, not that Shore that hath the dainty wife,   40
'Shore's wife', the flower of London for her beauty?
Shore. Yes, rebel, even the very same.
Spicing. Run, rascal, and fetch thy wife to our general
presently, or else all the gold in Cheapside cannot ransom
her. Wilt thou not stir when I bid thee?   45
Falconbridge. Shore, listen me. Thy wife is mine, that's flat.
This night, in thine own house, she sleeps with me.
Now, Crosby, Lord Mayor, shall we enter in?
Mayor. Crosby, the Lord Mayor, tells thee, proud rebel: no!
Falconbridge. No, Crosby? Shall I not? Then, doting lord,   50
I cram the name of rebel down thy throat.
There's not the poorest rascal in my camp,
But if he chance to meet thee in Cheapside,
Upon thy footcloth he shall make thee light,
And hold his stirrup while he mount thy horse;   55
Then lackey him which way he please to go.
Crosby, I'll make the citizens be glad
To send thee, and the Aldermen thy brethren,

54–5. *footcloth . . . horse*] The footcloth was an ornate covering for the
horse's back. Their use clearly indicated social standing: in Dekker's *The
Wonderful Year* (1603) the sextons were estimating that if the plague continued to generate such business 'they and their posteritie would all ryde
vppon footecloathes to the end of the world' (Grosart, I, 113), and Cade
considered the possession of one a sure sign of aristocratic greed (*Contention*,
1802–7). In the same play Suffolk recalled his executioner's having shown
exactly the kind of servility Falconbridge here envisages for Crosby: 'Hast
not thou kist thy hand and held my stirrope? / And barehead plodded by my
footecloth Mule . . . ?' (1524–5).

54. *light*] alight.

56. *lackey*] Fairly unusual use of the word as a verb, but cf. Dekker's (?)
Lust's Dominion (1620): 'Shall they thus tread thee down, which once wer
glad / To Lacquey by thy conquering Chariot wheeles?' (1.2.199–200). This
deployment—and the conjunction with chariot wheels—is a feature of plays
in which Dekker is involved; see also *The Virgin Martyr* (1620), 1.1.90–1, and
The Sun's Darling (1624), 2.1.277–8. But see also Heywood's *The Brazen Age*
(c.1613), B4v.

All manacled, and chained like galley-slaves,
To ransom them, and to redeem the city.   60
Mayor. Nay then, proud rebel, pause, and hear me speak.
There's not the poorest and meanest citizen,
That is a faithful subject to the King,
But, in despite of thy rebellious rout,
Shall walk to Bow, a small wand in his hand—   65
Although thou lie encamped at Mile End Green—
And not the proudest rebel of you all
Shall dare to touch him, for his damnèd soul.
Come, we will pull up our portcullises;
And let me see thee enter if thou dare.   70

[*The* MAYOR *and the Londoners climb to the upper stage.*]

Falconbridge. Spoken like a man—and true velvet-jacket;
And we will enter, or strike by the way.
                              Exeunt [*rebels, in several directions*].

---

72. strike] *Q2*; sticke *Q1*.

---

65. *Bow*] disrict of London just beyond Mile End.

wand] In Drayton's *Heroicall Epistles* (1597) Elinor Cobham complains that as part of her penance she was compelled 'Bare-foot to trudge before a Beadle's Wand' (l. 62), a procession formally attended, according to Stow's *Annals* by 'the Maior, Sherifes, and Crafts of London' (619). 'Wandes for the Lictors' is a property entry in the Revels Accounts for Christmas, 1573; A. Feuillerat (ed.), *Documents Relating to the Office of the Revels in the Time of Q. Elizabeth*, (rpt Vaduz, 1963), 200. These examples suggest that 'wand' may signify some piece of ceremonial regalia; equally, it may be a euphemistic term for the clubs to which the apprentices were ready to resort upon any provocation.

66. *Mile End Green*] A provocatively symbolic place for Falconbridge to choose; Mile End was historically an important marshalling area for the trained bands of London citizens. See *Survey*, I, 103, and a citizen's account of a 1538 muster preserved amongst Stow's papers printed in *Survey*, II, 284 (note).

71. *velvet-jacket*] Falconbridge is ridiculing the ceremonial punctilious-ness of Elizabethan London's governors; see John Strype's description of a muster, 1 July, 1559: 'the city of London entertained the queen . . . each company sending out a certain number of men at arms . . . they marched out of London in coats of velvet and chains of gold' (*Annals of the Reforma-tion*, 4 vols (Oxford, 1824), I, 287). Dekker's Simon Eyre characteristically envisages the holder of the Mayor's office leading 'a velvet life', *Shoemakers' Holiday*, 5.1.38.

[Scene 5]

Enter LORD MAYOR, RECORDER, *and* JOSSELYN [*above,*
and APPRENTICES *below*].

Mayor. Where's Master Recorder? And Master Josselyn?
Recorder. Here, my Lord Mayor. We now have manned the
    walls,
And fortified such places as were needful.
Mayor. Why, it is well, brothers and citizens;
    Stick to your city as good men should do.   5
    Think that in Richard's time, even such a rebel
    Was then by Walworth, the Lord Mayor of London,
    Stabbed dead in Smithfield;
    Then show yourselves as befits the time,
    And let this find a hundred Walworths now   10
    Dare stab a rebel, were he made of brass.
    And prentices: stick to your officers,
    For you may come to be as we are now.
    God and our king against an arrant rebel!
    Brothers, away: let us defend our walls.   15
1 Apprentice. My lord, your words are able to infuse
    A double courage in a coward's breast.
    Then fear not us, although our chins be bare;
    Our hearts are good. The trial shall be seen
    Against those rebels, on this champion green.   20
2 Apprentice. We have no tricks, nor policies of war,
    But by the ancient custom of our fathers
    We'll soundly lay it on, take't off that will.
    And, London prentices, be ruled by me:
    Die, ere ye lose fair London's liberty.   25

6–8. *in . . . Smithfield*] William Walworth headed Richard Johnson's list of
The Nine Worthies of London (1592), B3v–C1v. See also note to Scene 4, 32–4.
    12–13. *prentices . . . now*] The carrot of meteoric social elevation was often
dangled before recalcitrant apprentices by 'popular' writers and equally often
ridiculed by both Jacobean and Caroline court writers; see, for instance,
Jasper Mayne's *The City Match* (c.1638) 1.3 (A4v).
    16. *infuse*] instil. The language here is strikingly close to *3 Henry VI*:
'Methinks a woman of this valiant spirit / Should, if a coward hear her speak
these words, / Infuse his breast with magnanimity' (5.4.39–41).
    20. *champion*] Variant spelling of champaign; level, flat. Cf. Heywood's
Four Prentices, H1r.

[*Enter* SPICING, FALCONBRIDGE, SMOKE, *and other rebels.*]

Spicing. How now, my flatcaps, are ye grown so brave?
    'Tis but your words: when matters come to proof
    You'll scud, as 'twere a company of sheep.
    My counsel, therefore, is to keep your shops:
    'What lack you?' better will beseem your mouths   30
    Than terms of war. In sooth, you are too young.
1 Apprentice. Sirrah, go to; you shall not find it so.
    'Flatcaps', thou callst us? We scorn not the name,
    And shortly, by the virtue of our swords,
    We'll make your cap to sit upon your crown—   35
    As sconce, and cap, and all kiss the ground.
2 Apprentice. You are those desperate, idle, swaggering mates,
    That haunt the suburbs in the time of peace,
    And raise up alehouse brawls in the street;
    And when the rumour of the war begins,   40
    You hide your heads, and are not to be found.
    Thou termst it better that we keep our shops?
    It's good indeed we should have such a care;
    But yet, for all our keeping, now and then
    Your pilf'ring fingers break into our locks—   45
    Until at Tyburn you acquit the fault.
    Go to; albeit by custom we are mild,
    As those that do profess civility,
    Yet, being moved, a nest of angry hornets

42–51. Thou . . . hearts] *Q4–6 give as new speech by 1 Apprentice.*
42. termst] termest *Q1–6.*

---

26. *flatcaps*] Once a descriptive but by the 1590s clearly an abusive term for apprentices or artisans. Cf. Quicksilver's contemptuous references to Golding and Touchstone in *Eastward Ho* (1605), 1.1.101, 113.

28. *scud*] run in haste, as in *Shoemakers' Holiday*: 'she's fled out of doors with Hauns the shoemaker, I saw them scud, scud, scud, apace, apace' (4.4.35–6).

30. *What lack you*] the common cry of London vendors.

36. *sconce*] head.

37–41. *desperate . . . found*] Disturbances caused by disbanded servicemen were a constant source of concern to the civic authorities. The apprentice's use of the word 'mates' probably picks up the chronicles' suggestion that many of the rebels were, like Falconbridge, disaffected seafarers. See also Introduction, pp. 22–3, for the City government's fears of an alliance between such dispossessed figures and the apprentices.

46. *Tyburn*] notorious for its scenes of public execution.

Shall not be more offensive than we will;   50
We'll fly about your ears and sting your hearts.
Josselyn. He tells you truth, my friends—and so forth.
Falconbridge. Who can endure to be so braved? By boys!
1 Apprentice. Nay, scorn us not that we are prentices.
    The chronicles of England can report   55
    What memorable actions we have done;
    To which this day's achievement shall be knit,
    To make the volume larger than it is.
Mayor. Now, of mine honour, ye do cheer my heart;
    Brave English offsprings! Valiantly resolved!   60
2 Apprentice. My lord, return you back. Let us alone;
    You are our masters: give us leave to work!
    And if we do not vanquish them in fight,
    Let us go supperless to bed at night.

       Exeunt all but SPICING, SMOKE, *and their crew.*

Spicing. Smoke, get thee up on the top of St Botolph's steeple,   65
    and make a proclamation.
Smoke. What a plague should I proclaim there?
Spicing. That the bells be rung backward, and cutting of
    throats be cried 'Havoc!' No more calling of 'Lantern
    and Candlelight!' That maidenheads be valued at just   70
    nothing! And sack be sold by the sallet! That no piddling

---

65. *St Botolph's*] an Aldgate church. Holinshed is the only chronicler to
mention it though Stow, in the *Survey* only, notes that this church served as
a temporary stage of retreat for the rebels (I, 30).

68. *bells . . . backward*] Church bells ringing backwards were sometimes
used as a fire alarm—see *The City Match*, 2.3 (C1r)—but the context here
suggests an anticipation of Fletcher's comparison between 'bells rung backwards' and unruly children: 'Nothing but noise and giddiness'; *Wit Without
Money* (1614–20), 2.2.55–6.

69. *cried 'Havoc!'*] To 'cry havoc' was the signal to plunder or give no
quarter. The construction here lends credence to Furness's suggestion that
this order was supposed to be the monarch's prerogative; see the Variorum
Julius Caesar (Philadelphia, 1919) p. 161.

69–70. *'Lantern and Candlelight'*] The night-watchman's cry, warning
householders to hang up lights at their street doors; they were legally obliged
to do so as a crime prevention measure. There is an entry in the Stationers'
Register (1569/70) for a (lost) ballad thus entitled; Dekker's pamphlet of the
same name appeared in 1608.

71. *sack*] sweet Spanish wine.
sallet] helmet.

slave stand to pick a lock, but slash me off the hinges, as
one would slit up a cow's paunch!

Smoke. Let no man have less than a warehouse to his
wardrobe! Cry, 'a fig for a sergeant'! And walk by the   75
Counter like a lord! Pluck out the clapper of Bow Bell,
and hang up all the sextons of the city!

Spicing. Rantam, scantam, rogues! Follow your leader,
Cavalero Spicing, the maddest slave that ever pound
spice in a mortar!   80

Smoke. Take me an usurer by the greasy pouch, and shake
out his crowns, as a hungry dog would shake a haggis!
Bar 'foul play', rogues, and live by honest filching and
stealing! He that hath a true finger, let him forfeit his face

---

74–87.] *Qq give Smoke's speeches to Spicing, and vice versa.*

75. *wardrobe*] Smoke may refer to a dressing room, or he may use the
word in the more modern sense of a personal selection of clothing; Jonson
employs the latter for Mercury's caustic description of Hedon, 'furnish'd
with supplies for the retyring of his old wardrobe from pawne'; *Cynthia's
Revels* (1600/1), 2.1.57–8.

76. *Counter*] A generic term for a debtor's prison, of which Elizabethan
London boasted three. The most comprehensive description is in William
Fennor's *The Compters Common-wealth* (1617), but see also Dekker and
Middleton's *The Roaring Girl* (1611) for an equation of the Counter with
'an university', 3.3.78–102.

Pluck . . . Bell] another specifically barbed affront to London pride. Stow
tells how this famous bell was installed (and ordered to be rung nightly at
nine o'clock) during precisely this period of Edward's reign and also includes
a couple of rhymes about it (*Survey*, I, 255–6). That the definition of the true
Cockney as one born within the sound of Bow Bells was already current is
confirmed by Samuel Rowlands's *The Letting of Humors Blood in the Head-
Vaine* (1600), E1r.

77. *sextons*] This target may have been suggested by the previous one
because sextons were bell ringers as well as gravediggers; the latter occupation inevitably made them unpopular: see Sir Thomas Overbury's *Characters*
in E. F. Rimbault (ed.), *Miscellaneous Works* (London, 1856), pp. 145–6, for
a typical accusation of avarice—the topic with which Smoke resumes his
invective.

78. *Rantam, scantam*] OED cites but is unable to define; clearly an invocation of disorder.

79. *Cavalero*] Contemporary usage suggests a fantastical military figure,
as in *2 Henry IV*, 5.3.57, and *The Trial of Chivalry* (1605), *passim*.

84–5. *He . . . frying-pan*] This all sounds proverbial but Dent offers no
examples. The threat to fry those found honest presumably arises from
Smoke's name.

to the frying-pan! Follow your leader, rogues, follow your　85
leader!

Spicing. Assault! Assault, and cry 'a Falconbridge'!

　　　JOSSELYN *on the walls cries to them.*

Josselyn. Sirrah Spicing, if Spicing be thy name, we are here　90
for matters and causes, as it might seem, for the King;
therefore, it were good—and so forth.

Spicing. Open the gates, or if we be the picklocks, ye rogues,
we'll play the the mastiff dogs amongst you. If I worry
not a thousand of you with my teeth, let me be hanged　95
in a packthread—and so forth.

Josselyn. Fond fellow, justice is to be used—ay, marry, is it—
and law, in some sort, as it were, is to be followed; O,
God forbid else! This, our magistrate, hath power, as it
might seem—and so forth. For duty is to be observed,　100
and officers must be obeyed, in sort and calling—and so
forth.

Spicing. We'll talk more anon, good master 'and so forth'.

　　　Here is a very fierce assault on all sides, wherein the
　　　　　　prentices do great service.
　　　Enter FALCONBRIDGE, *angry with his men.*

Falconbridge. Why, this it is to trust these base rogues,
　　This dirty scum of rascal peasantry,
　　This heartless rout of base rascality;
　　A plague upon you all, you cowardly rogues!　105
　　You craven curs, you slimy, muddy clowns,
　　Whose courage but consists in multitude,
　　Like sheep and neat that follow one another,
　　Which, if one run away, all follow after.
　　This hedge-bred rascal, this filthy fry of ditches;　110

---

96. *packthread*] Stout thread for securing parcels; part of the miscellaneous junk Romeo notices in the apothecary's shop in Mantua, *Romeo and
Juliet*, 5.1.47.

101. *sort and calling*] In due order, with propriety. Shakespeare uses 'sort'
to distinguish the orderliness of the civic authorities from the swarming of
the plebeians in *Henry V*, Act 5, Prologue, 25.

108. *neat*] dumb cattle, usually oxen.

110. *fry*] offspring.

A vengeance take you all! This 'tis to lead you:
Now do you cry and shriek at every shock.
A hot consuming mischief follow you!
Spicing. S' wounds! Scale, rogues, scale! A Falconbridge! A
Falconbridge!

>   *Enter* LORD MAYOR *and his train* [*on the walls*].

Mayor. Set open the gates. Nay, then we'll sally out.   115
It never shall be said, when I was Mayor,
The Londoners were shut up in the city.
Then cry, 'King Edward!', and let's issue out.
Falconbridge. Now if you be true-hearted Englishmen,
The gates set open, and the portcullis up.   120
Let's pell mell in, to stop their passage out.
He that first enters, be possessed of Cheap;
I give it him freely—and the chiefest wench.
Spicing. That he can find; let that lie in the bargain. *Exeunt.*

[Scene 6]

>   *The* LORD MAYOR *and the citizens, having valiantly*
>   *repulsed the rebels from the city* [, *retire*]. *Enter*
>   FALCONBRIDGE *and* SPICING *and their train, wounded*
>   *and dismayed.*

Spicing. Hearst thou, General? There's hot drinking at the
Mouth at Bishopsgate, for our soldiers are all mouth; they

---

121. *pell mell*] A 'French word, and signifieth the mingling of men
together, buckling by the bosome one with another'; as defined in the 'Table'
of 'words and termes' which concludes Robert Barret's *The Theorike and
Practike of ModerneWarres* (1598), no pagination. Heywood uses it in this sense
in 2 *Iron Age* (B4r), and in *The Hierarchie of the Blessed Angells* (1634), 134.
    123. *chiefest*] choicest.
    124. *find . . . lie*] Both words indicate sexual innuendo. 'Lie' is obvious
enough, but, curiously, neither *OED* nor Partridge (*Shakespeare's Bawdy*)
offers a bawdy definition of 'find'; see, however, Heywood's *The Captives*, in
which Ashburne's wife denounces her husband as an 'owld ffornicator' who
can always 'ffind a yonge Colt's toothe abroad', ll. 2077–8. This joke may
have been remembered from Hand B's contribution to *The Book of Sir
Thomas More*; see Revels edition, p. 88, and Introduction, pp. 16–18.

    1–2. *the Mouth at Bishopsgate*] The Mouth Tavern stood in Bishopsgate
Street Without. Heywood refers to it in *2 If You Know Not Me* (1605), C2r,

lie like rascals, with their brains beaten out. Therefore,
since we are all like to feed hogs in Houndsditch, let us
retire our troops, and save our maimed men; or, if we   5
issue further, we are put to the sword, every mother's son
of us.

Falconbridge. Art thou that villain, in whose damnèd mouth
Was never heard of any word but wounds?
Whose recreant limbs are notched with gaping scars,   10
Thicker than any carking craftsman's score?
Whose very scalp is scratched and crazed and broken,
Like an old mazzer beaten on the stones?
And standst thou now to save our maimèd men?
A plague upon thee, coward!   15

Spicing. Why how now, base Thomas? S'wounds, wert thou a
bass viol, thou art but a rascal and a rebel as I am. Hearst

---

and again, as the resort of oyster women, in a song added to the later editions of *The Rape of Lucrece*—1638 edn, E1v. The tavern sign was presumably vividly illustrated; Dekker's *Lanthorne and Candle-light* (1608) describes
'the Father of Hell . . . looking verrie terribly with a paire of eies that stared
as wide as the mouth gapes at Bishops-gate'; Grosart, III, 212.

   4. *Houndsditch*] A disreputable quarter of London, adjacent to Bishopsgate. Greene had located the organizational centre of the 'fraternitie' of 'nips
and foists' (thieves) in the area: *Second part of conny catching*, D2v.

   11. *carking*] anxious, niggardly.

   score] table of credit.

   13. *mazzer*] a wooden bowl or drinking vessel, but also here with the
jocular sense of head, as in Brome's *The Love-sick Court* (1639/40): 'while
thou canst lift thy bottle / To that old Mazer'; J. Pearson (ed.), *Works*, 3 vols
(London, 1874), II, p. 150.

   17. *bass viol . . . rebel*] A curious passage; the 'bass' (base) viol was the
largest member of this family of stringed instruments and the word we might
have expected to justify the comparison would, for three reasons, have been
'rebec' (or rebeck), a small three-stringed instrument: firstly, the word could
connote a personification, as it had in Stephen Hawes's *The Pastime of Pleasure* (1509, reprinted four times in the sixteenth century)—see Percy Society,
vol. XVIII (1845), p. 61; secondly, it could mean resistance (*OED* sb. 3);
finally, the word was used as a verb, seemingly in a unique instance, in
Heywood's *A Woman Killed with Kindness* (1603), where the context requires
the interpretation, to resist or interfere with (Scene 3, l. 8). Perhaps the playwright wrote 'rebeck' and the unusual word defeated the compositor; it is
worth noting that in Heywood's hand 'ck' could be virtually indistinguish-
able from 'el': see, for instance, *The Captives*, l. 1256 and the corresponding
line in the photograph of the manuscript. Note also that Lucretius refers to
the disaffected statesmen of Rome as 'violes unstrung' (l. 501) in Heywood's

thou, if I do not turn true subject and leave thee, let me
be worried with dogs. S' wounds, dost thou impeach my
manhood? Tom Neville, thou hadst as good to have   20
damned thyself as uttered such a word. Flatly, I forsake
thee; and all that love Ned Spicing, follow me!

Here the rest offer to follow him.

Falconbridge. Come, come, ye testy fool! Thou see'st me
    grieved,
  Yet canst not bear with mine infirmity.
  Thou knowst I hold thee for as tall a man   25
  As any lives or breathes our English air.
  I know there lives not a more fiery spirit,
  A more resolved valiant—a plague upon it—
  Thou knowst I love thee! Yet, if a word escape
  My lips in anger, how testy then thou art!   30
  I had rather all men left me than thyself;
  Thou art my soul, thou art my Genius;
  I cannot live without thee, not an hour!
  Thus must I still be forced, against my will,   *Aside.*
  To sooth this dirty slave, this cowardly rascal!   35
  Come, come, be friends, ye testy firebrand;
  We must retire; there is no remedy.
Spicing. Nay, Tom, if thou wilt have me mount on the walls,
  And cast myself down headlong on their pikes,
  I'll do it; but, to impeach my valour!   40
  Had any man but thou spoke half so much,
  I would have split his heart. Still beware
  My valour; such words go hardly down.
  Well, I am friends. Thou thoughtst not as thou spakst.
Falconbridge. No, on my soul; thou thinkst not that I did.   45

---

22. that] *Q2;* y *Q1.*   29. knowst] knowest *Q1–6.*

The Rape of Lucrece (ed. A. Holaday, Urbana, 1950), although this could be
merely a garbled attempt at the familiar viol/vile pun.
  19. *impeach*] cast doubt upon.
  25. *tall*] brave.
  32. *Genius*] guardian spirit.

Sound a retreat there, I command ye straight.
But whither shall we retire?
Spicing. To Mile End Green. There's no fitter place.
Falconbridge. Then let us back retire to Mile End Green,
    And there expect fresh succour from our friends.   50
    With such supply as shall ere long assure,
    The city is our own. March on, away!   *Exeunt.*

[Scene 7]

Enter the LORD MAYOR *with his train, and prentices.*

Mayor. Ye have bestirred ye like good citizens,
    And showed yourselves true subjects to your king.
    You, worthily, prentices, bestirred yourselves,
    That it did cheer my heart to see your valour.
    The rebels are retired to Mile End Green?   5
Recorder. Where so we may not suffer them to rest,
    But issue forth upon them with fresh force.
Josselyn. My Lord Mayor, diligence doth well—and so forth.
    Matters must be looked into as they ought, indeed should
    they, when things are well done, they are—and so forth.   10
    For causes and things must indeed be looked into.
Mayor. Well, sir, we very well conceive your meaning,
    And you have shown yourself a worthy gentleman.
    See that our walls be kept with courts of guard,
    And well defended against the enemy;   15
    For we will now withdraw us to Guildhall,
    To take advice what further must be done.   *Exeunt.*

46. retreat] *Q2*; retrait *Q1*.

14. *courts of guard*] According to Barret's *Theorike and Practike of Modern
Warres* (end table) an anglicization of 'Corps de guard': 'the body of a watch,
of a certaine number of souldiers set for such purposes'.
16. *Guildhall*] The administative centre of London's power. For a lively
account of how Simon Eyre was chosen as Sheriff there, before the 'Lord
Maior, with the worshipfull Aldermen his brethren, with the whole
Communalitie of the honourable Citie', see *I The Gentle Craft*, in Deloney,
155–7.

[Scene 8]

Enter MASTER SHORE, *and* JANE, *his wife.*

Shore. Be not afraid, sweetheart, the worst is passed.
God have the praise: the victory is ours.
We have prevailed, the rebels are repulsed,
And every street of London soundeth joy.
Canst thou then, gentle Jane, be sad alone?   5
Jane. I am not sad now you are here with me:
My joy, my hope, my comfort, and my love,
My dear, dear husband, kindest Matthew Shore.
But when these arms, the circles of my soul,
Were in the fight so forward (as I heard),   10
How could I choose, sweetheart, but be afraid?
Shore. Why dost thou tremble now, when peril's passed?
Jane. I think upon the horror of the time.
But tell me why you fought so desperately.
Shore. First, to maintain King Edward's royalty.   15
Next, to defend the city's liberty.
But chiefly, Jane, to keep thee from the foil
Of him that to my face did vow thy spoil.
Had he prevailed, where then had been our lives?
Dishonoured our daughters; ravished our fair wives;   20
Possessed our goods, and set our servants free;
Yet all this nothing to the loss of thee.
Jane. Of me, sweetheart? Why, how should I be lost?
Were I by thousand storms of fortune tossed,
And should endure the poorest wretched life,   25
Yet Jane will be thy honest, loyal wife.
The greatest prince the sun did ever see

---

5. *be sad alone*] Can you be the only sad one? For the opposite sentiment but similarly tortuous syntax see Duke Senior's 'we are not all alone unhappy', *As You Like It*, 2.1.136.

9. *arms . . . soul*] Deyaneira uses the same image in Heywood's *The Brazen Age*, B4r; Marlowe was also fond of it—see *1 Tamburlaine*, 1.2.5–6, and *2 Tamburlaine*, 3.2.35.

17. *foil*] Several meanings are possible and may indeed be intended: firstly, a short sword; secondly, the act of overthrowing (from wrestling); thirdly, an act of defiling (usually chastity). Nashe quibbles on the first two meanings in *The Unfortunate Traveller* (1594), *Works*, II, 233; Shore implies the third in the ensuing lines.

Shall never make me prove untrue to thee.
Shore. I mean not fair means, but a rebel's force.
Jane. These hands shall make this body a dead corse   30
    Ere force or flattery shall mine honour stain.
Shore. True fame survives, when death the flesh hath slain.

        Enter an OFFICER *from the Lord Mayor.*

Officer. God save ye, Master Shore, and Mistress, by your
    leave.
    Sir, my Lord Mayor sends for ye by me,
    And prays your speedy presence at Guildhall.   35
    There's news the rebels have made head again,
    And have ensconced themselves upon Mile End,
    And presently our armèd men must out.
    You being captain of two companies,
    In honour of your valour and your skill,   40
    Must lead the vaward. God, and right, stand with ye.
Shore. Friend, tell my lord I'll wait upon him straight.
Jane. Friend, tell my lord he does my husband wrong,
    To set him foremost in the danger still.
    Ye shall not go, if I may have my will.   45
Shore. Peace, wife; no more. Friend, I will follow ye.
                      Exit [OFFICER].
Jane. I' faith, ye shall not. Prithee, do not go.
Shore. Not go, sweetheart? That were a coward's trick,
    A traitor's part, to shrink when others fight.
    Envy shall never say that Matthew Shore   50
    The goldsmith stayed, when other men went out
    To meet his king's and country's enemy.
    No, Jane; 'gainst all the rebels on Mile End,
    I dare alone King Edward's right defend.
Jane. If you be slain, what shall become of me?   55
Shore. Right well, my wench. Enough will marry thee;
    I leave thee worth at least five thousand pound.
Jane. Marry again? That word my heart doth wound.
    I'll never marry, nor I will not live   *She weeps.*
    If thou be killed. Let me go with thee, Mat.   60

---

37. *ensconced*] established a position for.
41. *vaward*] vanguard.

Shore. 'Tis idle talk, good Jane; no more of that.
　　Go to my Lady Mayoress, and the rest,
　　As you are still companion with the best;
　　With them be merry, and pray for our good speed.
Jane. To part from thee my very heart doth bleed.　*Exeunt.*　65

[Scene 9]

　　　　Enter FALCONBRIDGE *with his troops, marching,*
　　　　　　　　as being at Mile End.

Falconbridge. Yet stand we in the sight of upreared Troy,
　　And suck the air she draws. Our very breath
　　Flies from our nostrils, warm unto the walls.
　　We beard her bristling spires, her battled towers,
　　And proudly stand and gaze her in the face.　　　　　5
　　Look on me, and I doubt not ye imagine
　　My worth as great as any one of yours;
　　My fortunes, would I basely fawn on Edward,
　　To be as fair as any man's in England.
　　But he that keeps your sovereign in the Tower　　　10
　　Hath seized my land, and robbed me of my right.

---

63. *companion*] The lack of a pronoun here suggests that the noun is
perhaps being used as an adjective—an Heywoodian characteristic, although
Shakespeare uses the word quasi-adjectivally in *Richard II*, 1.3.93, and in
Pericles, 5.1.78.

　　1. *upreared Troy*] The legend that London had been founded as the new
Troy by Brute, a lineal descendant of Aeneas, was initiated by Geoffrey of
Monmouth and, in the sixteenth and seventeenth centuries became a literary commonplace. The child representing London in the earliest extant
(complete) Lord Mayor's pageant declares 'New Troye I hight'—Peele's *The
Device of the Pageant borne before Woolstone Dixi* (1585), A2v—and the myth
features prominently thereafter, from Munday's *The Triumphes of Re-united
Britania* (1605), A3v, B1v, B4v, through Dekker's 1612 and Webster's 1624
shows, to Heywood's *Londini Speculum* (1637), B1r–v. Stow opens the *Survey*
with an account of it *as* a legend. Perhaps the playwright is here remembering Marlowe's Aeneas, who, in a play much concerned with his efforts to
'build a statelier Troy', vows never to leave 'these new upreared walls'; *Dido,
Queen of Carthage* (1587–93), 5.1.2, 3.4.49.
　　4. *beard*] confront.
　　battled] embattled, fortified.
　　11. *seized . . . right*] A common enough accusation against Edward in the
chronicles, though not with respect to Falconbridge.

I am a gentleman as well as he;
What he hath got, he holds by tyranny.
Now, if you faint, or cowardly should fly,
There is no hope for anyone to live.   15
We hear the Londoners will leave the city,
And bid us battle here on Mile End Green;
Whom, if we vanquish, then we take the town,
And ride in triumph thorough Cheap to Paul's.
The Mint is ours; Cheap, Lombard Street our own;   20
The meanest soldier wealthier than a king.
Spicing. March fair, ye rogues; all kings or capknitters. Dost
    thou hear, Tom Falconbridge? I pray thee grant me one
    boon I shall ask thee.
Falconbridge. What is it, Ned? It's hard I should deny thee.   25
Spicing. Why, that when we have won the city—as we cannot
    choose but win it—that I may have the knighting of all
    these rogues and rascals.
Falconbridge. What then?
Spicing. What then? Zounds, I scorn your scurvy, wry-   30
    mouthed 'what then?' Now, a pox take me if I fight a blow.
Falconbridge. Why, this is fine. Go to. Knight whom thou wilt.
Spicing. Who? I knight any of them? I'll see them hanged first,
    for a company of tattered, ragged rascals! If I were a king,
    I would not knight one of them!   35
Chub. What, not me, Cavalero Chub?

---

19. *Paul's*] St Paul's. The cathedral church of London and its environs
played an important (and frequently alluded to) role in the City's pageantry;
see, for instance, Shirley's *A Contention for Honour and Riches* (1633), in A.
Dyce (ed.), *Works*, 6 vols (London, 1833), VI, 297.

20. *The Mint*] situated in the Tower until the nineteenth century.

Lombard Street] A street in the Cornhill district famous for money dealing,
running from Gracechurch Street to the Mansion House. Q1's spelling
(Lumbard) differs from Mistress Quickly's 'Lumbert' (*2 Henry IV*, 2.1.27,
Q only), and from Heywood's (Lumber) throughout *2 If You Know Not Me*.

22–42. *March . . . king*] An important exchange. Spicing's desire to issue
indiscriminate knighthoods to the winners in the conflict, his insistence on
not being denied his 'humour', his arbitrary designation of Falconbridge as
a king, and the repeated use of their abbreviated Christian names, Ned and
Tom, are all resonances picked up in later exchanges between 'Ned'
(Edward) and 'Tom' (Sellinger). See Introduction, pp. 24–6, 33.

22. *capknitters*] archetypal pliers of ill-paid cottage industry.

Spicing. Yes, I care not if I knight thee—and yet I'll see thee
hanged ere I'll honour thee so much. I care not so much
for the matter, but I would not be denied my humour.
Falconbridge. Why, what a perverse fellow art thou, Ned!   40
Spicing. Ho, my fine Tom, my brave Falconbridge, my mad
Greek, my lusty Neville: thou art a king, a Caesar! A
plague on thee! I love thee not—and yet I'll die with thee.

> *Enter the* LORD MAYOR, RECORDER, JOSSELYN,
> SHORE, *and their soldiers marching.*

Mayor. See how rebellion can exalt itself,
Pruning the feathers of sick discipline.   45
Recorder. They think they can out look our truer looks.
Shore. Mark but the scornful eye of Falconbridge.
Mayor. I rather think 'tis fear upon his cheek,
Deciphers pale disturbance in his heart.
Josselyn. Our coming forth hath—well, I say no more.   50
But, shall we take occasion—and so forth—
Rebellion should have no respite; oh, my lord,
The time hath been—but all is one for that.
Spicing. How like a troop of rank, o'er-ridden jades
You bushy-bearded citizens appear.   55
Chub. Nay, rather so many men in the moon,

---

39. *humour*] A term derived from medieval physiology, here meaning will,
as it does when Petruchio promises to curb Kate's in *The Taming of the Shrew*,
4.1.196.

41–2. *mad Greek*] An addition to Dekker's *Iests to Make You Merrie* (1607)
provides an appropriate gloss to both this phrase and the Spicing/
Falconbridge relationship: 'he that not an houre before had nothing but
daggers in his mouth, leaps about their necks, cals them mad Greekes, true
Troians, commaunds a gallon of sacke & suger . . . drinkes a health to them
all'; Grosart, II, 349.

45. *Pruning*] preening; cf. Braggadocchio in *The Faerie Queene*, II, iii, 36,
7–8.

49. *Deciphers*] reveals, indicates; cf. *Merry Wives*, 5.2.8–10.

56. *men in the moon*] The conjunction of this phrase and the word 'bush'
in the next line recalls two plays of the 1590s: at the end of Lyly's *The Women
in the Moone* (c.1593) Stesias is appointed to attend on Pandora as the Man
in the Moon and defiantly vows to 'beare this bush'—a metamorphosed
enemy—as a gesture of revenge (R. W. Bond (ed.), *Works*, 3 vols (Oxford,
1902), 5.1.317–19). Similarly, Robin Starveling, alias Moonshine, declares 'I

And every one a furzen bush in his mouth.
Spicing. The four and twenty wards? Now fair befall them!
Would anyone have thought before this hour
There had been such increase of muddy slaves?   60
Falconbridge. Peace, soldiers. They are resolute, you see;
And not to flatter us, nor favour them,
Such haughty stomachs seldom have been seen
Embodied in the breasts of citizens.
How sternly in their own peculiar strength,   65
Without the assistance of their ling'ring king,
Did they of late repulse us from their walls.
And now, again, how expeditiously
And unexpectedly they have met us here.
Were we more deadly incensed than we are,   70
I would not but commend their chivalry.
Spicing. Captain, shall we go challenge them to fight?
S' blood, we burn daylight! They'll think anon
We are afraid to see their glittering swords.

61–71.] *Qq give this speech to Spicing.*

the Man i' th' Moon; this thorn-bush my thorn-bush' (*A Midsummer Night's Dream*, 5.1.248–9). Perhaps, however, the allusion is more specific, referring to the hapless figure Dekker reproduces—and then ridicules the practice of reproducing—at the opening of *The Rauens Almanacke* (1609): 'At the beginning of euerie Almanacke, it is the fashion to haue the body of a man drawne as you see, and not onely baited, but bitten and shot at by wilde beasts and monsters. And this fellow, they . . . call the Man of the Moone'; Grosart, IV, 179–80.

57. *furzen*] Gorse-like, referring to their beards. Marston's Rossaline is similarly contemptuous: 'Oh, to have a husband . . . with a bush of furze on the ridge of his chin, ready still to slop into his foaming chaps; ah, 'tis more than most intolerable'; *Antonio and Mellida* (1599–1600), 5.1.45–8 (ed. G. K. Hunter (Lincoln, NE, 1965)).

58. *four and twenty wards*] There were actually twenty-five wards in Edward IV's London, and twenty-six in Elizabethan times; see Stow, *Survey*, I, 119.

64. *Embodied*] Given that 'haughty stomachs' = proud aggression, this use of the word, meaning 'given material expression', antedates *OED*'s earliest citation (1663).

68. *expeditiously*] speedily. This should be *OED*'s earliest example of this usage, notwithstanding its incorrect dating of *The Old Law* (1603).

73. *we burn daylight*] Proverbial, meaning 'waste time' (Dent, D123), as in *Merry Wives*, 2.1.52, and *Romeo and Juliet*, 1.4.43.

Chub. Tell them thay come instead of pudding pies   75
    And Stratford cakes, to make's a banquet here.
Falconbridge. Soft, give me leave. I will devise with words
    To weaken and abash their fortitude.
Recorder. The Bastard offers to come forth, my lord.
Mayor. I am the man intend to answer him.   80
Falconbridge. Crosby.
Mayor. Traitor.
[Rebels.] Traitor? Zounds, down with him!
Falconbridge. Be patient; give me leave, I say, to speak.
    I doubt not but the traitor's name shall rest   85
    With those that keeps their lawful king in bonds.
    Meantime, ye men of London, once again
    Behold! My warlike colours are displayed,
    Which I have vowed shall never be wrapped up
    Until your lofty buildings kiss our feet;   90
    Unless you grant me passage through your streets.
Recorder. Passage, sayst thou? That must be o'er our breasts,
    If any passage thou art like to have.
Falconbridge. Why, then, upon your bodies will I tread,
    And wade through standing pools of your lost blood.   95
Shore. We know thy threats, and reckon them as wind;
    Not of sufficient power to shake a reed.
Spicing. But we shook your gates not long ago,
    And made your walls to shake like Irish bogs.
Chub. Ay, and so terrified ye, that not one of ye durst come   100
    to fetch a pint of sack at the Mouth at Bishopsgate—no,
    not for your lives!
Josselyn. Ay, but you know what followed—and so forth.
Spicing. Et cetera? Are you there? Me thinks the sight

---

83. *Rebels.*] *all. Qq.*   104–7. Et cetera . . . all] *Qq print as prose.*

---

75. *pudding pies*] Custard pies; Massinger's Mary Frugal attributes a
vulgar partiality for pudding pies to 'Exchange-wenches' on Sunday outings:
The City Madam (1632), 4.4.37–9.

76. *Stratford cakes*] Stratford was a district one mile north-east of Mile
End. William Kemp in his *Nine Days Wonder* (1600) records the axiom that
'*Mile-end* is no walke without a recreatio at *Stratford Bow* with Creame and
Cakes', A3v.

95. *standing pools*] stagnant water; cf. *King Lear*, where Edgar's 'foul fiend'
drinks 'the green mantle of the standing pool', 3.4.130–1.

Of the dun bull, the Nevilles' honoured crest,   105
Should make you leave your broken sentences,
And quite forget ever to speak at all.
Shore. Nay, then, look upon our city's arms,
    Wherein is a bloody dagger. That is it,
    Wherewith a rebel like to Falconbridge   110
    Had his desert, meet for his treachery.
    Can you behold that, and not quake for fear?
Recorder. Since when it is successively decreed,
    Traitors with us shall never better speed.
Spicing. Captain, and fellow soldiers, talk no more,   115
    But draw your meaning forth in downright blows.
Falconbridge. Sound then alarum.
Mayor.   Do the like for us;
    And where the right is, there attend success.
Josselyn. Stay, and be better advised. Why, countrymen,
    What is this Falconbridge you follow so?   120
    I could instruct you—but you know my mind.
    And Falconbridge, what are these rusticals?
    Thou shouldst repose such confidence in glass.
    Shall I inform thee? No—thou art wise enough.
    Edward of York delays the time, you say,   125
    Therefore he will not come. Imagine so.
    The city's weak. Hold that opinion still.
    And your pretence, King Henry's liberty:
    True, but, as how? Shall I declare you? No.
    What then? You'll fight. A' God's name, take your choice;   130

---

105. *dun bull*] The usual Warwick crest was the Dun Cow, as it appears
in *Guy, Earl of Warwick* (printed 1661 but probably not later than 1618), B2r,
F3v, and as it is joked about in Marston's *Antonio and Mellida*, 4.1.230–9 (ed.
Hunter). In a play full of ironic echoes it is unlikely to be a coincidence that
Hobs's nag is called Dun.

108–11. *city's . . . treachery*] See note to Scene 4, ll. 32–4.

111. *meet*] appropriate reward.

122. *rusticals*] countryfolk, simpletons.

123.] Almost impenetrable. The clause should begin, presumably, with
'That'; the brittle nature of glass was a conventional analogue for the fragility
of power in homiletic literature (see, for example, *Mirror for Magistrates*, 'Cardinal Wolsey', l. 467), and Josselyn is probably linking that volatility to the
unreliability of the rustics. See also, however, Isabella's difficult speech about
man's over-confidence in his 'glassy essence', *Measure for Measure*,
2.2.118–24.

I can no more but give you mine advice.
Falconbridge. Away with this parenthesis of words.
    Crosby, courage thy men, and on this green,
    Whose cause is right, let it be quickly seen.
Mayor. I am as ready as thou canst desire.   135
    On then, a' God's name.

         They fight; the rebels drive them back. Then enter
         FALCONBRIDGE *and* SPICING.

Falconbridge. This was well fought. Now, Spicing, list to me.
    The citizens thus having given us ground,
    And therefore somewhat daunted, take a band
    Of Essex soldiers, and with all the speed   140
    Thou possibly canst make, withdraw thyself,
    And get between the city gates and them.
Spicing. O brave Tom Neville, gallant Falconbridge,
    I aim at thy intended policy.
    This is thy meaning: while thou art employed,   145
    And holdst them battle here on Mile End Green,
    I must provide as harbinger, before
    There be not only clear and open passage,
    But the best merchants' houses to receive
    Us and our retinue. I am proud of that,   150
    And will not sleep upon thy just command.
Falconbridge. Away then. I will follow as I may;
    And doubt not but that ours will be the day.   *Exeunt.*

         After some excursions, enter LORD MAYOR *and*
         MASTER SHORE.

Mayor. We have recovered what before we lost,
    And heaven stands with the justice of our cause.   155

153.01. *Exeunt*] *MS annotation to Dyce (1) copy of Q3; not in Qq.*

---

    132. *parenthesis*] 'A passage introduced into a context with which it has
no connection; a digression' (*OED* 1b, citing this example).
    133. *courage*] commonly used as a verb in the sixteenth century; could
mean either 'encourage' or instil with courage.
    144. *aim*] guess.
    151. *sleep upon*] be slow to perform.
    153.01 *excursions*] rapid entrances and exits of combatants, probably
accompanied by sounds of battle produced offstage.

But this I noted in the fight e'en now:
That part of this rebellious crew is sent—
By what direction, or for what intent
I cannot guess, but may suspect the worst—
And, as it seems, they compass it about   160
To hem us in, or get the gate of us.
And therefore, cousin Shore, as I repose
Trust in thy valour and thy loyalty,
Draw forth three hundred bowmen, and some pikes,
And presently encounter their assault.   165
Shore. I have your meaning; and effect, my lord,
I trust shall disappoint them of their hope.   [*Exeunt.*]

> *After an alarum, enter* SPICING *with drum and*
> *certain soldiers.*

Spicing. Come on, my hearts! We will be kings tonight,
Carouse in gold, and sleep with merchants' wives
While their poor husbands lose their lives abroad.   170
We are now quite behind our enemies' backs,
And there's no let or hindrance in the way,
But we may take possession of the town.
Ah, you mad rogues, this is the wishèd hour;
Follow your leader, and be resolute.   175

> *As he marcheth, thinking to enter,* SHORE *and his soldiers*
> *issue forth and repulse him. After excursions, wherein the*
> *rebels are dispersed, enter* MAYOR, RECORDER, SHORE,
> JOSSELYN, *and a Messenger talking with the* MAYOR.

Mayor. Ay, my good friend, so certify his grace:
The rebels are dispersèd all and fled,
And now his highness meets with victory.
                                          Exit Messenger.
Marshal yourselves, and keep in good array,
To add more glory to this victory: 180
The King in person cometh to this place.

---

160. *compass it about*] contrive; but also with the secondary senses of
aggressively encircling, gaining advantage. Heywood is fond of the word: see
SD in *The Golden Age*, K1r, '*Enter Ganimed compast in with soldiers*', and *1
Fair Maid of the West*, F2v: 'you have trickes to compasse these gay cloaths'.
172. *let*] impediment.

How great an honour have you gained today?
And how much is this city famed for ever,
That twice, without the help either of king,
Or any, but of God and our own selves,   185
We have prevailed against our country's foes?
Thanks to his majesty assisted us,
Who always helps true subjects in their need.

The trumpets sound, then enters KING EDWARD, LORD
HOWARD, SELLINGER, *and the train.*

Edward. Where is my Lord Mayor?
Mayor.   Here, dread sovereign.
I hold no lordship nor no dignity   190
In presence of my gracious lord the King,
But all I humble at your highness' feet;
With the most happy conquest of proud rebels,
Dispersed and fled, that now remains no doubt
Of ever making head to vex us more.   195
Edward. You have not ta'en the bastard Falconbridge—
Or is he slain?
Mayor.   Neither, my gracious lord.
Although we laboured to our uttermost,
Yet all our care came over-short,
For apprehending him or Spicing either;   200
But some are taken, others on proffered grace
Yielded themselves, and at your mercy stand.
Edward. Thanks, good Lord Mayor. You may condemn us
Of too much slackness in such urgent need;
But we assure you on our royal word,   205
So soon as we had gathered us a power
We dallied not, but made all haste we could.
What order have ye ta'en for Falconbridge
And his confederates in this rebellion?
Mayor. Under your leave, my liege, we have proclaimed   210

190–1. *I . . . King*] Cf. Scene 4, l. 28 and commentary; Scene 16, ll. 1–8
and commentary.

201. *on proffered grace*] with the promise of pardon; cf. *Edmund Ironside*,
l. 909.

208. *ta'en*] issued.

210–11. *proclaimed . . . bringeth*] A common construction which omits
'that he' before 'Who bringeth'.

Who bringeth Falconbridge alive or dead,
Shall be requited with a thousand marks;
As much for Spicing; others of less worth
At easier rates are set.
Edward.   Well have ye done,
And we will see it paid from our Exchequer.   215
Now leave we this, and come to you
That have so well deserved in these affairs—
Affairs, I mean, of so main consequence.
Kneel down, and all of you receive in field
The honour you have merited in field.   220

There he draws his sword and knights them.

Arise, Sir John Crosby, Lord Mayor of London, and
    knight.
Arise up, Sir Ralph Josselyn, knight.
Arise, Sir Thomas Urswick, our Recorder of London,
    and knight.
Now, tell me which is Master Shore.
Mayor.   This same, my lord,
And hand to hand he fought with Falconbridge.   225
Edward. Shore, kneel thou down. What call ye else his name?
Recorder. His name is Matthew Shore, my lord.
Edward.   Shore,
Why kneelst thou not, and at thy sovereign's hand
Receive thy right?
Shore.   Pardon me, gracious lord.
I do not stand contemptuous, or despising   230
Such royal favour of my sovereign,
But to acknowledge mine unworthiness.
Far be it from the thought of Matthew Shore

228. kneelst] kneelest *Q1–6.*

---

218. *of so main consequence*] of such importance.
227–39.] Shore's refusal of a knighthood may have been inspired by Stow's
brusque insistence on William Walworth's reluctance to accept the same
honour: this mayor stated that 'hee was neither worthie nor able to take
such estate vpon him, for he was but a Marchant, and had to liue by his
Marchandise onely'; *Survey*, I, 220. Deloney's Jack of Newbury declined a
similar offer (p. 49) but the playwright sacrifices the conventional anti-court
satire of the prose fiction in order to exploit fully the dramatic irony
triggered by Edward's response.

That he should be advanced with Aldermen,
With our Lord Mayor, and our right grave Recorder.   235
If any thing hath been performed by me,
That may deserve your highness' meanest respect,
I have enough, and I desire no more.
Then let me crave that I may have no more.
Edward. Well, be it as thou wilt. Some other way   240
We will devise to quittance thy deserts,
And not to fail therein, upon my word.
Now, let me tell ye, all my friends at once,
Your king is married since you saw him last,
And haste to help you in this needful time   245
Made me on sudden to forsake my bride.
But seeing all things are fallen out so well,
And there remains no further doubt of ill,
Let me entreat you would go boot yourselves,
And bring your king a little on his way.   250
How say you, my lord, shall it be so?
Mayor. Now God forbid but that my lord the king
Should always have his subjects at command.
Josselyn. Forbid, quotha? Ay, in good sadness, your majesty
shall find us always ready—and so forth.   255
Edward. Why then, set forward, gentlemen;
And come, Lord Mayor, I must confer with you.

                                        Exeunt.

[Scene 10]

            Enter FALCONBRIDGE *and* SPICING *with their weapons*
                              in their hands.

Spicing. Art thou the man whose victories drawn at sea
    Filled every heart with terror of thy name?

---

234. *with*] equally with.

241. *quittance*] Repay, reward. Fairly unusual use of the verb; Shakespeare
employed it to imply 'revenge' (*1 Henry VI*, 2.1.14), but Heywood exactly
reproduced the sense here, complete with irony, in *Gunaikeion* (1624): 'to
quittance this, / He guerdons Midas with his golden wish', I, 54.

249. *boot yourselves*] Do yourselves a favour, with the implication of
enrichment, as in *Antony and Cleopatra*, 2.5.71-2: 'And I will boot thee with
what gift beside / Thy modesty can beg.'

1. *drawn*] The following line suggests that Spicing means an oral rather
than an actual pictorial description of Falconbridge's piracy.

Art thou that Neville whom we took thee for?
Thou art a louse, thou bastard Falconbridge!
Thou baser than a bastard, in whose birth   5
The very dregs of servitude appears!
Why, tell me, liver of some rotten sheep,
After by thy allurements we are brought
To undertake this course, after thy promises
Of many golden mountains to ensue,   10
Is this the greatest comfort thou canst give?
Hast thou ensnared our heedless feet with death,
And brought us to the gibbet of defame,
And now dost bid us shift, and save ourselves?
No, craven; were I sure I should be ta'en,   15
I would not stir my feet until this hand
Had venged me on thee for misguiding us.
Falconbridge. Opprobrious villain, stable excrement,
That never dreamst of other manhood yet
But how to jerk a horse, until my words   20
Infused into thee resolution's fire,
Controlst thou me for that wherein thy self
Art only the occasion of mishap?
Hadst thou—and they—stood to't as well as I,
The day had been our own, and London now   25
That laughs in triumph should have wept in tears.
But, being backed by such faint-hearted slaves,
No marvel if the lion go to wrack,
As though it were not incident to kings
Sometime to take repulse. Mine is no more;   30
Nor is not for that muddy brain of thine
To tutor me how to digest my loss.

---

13. *gibbet*] any kind of frame or post from which criminals were hanged.

18. *stable*] Either Spicing is being compared to horse dung or this is a rare pejorative usage of the adjective: 'incapable of change', 'irredeemable piece of'.

20. *jerk*] ride violently, as in line 40.

22. *Controlst thou*] Dare you rebuke me? Cf. Skelton's unsuccessful confrontation with the violator of his church: 'I hym controld; / But he sayde that he wolde / Agaynst my mynde and wyll / In my church hawke styll'; 'Ware the Hawke', in J. Scattergood (ed.), *Complete English Poems* (London, 1983), 64, ll. 96–9.

30. *Mine is no more*] my situation is no different.

Then fly with those that are already fled,
Or stay behind, and hang all but the head.
Spicing. O prejudice to Spicing's conquering name!   35
    Whose valour even the hacks this sword has made
    Upon the flint and iron bars at Aldgate
    Like mouths will publish whiles the city stands;
    That I shrunk back? That I was never seen
    To show my manly spleen but with a whip?   40
    I tell thee, Falconbridge, the least of these
    Do challenge blood before they be appeased.
Falconbridge. Away, ye scoundrel! Tempt not my resolve;
    The courage that survives in Falconbridge
    Scorns the encounter of so base a drudge.   45
Spicing. By the pure temper of this sword of mine,
    By this true flesh and blood that grips the same,
    And by the honour I did win of late
    Against those frosty-bearded citizens,
    It shall be tried before we do depart   50
    Whether accuseth other wrongfully,
    Or which of us two is the better man.
Falconbridge. I shall but quit the hangman of a labour.
    Yet rather than to be upbraided thus,
    The eagle once will stoop to feed on carrion.   55

They fight. Enter CHUB.

Chub. Hold, if ye be men! If not, hold as ye are! Rebels, and
    strong thieves: I bring you news of a proclamation. The
    King hath promised that whosoever can bring the head
    of Falconbridge, or Spicing, shall have for his labour a
    thousand crowns. What mean you then to swagger? Save   60
    yourselves!
Spicing. [*Aside*] This proclamation's come in happy time.
    I'll vanquish Falconbridge, and with this sword

36–8.] Spicing suggests that the indelible marks he has made on the
fabric of the city's defensive walls provide an eloquent testimony to his
courage.
    49. *frosty-bearded*] Contemptuous reference to the gravity of the senior
Londoners; cf. E. K's enthusiastic explication of Thenot's 'Embleme': 'So
the old man checketh the rashheaded boy, for despysing his gray and frostye
heares', *Shepheardes Calender*, 'February', ll. 248–9.

Cut off his head and bear it to the King;
So, not alone shall I be pardoned,   65
But have the thousand crowns is promisèd.
Falconbridge. [*Aside*] This rascal was ordained to save my life.
For now when I have overthrown the wretch,
Even with his head I'll yield me to the King.
His princely word is passed to pardon me,   70
And though I was the chief in this rebellion,
Yet this will be a means to make my peace.
Chub. [*Aside*] O, that I knew how to betray them both!
Falconbridge. How sayst thou, Spicing? Wilt thou yield thyself?
For I have vowed, either alive or dead   75
To bring thee to King Edward.
Spicing. And I have vowed the like by thee.
How will these two bad contraries agree?
Chub. And I the same by both of you.
Falconbridge. Come, sir, I'll quickly rid you of that care.   80
Spicing. And what thou lottest me shall be thy share.

[*Enter* MILLER.]

Chub. Here comes a miller. Help to part the fray.
These are the rebels, Falconbridge and Spicing;
The worst of them is worth a thousand crowns.
Miller. Marry, and such a booty would I have.   85
Submit, submit! It is vain to strive.
                                        Exit FALCONBRIDGE.
Spicing. Why, what art thou?
Miller.   One that will hamper you.
But what's the other that is fled away?
Chub. O, miller, that was Falconbridge,
And this is Spicing, his companion.   90
Spicing. I tell thee, miller, thou hast been the means
To hinder the most charitable deed
That ever honest Christian undertook.
Chub. Thou canst bear me witness, I had ta'en
That most notorious rebel but for him.   95
Miller. But I have taken thee, and the world knows

81. thy] *Q2*; my *Q1*. 85. would] *Q1, 3–6*; should *Q2*.

___

81. *lottest*] Allots. Unusual abbreviation, but see Heywood's *Escapes of
Jupiter*, l. 329.

That Spicing is as bad as who is best.
Spicing. Why, thou mistak'st; I am a true subject.
Chub. Miller, he lies. Be sure to hold him fast.
Spicing. Dost thou accuse me? Apprehend him too,   100
    For he's as guilty as any of us.
Miller. Come. You shall both together answer it
    Before my Lord Mayor; and here he comes.

       Enter LORD MAYOR, JOSSELYN *and other attendants.*

Mayor. Sir Ralph Josselyn, have you ever seen
    A prince more affable than Edward is?   105
    What merry talk he had upon the way.
Josselyn. Doubtless, my lord, he'll prove a royal king.
    But how now, what are these?
Miller.   God save your honour.
    Here I present unto you, my Lord Mayor,
    A pair of rebels, whom I did espy   110
    As I was busy grinding at my mill;
    And taking them for vagrant idle knaves
    That had beset some true man from his house,
    I came to keep the peace; but afterward
    Found that it was the bastard Falconbridge,   115
    And this, his mate, together by the ears.
    The one, for all that I could do, escaped;
    The other standeth at your mercy here.
Mayor. It is the rebel, Spicing.
Spicing.   It is indeed.
    I see you are not blind; you know me then.   120
Mayor. Well, miller, thou hast done a subject's part,
    And worthily deserv'st that recompense
    As publicly proclaimèd by the King.
    But what's this other? I have seen his face
    And, as I take it, he is one of them.   125
Miller. I must confess, I took them both together;
    He aided me to apprehend the rest.

104–6. Sir . . . way] *Qq print as prose.*

    107. *prove . . . king*] Including the brief period of Henry's restoration to
the throne Edward historically had been king for ten years.
    113. *beset*] surrounded with hostile intent, but could also mean (as
implied here) 'deny access'.

Chub. 'A tells you true, my lord; I am Chub the chandler, and
    I curse the time that ever I saw their faces, for if they had
    not been, I had lived like an honest man in mine own   130
    country, and never come to this.
Spicing. Out, rogue! Dost thou recant for fear of death?
    Ay, Mayor, I am he that sought to cut your throat,
    And since I have miscarried in the fact,
    I'll ne'er deny it. Do the worst you can.   135
Mayor. Bring him away. He shall have martial law,
    And at the next tree we do come unto,
    Be hanged, to rid the world of such a wretch.
    Miller, thy duty is a thousand marks,
    Which must be shared betwixt thee and this poor   140
    Fellow, that did reveal him. And, sirrah,
    Your life is saved, on this condition:
    That you hang up Spicing. How sayest thou?
    Wilt thou do it?
Chub. Will I do it? What a question is that? I would hang him   145
    if he were my father, to save my own life.
Mayor. Then when ye have done it, come home to my house,
    and there ye truly shall have your reward.

        Exit MAYOR [*with* JOSSELYN *and attendants*].

Spicing. Well, sirrah, then thou must be my hangman?
Chub. Ay, by my troth sir, for fault of a better.   150
Spicing. Well, commend me to little Pym, and pray her to
    redeem my pawned hose; they lie at the Blue Boar for

136–44. Bring . . . it?] *Qq print 134–7 as verse, but without capitals at line
beginnings; 138–42 are printed as prose.*   148.01. *Exit*] *MS annotation to Dyce
(1) copy of Q3; not in Qq.*

---

131. *country*] county.
139. *duty*] reward.
151–5. *commend . . . score*] Comical details of domestic life did (and do)
actually surface in such moments of crisis and even found their way into official records; see, for example, the case in June 1596 where a hard-pressed
deponent responded to an examination concerning seditious words against
Cecil by observing that 'he should not now take care for the payment of the
9 l. which he owed Polly', *CSPD, 1595–1597,* 237.
152. *Blue Boar*] There were at least two East London taverns so named
but John Taylor's recording that 'The Waggons from Chelmsford in Essex,

eleven pence, and if my hostess will have the other odd
penny, tell her she is a damned bawd, and there is no
truth in her score.   155
Chub. Take no thought for your pawned hose, sir; they are
    lousy, and not worth the redeeming.
Spicing. There is a constable sticks in my mind; he got my
    sword from me, that night I should have killed Black
    Ralph. If I had lived, I would have been meet with him.   160
Chub. Ay, sir, but here's a thing shall take an order for that.
Spicing. Commend me to Black Luce, bouncing Bess, and
    lusty Kate, and all the other pretty morsels of man's flesh.
    Farewell, pink and pinnace, flyboat and carvell, Turnbull
    and Spittle; I die like a man.   165

---

come on Wednesdaies to the signe of the blew Boare without Algate' suggests that this would have been Spicing's haunt; *The Carriers Cosmographie*
(1637), Biv.

161. *been meet with*] come face to face with, encountered aggressively.

161. *take an order*] Usually meant 'make arrangements'; here Chub simply
implies that the noose will resolve (or render irrelevant) Spicing's outstand-
ing worries.

163. *morsels . . . flesh*] Sixteenth-century parlance for 'a bit of skirt', with
the sexism reinforced by the biblical allusion to woman as 'Adam's rib'. The
term was not exclusive to any particular social rank: Mistress Overdone and
Cleopatra were both 'morsels'.

164. *pink*] a small sailing ship.

pinnace] another small sailing vessel but one with some pretensions to
grandeur, as can be seen on the title page of Peele's *Descensus Astraeae* (1591),
which describes a nymph presenting 'a Pinesse on the water brauely rigd and
mand, to the Lord Maior'. The term quickly became common currency for
a woman of dubious morality: see Dekker and Webster's *Northward Ho*
(1605), 5.1.424, 443-4, and Jonson's *Bartholomew Fair* (1614), 2.2.72-4.

flyboat] a small, fast, trading ship. Used figuratively by Marston: 'Here's
such a company of flyboats hulling about this galleas of greatness that there's
no boarding him'; *Antonio and Mellida*, 5.2.127-8 (ed. Hunter).

carvell] trading vessel, usually Iberian; mentioned by Heywood in *1 Fair
Maid*, G4r, and *The Life of Merlin* (1640), p. 269.

Turnbull] Street (later Turnmill Street) in West Smithfield. Falstaff is irri-
tated by Shallow's reminiscences of youthful antics there, *2 Henry IV*,
3.2.298-300, and the outraged steward of Fletcher's *The Scornful Lady* (1613)
remarks: 'here has beene such a hurry, such a din, such dismall drinking,
swearing, and whoring . . . we haue al liu'd in a continuall *Turneball* streete',
3.2.143-5.

165. *Spittle*] A charitable hospital, one which dealt with the poor generally, those with leprosy, and, in the estimate of the dramatists, those with

Chub. O Captain Spicing, thy vain enticing
 Brought me from my trade;
 From good candles-making, to this pains-taking,
 A rebel to be made.
 Therefore, Ned Spicing, to quit thy enticing,   170
 This must be thy hope:
 By one of thy fellows, to be led to the gallows,
 To end in a rope.   *Exeunt.*

[Scene 11]

     Enter HOBS *the tanner of Tamworth.*

Hobs. Dudgeon! Dost thou hear? Look well to Brock, my
 mare; drive Dun and her fair and softly down the hill,
 and take heed the thorns tear not the horns of my
 cowhides as thou goest near the hedges. Ha? What sayst
 thou, knave? Is the bull's hide down? Why, lay it up again; 5
 what care I? I'll meet thee at the stile, and help to set all
 straight. And yet, God help, it's a crooked world, and an
 unthrifty, for some that have ne'er a shoe had rather go

---

venereal disease. Mistress Openwork refers to her husband's supposed
suburb-whoring as 'spittle dealing', *Roaring Girl*, 2.1.299. See also *Henry V*,
2.1.74, 5.1.85, and Dekker's 2 *Honest Whore* (1605), 4.1.199, 5.2.279.
 170–3. *Ned . . . rope*] The wording of *The Great Chronicle* is similar: 'that
othir Capytayn namyd Quyntin was hangid & hedyd, and aftyr ⟨his hede
was⟩ sett vpon Algate, by Spysyng his ffelaw' (221), though 'by' turns out to
mean 'next to'.

 0.1. Tamworth] a market town which, as described by Leland, had one
end of its principal street in Warwickshire and the other in Staffordshire, *Itinerary*, II,104.
 1. *Dudgeon*] Hobs is addressing his serving-man, who does not appear
onstage until Scene 14. The name derived from a composite insult. Dudgeon
was the wood from which the handle of a knife was made, thus implying
inflexibility or stupidity; but the word was also beginning to be used to indicate ill-humour, and it was in this sense that Nashe complained of the
'dudgen scorne' with which Greek oligarchies refused Homer patronage; see
Lenten Stuffe, in *Works*, III, 155.

barefoot than buy clout-leather to mend the old, when
they can buy no new, for they have time enough to mend   10
all, they sit so long between the cup and the wall. Well,
God amend them, God amend them. Let me see, by my
executor here, my leather pouch, what I have taken, what
I have spent; what I have gained, what I have lost; and
what I have laid out. My taking is more than my spend-   15
ing, for here's store left. I have spent but a groat; a penny
for my two jades, a penny to the poor, a penny pot of ale,
and a penny cake for my man and me. A dicker of
cowhides cost me—

> *Here enter* [2 HUNTSMEN,] *the* QUEEN *and* DUCHESS
> *with their riding rods, unpinning their masks;* HOBS
> *goes forward.*

S' nails, who comes here? Mistress Ferris, or mistress what-   20
call-ye-her? Put up, John Hobs; money tempts beauty.
Duchess. Well met, good fellow; sawst thou not the hart?
Hobs. My heart? God bless me from seeing my heart.
Duchess. Thy heart? The deer, man, we demand the deer.

---

9. buy] *Q2*; by *Q1*.

---

9. *clout-leather*] patches specifically for mending shoes. The term appears
in both the ballad and the 'history' but only in their probable source, *The
King and the Barker*, early versions of which survive in MS only, does the
tanner complain of such parsimony; see stanza 27 in Child's transcript, V,
79.
    11. *between the cup and the wall*] This sounds proverbial but although Dent
lists it he cites no other examples and provides no gloss. The tanner's allegation is clearly that the feasting is over-indulgent and over-long.
    18. *dicker*] a batch of ten hides. Q1 lacks punctuation here, indicating that
the royal entrance interrupts Hobs's reckoning.
    19.02. *riding rods*] switches, crops.
    masks] made of velvet or silk, worn by women of middle and high rank.
Susan Mountford, prior to her impoverishment, never 'tasted a rough winters
blast' without one; *A Woman Killed with Kindness*, Scene 7, l. 41. See also note
to ll. 48–9, below.
    20. *S'nails*] abbreviation of the mild oath 'God's nails'.
    Mistress Ferris] Probably a variant form of Ferrers; for the significance of
this name see the Introduction, pp. 37–8.
    21. *money tempts beauty*] Probably gestures towards the proverb (Dent,
B174) as expounded in Lyly's *Euphues and his England* (1580): 'beautie
without riches, goeth a begging'; Lyly, II, 72.

Hobs. Do you demand what's dear? Marry, corn, and   25
  cowhides. Mass, a good smug lass, well like my daughter
  Nell. I had rather than a bend of leather she and I might
  smutch together.

Duchess. Cam'st thou not down the wood?

Hobs. Yes, mistress, that I did.   30

Duchess. And sawst thou not the deer embossed?

Hobs. By my hood, ye make me laugh. What the dickens? Is
  it love that makes ye prate to me so fondly? By my father's
  soul, I would I had jobbed faces with you.

1 Huntsman. Why, how now Hobs, so saucy with the Duchess   35
  and the Queen?

Hobs. Much queen, I trow! These be but women, and one of
  them is like my wench. I would she had her rags; I would
  give a load of hair and horns, and a fat of leather, to
  match her to some Justice, by the meg holly.   40

2 Huntsman. Be silent, tanner, and ask pardon of the Queen.

Hobs. And ye be the Queen, I cry ye mercy, good mistress
  Queen.

Queen. No fault, my friend. Madam, let's take our bows,
  And in the standing seek to get a shoot.   45

---

39. hair] *Q2*; heare *Q1*.

26. *smug*] Pretty, good-looking; the word did not yet mean self-satisfied.
Vulcan explains that he was born 'A pretty smug knaue', *Brazen Age*, 11r;
Rusticano drools over one of the 'smuggest lasses' in *Tom a Lincoln*, 430.

27. *bend*] the thickest and stoutest kind of leather, from the back and
flanks; another northern dialect form.

28. *smutch*] kiss.

31. *the deer embossed*] The Duchess is using a hunting term, meaning that
the quarry is exhausted or foaming at the mouth; cf. *The Taming of the Shrew*,
Ind., 1. 15. Hobs, however, takes 'deere' to be an affectionate appellation
aimed in his direction and possibly goes on, vulgarly, to construe 'imbost' as
bulging or protruding.

33. *fondly*] foolishly.

34. *jobbed faces*] kissed. Child prints a ballad of indeterminate date in
which Robin Hood and Maid Marian meet 'With kind imbraces, and jobbing
of faces'; III, 219, st. 14.

37. *trow*] Think; modern usage would add 'not!'.

39. *fat*] a substantial measure of capacity, though usually used of grain or
liquids.

40. *by the meg holly*] a possibly unique oath, a distortion of 'Holy Mary'.

45. *standing*] concealed vantage point in hunting.

Duchess. Come, bend our bows, and bring the herd of deer.

               Exeunt [QUEEN, DUCHESS *and* HUNTSMEN].

Hobs. God send ye good standing, and good striking, and fat
    flesh! See if all gentlewomen be not alike when their black
    faces be on. I took the Queen, as I am true tanner, for
    Mistress Ferris.   50

          Enter SELLINGER *and* HOWARD *in green.*

    Soft, who comes here? More knaves yet?

Sellinger. Ho, good fellow, sawst thou not the King?

Hobs. No, good fellow, I saw no king. Which king dost thou
    ask for?

Howard. Why, King Edward. What king is there else?   55

Hobs. There's another king and ye could hit on him: one
    Harry, one Harry, and, by our Lady, they say he's the
    honester man of the two.

Sellinger. Sirrah, beware you speak not treason.

Hobs. What if I do?   60

Sellinger. Then thou'lt be hanged.

Hobs. A dog's death; I'll not meddle with it. For, by my troth,
    I know not when I speak treason, when I do not. There's
    such halting betwixt two kings that a man cannot go
    upright but he shall offend t' one of them. I would God   65
    had them both for me.

Howard. Well, thou sawst not the King?

Hobs. No. Is he in the country?

Howard. He's hunting here at Drayton Basset.

Hobs. The devil he is, God bless his mastership! I saw a   70
    woman here that they said was the Queen; she's as like

    48–9. *black faces*] Cf. the Clown's tactless banter with the disfigured
Bellamira in *The Trial of Chivalry*: 'you think a bald face hath no need of a
black mask', GIV.

    62–5. *dog's . . . them*] This passage closely anticipates the scene in *1 If You
Know Not Me* in which the soldiers instructed to convey the Princess Elizabeth to the Tower discuss the dangers of speaking treason and develop osten-
sibly naive strategies to circumvent the problem, C2r–C3r. The connection
between hanging and a dog's death was proverbial (see Dent, D509), but cf.
also the intriguing entry for 'Chien' in Randle Cotgrave's *Dictionarie of the
French and English Tongues* (1611): 'When a bad Prince would be rid of a
good subiect, or seruant, the tricke is, to lay treason to his charge'.

    64. *halting*] wavering.

my daughter—but my daughter is the fairer—as ever I
see.

Sellinger. Farewell, fellow. Speak well of the King.

Exeunt [HOWARD *and* SELLINGER].

Hobs. God make him an honest man. I hope that's well   75
spoken, for by th' mouse foot, some give him hard words,
whether he 'serves 'um or not. Let him look to that; I'll
meddle of my cowhide, and let the world slide.

Enter the KING *disguised.*

The devil in a dung cart! How these roysters swarm in
the country now the King is so near! God 'liver me from   80
this, for this looks like a thief. But a man cannot tell
amongst these courtnoles who's true.

Edward. Holla, my friend. [Hobs *makes to go.*] Good fellow,
pray thee stay.

Hobs. No such matter, I have more haste of my way.   85

Edward. If thou be a good fellow, let me borrow a word.

Hobs. My purse, thou meanest. I am no good fellow, and I
pray God thou beest not one.

---

76. *by th' mouse foot*] An oath also found in *The London Prodigal* (1605),
C1r, but one so mild that even the Puritan Arthur Dent excused its use; see
the note in Heywood's *Works* (P), I, 356.

77. *'serves*] deserves.

78. *let the world slide*] Proverbial (see Dent's 'Let the world wag', W879),
a sentiment much favoured by Christopher Sly—see *The Taming of the Shrew*,
Ind., 1.5, 2.141–2—and even finding its way into Cotgrave's *Dictionarie*, s.v.
'Charge': 'To take no thought, passe the time merrily, let the world slide'.

79. *roysters*] Swaggerers, boisterous revellers. A common enough term,
not found in the 'Tanner' sources but used repeatedly to describe King Alfred
and his entourage in the generically similar ballad 'The Shepherd and the
King'. (The copy consulted was probably issued in the 1670s, in London,
and was printed by the partnership—Thomas Vere and John Wright
(junior)—which bought the rights to five Heywood plays in 1673.) Heywood
uses the verb 'roysting' in *A Woman Killed with Kindness*, Scene 9, l. 33.

82. *courtnoles*] A contemptuous term for a courtier. Not found in the
'Tanner' sources but in one of their antecedents, 'The King and the Miller';
see Percy, II, 147–57, ll. 79–80. Its use is perhaps intended to suggest a certain
rusticity in the speaker; cf. its appearance twice in sustained passages of
dialect in another play printed in 1599, *Clyomon and Clamydes*, where the
shepherd Corin confronts the disguised Neronis: 'You courtnoll crackropes,
wod be hangd, you do nothing now and then / But come vp and downe the
country, thus to flout poore men', 1311–12.

Edward. Why, dost thou not love a good fellow?

Hobs. No, good fellows be thieves.   90

Edward. Dost thou think I am one?

Hobs. Thought is free, and thou art not my ghostly father.

Edward. I mean thee no harm.

Hobs. Who knows that but thyself? [*Aside*] I pray God he spy
   not my purse.   95

Edward. On my troth, I mean thee none.

Hobs. Upon thy oath I'll stay. Now, what sayst thou to me?
   Speak quickly, for my company stays for me beneath at
   the next stile.

Edward. The King is hunting hereabouts; didst thou see his   100
   majesty?

Hobs. His majesty? What's that? His horse, or his mare?

Edward. Tush, I mean his grace.

Hobs. Grace, quotha? Pray God he have any. Which king dost
   thou 'quire for?   105

Edward. Why, for King Edward. Knowst thou any more kings
   than one?

---

92. *Thought is free*] The phrase is proverbial (Dent, T244) and was probably by this time established as the refrain of a catch; Maria teases Sir
Andrew with it—*Twelfth Night*, 1.3.67—and Caliban and Ariel are familiar
with both tune and lyric (*The Tempest*, 3.2.121). Sir John Hayward nervously
refers to it in 1599 as 'a common saying', J. W. Manning (ed.), *The Life and
Raigne of King Henrie IIII* (London, 1991), 102.

   ghostly father] priest, and thus the trusted custodian of confession. Romeo
so terms Friar Laurence, 2.2.192 (Q1 only) and 2.3.41, and the disguised
Duke Vincentio is similarly designated in *Measure for Measure*, 4.3.47. Interestingly, Edward IV, during his wooing of Lady Grey, is scurrilously referred
to in this way by Richard of Gloucester, *3 Henry VI*, 3.2.107; the pejorative
sense of the phrase can be seen in a letter from William Atkinson to Cecil
(February 1595), in which he offers to poison Tyrone by posing as one of the
Irish rebel's 'ghostly fathers', *CSPD, 1595–1597*, 14.

   101–10. *majesty . . . highness*] Though the Shakespearean scenes to which
this episode most closely relates do not reproduce the Tanner's obtuse
'semantic' quibbles on 'majesty', the word occurs, as a resonant counterpart
to 'fellow', no fewer than eighteen times in less than 140 lines; see *Henry V*,
4.7.94–4.8.58.

   103–4. *grace . . . Grace*] Hobs repeats the Falstaffian quibble on 'Grace',
signifying either a form of address to the nobility or spiritual grace; cf. *1
Henry IV*, 1.2.16–18.

   105. *'quire*] enquire.

Hobs. I know not so many, for I tell thee I know none. Marry,
  I hear of King Edward.

Edward. Didst thou see his highness?   110

Hobs. By my holidame, that's the best term thou gav'st him
  yet! He's high enough, but he has put poor King Harry
  low enough.

Edward. How low hath he put him?

Hobs. Nay, I cannot tell, but he has put him down, for he has   115
  got the crown; much good do't him with it.

Edward. Amen. I like thy talk so well, I would I knew thy
  name.

Hobs. Dost thou not know me?

Edward. No.   120

Hobs. Then thou knowst nobody. Didst never hear of John
  Hobs, the tanner of Tamworth?

Edward. Not till now, I promise thee; but now I like thee well.

Hobs. So do not I thee. I fear thou art some out-rider, that
  lives by taking of purses here on Basset's Heath, but I fear   125
  thee not, for I have wared all my money in cowhides at
  Coleshill market; and my man and my mare are hard by
  at the hill foot.

Edward. Is that thy grey mare, that's tied at the stile with the
  hides on her back?   130

Hobs. That's Brock, my mare, and there's Dun, my nag, and
  Dudgeon, my man.

---

115. *Hobs.*] *No speech prefix in Qq.*

111. *holidame*] Originally 'haligdom', the state of holiness; the suffix
'dame' seems to have been grafted on to render the oath a variant form of
'By Our Lady'. The King uses the oath, in the supremely inappropriate
context of an interview with Cranmer, in *Henry VIII*, 5.1.116.

119–22. *Dost . . . Tamworth*] Hobson is similarly amazed that Queen Elizabeth is unaware of his eminence in Heywood's play that takes its title from
this episode: *2 If You Know Not Me*, H1v.

124. *out-rider*] Hobs clearly means a highwayman but may also, in this
context, glance at the technical term for 'bayliffe errants' or officers of the
sheriff's court, as caustically defined by the legal theorist John Cowell in his
(suppressed) *The Interpreter* (1607), Zz4v; either way, a swipe at the execu-
tors of the King's 'justice', in keeping with the Tanner's opinions on the more
immediate royal entourage, at Scene 14, ll. 44–8.

126. *wared*] invested.

127. *Coleshill*] a small Warwickshire town; 'It is countyd almoste the midle
way betwixt Tamworthe and Coventrye', Leland's *Itinerary*, II, 106.

Edward. There's neither man nor horse, but only one mare.

Hobs. God's blue bodkin, has the knave served me so?
Farewell, I may lose hides, horns, and mare and all by   135
prating with thee.

Edward. Tarry, man, tarry. They'll sooner take my gelding
than thy grey mare, for I have tied mine by her.

Hobs. That will I see, afore I'll take your word.

Edward. I'll bear thee company.   140

Hobs. I had as lief go alone.   *Exeunt.*

[Scene 12]

Enter the two HUNTSMEN *again, with the bows.*

1 Huntsman. Now, on my troth, the Queen shoots passing
well.

2 Huntsman. So did the Duchess, when she was as young.

1 Huntsman. Age shakes the hand, and shoots both wide
and short.

2 Huntsman. What have they given us?

1 Huntsman.   Six rose nobles just.

2 Huntsman. The Queen gave four.

1 Huntsman.   True, and the Duchess, twain.   5

2 Huntsman. O, were we ever so paid for our pain?

1 Huntsman. Tut, had the King come, as they said he would,
He would have rained upon us showers of gold.

2 Huntsman. Why, he is hunting somewhere here about.
Let's first go drink, and then go seek him out.   *Exeunt.*   10

1–10.] *Qq print whole scene as prose.*

134. *God's blue bodkin*] an oath the literal meaning of which is 'God's blue
body'; cf. *Hamlet*, 2.2.524.

141. *as lief*] just as soon.

4. *rose nobles*] Coins introduced by Edward as part of his controversial
manipulation of the coinage; they were to be worth 10 shillings, whilst
'angels' were worth 6s 8d. See Scofield, I, 360–3.

8. *showers of gold*] Edward's 'largesse' was legendary but here there may
also be a glancing allusion—which will later be expanded—to one of the
amorous conquests of Jupiter, the seduction of Danae.

[Scene 13]

Enter KING EDWARD *again, and* HOBS.

Edward. How sayst thou, tanner, wilt thou take my courser
for thy mare?

Hobs. Courser, callst thou him? So ill mought I fare! Thy skit-
tish jade will never abide to carry my leather, my horns,
nor hide. But if I were so mad to scorse, what boot   5
wouldst thou give me?

Edward. Nay boot that's boot-worthy; I look for boot of thee.

Hobs. He, ha, a merry jig! Why man, Brock my mare knows
'ha and ree', and will stand when I cry 'ho', and let me
get up and down, and make water when I do.   10

Edward. I'll give thee a noble if I like her pace. Lay thy
cowhides in my saddle, and let's jog towards Drayton.

Hobs. 'Tis out of my way, but I begin to like thee well.

Edward. Thou wilt like me better before we do part. I pray
thee tell me, what say they of the King?   15

Hobs. Of the kings, thou meanst. Art thou no blab, if I tell
thee?

Edward. If the King know't not now, he shall never know it
for me.

Hobs. 'Mass, they say King Harry's a very advowtry man. 20

Edward. A devout man? And what's King Edward?

5–6. But . . . me?] *Q2; Q1 gives as new speech by the King.*   7. *Edward.*] *Q2;*
Hobs. Q1.

---

3. *mought*] archaic form of 'may'.

5. *scorse*] make an exchange; there may also be an oblique pun since the
word's etymological derivation is from 'horse-[s]courser'.

7. *boot . . . thee*]Edward puns on 'boot' as bounty or financial reward, as
opposed to the footwear he might expect a tanner to provide.

9. *ha and ree*] calls indicating that a horse should change direction; the
phrase turns up in Nashe's *Summers Last Will and Testament* (1600), *Works*,
III, 261, and in *Micro-Cynicon* (1599), Middleton VIII, 121, but see also a
probably Heywoodian section of *Fortune by Land and Sea* (1607–9), B4v.

16. *blab*] tell-tale, informer. The word occurs again in Part Two, and had
featured earlier in *Edmund Ironside*, l. 1762. Phoebus feels he is unjustly
'term'd a tel-tale and a blab', *Brazen Age*, H3v.

20. *advowtry*] The King correctly decodes the Tanner's malapropism but
the comedy lies not simply in Hobs's muddled vocabulary but in the fact
that his description is ironically and grotesquely misplaced; advowtry,
meaning adultery, will be Edward's province.

Hobs. He's a frank franion, a merry companion, and loves a
    wench well. They say he has married a poor widow
    because she's fair.

Edward. Dost thou like him the worse for that?   25

Hobs. No, by my feckens, but the better; for though I be a
    plain tanner, I love a fair lass myself.

Edward. Pray thee tell me, how love they King Edward?

Hobs. Faith, as poor folks love holidays: glad to have them
    now and then, but to have them come too often will undo   30
    them. So, to see the King now and then, 'tis comfort, but
    every day would beggar us. And, I may say to thee, we
    fear we shall be troubled to lend him money, for we doubt
    he's but needy.

Edward. Wouldst thou lend him no money, if he should need?   35

Hobs. By my halidom, yes; he shall have half my store, and
    I'll sell sole leather to help him to more.

Edward. Say'th whether lovest thou better Harry or Edward.

Hobs. Nay, that's counsel; and two may keep it, if one be away.

Edward. Shall I say my conscience? I think Harry is the true   40
    king.

Hobs. Art advised of that? Harry's of the old house of
    Lancaster, and that progenity do I love.

Edward. And thou dost not hate the house of York?

---

32. may say to] *Q4*; may to *Q1–3*.

---

22. *franion*] A recklessly exuberant person. Spenser uses it of a 'loose'
woman, *Faerie Queene*, V, iii, 22, 7; a parasitical courtier in *The Rare Triumphs
of Love and Fortune* (possibly in the repertoire of Derby's Men c.1582)
proudly describes himself as a 'franke franion', only to have the term deri-
sively spat back at him by a loyal retainer, ll. 689–91.

26. *by my feckens*] probably a dialect expansion of 'fecks', meaning faith,
as in *The Winter's Tale*, 1.2.120.

29–32. *Faith . . . us*] This sentiment is related to the proverb 'Every day
is not holiday' (Dent, D68), and possibly to Prince Henry's chilling employ-
ment of it, *1 Henry IV*, 1.2.199–202; it is typical, however, that Hobs should
extend his pragmatic approach to the regulation of holiday into a critique of
royal 'progresses'.

33. *doubt*] suspect.

39. *counsel*] a secret; proverbial (see Dent, T257).

42. *advised*] sure, as in Gloucester's whispered taunt to the Cardinal in *2
Henry VI*, 2.1.49.

43. *progenity*] Hobs means progeny.

Hobs. Why no, for I am just akin to Sutton windmill: I can   45
    grind which way so e'er the wind blow. If it be Harry, I
    can say 'well fare Lancaster'; if it be Edward, I can sing
    'York, York, for my money'.

Edward. Thou art of my mind. But I say Harry is the lawful
    king; Edward is but an usurper, and a fool, and a coward.   50

Hobs. Nay, there thou liest; he has wit enough, and courage
    enough. Dost thou not speak treason?

Edward. Ay, but I know to whom I speak it.

Hobs. Dost thou? Well, if I were constable, I should be for-
    sworn if I set thee not in the stocks for it.   55

Edward. Well, let it go no further; for I did serve King Harry,
    and I love him best, though now I serve King Edward.

Hobs. Thou art the arranter knave to speak ill of thy master.
    But, sirrah, what's thy name? What office hast thou? And
    what will the King do for thee?   60

Edward. My name is Ned. I am the King's butler, and he will
    do more for me than for any nobleman in the court.

Hobs. The devil he will! He's the more fool, and so I'll tell
    him, if e'er I see him; and I would I might see him in my
    poor house at Tamworth.   65

Edward. Go with me to the court, and I'll bring thee to the
    King, and what suit so e'er thou have to him, I'll warrant
    thee to speed.

---

45. *Sutton*] Sutton Coldfield.

48. *York, York . . . money*] The refrain from a ballad entered in the
Stationer's Register in November 1582 (Arber, II, 416). It celebrates not
only the city but the continuing tradition of archery contests, particularly as
patronized by the young Earl of Essex; it is reprinted in *Roxburghe Ballads*,
I, 4–9. Hobs unashamedly conforms to the image of the windblown multitude as imagined by the deposed King Henry, *3 Henry VI*, 3.1.83–95.
Heywood features several advocates of this position: Valerius in *The Rape of
Lucrece*, ll. 164–7, and the Clown in *Fortune by Land and Sea*, B2r. For the
possible allusion to 'Jack Miller's Song', see Intoduction, pp. 26–7.

51. *he . . . courage*] The Tanner's opinion is supported by even the least
sympathetic chroniclers; see, for instance, Stow's *Annals*, where Edward is
accounted 'a man of noble courage and great wit', 680.

61. *Ned*] 'Ned' may have become a kind of occupational tag, judging by
its appearance in *The Book of Sir Thomas More*, 5.2.2.

68. *speed*] prosper.

Hobs. I ha' nothing to do at court. I'll home with my
    cowhides, and if the King will come to me, he shall be   70
    welcome.

Edward. Hast thou no suit, touching thy trade? To transport
    hides, or sell leather only in a certain circuit? Or about
    bark, or such like? To have letters patents?

Hobs. By the mass and the matins, I like not those pattens!   75
    Sirrah, they that have them do as the priests did in old
    time: buy and sell the sins of the people. So they make
    the King believe they mend what's amiss, and, for money,
    they make the thing worse than it is. There's another thing
    in't too, the more is the pity.   80

Edward. What pity, John Hobs? I pray thee, say all.

Hobs. Faith, 'tis pity that one subject should have in his hand,
    that might do good to many through the land.

Edward. Sayst thou me so, tanner? Well, let's cast lots, whether
    thou shalt go with me to Drayton, or I go home with thee   85
    to Tamworth.

---

72. Hast] *Q2*; Haste *Q1*.

---

73. *sell . . . circuit*] An awkward construction: 'only in' means something
like 'with exclusive rights within'. This allusion to restictive trading practices
is a pointedly anachronistic touch, since the practice of raising royal revenue
by the granting of monopoly patents only reached its 'scandalous phase'
between 1580 and 1624 (J. Thirsk, *The Agrarian History of England and Wales,
IV: 1500–1640* (Cambridge, 1967), *passim*). The *Remembrancia* (1878) documents a sequence of heated exchanges between the City and the government
over the leather monopoly, mostly from 1580 until 1595, but still rumbling
in 1614, and again in 1634. There was an explosive parliamentary campaign
against monopolies in 1597—see J. E. Neale, *Elizabeth I and her Parliaments,
1584–1601* (London, 1957), 352–6—and Sir Robert Wroth still angrily
included 'hornes' and 'transportation of leather' in an acrimonious
Commons debate of 1601; R. H. Tawney, E. Power (eds), *Tudor Economic
Documents*, 3 vols (London, 1924), II, 279. Dramatists frequently attacked the
practice—see, for instance, Greene's *James IV* (c.1591), 2.1.768–80, and the
scurrilous episode in 3.1—and the term 'letters patent' soon came to carry
automatically a sense of moral opprobrium, as in the opening scene of *Arden
of Faversham*.

74. *bark*] residue from the bark of trees, used in the tanning process.

75. *By . . . pattens*] The Tanner's rhyming assault may be anachronistic
but he did have medieval linguistic precedents for linking patents with
the sale of indulgences: see *Piers Plowman* (B), VII, 184–94, and Chaucer's
Pardoner's Prologue, 335–40.

Hobs. Lot me no lotting. I'll not go with thee. If thou wilt go
  with me, 'cause thou art my liege's man—and yet I think
  he has many honester—thou shalt be welcome to John
  Hobs. Thou shalt be welcome to beef and bacon, and   90
  perhaps a bagpudding; and my daughter Nell shall pop a
  posset upon thee when thou go'st to bed.
Edward. Here's my hand. I'll but go and see the King served,
  and I'll be at home as soon as thyself.
Hobs. Dost thou hear me, Ned? If I shall be thy host,   95
  Make haste, thou art best, for fear thou kiss the post.
                                                Exit HOBS.
Edward. Farewell, John Hobs, the honest true tanner.
  I see plain men, by observation
  Of things that alter in the change of times,
  Do gather knowledge; and the meanest life,   100
  Proportioned with content sufficiency,
  Is merrier than the mighty state of kings.

                Enter HOWARD *and* SELLINGER.

  How now? What news bring ye, sirs?
  Where's the Queen?
Sellinger. Her highness and your mother, my dread lord,   105
  Are both invited by Sir Humphrey Bowes,
  Where they intend to feast and lodge this night,
  And do expect your grace's presence there.
Edward. Tom Sellinger, I have other business.
  Astray from you and all my other train   110
  I met a tanner; such a merry mate,

---

94. and] *Q2*; and and *Q1*. 96. SD] *Q2*; *omitted in Q1*.

---

91. *bagpudding*] Rusticano reveals a penchant for these (with bacon) in
Tom a Lincoln, 470, and later refers to the combination as a 'clownicall
dinner', 1298.

92. *posset*] Spiced drink of milk and wine; both John Rugby and Falstaff
are promised one, *Merry Wives*, 1.4.7, 5.5.171–2.

96. *kiss the post*] proverbial (Dent, P494), meaning 'be shut out'. The
derivation of the phrase and its implications are more searchingly examined
in *A Woman Killed with Kindness*, 8.162ff.

98–102. *I . . . kings*] A characteristically flippant variation on what had
become an almost obligatory trope of the chronicle play; cf. *3 Henry VI*,
2.5.21–54, and *2 Henry IV*, 3.1.4–31 (Folio only). In the latter instance the
'gravitas' of the sentiment has already been undermined by Falstaff's parody,
2.4.371–3, and the disguised Henry V's version is also profoundly problematic.

So frolic, and so full of good conceit
That I have given my word to be his guest,
Because he knows me not to be the King.
Good cousin Howard, grudge not at the jest,   115
But greet my mother and my wife from me;
Bid them be merry. I must have my humour.
Let them both sup and sleep when they see time.
Commend me kindly to Sir Humphrey Bowes:
Tell him, at breakfast I will visit him.   120
This night Tom Sellinger and I must feast
With Hobs the tanner; there, plain 'Ned' and 'Tom';
No 'King', nor 'Sellinger', for a thousand pound.

Enter a Messenger booted, with letters, and kneeling gives
them to the King.

Howard. [*While the King reads*] The Queen and Duchess
    will be discontent
    Because his highness comes not to the feast.   125
Sellinger. Sir Humphrey Bowes may take the most conceit;
    But what's the end? The King will have his pleasure.
Edward. Good news, my boys: Harry the Sixth is dead.
    Peruse that letter. [*To Messenger*] Sirrah, drink you that,
                                                [*He*] *gives his purse.*
    And stay not, but post back again for life,   130
    And thank my brother Gloucester for his news;
    Commend me to him; I'll see him tomorrow night.
    How like ye it, sirs?

                                                Exit Messenger.

128–34. Good . . . news] *Qq print as prose.*

---

117. *must . . . humour*] The King's insistence on being allowed his
'humour' recalls Spicing's similar wilfulness (Scene 9, l. 39), just as it is no
accident that 'plain Ned and Tom' (l. 108) are the names still resonating from
the rebel leaders' exchanges.

118. *see time*] see fit.

123.01. booted] Wearing riding boots; the bearer of such important news
is supposed to have rapidly covered the considerable distance from London.

126. *take . . . conceit*] be the person most grievously offended.

128–31. *Good . . . news*] The chroniclers were virtually unanimous in
acknowledging Richard's involvement in Henry's death—Shakespeare had
staged it vividly—and Edward's complicity is glanced at by most, though not
More; this degree of callousness is, however, implied only by Virgil, 155–6.

130. *post . . . life*] ride as if your life depended on it.

Sellinger.   O, passing well, my liege.
You may be merry for these happy news.
Edward. The merrier with our host the tanner, Tom.   135
[*To Howard*] My lord, take you that letter to the ladies.
Bid them be merry with that second course,
And if we see them not before we go,
Pray them to journey easily after us.
We'll post to London. So, good night, my lord. *Exeunt.*   140

[Scene 14]

Enter HOBS *and his daughter* NELL.

Hobs. Come Nell, come daughter; is your hands and face
washed?
Nell. Ay, forsooth, father.
Hobs. Ye must be cleanly, I tell ye, for there comes a courtnole hither tonight, the King's mastership's butler, Ned;   5
a spruce youth, but beware ye be not in love, nor over-
taken by him, for courtiers be slippery lads.
Nell. No, forsooth, father.
Hobs. God's blessing on thee, that half year's schooling in
Lichfield was better to thee than house and land, it has   10
put such manners into thee: 'ay forsooth', and 'no for-

---

137. *second course*] When Macbeth refers to 'great nature's second course'
(2.2.38) he means sleep; since the King has already been concerned with the
overnight lodging of the royal ladies—'Let them both sup and sleep' (103)—
perhaps the suggestion here is 'having feasted, let them sleep all the more
soundly for this news'.

9–12. *half . . . word*] Comic effect notwithstanding, the tanner's views on
education are those of an enlightened craftsman of the late Elizabethan
period rather than those of his 1470s counterpart. John Brinsley's account
of his 1590s experience as a teacher in the adjacent county of Leicestershire
reveals that village and market town schooling had recently become
more widely available to both sexes; see *A Consolation for our Grammar
Schools* (1622), *passim*, and J. Simon, *Education and Society in Tudor England*
(Cambridge, 1966), 375–7. On the other hand Lichfield's educational provision for the poor was minimal; six pupils were allowed £1 6s 8d each for
books, provided they also brought brooms to sweep out the school; see
A. M. Stowe, *English Grammar Schools in the Reign of Queen Elizabeth* (New
York, 1908), 126.

sooth' at every word. Ye have a clean smock on, I like your
apparel well. Is supper ready?

Nell. Ay, forsooth, father.

Hobs. Have we a good barley bagpudding, a piece of fat   15
bacon, a good cow heel, a hard cheese, and a brown loaf?

Nell. All this, forsooth, and more. Ye shall have a posset, but
indeed the rats have spoiled your hard cheese.

Hobs. Now the devil choke them! So they have eat me a far-
thing candle the other night.   20

Dudgeon. (within) What, master, master!

Hobs. How now knave? What sayst thou, Dudgeon?

Dudgeon. Here's guests come. Where's Helen?

Hobs. What guests be they?

Dudgeon. A courtnole: one Ned, the King's butcher, he says, 25
and his friends too.

Hobs. Ned, the King's butcher? Ha, ha, the King's butler!
Take their horses and walk them, and bid them come near
house. Nell, lay the cloth, and clap supper o' th' board.

                                                Exit NELL.

                Enter KING EDWARD *and* SELLINGER.

Mass, here's Ned indeed—and another misproud ruf-   30
fian. Welcome, Ned. I like thy honesty, thou keepest
promise.

Edward. I'faith, honest tanner, I'll ever keep promise with
thee. Pray thee, bid my friend welcome.

Hobs. By my troth, ye are both welcome to Tamworth. Friend, 35
I know not your name.

Sellinger. My name is Tom Twist.

Hobs. Believe ye that list. But ye are welcome both, and I like
ye both well but for one thing.

Sellinger. What's that?   40

---

30. *misproud*] arrogant.

37. *Tom Twist*] Clearly a quasi-proverbial inversion of 'Tom Telltroth',
although to 'twist' in the sense of to distort meaning was not in use for at
least another century and I can find no comparable contemporary example.

38. *Believe . . . list*] proverbial expression of incredulity (Dent, B264.11);
it had occurred in an exchange concerning doubtful identity in George Gas-
coigne's *Supposes* (1566), in J. W. Cunliffe (ed.), *Works*, 2 vols (Cambridge,
1907–10), I, 4.5.36.

Hobs. Nay, that I keep to myself; for I sigh to see, and think,
  that pride brings many a one to extruction.
Edward. Pray tell us thy meaning.
Hobs. Troth, I doubt ye ne'er came truly by all these gay rags.
  'Tis not your bare wages and thin fees ye have of the   45
  King can keep ye thus fine, but either ye must rob the
  King privily, or his subjects openly, to maintain your
  probicality.
Sellinger. Thinkest thou so, tanner?
Hobs. 'Tis no matter what I think. Come, let's go to supper.   50
  What, Nell! What, Dudgeon! Where be these folks?

  Enter NELL *and* DUDGEON, *with a table covered.*

  Daughter, bid my friends welcome.
Nell. Ye are welcome, gentlemen, as I may say.
Sellinger. I thank ye, fair maid.   *kiss her both.*
Edward. A pretty wench, by my fay.   55
Hobs. How likest her, Ned?
Edward. I like her so well, I would ye would make me your
  son-in-law.
Hobs. And I like thee so well, Ned, that hadst thou an occu-

---

42. *pride . . . extruction*] Variation on the proverb 'Pride will have a fall'
(Dent, P581); Hobs's conflation of 'destruction' and 'extrusion' is not inappropriate since the latter could mean forcible expulsion from a privileged
position, as in Wyatt's letter to Cromwell, *Life and Letters*, ed. K.Muir
(Liverpool, 1963), 141.

44–8. *I . . . probicality*] The Tanner's mispronunciation of 'prodigality'
diminishes neither the specificity nor the force of his critique. The dramatist
has carefully inverted the usual strategies of his generic forebears,
particularly as regards costume; the King and Sellinger are incognito but,
rather than being disguised in a style which is socially levelling (e.g. a huntsman, a travelling artisan) or indeterminate, they are still conspicuously
courtiers. The distinction, visually and ultimately politically, is crucial; for an
example of the more orthodox approach, and the consequent emergence of
an innocuous financial joke which is the exact obverse of that found here,
see the ballad *The King and a Poore Northerne Man* (earliest surviving text
1640 but in an earlier form almost certainly the source of the lost Admiral's
play of 1601, *Too Good to Be True*), 12. For an analysis of the actual situation
which provoked Hobs's observation see J. E. Neale, *Essays in Elizabethan
History* (London, 1958), 61–79.

55. *fay*] already archaic form of 'faith'.

59–60. *occupation*] Hobs may be stumbling inadvertently (though suitably
given Edward's appetites) over a sexual innuendo which, as Jonson complained (VIII, 610), constantly attended the word 'occupy'.

pation—for 'service is no heritage': 'a young courtier, an   60
old beggar'—I could find in my heart to cast her away
upon thee. And, if thou wilt forsake the court, and turn
tanner, or bind thyself to a shoemaker in Lichfield, I'll
give thee twenty nobles ready money, with my Nell, and
trust thee with a dicker of leather, to set up thy trade.   65
Sellinger. Ned, he offers ye fair, if ye have the grace to take it.
Edward. He does indeed, Tom, and hereafter I'll tell him
more.
Hobs. Come, sit down to supper. Go to, Nell, no more sheep's
eyes. Ye may be caught, I tell ye; these be liquorish lads.   70
Nell. I warrant ye, father. Yet in truth, Ned is a very proper
man, and t' other may serve—but Ned's a pearl in mine
eye.
Hobs. Daughter, call Dudgeon and his fellows. We'll have a
three-men song to make our guests merry.   *Exit* NELL.   75
'Nails, what courtnoles are ye? Ye'll neither talk nor eat.
What news at the court? Do somewhat for your meat.
Edward. Heavy news there. King Henry is dead.
Hobs. That's light news, and merry, for your master King
Edward.   80
Edward. But how will the commons take it?

60–1. *service . . . beggar*] Two proverbs juxtaposed: 'service is no heritage'
(Dent, S253) occurs in Day's *Isle of Gulls* (1606), E4v, and 'a young courtier,
an old beggar' (Dent, C737), is mentioned to impressionable women in both
The Revenger's Tragedy (c.1606), 4.4.142–3 and *The Devil's Law-Case* (c.1617),
1.2.72–4.

63. *bind*] apprentice.

69–70. *sheep's eyes*] Amorous glances; the clown in Heywood's *The Rape
of Lucrece* denies having 'flung' any at the heroine's maid, E1r.

70. *liquorish*] The Tanner makes a hash of 'leckerous', a common variant
form of 'lecherous', but in so doing contrives to cast another aspersion:
liquorish was a gauche remedy for clearing the throat and improving the
voice, as in Beaumont's *The Knight of the Burning Pestle*, 1.1.70–1, so the hint
is perhaps at smooth talking.

71–6. *Ned . . . eat*] There are two ironic anticipations here; Nell's innocent cliché comparing Edward to a pearl foreshadows the more ominous
jewel imagery of Jane's seduction, and the courtiers' failure to eat in Hobs's
house prefigures the more flagrant violation of hospitality at the Lord
Mayor's banquet.

71. *proper*] handsome.

Hobs. Well, God be with good King Henry.
    Faith, the commons will take it as a common thing.
    Death's an honest man, for he spares not the king;
    For, as one comes, another's ta'en away—   85
    And seldom comes the better, that's all we say.
Sellinger. Shrewdly spoken, tanner, by my fay.

            [*Enter* NELL *again.*]

Hobs. Come, fill me a cup of Mother Whetstone's ale:
    I may drink to my friends, and drive down my tale.
    Here, Ned and Tom, I drink to ye. And yet if I come to   90
    the court, I doubt you'll not know me.
Edward. Yes, Tom shall be my surety, tanner; I will know thee.
Sellinger. If thou dost not, Ned, by my troth, I beshrew thee.
Edward. I drink to my wife that may be.
Sellinger. Faith, Ned, thou mayst live to make her a lady.   95
Edward. Tush, her father offers nothing, having no more chil-
    dren but her.

83–4. *commons . . . king*] Hobs offers a punning conflation of two widely
known proverbs, 'Death is common to all' (Dent, D142), and 'Death is the
great Leveller' (Dent, D143). Both feature prominently in chronicle plays;
the first, for instance, in Audley's bolstering speech to Prince Edward in
Edward III, H3v, and the second in the closing moments of Peele's *Edward
I*, 5.870. Typically, Hobs regards death's lack of social discrimination as the
quality of an 'honest man', unlike, for example, the author of *The Valiant
Welshman* (1612), who finds this same quality the attribute of a 'saucy knave',
B3v.
    86. *seldom . . . better*] also proverbial (Dent, B332).
    88. *Mother Whetstone's ale*] possibly an invented name, but I suspect an
oblique reference to the same in *Westward Ho*, 2.2.22. Whetstone is an incor-
rigible liar in Heywood and Brome's *The Late Lancashire Witches* (1634), who
claims that his mother was a witch. A bawdy joke could also be alluded
to; this is certainly the case with the song 'Mother Watkins' Ale', which
concerns the pregnancy of young girls. It aroused Chettle's indignation
(*Kind Hartes Dreame* (1592), C2r); the song can be found in Bodleian MS.
Rawlinson Poet. 185, and is printed in *Archiv für das Studium der Neueren
Sprachen und Literaturen*, 114 (1905), 346–7.
    89. *drive . . . tale*] perhaps 'banish the sadness my story has aroused';
cf. Pisanio's remedy for sea-sickness: 'a dram of this / Will drive away dis-
temper', *Cymbeline*, 3.4.192–3.
    93. *beshrew*] curse.

Hobs. I would I had not, condition she had all. But I have a
knave to my son. I remember him by you: even such an
unthrift as one of you two, that spends all on gay clothes   100
and new fashions, and no work will down with him, that
I fear he'll be hanged. God bless you from a better
fortune. Yet you wear such filthy breeks! Lord, were not
this a good fashion? Yes, and would save many a fair
penny.   105

Edward. Let that pass, and let us hear your song.

Hobs. Agreed, agreed. Come, sol, sol, sol, fa, fa, fa. Say,
Dudgeon!

>   [*Enter* DUDGEON *and another servant.*] *Here they sing*
>   *the threemen's song.*

>   *Agincourt, Agincourt, know ye not Agincourt?*
>   *Where the English slew and hurt*   110
>   *All the French foe-men;*
>   *With our guns and bills brown,*
>   *O, the French were beaten down,*
>   *Morris pikes and bowmen, etc.*

---

101. *no work . . . him*] he will settle to no occupation.
103. *breeks*] breeches.
109–14. Agincourt, Agincourt] An eleven-stanza ballad, with some variants in this first stanza, is reprinted as an appendix to Percy, II, 595. The
fourth stanza encapsulates the levelling fantasy this episode gestures towards:
'*English of every sort* / *High men and low men* / *Fought that day wondrous well,*
as / *All our old stories tell us* / *Thanks to our bowmen.*' The earliest 'extant' copy
is, on the dubious authority of Collier, said to be a black-letter publication
of the 1630s–60s, printed by Henry Harper. I can find no trace of it and, significantly, it does not appear amongst the numerous other literary celebrations which constitute the appendices to Sir Nicholas Harris Nicolas's
splendid *History of the Battle of Agincourt* (1832). Whatever its original
content, its appearance here clearly establishes a context against which the
action of Part Two will be defined.
112. bills brown] A foot soldier's hand weapon, with a blade. The form
varied; Drayton distinguishes the 'Browne Bill' from the pike and the spear
in *Barons Warres*, II, 37 (*Works*, II, 36).
114. Morris pikes] The weapon itself was a pike thought to be of
'Moorish' design. Munday has the juxtaposition of brown bills and morris
pikes in *Deliuery of 266 Christians by J. Reynard . . .* (1608), B1r. The last line
of the 'Percy' stanza has simply 'shot by our bowmen'.

Sellinger. Well sung, good fellows! I would the King heard ye.   115
Hobs. So would I, faith; I would strain a note for him. Come,
    take away,

[NELL, DUDGEON *and servant take the table out.*]

and let's to bed. Ye shall have clean sheets, Ned, but they
be coarse, good, strong hemp, of my daughter's own spin-
ning. And I tell thee, your chamber pot must be a fair   120
horn (a badge of our occupation), for we buy no bending
pewter, nor bending earth.
Edward. No matter, Hobs; we will not go to bed.
Hobs. What, then?
Edward. Even what thou wilt, for it is near day.   125
    Tanner, grammercies for our hearty cheer.
    If e'er it be thy chance to come to court,
    Enquire for me, Ned, the King's butler,
    Or Tom, of the King's chamber, my companion;
    And see what welcome we will give thee there.   130
Hobs. I have heard of courtiers have said as much as you, and
    when they have been tried, would not bid their friends
    drink.
Sellinger. We are none such. Let our horses be brought out,
    For we must away. And so, with thanks, farewell.   135

---

122. bending] *Q1–5*; breaking *Q6.*

116–21. *Come ... horn*] In the printed sources the King does not visit the
Tanner's house but cf. the MS 'Kinge and the Miller', in which the Miller's
wife promises King Henry: 'fresh straw I will lay vpon your bed so braue, /
good browne hempen sheetes likewise' (ll. 63–4).
   120–1. *Chamber ... horn*] Obscure. Hobs could be intending to utilize a
discarded animal horn from his trade, but is more probably referring to a
multi-purpose drinking horn made from leather; all manner of durable pots
and bottles were manufactured this way. On this whole passage, see Introduction, pp. 30, 35–6.
   121. *bending*] Again, obscure. The sense of pliable, having the capacity to
be moulded or bent into shape, is supported by examples in *OED*, but it
also seems that 'bending' could bear the pejorative sense of adulterated or
improperly prepared, when used of the leather trade (cf. Scene 11, l. 27
and commentary); a tanner was fined in the 1630s for 'seling of Bend^g leath'"
(C. P. Whiting (ed.), *The Book of the Tanners' Company, Durham, 1612–55*
(Surtees Society, 1945), 127). Q6's 'breaking' fails to clarify.
   122. *earth*] earthenware.

Hobs. Farewell to ye both. Commend me to the King, and
tell him I would have been glad to have seen his worship
here.   *Exit* [HOBS].
Edward. Come, Tom: for London, horse, and hence away.
                                                                Exeunt.

[Scene 15]

> *Enter the* VICE-ADMIRAL [MORTON] *and the* CAPTAIN
> OF THE ISLE OF WIGHT, *with* FALCONBRIDGE *bound,*
> *the* HEADSMAN *bearing the axe before him.*

Morton. Thomas Neville: yet hast thou gracious time
Of dear repentance. Now discharge thy conscience;
Lay open thine offences to the world,
That we may witness thou dost die a Christian.

0.1–2.] Since the stage direction fails to name the Vice-Admiral and since
he is not named in the dialogue until l. 5, the speech-prefix 'Mor' at l. 1
points to the author's MS as the printer's copy here; but the specification,
designation and characterization of Falconbridge's captors in this scene are
also indicative of the author's treatment of his source material. The chronicles all attribute—if rather vaguely—Falconbridge's capture to the efforts of
the King. Most mention Southampton as the location of the arrest and imply
that this was also the place of execution (Stow is the exception, asserting
that the Bastard was killed in Yorkshire; *Annals*, 698). None, however, specifies the individual officers involved—Stow does mention a 'Vice-admirall'
but not only suggests that Edward initially pardoned Falconbridge but
further that the King gave the *rebel* this appointment (*Annals* only, 698)—
nor do they mention the Isle of Wight; Sir Harry Morton, indeed, is an
invented name with no historical authority whatever, and no discernible
Elizabethan resonance. On the one hand, the omission of Edward's personal
contribution to the apprehension of the rebels deflects attention away from
the ferocity and avariciousness which the most caustic of the chroniclers
ascribed to the King's retribution: 'Such as were Rych were hangid by the
purs, and the othir that were nedy were hangid by the nekkis, By meane
whereof [the] Cuntre was gretly enpoverysshid and the kyngys coffyrs
somdele encreasyd' (*Great Chronicle*, 221). This displacement is consolidated
by the playwright's investing the military authorities with the philanthropic
intentions which will assume such importance in the ensuing scenes
concerning the civil authorities in the capital (ll. 109–11). On the other hand,
the dramatist has absorbed and reproduced an uneasy juxtaposition which
existed particularly in the printed sources: sandwiched between the account
of the successful defence of London from the insurgents and the deserved
punishment of the ringleaders are the inconclusive narratives of Henry
VI's death and the hesitant eulogies of his achievements. The confusion

Falconbridge. Why, Sir Harry Morton, have you arraigned,   5
    Condemned, and brought me to this place
    Of bloody execution, and now ask
    If I be guilty? Therein doth appear
    What justice you have used. Call you this law?
Captain. Thou dost mistake our meaning, Falconbridge.   10
    We do not ask as being ignorant
    Of thy transgression, but as urging thee
    To hearty sorrow for thy vile misdeeds,
    That heaven may take compassion on thy soul.
Falconbridge. How charitable you would seem to be.   15
    I fear anon you'll say it is for love
    You bind me thus, and bring me to the block;
    And that of mere affection you are moved
    To cut my head off. Cunning policy!
    Such butchers as yourselves do never want   20
    A colour to excuse your slaughterous minds.
Morton. We butcher thee? Canst thou deny thyself
    But thou hast been a pirate on the sea?
    Canst thou deny but with the communalty
    Of Kent and Essex thou didst rise in arms,   25
    And twice assault the city, London, where
    Thou twice didst take repulse? And since that time,
    Canst thou deny that being fled from thence
    Thou joinèdst in confederacy with France,
    And cam'st with them to burn Southampton here?   30
    Are these no faults, thou shouldst so much presume
    To clear thyself, and lay thy blood on us?
Falconbridge. Hear me, Sir Harry, since we must dispute.
Captain. Dispute, uncivil wretch? What needs dispute?
    Did not the Vice-Admiral here and I,   35
    Encount'ring with the navy of the French,

---

filters into this scene partly through the vagueness of the Messenger's information and Morton's evasive response to it (ll. 126–33), and partly through
Falconbridge's obduracy, and his insistence on the divine authority of
Henry's rule and the sacrilegious nature of Edward's usurpation. No
chronicle so much as hints at any of this; there, as in most of the play's earlier
scenes, the rebels were and remain a disorderly rout of desperate and traitorous outlaws.

  11. *as being*] as if we were.
  21. *colour*] pretext.

Attach thee in a ship of Normandy?
And wilt thou stand upon thine innocence?
Dispatch: thou art as rightfully condemned
As ever rebel was. And thou shalt die.   40
Falconbridge. I make no question of it: I must die.
But, let me tell you how I scorn your threats.
So little do I reckon of the name
Of ugly death, as, were he visible,
I'd wrestle with him for the victory,   45
And tug the slave, and tear him with my teeth,
But I would make him stoop to Falconbridge.
And for this life, this paltry, brittle life,
This blast of wind, which you have laboured so—
By juries, sessions and I know not what—   50
To rob me of, is of so vile repute
That, to attain that I might live mine age,
I would not give the value of a point.
You cannot be so cruel to afflict,
But I will be as forward to endure.   55
Morton. Go to, leave off these idle braves of thine,
And think upon thy soul's health, Falconbridge.
Captain. Submit, and ask forgiveness of thy king.
Falconbridge. What king?
Morton.   Why, Edward, of the house of York.
Falconbridge. He is no king of mine. He does usurp;   60
And if the destinies had giv'n me leave,
I would have told him so before this time,
And pulled the diadem from off his head.
Morton. Thou art a traitor! Stop thy traitor's mouth!
Falconbridge. I am no traitor: Lancaster is king.   65
If that be treason, to defend his right,
What is't for them that do imprison him?
If insurrection to advance his sceptre,
What fault is theirs that step into his throne?

---

37. *Attach*] arrest.
38. *stand*] insist.
52. *mine age*] normal span of life.
53. *point*] laces or cords for fastening, especially the hose or breeches to
the doublet.
55. *forward*] ready, eager.

O God, thou pouredst the balm upon his head: 70
Can that pure unction be wiped off again?
Thou once did crown him in his infancy:
Shall wicked men now, in his age depose him?
O, pardon me, if I expostulate
More than becomes a sinful man to do;   75
England, I fear thou wilt thy folly rue.
Captain. Thou triflest time, and dost but weary us
    With dilatory questions. Make an end.
Falconbridge. Indeed, the end of all kingdoms must end.
    Honour, and riches, all must end.   80
    And he that thinks he doth the most prevail,
    His head once laid, there resteth but a tale.
    Come, fellow, do thy office. What, me thinks
    Thou lookst as if thy heart were in thy hose.
    Pull up thy spirits! It will be quickly done: 85
    A blow or two at most will serve the turn.
Headsman. Forgive me, sir, your death.
Falconbridge. Forgive thee? Ay, and give thee too:
    Hold, there is some few crowns for thee to drink.
                             [He gives money.]
    Tush, weep not, man; give losers leave to plain.   90
    And yet, i'faith, my loss I count a gain.
    First, let me see: is thy axe sharp enough?
    I am indifferent. Well, a' God's name, to this gear.
Headsman. Come, and yield your head gently to the block.
Falconbridge. Gently, sayst thou? Thou wilt not use me so.   95
    But all is one for that. What strength hast thou
    Throughout the whole proportion of thy limbs,
    Revoke it all into thy manly arms;

70–3. *God . . . him?*] Cf. *Richard II*: 'Not all the water in the rough rude
sea / Can wash the balm off from an annointed king; / The breath of worldly
men cannot depose / The deputy elected by the Lord' (3.2.34–7).
   71. *unction*] the oil of consecration.
   78. *dilatory*] delaying; a dilatory plea was a quasi-technical term for inter-
rupting the legal process.
   82. *there . . . tale*] There remains only his story.
   90. *plain*] complain.
   93. *to . . . gear*] 'Let's get on with the business'.
   98. *Revoke*] unusual use of the word in that all *OED* citations contain the
sense of calling something back; here the word simply means 'summon'.

And spare me not: I am a gentleman,
A Neville, and a Falconbridge beside.   100
Then, do thy work. Thou mayst get credit by it;
For if thou dost not, I must tell thee plain,
I shall be passing angry when 'tis done.
Headsman. I warrant you, sir, none in the land shall do it
    better.
Falconbridge. Why now thou pleasest me. England, farewell.   105
And old Plantagenet, if thou survive,
Think on my love, although it did not thrive.

                    He is led forth.

Morton. As for his head, it shall be sent with speed
To London, and the promisèd reward
Allotted for the apprehending him   110
Be given unto the poor of Southampton here.
How say you, captain? Are you so content?
Captain. With all my heart. But I do marvel much
We hear not of the messenger we sent
To give the King intelligence of this.   115
Morton. Take truce with your surmises; here he comes.

                    Enter a MESSENGER.

Fellow, it seems that thou art slow of gait,
Or very negligent in our affairs.
What says King Edward to our service done?
Messenger. To answer you directly and as briefly: 120
I spoke not with him. For, when I was come
To Drayton Basset, where they said he was,
'Twas told me there that e'en the night before,
His highness in all haste was rid towards London.
The occasion: Henry's death within the Tower—   125
Of which the people are in sundry tales,
Some thinking he was murdered, some again
Supporting that he died a natural death.
Morton. Well, how so e'er, that concerns not us.
We have to do with no man's death, but his   130

107.1. led forth] taken away.
116. *take truce with*] Make peace with, cease worrying about; cf. *King John*, 3.1.17.

That for his treason here hath lost his head.
Come, let us give direction as before,
And afterward make back unto the shore.   *Exeunt.*

[Scene 16]

Enter the LORD MAYOR *in his scarlet gown, with a gilded*
rapier by his side.

Mayor. Ay, marry, Crosby, this befits thee well.
But some will marvel that with a scarlet gown
I wear a gilded rapier by my side.
Why, let them know I was knighted in the field
For my good service to my lord, the King;   5
And therefore I may wear it lawfully
In court, in city or at any royal banquet.
But soft, John Crosby, thou forgetst thyself
And dost not mind thy birth and parentage:
Where thou wast born, and whence thou art derived.   10
I do not shame to say the Hospital
Of London was my chiefest fost'ring place.

0.1.] The King's violation of the Lord Mayor's hospitality is an important
invention of the dramatist. If he was prompted to include a banquet scene
by the chronicles, he chose to reverse the relationship between host and guest
and to emphasize division rather than unity; Fabyan, for instance, writes of
a pastoral feast of thanksgiving at which the King magnificently entertained
the Mayor and alderman as a reward for their loyalty and the customs money
he farmed from them (512). That hospitality between the court and the City
continued to be of symbolic significance to Londoners is clear from Anthony
Munday's additions to Stow's *Survey*: see in particular his enraptured
account of the feast in 1617 at which the Mayor and aldermen entertained
leading members of the Privy Council including Sir Francis Bacon and
Archbishop Abbot; *The Survay of London* (1618 edition), Y2r.
    3–6. *gilded . . . lawfully*] See Introduction, pp. 49–50.
    9. *mind*] remember.
    11–12. *Hospital . . . London*] In neither the 1470s nor the 1590s was there
actually a hospital so called; the context suggests that Crosby is referring to
St Bartholomew's, a large establishment offering relief to the poor which was
less than a quarter of a mile from Cow Cross (l. 14). It was still functioning
on behalf of 'poore fatherless children' in Elizabethan times, and was 'furnished at the charges of the Cittizens' (*Survey*, II, 25).

There did I learn that near unto a cross,
Commonly called Cow Cross, near Islington,
An honest citizen did chance to find me.   15
A poor shoemaker by trade he was,
And doubting of my Christendom or no,
Called me according to the place he found me:
John Crosby, finding me so by a cross.
The Masters of the Hospital at further years   20
Bound me apprentice to the Grocers' trade,
Wherein God pleased to bless my poor endeavours,
That, by his blessings, I am come to this.
The man that found me I have well requited,
And to the Hospital, my fost'ring place,   25
An hundred pound a year I give, for ever.
Likewise, in memory of me, John Crosby,
In Bishopsgate Street a poor house have I built,
And, as my name, have called it Crosby House;
And when as God shall take me from this life,   30
In little St Helen's will I be buried.
All this declares I boast not of my birth,
But, found on earth, I must return to earth.
But, God for his pity, I forget myself!
The King, my sovereign lord, will come anon,   35

13–19. *near . . . cross*] Stow (*Survey*, I,173) contemptuously dismisses this etymology as a mere 'fable', even offering Crosby a putative father or grand-father from records dating 1406.

14. *Cow Cross*] Cow Cross Lane connected Turnmill Street and St John Street and was 'near Islington', but actually in the district of Clerkenwell.

17. *doubting . . . Christendom*] either 'doubting whether I had been bap-tized or not', or 'uncertain of my true (Christian) name'. Nashe uses the word in both senses, in *Have With You to Saffron-Walden* (1596), and in *Lenten Stuffe* (1599); *Works*, III, 71, 161.

25–6. *to . . . ever*] Crosby was certainly a generous benefactor to several institutions—Stow documents donations to St Helen's Church, to 'the wirkes of the newe towre of stone at the sowthe ende of London bridge', and to St Peter's Library in Cornhill (*Survey*, I, 173; II, 278; I, 194)—but this munificence is an invention of the playwright.

28–31. *In . . . buried*] Crosby Place was in no sense a 'poor' house; some-time home to Sir Thomas More and Sir Walter Ralegh, it was still a formi-dable building in the 1590s, standing opposite another famous institution founded by a civic dignitary celebrated by Heywood, Gresham College. Stow (*Survey*, I, 172) calls it 'verie large and beautifull'; he also records Crosby's burial in St Helen's Church which was right next to Crosby Place.

And nothing is as yet in readiness.
Where are ye, cousin Shore? Nay, where is Mistress Shore?
O, I am sorry that she stays so long;
See what it is to be a widower,
And lack a Lady Mayoress in such need!   40

    Enter MASTER SHORE *and* MISTRESS SHORE.

O, are ye come? Welcome, good cousin Shore.
But you indeed are welcome, gentle niece:
Needs must you be our Lady Mayoress now,
And help us, or else we are shamed for ever.
Good cousin, still thus am I bold with you.   45
Shore. With all my heart, my lord, and thank ye too
    That you do please to use our homely help.
Mayor. Why, see how neatly she bestirs herself,
    And in good sooth makes huswifery to shine.
    Ah, had my Lady Mayoress lived to see   50
    Fair Mistress Shore thus beautify her house,
    She would have been not little proud thereof.
Jane. Well, my Lord Mayor, I thank you for that flout;
    But let his highness now come when he please,
    All things are in a perfect readiness.   55

    They [servants] bring forth a table, and serve
        in the banquet.

Mayor. The more am I beholding, niece, to you,
    That take such pains to save our credit now.
    My servants are so slack, his majesty
    Might have been here before we were prepared—
    But peace, here comes his highness!   60

    The trumpets sound, and enters KING EDWARD,
      HOWARD, SELLINGER *and the train.*

Edward. Now my Lord Mayor, have we not kept our word?
    Because we could not stay to dine with you
    At our departure hence, we promised,

---

53. *flout*] Jane is presumably gently mocking the extravagance of Crosby's
praise, but 'flout' is odd in this context; the word invariably connoted a
serious insult in the period, and Heywood's usage elsewhere is no exception;
see, for example, *The Captives*, ll. 960, 1223.

First food we tasted at our back return
Should be with you; still yielding hearty thanks   65
To you, and all our London citizens,
For the great service which you did perform
Against that bold-faced rebel, Falconbridge.
Mayor. My gracious lord, what then we did
    We did account no more than was our duty,   70
    Thereto obliged by true subjects' zeal;
    And may he never live that not defends
    The honour of his king and country.
    Next, thank I God, it likes your majesty
    To bless my poor roof with your royal presence;   75
    To me could come no greater happiness.
Edward. Thanks, good Lord Mayor. But where's my lady
        mayoress?
    I hope that she will bid us welcome too.
Mayor. She would, my liege, and with no little joy,
    Had she but lived to see this blessèd day;   80
    But in her stead this gentlewoman here,
    My cousin's wife, that office will supply.
    How say you Mistress Shore?
Edward. How? Mistress Shore? What, not his wife
    That did refuse his knighthood at our hand?   85
Mayor. The very same, my lord, and here he is.
Edward. What, Master Shore? We are your debtor still,
    But by God's grace, intend not so to die.
    And, gentlewoman, now before your face
    I must condemn him of discourtesy—   90
    Yea, and of great wrong that he hath offered you;
    For you had been a lady but for him.
    He was in fault; trust me, he was to blame
    To hinder virtue of her due by right.
Jane. My gracious lord, my poor and humble thoughts   95
    Ne'er had an eye to such unworthiness;
    And though some hold it as a maxim
    That women's minds by nature do aspire,

77–8. Thanks . . . too.] *Qq print as prose.*

90–4. *I . . . right*] For the relationship between the play's handling of
Edward's attempt on Jane and Drayton's treatment in *Englands Heroicall
Epistles*, see Introduction, pp. 45–7.

Yet how both God and Master Shore I thank
For my continuance in this humble state—   100
And likewise how I love your majesty
For gracious sufferance that it may be so—
Heaven bear true record of my inward soul.
Now it remains, on my Lord Mayor's behalf,
I do such duty as becometh me,   105
To bid your highness welcome to his house:
Were welcome's virtue powerful in my word,
The King of England should not doubt thereof.
Edward. Nor do I, Mistress Shore. Now, my Lord Mayor,
Edward dare boldly swear that he is welcome;   110
You spake the word well—very well, i' faith—
But Mistress Shore, her tongue hath gilded it.
Tell me, cousin Howard, and Tom Sellinger,
Had ever citizen so fair a wife?
Howard. Of flesh and blood I never did behold   115
A woman every way so absolute.
Sellinger. Nor I, my liege. Were Sellinger a king,
He could afford Shore's wife to be a queen.
Edward. Why, how now Tom? [*Aside*] Nay, rather how now
    Ned?
What change is this? Proud, saucy, roving eye,   120
What whisperst in my brain? That she is fair?
I know it, I see it. Fairer than my queen?
Wilt thou maintain it? What, and thou, traitor heart,
Wouldst thou shake hands in this conspiracy?
Down, rebel! Back, base treacherous conceit,   125
I will not credit thee. My Bess is fair,
And Shore's wife but a blowze compared to her.
—Come, let us sit. Here will I take my place.
And, my Lord Mayor, fill me a bowl of wine,

---

116. *absolute*] consummate, perfect.

118. *afford*] Sinisterly ambiguous; 'afford' could mean 'allow, grant' (*OED* 5), but also 'be rich enough to procure' (*OED* 3).

123. *maintain*] Again, alternative meanings are evoked; either 'persevere with' (*OED* 1), or 'justify one's position' (in a quasi legal or even a pugilistic sense, *OED* 14).

127. *blowze*] Normally glossed as 'ruddy faced wench' (as in Arden and Oxford commentaries on *Titus Andronicus*, 4.2.72), but *OED*'s examples suggest that low social rank determined usage as much as complexion.

That I may drink to your elected Mayoress.   130
And Master Shore, tell me how you like this:
My Lord Mayor makes your wife his Lady Mayoress?
Shore. So well, my lord, as better cannot be:
All in the honour of your majesty.

> The LORD MAYOR *brings a bowl of wine, and humbly,*
> *on his knees, offers it to the King.*

Edward. Nay, drink to us, Lord Mayor! We'll have it so.   135
Go to, I say; you are our taster now!
Drink, then, and we will pledge ye.
Mayor. All health and happiness to my sovereign. *He drinks.*
Edward. Fill full our cup. And Lady Mayoress,
This full carouse we mean to drink to you;   140
And you must pledge us, but yet no more
Than you shall please to answer us withal.

> He drinks, and the trumpets sound; then wine is brought
> to her, and she offers to drink.

Nay, you must drink to somebody. Yea, Tom,
To thee? Well, sirrah, see you do her right,
For Edward would. [*Aside*] O would to God he might!   145
Yet, idle eye, wilt thou be gadding still?
Keep home, keep home, for fear of further ill.

> *Enter a* MESSENGER *with letters.*

How now? Letters to us? From whom?
Messenger. My liege, this from the Duke of Burgundy,
And this from the Constable of France.   150
Edward. What news from them?

> *He opens the letter and reads.*

143–4.] *Qq line*: thee? / Well.

---

135. *to us*] before us.

141–2. *but . . . withal*] More innuendo; the phrase could mean 'no more
than you are willing to pay back in kind', i.e. drink the same toast, but 'withal'
could also suggest 'in addition' (this is how Heywood customarily deploys
the word, as in *The Captives*, ll. 887, 2072); see also the last speech of Part
One of the play. The comma at the end of 141, common to all Qs, seriously
obscures the sense of the lines.

> To claim our right in France?
And they will aid us. Yea, will ye so?
But other aid must aid us ere we go:

He seems to read the letters, but glances on MISTRESS
SHORE *in his reading.*

A woman's aid, that hath more power than France
To crown us, or to kill us with mischance.   155
If chaste resolve be to such beauty tied,
Sue how thou canst, thou wilt be still denied.
Her husband hath deserved well of thee;
Tut, love makes no respect where e'er it be.
Thou wrongst thy queen; every enforcèd ill   160
Must be endured where beauty seeks to kill.
Thou seemst to read, only to blind their eyes
Who, knowing it, thy folly would despise.

He starts from the table.

Thanks for my cheer, Lord Mayor. I am not well.
I know not how to take these news—this fit, I mean,   165
That hath bereft me of all reason clean.
Mayor. God shield my sovereign.
Edward. Nay, nothing. I shall be well anon.
Jane. May it please your highness sit.
Edward. [*Aside*] Ay, fain with thee.—Nay, we must needs be
    gone.   170
Cousin Howard, convey these letters to our Council,
And bid them give us their advice of them.
Thanks for my cheer, Lord Mayor; farewell to you.
And farewell Mistress Shore—Lady Mayoress, I should
    say;
'Tis you have caused our parting at this time.   175
Farewell, Master Shore; farewell to all;
We'll meet once more to make amends for this.

Exeunt KING, HOWARD *and* SELLINGER.

Mayor. O God! Here to be ill?
My house to cause my sovereign's discontent?
Cousin Shore, I had rather spent.   180

---

180. *spent*] died.

Shore. Content yourself, my lord. Kings have their humours.
       The letters did contain somewhat, no doubt,
       That did displease him.
Jane.   So, my lord, think I,
       But by God's help he will be well again.
Mayor. I hope so too. Well, cousin, for your pains   185
       I can but thank ye; chiefly you, fair niece.
       At night I pray ye both come sup with me.
       How say ye? Will ye?
Shore.   Yes, my lord, we will.
       So, for this time, we humbly take our leave.
                              Exeunt SHORE *and his wife.*
Mayor. O, how the sudden sickness of my liege   190
       Afflicts my soul with many passions!
       His highness did intend to be right merry;
       And God, he knows how it would glad my soul
       If I had seen his highness satisfied
       With the poor entertainment of his Mayor—   195
       His humble vassal, whose lands, whose life and all
       Are, and in duty must be always his.
       Well, God I trust will bless his grace's health,
       And quickly ease him of his sudden fit.
       Take away, there, ho!
                         [*Servants carry out the banquet.*]
                         Rid this place;   200
       And God of heaven bless my sovereign's grace.   *Exit.*

[Scene 17]

       Enter two APPRENTICES, *preparing the goldsmith's*
                        shop with plate.

1 Apprentice. Sirrah Jack, come, set out.
2 Apprentice. You are the elder 'prentice; I pray you do it, lest
       my mistress talk with you when she comes down. What
       is it a' clock?
1 Apprentice. Six, by All Hallows.   5

---

3. *talk with*] scold.
5. *All Hallows*] parish church at the eastern end of Lombard Street.

2 Apprentice. Lying and stealing will bring ye to the gallows.
   Is here all the plate?
1 Apprentice. Ay, that must serve today. Where is the weights
   and balance?
2 Apprentice. All ready. Hark, my mistress comes.   10

Exit 1 APPRENTICE.

Enter MISTRESS SHORE with her work in her hand.

Jane. Sir boy, while I attend the shop myself,
   See if the workman have dispatched the cup.
   How many ounces weighs it?
2 Apprentice. Twenty, forsooth.
Jane. What said the gentleman to the fashion?   15
2 Apprentice. He told my master; I was not within.
Jane. Go sir, make haste. Your master is in Cheapside;
   Take heed, ye were best, your loit'ring be not spied.

The boy departs, and she sits sewing in her shop.
Enter the KING, disguised.

Edward. Well fare a case, to put a king in yet.
   Good Mistress Shore, this does your love procure.   20
   This shape is secret, and I hope 'tis sure;
   The watermen, that daily use the court
   And see me often, knew me not in this.
   At Lion Quay I landed in their view,
   Yet none of them took knowledge of the King.   25

   10.01. work] needlework.
   17. *Cheapside*] This street had housed 'Goldsmiths' Row' for centuries; it is discussed in Stow (*Survey*, I, 345), marvelled at by the German traveller Paul Hentzner (*Travels in England During the Reign of Queen Elizabeth* (1889 edition), 44), and ridiculed in, amongst other plays, Marston's *The Malcontent*, Induction, ll. 105–10.
   19. *case*] The ostensible meaning is 'garb' (the word invariably conveying some sense of disguise, as in Shakespeare's *The Lover's Complaint*, 116). But the phrase as a whole is proleptically ironic, since 'case' was also frequently employed as slang for the female genitals; see, for example, the extended punning in Dekker's *Match Me in London*, 2.4.112, 5.2.101.
   21. *shape*] costume, disguise.
   sure] safe, secure.
   24. *Lion Quay*] linked the river to Thames Street in Billingsgate.

If any gallant strive to have the wall,
I'll yield it gently. Soft. Here I must turn:
Here's Lombard Street, and here's the Pelican;
And there's the phoenix in the pelican's nest.
O, rare perfection of rich Nature's work!   30
Bright twinkling spark of precious diamond,
Of greater value than all India.
Were there no sun, by whose kind, lovely heat
The earth brings forth those stones we hold of prize,
Her radiant eyes, dejected to the ground,   35
Would turn each pebble to a diamond.
Gaze, greedy eyes, and be not satisfied
Till you find rest, where heart's desire doth bide.
Jane. What would you buy, sir, that you look on here?

---

26. *If . . . wall*] Taking the wall of a person was an aggressive assertion of
superiority, in which a gallant would insist on walking nearest the wall and
thus furthest from the stinking gutters; Nashe describes an Italian braggart
doing this to Sidney in *Have With You to Saffron-Walden, Works*, III, 76–7.

28. *Pelican*] Probably a tavern; a sign of the pelican still hangs in Lombard
Street. This is a suggestive detail not found in other treatments of the story
(Deloney's ballad (c.1593), for instance, gives the 'Flower-de-luce' as Jane's
unmarried quarters (302)—and see Part Two, Scene 13, ll. 84–94—but no
other writer offers further information). The pelican was a powerful symbol
which could be read in two diametrically opposed ways. It could represent
the very essence of self-sacrifice in the image of the parent which opens its
own breast to sustain its offspring with life-giving blood. In this sense the
bird became synonymous with Christian (and Christ-like) charity, and the
myth appears thus in Dekker's *2 Honest Whore* (1.2.173–6), and in his *Foure
Birds of Noahs Arke* (1609), *passim*; see also Munday's *Chrysanaleia: The
Golden Fishing* (1616), B2r, and Webster's *Monuments of Honor* (1624), *Works*,
III, 324. On the other hand, the birds were proverbial for their patricidal
cruelty (hence Goneril and Regan are Lear's 'pelican daughters', 3.4.70) and
selfishness; Middleton rather incoherently juxtaposed both views in *The
Wisdom of Solomon Paraphrased* (1597); *Works*, VIII, 263, 293.

29. *phoenix*] The phoenix was the type of constant love and the only one
of her kind; in Robert Chester's collection *Loves Martyr* (1601) the pelican
became the privileged witness of the Phoenix's self-immolation, S2r–S3r.

31. *diamond*] Cf. Drayton's 'Edward the Fourth to Mistres Shore', in
which the King writes that she 'Is like an un-cut Diamond in Lead, / Ere it
be set in some high-prized Ring' (ll. 28–9).

35–6. *Her . . . diamond*] Again, cf. Drayton's l. 44: 'Whose sparkling radi-
ance shadowed but thine eye' (1597–1600 texts, altered in the later text
printed by Hebel in *Works*).

dejected to] bent towards; unusual usage, but cf. Heywood's *1 If You Know
Not Me*, B4v.

Edward. Your fairest jewel, be it not too dear.   40
　　First, how this sapphire, mistress, that you wear?
Jane. Sir, it is right, that will I warrant ye;
　　No jeweller in London shows a better.
Edward. No, nor the like. You praise it passing well.
Jane. Do I? No, if some lapidary had the stone,   45
　　More would not buy it than I can demand.
　　'Tis as well set, I think, as ere ye saw.
Edward. 'Tis set, indeed, upon the fairest hand
　　That e'er I saw.
Jane.　　　　　You are disposed to jest.
　　But, for the value, his majesty might wear it.   50
Edward. Might he, i' faith?
Jane.　　　　　Sir, 'tis the ring I mean.
Edward. I meant the hand.
Jane.　　　　　You are a merry man.
　　I see you come to cheap, and not to buy.
Edward. Yet he that offers fairer than I'll do
　　Shall hardly find a partner in his bargain.   55
Jane. Perhaps of buying things of so small value?
Edward. Rather because no wealth can purchase it.
Jane. He were too fond, that would so highly prize
　　The thing which once was giv'n away for love.
Edward. His hap was good that came so easily by it.   60

45–50. Do . . . it] *Qq print as prose.*　54–5. Yet . . . bargain] *Q6; Q1–5 print
as prose.*

41. *sapphire*] Drayton's king compares Mistress Shore to a sapphire, l. 48.
　42. *right*] the genuine article. Relatively uncommon usage but 'right' in
the sense of 'not counterfeit' also occurs in an exchange about a jewel in
Henry VIII, 5.2.137.
　45–6. *if . . . demand*] Awkward construction but the sense seems to be 'if
the jewel were being offered by a lapidary (an expert in stones) he would
extract a greater price than I can'.
　50. *wear*] The King may be choosing to invest 'wear' with the quasi-
bawdy sense it has in the proverbial phrase 'Win it and wear it' (Dent, W408);
'it' is usually a woman whose favours the 'victor' flourishes as his own
possession.
　53. *cheap*] haggle, bargain.
　57. *no . . . it*] Cf. Drayton: 'That I might not for Love or Money buy it',
l. 42.
　58. *fond*] foolish.
　60. *hap*] fortune.
　easily] As at l. 67, the word is pronounced with two syllables.

Jane. The gift so small, that asked, who could deny it?
Edward. O, she gave more, that such a gift then gave,
    Than earth e'er had, or world shall ever have.
Jane. His hap is ill, should it be as you say,
    That having given him what you rate so high,   65
    And yet is still the poorer by the match.
Edward. That easily proves he doth not know the worth.
Jane. Yet having had the use of it so long,
    It rather proves you over-rate the thing,
    He being a chapman—as it seems you are.   70
Edward. Indeed, none should adventure on the thing
    That's to be purchased only by a king.
Jane. If kings love that which no man else respects,
    It may be so; else do I see small reason
    A king should take delight in such coarse stuff.   75
Edward. Lives there a king that would not give his crown
    To purchase such a kingdom of content?
Jane. In my conceit, right well you ask that question.
    The world, I think, contains not such fond king.
Edward. Why, Mistress Shore, I am the man will do it.   80
Jane. It's proudly spoke, although I not believe it;
    Were he King Edward that should offer it.
Edward. But shall I have it?
Jane. Upon what acquaintance?
Edward. Why, since I saw thee last.   85
Jane. Where was that?
Edward. At the Lord Mayor's, in the presence of the King.
Jane. I have forgotten that I saw you there,
    For there were many that I took small note of.
Edward. Of me you did, and we had some discourse.   90
Jane. You are deceived, sir. I had then no time,
    For my attendance on his majesty.

---

67. *That . . . worth*] Drayton's king suggests the same of Jane's husband, 'Who having all, yet knowes not what is had', l. 20.

70. *chapman*] Catch-all term for anyone involved in trade or barter; it could apply to both shopkeepers and customers, and Jane may be alluding to both here.

73. *respects*] values.

76–7. *Lives . . . content*] Cf. Drayton: 'Would not my Treasure serve, my Crowne should goe, / If any Jewell could be prized so!', ll. 45–6.

92. *For*] because of.

Edward. I'll 'gage my hand unto your hand of that;
Look well upon me.

He discovers himself.

Jane. Now I beseech you, let this strange disguise   95
Excuse my boldness to your majesty.   *She kneels.*
Whatever we possess is all your highness',
Only mine honour, which I cannot grant.
Edward. Only thy love, bright angel, Edward craves,
For which I thus adventured to see thee.   100

Enter MASTER SHORE.

Jane. But here comes one to whom I only gave it,
And he I doubt will say you shall not have it.
Edward. [*Aside*] Am I so soon cut off? O spite!—
How say ye, mistress? Will ye take my offer?
Jane. Indeed I cannot, sir, afford it so.   105
Edward. You'll not be offered fairlier, I believe.
Jane. Indeed, you offer like a gentleman,
But yet the jewel will not so be left.
Shore. Sir, if you bid not too much under-foot,
I'll drive the bargain 'twixt you and my wife.   110
Edward. Aside. Alas, good Shore, myself dare answer 'No';
[*To him*] Nothing can make thee such a jewel forgo.
She say'th you shall be too much loser by it.
Shore. See in the Row, then, if you can speed better.
Edward. See many worlds arow, affords not like.   115

[*Exit* EDWARD.]

As he goes forth, SHORE *looks earnestly, and perceives it is
the King, whereat he seemeth greatly discontented.*

---

93. *of*] 'to prove'.

98. *Only*] Means 'except' in this line, 'only' in the next, and 'exclusively'
in l. 101.

109. *under-foot*] Under (the real) value. Rather unusual adverbial use—
OED (3) cites *The Death of Usurie* (1594) as its earliest example—although
Nashe accused Harvey of being 'vnder-foot' in his commendation of Sidney,
III, 49.

113. *loser*] Both Q's spelling—'looser'—and the lack of the preposition
'the' are anticipated in *2 Henry IV*, Q1, G3r (4.2.91).

114. *Row*] Goldsmiths' Row.

115. *arow*] one after another.

Jane. Why lookst thou, Mat? Knowst thou the gentleman?
Alas, what ails thee that thou lookst so pale?
What cheer, sweetheart? Alas, where hast thou been?
Shore. Nay, nothing, Jane. Know you the gentleman?
Jane. Not I, sweetheart. Alas, why do you ask?   120
Is he thine enemy?
Shore.   I cannot tell.
What, came he here to cheapen at our shop?
Jane. This jewel, love.
Shore. Well, I pray God he came for nothing else.
Jane. Why, who is it? I do suspect him, Shore,   125
That you demand thus doubtfully of me.
Shore. Ah, Jane, it is the King.
Jane. The King? What then? Is it for that thou sighst?
Were he a thousand kings, thou hast no cause
To fear his presence, or suspect my love.   130
Shore. I know I have not. See, he comes again.

The KING *enters again, muffled in his cloak.*

Edward. [*Aside*] Still my hind'rer there? Be patient, heart;
Some fitter season must assuage the smart.—
What, will ye take that, mistress, which I offered ye?
I come again, sir, as one willing to buy.   135
Jane. Indeed I cannot sir. I pray ye
Deal with my husband; hear what he will say.
Shore. I'll sell it worth your money. If you please,
I pray ye come near, sir.
Edward. Aside. I am too near already, thou so near.—   140

140. *Aside*] MS *annotation to Dyce (1) copy of Q3; not in Qq.*

---

122. *cheapen*] trade, bargain for.
126. *doubtfully*] suspiciously; Q2's 'doubtedly' means the same.
137. *Deal*] Both here and six lines later the usage is ironic; 'deal' could
mean simply 'negotiate' but it was also beginning to acquire more ominous
connotations. It is, for instance, the key word in Bacon's essay 'Of Negoti-
ating' (1597), where the context insistently suggests furtive activity.
Heywood, moreover, plays extensively with the sexual possibilities of the
word in *A Woman Killed With Kindness*, 8.167–93; cf. also the song in his *The
Rape of Lucrece*: 'Some love the rough, and some th'smooth, / Some great, and
others small things, / But your lecherous* Englishman: / *Hee loves to deale in all
things*' (1767–70). (The same song with slight variants also appears in the
fifth act of his *A Challenge for Beauty* (c.1635).) See also my commentary to
Marlowe's *Edward II* (Oxford, 1994), Scene 16, 37–40.

Nay, nay, she knows what I did offer her,
And, in good sadness, I can give no more.
So, fare ye well, sir. I will not deal with you.   *Exit.*
Jane. You are deceived, sweetheart; 'tis not the King.
Think you he would adventure thus, alone?   145
Shore. I do assure thee, Jane, it is the King.
O God, 'twixt the extremes of love and fear,
In what a shivering ague sits my soul!
Keep we our treasure secret, yet so fond
As set so rich a beauty as this is   150
In the wide view of every gazer's eye?
O traitor, beauty! O deceitful good,
That dost conspire against thyself and love;
No sooner got, but wished again of others;
In thine own self, injurious to thyself.   155
O rich, poor portion, thou good, evil thing:
How many joyful woes still dost thou bring.
Jane. I pray thee come, sweet love, and sit by me.
No king that's under heaven I love like thee.   *Exeunt.*

[Scene 18]

> *Enter* SIR HUMPHREY BOWES *and* MASTER ASTON,
> *being two Justices,* HARRY GRUDGEN, ROBERT
> GOODFELLOW, [MASTER HADLAND,] *and*
> JOHN HOBS *the tanner.*

Bowes. Neighbours and friends, the cause that you are called
Concerns the King's most excellent majesty,
Whose right, you know, by his progenitors
Unto the crown and sovereignty of France

---

159. *Exeunt.*] *exit. Qq.*

142. *in good sadness*] seriously.
150. *As set*] Modern idiom requires the preposition 'to' between these words.
152–7. *beauty . . . bring*] These lines offer a different perspective on an idea prominent in Drayton's poem; cf. particularly, ll. 9–10, 145–6.
154. *wished . . . of*] desired immediately by.

Is wrongfully detainèd by the French;   5
Which, to revenge and royally regain,
His highness means to put himself in arms,
And in his princely person to conduct
His warlike troops against the enemy.
But, for his coffers are unfurnishèd   10
Through civil discord and intestine war—
Whose bleeding scars our eyes may yet behold—
He prays his faithful loving subjects' help
To further this, his just, great enterprise.

Hobs. So, the feck and meaning whereby, as it were, of all your   15
long purgation, Sir Humphrey, is no more in some
respect, but the King wants money, and would have some
of his commenty.

Bowes. Tanner, you rightly understand the matter.

Aston. Note this withal: where his dread majesty,   20
Our lawful sovereign, and most royal King,
Might have exacted or imposed a tax,
Or borrowed greater sums than we can spare—
For all we have is at his dread command—

---

5. *detainèd*] unusual deployment of the word when it refers specifically to keeping a person from his right. *OED* (2b) offers only a single example (from Stubbes's *The Anatomie of Abuses*, 1583) but cf. *The Captives*: 'where my right is deteind mee by ffayre / meanes. I will have it by fforce', ll. 2012–13. Holinshed's wording is the source; he writes of Edward's right which the French king 'wrongfullie deteined from him', III, 330.

10. *for*] because.

11. *intestine*] internal; the word was originally used in this context, relating particularly to the body politic; cf. *1 Henry IV*, 1.1.12.

15. *feck*] substance.

16. *purgation*] It is probable that an audience is supposed to register another mispronunciation here, either a very inaccurate attempt at 'oration', or a rather closer (and more appropriate) attempt at 'prorogation', the act of prolongation or protraction. 'Purgation' itself, however, is, in the legal sense, even more apt: 'the action of clearing oneself of an accusation or suspicion of crime or guilt' (*OED* 4).

18. *commenty*] commonality.

22–6. *tax . . . benevolence*] The dramatist is adhering closely to both the tone and vocabulary of Holinshed's account here, and in so doing draws the important distinction between the taxes or subsidies authorized by Parliament and the 'voluntary' financing of the Crown by willing subjects. He is also chronologically accurate in a way that some contemporary dramatists and historians conspicuously and contentiously were not. The Attorney General Coke, for instance, pounced on the anachronistic appearance of

He doth not so; but mildly doth entreat   25
Our kind benevolence: what we will give,
With willing minds, towards this mighty charge.

Enter LORD HOWARD.

Which to receive, his noble counsellor
And kinsman, the Lord Howard, here is come.
Howard. Now, good Sir Humphrey Bowes, and Master Aston,   30
Have ye declared the King's most gracious pleasure?
Bowes. We have, my lord.
Howard.   His highness will not force,
As loan or tribute, but will take your gift
In grateful part, and recompense your love.
Bowes. To show my love, though money now be scarce,   35
A hundred pound I'll give his majesty.
Howard. 'Tis well, Sir Humphrey.
Aston.   I, a hundred marks.
Howard. Thanks, Master Aston; you both show your love.
Now ask your neighbours what they will bestow.
Hadland. O good Sir Humphrey, do not rack my purse.   40
You know my state; I lately sold my land.
Aston. Then you have money; let the King have part.
Hobs. Ay, do, Master Hadland, do. They say you sold a foul
deal of dirty land for fair gold and silver. Let the King

'benevolences' in Sir John Hayward's *The Life and Raigne of King Henrie IIII* (1599; ed. Manning, 23, 108), a historical error purposefully anticipated several times on the London stage; see *Jack Straw* (ll. 188–93), *Woodstock* (1591–95, *passim*) and *Richard II* (1595, 2.1.249–50). The distinction was still a sensitive one; in the acrimonious debate on supply in the 1593 Parliament Cecil justified the granting of a triple subsidy on the grounds that Elizabeth would 'never accept any thing that is given her unwillingly of her subjects', and reminded the House that she had once 'refused a benevolence offered her, because she had no need of it, and would not charge her people'; Tawney, Power, *Tudor Economic Documents* (London, 1924), II, 242. Many Elizabethan Londoners were also probably familiar with the word in a more personal way; 'benevolences' was invariably the term used to describe the money collected from the wealthier citizens in the increasingly desperate struggle to relieve the poor, particularly in the plague years 1592–94, and during the serious dearths of 1595–97; see Archer, 198–203.

27.01. *HOWARD*] Howard was treasurer of Edward's royal household from 1467 to 1471, but not a 'kinsman'.

37. *marks*] A mark's value was two-thirds of a pound.

have some now, while you have it, for if ye be forborne a   45
while, all will be spent; for he that cannot keep land that
lies fast will have much ado to hold money. It's slippery
ware, 'tis melting ware, 'tis melting ware.

Howard. Grammercy, tanner.

Bowes. [*to Hadland*]   Say, what shall we have?

Hadland. My forty shillings.

Aston.   Robert Goodfellow,   50
I know you will be liberal to the King.

Goodfellow. O Master Aston, be content, I pray ye.
You know my charge: my household very great,
And my housekeeping holds me very bare.
Threescore uprising, and down-lying, sir,   55
Spends no small store of victuals in a year;
Two brace of greyhounds, twenty couple of hounds,
And then my jades, devour a deal of corn;
My Christmas cost, and then my friends that come,
Amounts to charge: I am Robin Goodfellow,   60
That welcomes all and keeps a frolic house.
I have no money; pray ye, pardon me.

Howard. Here's a plain tanner can teach ye how to thrive:
Keep fewer dogs, and then ye may feed men.
Yet feed no idle men; 'tis needless charge.   65
You that on hounds and hunting mates will spend,
No doubt but something to your King you'll lend.

Goodfellow. My brace of angels. By my troth, that's all.

Hobs. Mass, and 'tis well thy curs have left so much; I thought
they would have eaten up thy house and land ere this.   70

Bowes. Now, Harry Grudgen.

---

67. lend] *Q2*; send *Q1*.

---

45. *forborne*] tolerated, left to your own devices.

47. *fast*] secure.

55. *uprising . . . down-lying*] originally a comprehensive term indicating
the living-in members of a household. According to the petitioner of *Certayne causes . . . wherin is shewed the decaye of England* (c.1550), 'euery plough
was able to keepe vi. persons downe lyinge and vprisynge in hys house' (ed.
J. Meadows Cowper, EETS (ES), XIII (London, 1871), 98); cf. ll. 78–9. The
phrase also had bawdy implications which are developed in Dekker's *Westward Ho*, 5.4.251–3.

68. *angels*] coins worth just over a third of a pound.

Grudgen. What would you have of me? Money I have none,
and I'll sell no stock. Here's old polling, subsidy, fifteen,
soldiers, and to the poor. And ye may have your will,
you'll soon shut me out a' door.   75
Hobs. Hear ye, worships, will ye let me answer my neighbour
Grudgen? By my halidom, Harry Grudgen, th' art but a
grumbling, grudgeling churl! Thou hast two ploughs
going, and ne'er a cradle rocking; th'ast a peck of money!
Go to, turn thee loose. Thou'lt go to law with the vicar   80
for a tithe-goose, and wilt not spare the King four or five
pound!
Grudgen. Gep, goodman tanner, are ye so round? Your prolicateness has brought your son to the gallows, almost; you
can be frank of another man's cost!   85
Hobs. Th' art no honest man to twit me with my son. He may
outlive thee yet, for aught that he has done. My son's in
the gaol; is he the first has been there? And thou wert a
man, as th' art a beast, I would have thee by the ears!
                                                             Weeping.

73–4. *old . . . poor*] Grudgen is suggesting that the 'benevolence' is no different from other forms of compulsory taxation ('old' = 'same old', 'poll' =
'poll tax'). The 'fifteen' was a tax of one-fifteenth levied on personal property (cf. the wild accusations of extortion made of the Lord Say in *2 Henry
VI*, 2.7.18–21); 'soldiers' could be the number of able-bodied men repeatedly required of the parish for military service during the decade following
1588; 'and to the poor' either means 'and all this burden falls primarily on
the poor', or Grudgen is mimicking the attitude he attributes to the collectors, which would require an offensive or dismissive gesture before 'to'.
74. *And*] and if.
77. *halidom*] by the sacred relics; a mild oath.
79. *peck*] substantial amount.
80–1. *go . . . goose*] Even more parsimonious than Bosola's vicar who goes
'to law for a tithe-pig' (*Duchess of Malfi*, 2.1.105); according to Harrison's
Description of England (1587) the only qualities of geese that were prized at
all were their feathers (cited in *Shakespeare's England* (Oxford, 1917), I, 488).
83. *Gep*] exclamation of derision: 'get out of here!'
round] blunt.
prolicateness] Grudgen's malapropism could be an error for either prolix-
ity or profligacy.
85. *of*] at.
86. *twit*] taunt.
88. *And*] if.

Howard. Friend, thou wantst nurture, to upbraid a father   90
    With a son's fault. We sit not here for this.
    What's thy benevolence towards his majesty?
Hobs. His benegligence? Hang him; he'll not give a penny
    willingly.
Grudgen. I care not much to cast away forty pence.   95
Howard. Out, grudging peasant! Base, ill-natured groom!
    Is this the love thou bearst unto the King?
    Gentlemen, take notice of the slave,
    And if he fault let him be soundly plagued.
    Now, frolic tanner, what wilt thou afford?   100
Hobs. Twenty old angels, and a score of hides. If that be too
    little, take twenty nobles more. While I have it, my King
    shall spend of my store.
Howard. The King shall know thy loving, liberal heart.
Hobs. Shall he, i' faith? I thank ye heartily, but hear ye, gen-   105
    tlemen: you come from the court?
Howard. I do.
Hobs. Lord, how does the King? And how does Ned, the
    King's butler, and Tom of his chamber? I am sure ye know
    them?   110
Howard. They do very well.
Hobs. For want of better guests, they were at my house one
    night.
Howard. I know they were.
Hobs. They promised me a good turn for kissing my daugh-   115
    ter Nell, and now I ha' cagion to try them. My son's in
    Dybell here in Caperdochie, i' the gaol, for peeping into

---

112. guests] *Q2*; guesse *Q1*.

---

99. *fault*] Either 'default' (*OED* 4) or 'transgress' (in some other way,
OED 5). The reprisals attendant on those who failed to respond to the benevolences are discussed in *Woodstock*, 1253–79.

102. *nobles*] coins worth just over ten shillings.

112. *guests*] Q2's 'modernization' is accepted here although Q1's 'guesse'
was an acknowledged (if archaic) form of the same word.

115. *turn*] Ironically bawdy; 'turn' often meant illicit copulation, as in
Othello, 4.1.248–50.

116. *cagion*] occasion.

117. *Dybell . . . Caperdochie*] The Tanner's words are difficult not only
because of their dialect forms but also because they are tautological. 'Dybell'
is presumably a corruption of 'Devil', and 'Caperdochie' of 'Cappadochio';

another man's purse, and outstep the King be miserable,
he's like to totter. Can that same Ned the butler do any-
thing with the King?   120
Howard. More than myself, or any other lord.
Hobs. A halter, he can! By my troth, ye rejounce my heart to
hear it.
Howard. Come to the court, I warrant thy son's life;
Ned will save that, and do thee greater good.   125
Hobs. I'll wean Brock my mare's foal, and come up to the
King; and it shall go hard but two fat hens for your pains
I will bring.
Bowes. My lord, this fellow gladly now will give
Five pounds, so you will pardon his rude speech.   130
Howard. For five and five I cannot brook the beast.
Grudgen. What gives the tanner? I am as well able as he.
Aston. He gives ten pound.
Grudgen.   Take twenty then of me.
I pray ye, my lord, forgive my rough-heaved speech:
Iwis, I meant no hurt unto my liege.   135
Bowes. Let us entreat your lordship's patience.
Howard. I do at your request remit th' offence.
So, let's depart; here's all we have to do.
Aston. 'Tis for this time and place, my lord. [*To Grudgen*]
Sirrah, bring your money.
Hobs. What have ye saved now, goodman Grudgen, by your   140
hinching and pinching? Not the worth of a black
pudding.   *Exeunt.*

129–30. My . . . speech] *Qq print as prose.*

both are cant terms for prison. Cf. Middleton's (?) *The Puritaine*, 1.3.56 (C.
F. Tucker Brooke (ed.), *The Shakespeare Apocrypha* (Oxford, 1908)).
   118. *outstep . . . miserable*] 'outstep' is Hobs's idiosyncratic rendering of
'unless'; 'miserable' is used in the rare but not unprecedented sense of 'compassionate' (*OED* 7); cf. *The Three Ladies of London* (c.1581), F1v.
   122. *rejounce*] rejoice.
   131. *brook*] tolerate.
   134. *rough-heaved*] rough-hewed.
   135. *Iwis*] assuredly, as in *Taming of the Shrew*, 1.1.62.
   137. *remit*] the original sense: pardon, forgive (*OED* 1).
   141. *hinching*] Merely a rhyming synonym for 'pinching'; the same
conjunction is found in Robert Greene's *Neuer Too Late* (1590), D2v.

[Scene 19]

    Enter MISTRESS SHORE and MISTRESS BLAGE.

M. Blage. Now, Mistress Shore, what urgent cause is that
    Which made ye send for me in such great haste?
    I promise ye, it made me half afraid
    You were not well.
Jane.   Trust me, nor sick, nor well,
    But troubled still with the disease I told ye.   5
    Here is another letter from the King.
    Was never poor soul so importunèd.
M. Blage. But will no answer serve?
Jane. No, Mistress Blage, no answer will suffice.
    He, he it is, that with a violent siege,   10
    Labours to break into my plighted faith.
    O, what am I, he should so much forget
    His royal state, and his high majesty?
    Still doth he come disguisèd to my house,
    And in most humble terms bewrays his love.   15
    My husband grieves: alas, how can he choose,
    Fearing the dispossessment of his Jane?
    And, when he cannot come—for him—he writes,
    Offering beside incomparable gifts,
    And all to win me to his princely will.   20
M. Blage. Believe me, Mistress Shore, a dangerous case,
    And every way replete with doubtful fear.
    If you should yield, your virtuous name were soiled,
    And your beloved husband made a scorn.
    And if not yield, it's likely that his love,   25
    Which now admires ye, will convert to hate;
    And who knows not, a prince's hate is death?

1–7. Now . . . importunèd] *Qq print as prose.*

    15. *bewrays*] reveals, discloses the nature of.
    17. *dispossessment*] The meaning is obvious but the word is rare; this is *OED*'s only example.
    18. *for him*] because of Matthew Shore's presence.
    21. *case*] For the possible sexual innuendo see the commentary to Scene 17, l. 19.
    27. *who . . . death?*] proverbial (Dent, P589); cf. Marston's *The Malcontent*, 2.5.72–3 (ed. G. K. Hunter (Manchester, 1975)).

Yet, I will not be she shall counsel ye:
Good Mistress Shore, do what ye will, for me.
Jane. Then counsel me what I were best to do.   30
M. Blage. You know his greatness can dispense with ill,
    Making the sin seem lesser by his worth.
    And you yourself, your children and your friends,
    Be all advanced to worldly dignity
    And this world's pomp, you know is a goodly thing.   35
    Yet, I will not be she shall counsel ye:
    Good Mistress Shore, do what ye will, for me.
Jane. Alas, I know that I was bound by oath
    To keep the promise that I made at first;
    And virtue lives, when pomp consumes to dust.   40
M. Blage. So we do say, dishonour is no shame,
    When slander does not touch th' offender's name.
    You shall be folded in a prince's arms,
    Whose beck disperseth e'en the greatest harms.
    Many that sit themselves in high degree   45
    Will then be glad to stoop and bend the knee;
    And who is't, having plenty in the hand,
    Never commanded, but doth still command,
    That cannot work in such excess of things
    To quit the guilt one small transgression brings?   50
    Yet, I will not be she shall counsel ye:
    Good Mistress Shore, do what ye will, for me.
Jane. Here do I live, although in mean estate,
    Yet with a conscience free from all debate;
    Where higher footing may in time procure   55

---

29. *do . . . me*] 'Do what you like as far as I'm concerned'.
31. *dispense with*] A quasi-legal term, meaning to grant a dispensation for
an offence. Mistress Blage's sophistry anticipates Claudio's: 'Nature dispenses with the deed so far / That it becomes a virtue', *Measure for Measure*,
3.1.134–5.
40. *consumes*] rots away (*OED*, 6a).
44. *beck*] 'The slightest indication of will or command' (*OED*, 2); the
pimp's absolute authority over his girls is denied—'no not a beck or nod'—
in *The Captives*, l. 1565.
49. *work . . . things*] manage, surrounded by such abundance.
50. *quit*] expiate.
54. *debate*] The sixteenth-century sense was far more pejorative; the word
more often meant 'strife' or even 'violent altercation' than 'dispassionate
discussion'.

A sudden fall, and mix my sweet with sour.
M. Blage. True, I confess a private life is good,
    Nor would I otherwise be understood.
    To be a goldsmith's wife is some content;
    But days in court more pleasantly are spent.   60
    A household's government deserves renown;
    But what is a companion to a crown?
    The name of 'Mistress' is a pretty thing;
    But 'Madam' at each word doth glory bring.
    Yet I will not be she shall counsel ye: 65
    Good Mistress Shore, do what ye will, for me.
Jane. O, that I knew which were the best of twain;
    Which for I do not, I am sick with pain.

Enter her [Jane's] BOY.

How now, sir boy, what is the news with you?
Boy. The gentleman, forsooth, the other day,   70
    That would have bought the jewel at our stall,
    Is here to speak with ye.
Jane. O God, it is the King.
    Good Mistress Blage, withdraw ye from this place:
    I'll come anon, so soon as he is gone.   75
    And sirrah, get you to the shop again.

Exit BOY.

MISTRESS BLAGE *departs, and the* KING *enters in his
former disguise.*

Edward. Thou mayst convict me, beauty's pride, of boldness,
    That I intrude like an unbidden guest;
    But love being my guide, my fault will seem the less.
Jane. Most welcome to your subject's homely roof: 80
    The foot, my sovereign, seldom doth offend,
    Unless the heart some other hurt intend.
Edward. The most thou see'st is hurt unto myself:

---

57. private] *Q2*; priuately *Q1*.

---

  57. *private*] sheltered, inconspicuous.
  62. *companion*] The word frequently implied sexual misconduct; Gaveston's associates are so called by Mortimer in Marlowe's *Edward II* (ed. R. Rowland (Oxford, 1994)), Scene 9, l. 72.
  68. *Which for*] and because.

How, for thy sake, is majesty disrobed!
Riches made poor, and dignity brought low,   85
Only that thou mightst our affection know.
Jane. The more the pity, that, within the sky,
The sun, that should all other vapours dry
And guide the world with his most glorious light,
Is muffled up himself in wilful night.   90
Edward. The want of thee, fair Cynthia, is the cause:
Spread thou thy silver brightness in the air,
And straight the gladsome morning will appear.
Jane. I may not wander. He that guides my car
Is an immovèd, constant, fixèd star.   95
Edward. But I will give that star a comet's name,
And shield both thee and him from further blame.
Jane. How if the host of heaven at this abuse
Repine? Who can the prodigy excuse?
Edward. It lies within the compass of my power   100

88–90. *The sun . . . night*] Jane contrasts Edward's behaviour with the traditional trope of monarch as sun; 'wilful' (l. 90) evokes both the notion of arbitrary power (*OED*, 4b) and the exercise of illicit sexuality, as in Webster's *The White Devil*, 2.1.41–2.

91. *Cynthia*] English poetry of the 1590s offers countless appearances of this goddess of the moon and chastity. Darkness prevails in *Venus and Adonis* because 'Cynthia for shame obscures her silver shine' (l. 728); Britomart's restorative beauty is compared to Cynthia's 'siluer beames' in *The Faerie Queene*, III, i, 43; the second section of Chapman's *The School of Night* (1594) is an 'Hymnus In Cynthiam'; and the heroine's complexion has some of Cynthia's 'siluer white' in T. H.'s (possibly Heywood's) *Oenone and Paris* (1594); see the edition by J. Q. Adams (Washington, 1943), ll. 497–8. By 1599, in short, the trope was stale as well as inappropriate.

94. *car*] The word means carriage or chariot and is odd in this context; the term in sixteenth-century poetry is invariably associated with Phoebus, the sun god, and so might be more appropriate to Edward than to Jane.

95. *immovèd*] Unmoving; the word may have been Heywood's coinage since *OED*'s only other citation is from his *A Mayden-head Well Lost* (c.1634), B4r.

99. *Repine*] React with disapproval, rather than the more usual modern sense of discontented longing.

prodigy] May simply mean a momentous event with serious (in this case ominous) repercussions, but the dramatist may also be gesturing toward the unnatural or monstrous offspring that such an illicit union might produce. Many pamphlets testify to Renaissance London's appalled fascination with such 'prodigies'; see, for example, I.R, *A Most Strange and True Discourse of the Wonderfull Iudgement of God* (1600).

To dim their envious eyes, dare seem to lour.
But leaving this, our enigmatic talk:
Thou must, sweet Jane, repair unto the court.
His tongue entreats, controls the greatest peer;
His hand plights love, a royal sceptre holds;   105
And in his heart he hath confimed thy good;
Which may not, must not, shall not be withstood.
Jane. If you enforce me, I have nought to say;
But wish I had not lived to see this day.
Edward. Blame not the time: thou shalt have cause to joy.   110
Jane, in the evening I will send for thee,
And thou and thine shall be advanced by me.
In sign whereof, receive this true love kiss:
Nothing ill-meant, there can be no amiss.
                                     Exit [the KING].
Jane. Well, I will in; and ere the time begin,   115
Learn how to be repentant for my sin.   *Exit.*

[Scene 20]

Enter LORD MAYOR, MASTER SHORE *and*
FRANCIS EMERSLEY.

Mayor. But cousin Shore, are ye assured
It was the King you saw in such disguise?
Shore. Do I know you, the uncle to my wife?
Know I Frank Emersley, her brother, here?
So surely do I know that counterfeit   5
To be the King.

1–11. But . . . thereat] *Qq print as prose.*   6. be the king] *Q5;* be king *Q1–4.*

101. *dare . . . lour*] Modern idiom would require 'that' before 'dare'.
102. *enigmatic*] Antedates *OED*'s earliest example (1627); the more usual form in the period was 'enigmatical'.

0.1. FRANCIS EMERSLEY] an invented name of no obvious significance.
6–11. *Well . . . thereat*] Not everyone in the period was as complacent about the morality and legitimacy of a ruler's anonymous scrutiny of his subjects as this. Shakespeare had already explored the problematic nature of such encounters in the second Henriad, and would do so again in *Measure for Measure*; Marston would shortly do the same in *The Malcontent* and *The Fawn.*

Emersley.   Well, admit all this;
   And that his majesty in such disguise
   Please to survey the manners of our city,
   Or what occasion else may like himself:
   Me thinks you have small reason, brother Shore,   10
   To be displeased thereat.
Mayor.   O, I have found him now.
   Because my niece, his wife, is beautiful,
   And well reputed for her virtuous parts,
   He, in his fond conceit, misdoubts the King
   Doth dote on her in his affection.   15
   I know not, cousin, how she may be changed,
   By any cause in you procuring it,
   From the fair carriage of her wonted course:
   But well I wot—I have oft heard you say—
   She merited no scruple of mislike.   20
   If now some giddy fancy in your brain
   Make you conceive sinisterly of her,
   And with a person of such difference,
   I tell you, cousin, more for her respect
   Than to sooth you in such a sottishness,   25
   I would reveal ye open to the world,
   And let your folly justly plague yourself.
Shore. Uncle, you are too forward in your rage,
   And much mistake me in this suddenness.

---

8. manners] *Q1*; maner *Q2*.

---

11. *found him*] discovered his real motivation.

14. *misdoubts*] suspects; cf. Heywood's *Pleasant Dialogues and Drammas* (1637), ll. 3893.

17. *any . . . it*] Anything you have done. Since the talk is about Jane's sexual virtue it is possible that the dramatist intends the Mayor to gesture unwittingly towards 'procuring''s evolving sense of obtaining women for sex; *OED*'s earliest example of this usage is from *Measure for Measure* (3.2.52-3), and it was certainly established by the time Dekker wrote the bawdy exchange in 2 *Honest Whore* (1604/5), 3.3.19-24.

18. *wonted*] accustomed.

19. *wot*] know.

22. *sinisterly*] in an unfavourable way.

23. *difference*] The Mayor is referring to the difference in social rank between Jane and the King.

25. *sottishness*] foolishness.

Your niece's reputation have I prized,   30
And shrined as devoutly in my soul
As you, or any that it can concern.
For, when I tell you that it is the King
Comes muffled like a common servingman,
Do I infer thereby my wife is false,   35
Or swerves one jot from wonted modesty?
Though in my shop she sit, more to respect
Her servants' duty than for any skill
She doth or can pretend in what we trade,
Is it not strange that ever when he comes   40
It is to her, and will not deal with me?
Ah, uncle Frank, nay, would all her kin
Were here to censure of my cause aright:
Though I misdeem not her, yet give me leave
To doubt what his sly walking may intend.   45
And let me tell ye, he that is possessed
Of such a beauty fears undermining guests;
Especially a mighty one like him,
Whose greatness may gild over ugly sin.
But, say his coming is not to my wife: 50
Then hath he some sly aiming at my life,
By false compound metals, or light gold,
Or else some other trifle to be sold.
When kings themselves so narrowly do pry
Into the world, men fear; and why not I?   55
Emersley. Believe me, brother; in this doubtful case
I know not well how I should answer ye.
I wonder in this serious, busy time—
Of this great gatherèd benevolence

---

31. *shrined*] venerated, but also possibly with the additional sense of
enclosing, as a shrine does the image of a saint.

37–8. *respect . . . duty*] observe carefully (*OED* 2b) her servants performing their work.

39. *doth*] has.

44. *misdeem*] entertain suspicion.

47. *undermining*] insidiously plotting. The word was frequently associated
with seduction; Bellamont explains how to 'vndermine' for a friend in Dekker
and Webster's *Northward Ho*: 'Ile so whet the wenches stomack, and make
her so hungry, that she shall haue an appetite to him' (5.1.402–4); cf. also
All's Well That Ends Well, 1.1.116–19.

For his regaining of his right in France,   60
The day and nightly turmoil of his lords,
Yea, of the whole estate in general—
He can be spared from these great affairs,
And wander here disguisèd in this sort.
But is not this your boy?   65

Enter the BOY.

Shore. Yes, marry, is it. How now, what news with thee?
Boy. Master, my mistress by a nobleman
   Is sent for to the King in a close coach.
   She's gone with him. These are the news I bring.
Mayor. How? My niece sent for to the King?   70
   By a nobleman? And she is gone with him?
   Nay, then, I like it not.
Shore. Be patient, uncle. Storm not, gentle Frank.
   The wrong is mine. By whom? A king.
   To talk of such, it is no common thing.   75
   She is gone, thou sayst?
Boy.   Yes, truly, sir, 'tis so.
Shore. I cannot help it. A' God's name, let her go.
   You cannot help it, uncle; no, nor you;
   Where kings are meddlers, meaner men must rue.
   I storm against it? No. Farewell, Jane Shore: 80
   Once thou wast mine, but must be so no more.
Mayor. Gone to the court?   *Exit* MAYOR.
Shore.   Yet, uncle, will ye rage?
   Let mine example your high heat assuage:
   To note offences in a mighty man

---

64. *sort*] manner.
68. *close coach*] Anachronistic. Stow reckoned a coach made in 1555 was the first 'that euer was made in England'; *A Summarie of English Chronicles Abridged* (1604), 260. Writers were quick to note their potential uses and John Taylor was typical, arguing that a coach 'is neuer vnfurnished of a bedde and curtaines, with shop-windowes of leather to buckle Bawdry vp as close in the midst of the street, as it were in the Stewes'; *The World runnes on Wheeles*, in *All the workes of J. Taylor the Water Poet* (1630), Bbb3r. See also *The Roaring Girl* (1611), 3.1.59–60, and *Bartholomew Fair*, 4.5.96–100.
79. *meddlers*] The word covers anyone who interferes but frequently a specifically sexual involvement was inferred. Shakespeare extracts comic mileage from the pun during the Aguecheek/Cesario 'duel' in *Twelfth Night*, 3.4.255, 285, but darker use is made of it in *2 Honest Whore*, 3.1.15ff.

It is enough; amend it, he that can.   85
Frank Emersley, my wife thy sister was.
Lands, goods, and all I have, to thee I pass,
Save that poor portion must along with me,
To bear me from this badge of obloquy.
It never shall be said that Matthew Shore   90
A king's dishonour in his bonnet wore.
Emersley. Good brother—
Shore. Strive not to change me for I am resolved,
And will not tarry. England, fare thou well;
And Edward, for requiting me so well—   95
But dare I speak of him? Forbear, forbear.
Come, Frank, I will surrender all to thee;
And then abroad, where e'er my fortunes be.   *Exeunt.*

[Scene 21]

        Enter KING EDWARD, HOWARD, SELLINGER
           [, *and attendants*].

Edward. And have our country subjects been so frank
And bountiful in their benevolence
Toward our present expedition?
Thanks, cousin Howard, for thy pains therein:
We will have letters sent to every shire   5
Of thankful gratitude, that they may know
How highly we respect their gentleness.
                  [*Exeunt attendants with letters.*]

---

87. *all I have*] Either here, or possibly at l. 97, Matthew might visually
place his 'boy' (for whom no exit is marked) under Emersley's protection.

91. *king's . . . wore*] Shore seems to be asserting that he will not stay to be
jeered at because of the cuckold's horns (however royally bestowed) which
will disfigure his headwear. Williams, another commoner deeply unimpressed
by royalty, is given a glove by his king and told to 'wear it for an honour in
thy cap' (*Henry V*, 4.8.58).

98. *abroad*] often means simply 'away' in early modern usage, but here,
as Part Two makes clear, Matthew means 'overseas'.

0.1. and attendants] The quartos have merely '*etc*' here. Extra courtiers
for the opening lines of the scene would emphasize its public nature, and
their departure at l. 7, apart from registering a response to the King's injunc-
tion, signals a shift to greater intimacy.

Howard. One thing, my lord, I had well near forgot:
Your pleasant host, the tanner of Tamworth.
Edward. What of him, cousin?
Howard.   He was right liberal;   10
Twenty old angels did he send your grace,
And others seeing him so bountiful
Stretched further than otherwise they had done.
Edward. Trust me, I must requite that honest tanner.
O, had he kept his word and come to court,   15
Then, in good sadness, we had had good sport.
Howard. That is not long, my lord, which comes at last.
He's come to London, on an earnest cause:
His son lies prisoner in Stafford gaol,
And is condemnèd for a robbery.   20
Your highness pardoning his son's offence
May yield the tanner no mean recompence.
Edward. But who hath seen him since he came to town?
Sellinger. My lord, in Holborn 'twas my hap to see him
Gazing about. I sent away my men,   25
And clapping on one of their livery cloaks,
Came to him, and the tanner knew me straight.
'How dost thou, Tom? And how doth Ned?', quoth he;
'That honest merry hangman, how doth he?'
I, knowing that your majesty intended   30
This day in person to come to the Tower,
There bad him meet me, where 'Ned' and I
Would bring him to the presence of the King,
And there procure a pardon for his son.
Edward. Have then a care we be not seen of him   35
Until we be provided for the purpose,
Because once more we'll have a little sport.
Tom Sellinger, let that care be yours.
Sellinger. I warrant ye, my lord, let me alone.

Enter the LORD MAYOR.

---

13. *Stretched further*] Remembering the threats made by Howard to the
reluctant Grudgen (Scene 18, ll. 98–9), his words here—perhaps reinforced
by gesture—might suggest a more physical form of persuasion.
   17. *That . . . last*] 'Long looked for comes at last' is proverbial (Dent,
L423); cf. Day's *Isle of Gulls*, D3r.
   39. *let . . . alone*] leave it to me.

Edward. Welcome, Lord Mayor; what, have you signified   40
  Our thankfulness unto our citizens
  For their late gathered benevolence?
Mayor. Before the citizens, in our Guildhall,
  Master Recorder made a good oration
  Of thankful gratitude unto them all;   45
  Which they received with so kind respect
  And love unto your royal majesty,
  As it appeared to us they sorrowed
  Their bounty to your highness was no more.
Edward. Lord Mayor, thanks to yourself, and them.   50
  And go ye with us now into the Tower,
  To see the order that we shall observe
  In this so needful preparation;
  The better may you signify to them
  What need there was of their benevolence.   55
Mayor. I'll wait upon your gracious majesty.
  —Yet there is one thing that much grieveth me.   *Aside.*
                                                    Exeunt.

[Scene 22]

  Enter SHORE, *and two* WATERMEN *bearing his trunks.*

Shore. Go, honest fellow; bear my trunks abroad,
  And tell the master I'll come presently.

  Enter MISTRESS SHORE, *ladylike attired, with diverse*
  supplications in her hand; she unpinning her mask, and
  attended on by many suitors [AIRE, PALMER, RUFFORD
  etc.; and JOCKIE].

1 Waterman. We will sir. But what lady have we here?
  Belike she is of no mean countenance,

---

52. *order*] procedures.

2.02. supplications] formal petitions.
mask] See note to Scene 11, l. 18.02.
4. *countenance*] estimation, reputation in the world (*OED*, sb.III, 9); the
word was also often used to indicate a person's perceived social rank, as in
Merry Wives, 2.2.4–5.

That hath so many suitors waiting on her.   5
Shore. Go, one of you, I pray ye; enquire her name.
                    [*Exeunt* WATERMEN *carrying Shore's trunks;*
                            one addresses AIRE *as he goes off.*]
1 Waterman. My honest friend, what lady call ye this?
Aire. Her name is Mistress Shore, the King's beloved:
A special friend to suitors at the court.
Shore. 'Her name is Mistress Shore, the King's beloved'?   10
Where shall I hide my head, or stop mine ears,
But like an owl I shall be wondered at?
When she with me was wont to walk the streets,
The people then, as she did pass along,
Would say 'There goes fair, modest, Mistress Shore';   15
When she attended like a city dame,
Was praised of matrons, so that citizens
When they would speak of aught unto their wives,
Fetched their example still from Mistress Shore.
But now she goes decked in her courtly robes.   20
This is not she, that once in seemly black
Was the chaste, sober wife of Matthew Shore,
For now she is King Edward's concubine.
O great-ill title, honourable shame!
Her good I had; but, King, her ill is thine: 25
Once Shore's true wife, now Edward's concubine.
Amongst the rest, I'll note her new behaviour.

All this while she stands conferring privately with her
suitors, and looking on their bills.

---

12. *like . . . at?*] Traditionally the nocturnal owl was thought to be ostracized or persecuted by the birds of day; see Ovid's *Metamorphoses*, II, 742–52,
VI, 25–6; cf. also *Edmund Ironside*, ll. 637–8, *The True Tragedie of Richard III*,
xxiv, 29–30, and Marlowe's *Edward II* (ed. Rowland), Scene 20, ll. 6–7. A
long passage on the owl in Nashe's *Christs Teares ouer Ierusalem* (1593) shows
that the bird also symbolized desolation and isolation (II, 58); Matthew's
sense of alienation is not simply that of the cuckold.
    19. *still*] always.
    21. *seemly black*] Richard Barnfield's *The Affectionate Shepheard* (1594)
provides an apt gloss: 'Blacke is the badge of sober Modestie, / The wonted
weare of ancient Gravetie'; G. Klawitter (ed.), *Complete Poems* (Toronto,
1990), p. 94, ll. 299–300. Shore's linking of Jane's costume with her chastity
within marriage here locates him amongst the most earnest protestants.
    27.02. bills] petitions.

Aire. Good Mistress Shore, remember my son's life.

Jane. What is thy name?

Aire.   My name is Thomas Aire.

Jane. There is his pardon, signèd by the King.   30

Aire. In sign of humble, hearty thankfulness,

   Take this: in angels, twenty pound.

Jane. What? Think ye that I buy and sell for bribes

   His highness' favour, or his subjects' blood?

   No. Without gifts, God grant I may do good.   35

   For all my good cannot redeem my ill;

   Yet to do good I will endeavour still.

Shore. Yet all this good doth but gild o'er thy ill.   *Aside.*

Palmer. Mistress, the restitution of my lands,

   Taken perforce by his highness' officers.   40

Jane. The King is content your goods shall be restored,

   But the officers will hardly yield thereto;

   Yet be content, I'll see ye have no wrong.

Shore. [*Aside*] Thou canst not say to me so. I have wrong.

Jockie. Mistress, gude faith, giff ye'll help me til my land,   45

   whilk the fause loun Billy Grime of Glendale hauds

---

45. giff] *Q6* (giffe); gin *Q1–2*; giue *Q3–5*.

40. *perforce*] forcibly, with violence.

42. *will hardly*] are reluctant to.

45. Jockie] Northern or Scottish dialect form; a diminutive rendering of John or Jack which came to be used as a contemptuous term inferring low social rank. An example was a Puritan libel on the late Archbishop of Canterbury and the Lord Bishop of London discovered in 1605; its title was *The lamentation of Dickie for the death of his brother Jockey*; see L. Rostenberg, *The Minority Press and the English Crown: A Study in Repression* (Nieuwkoop, 1971) p. 186. Cf. also *Richard III*, 5.3.305.

giff] If. Q6's reading—'giffe'—is adopted as being closer to the modern meaning, but Q1's 'gin' is a Scottish dialect form (of obscure origin) of the same, although this example would antedate *OED*'s earliest (1674).

46. *whilk*] which.

fause] false.

loun] rogue or person of the lowest rank. The spelling again suggests Scottish dialect form, as is the case with Iago's song about 'low degree' in *Othello*, 2.3.83–90; cf. also *Edward II* (ed. Rowland), Scene 4, l. 82.

hauds] Q1's 'haudr' is certainly a compositor's error, but even the later quartos' readings adopted here are unusual; the word should probably be 'haulds', a Scottish form of 'holds'.

wranfully frea me, I'll quite your gudeness with a bonny
nag, sal swum away so deftly as the wind.
Jane. Your suit, my friend, requires a longer time;
    Yet since you dwell so far off, to ease your charge,   50
    Your diet with my servants you may take,
    And some relief I'll get thee of the King.
Shore. [*Aside*] It's cold relief thou getst me from the King.
Jockie. Now God's blessing light on that gudely fair face! I's
    be your true beadsman, mistress, ay indeed, sall I!   55
Palmer. God bless the care you have of doing good.
Aire. Pity she should miscarry in her life,
    That bears so sweet a mind in doing good.
Shore. [*Aside*] So say I too. Ah, Jane, this kills my heart:
    That thou recks others', and not ru'st my smart.   60
Rufford. Mistress, I fear you have forgot my suit?
Jane. O, 'tis for a licence to transport corn

62–70. O . . . punishèd] *Qq print as prose.*

47. *wranfully*] Q2's spelling is closer to the modern equivalent,
'wrongfully'.

    quite] Qq read 'white'. The context seems to require the sense 'repay' or
'reward' but *OED* records no such usage. 'White' could be a variant spelling
of 'wite', an obsolete verb which could mean to preserve or defend, but the
latest citation dates from 1440. On the assumption that all the quartos may
retain an initial compositorial error, in that 'white' should read 'quite'
(requite), I have emended.

    48. *swum*] dialect form of 'swim'.

    deftly] 'Finelye and nimbly', as defined in E. K.'s gloss on 'April', l. 111
in Spenser's *The Shepheardes Calendar.*

    55. *beadsman*] Either one who prays for the welfare of another, as Proteus
promises to do for Valentine in *The Two Gentlemen of Verona*, 1.1.18, or the
word could be used as the term by which petitioners designated themselves
when addressing their patrons or superiors; for example, Edmund Bonner
subscribed himself this way in a letter to Cardinal Poole in 1556 (Holinshed,
III, 1164).

    60. *recks*] takes trouble over, shows concern for.

    62–3. *licence . . . realms*] The exporting of corn was a highly sensitive issue
of the 1590s rather than the 1470s. Four consecutive harvest failures up to
1597 led to serious food shortages, particularly in London, and there were
countless appeals for restraints on exports and curbs on the activities of pur-
veyors. The City authorities themselves made strenuous interventions on the
issue; in 1597, for example, the livery companies were instructed to sell meal
to the 'poorer sort' at 4*d* per bushel below the prices prevailing in the
markets; see Archer, 201. Jane's action here (and her background as the wife
of a prominent citizen trader) serves also to defuse suspicions which an

From this land, and lead to foreign realms.
I had your bill, but I have torn your bill;
And 'twere no shame I think to tear your ears,   65
That care not how you wound the commonwealth.
The poor must starve for food to fill your purse,
And the enemy bandy bullets of our lead?
No, Master Rufford, I'll not speak for you—
Except it be to have you punishèd.   70
Jockie. By the mess, a deft lass; Christ benison light on her!

*She espies her husband walking aloof off, and not knowing
him, takes him for another suitor.*

Jane. Is that another suitor? I have no bill of his.
Go, one of you, and know what he would have.
Shore. Yes, Jane, the bill of my obligèd faith;
And I had thine, but thou hast cancelled it.   75

Here she knows him, and lamenting, comes to him.

Jane. O God, it is my husband, kind Matthew Shore.
Shore. Ah, Jane, what's he dare say he is thy husband?
Thou wast a wife, but now thou art not so.

---

audience might have about the integrity of the civic authorities; the anxieties
of the governors of London were well expressed by the Lord Mayor in 1596
who feared that the 'poorer sort who ar soon mooved both to conceave and
report amisse of the magistrate specially in matter of this sort' might be
'moved to exclaime against us as if wee enhaunced the price of corne for our
own gaine'; *HMC, Hatfield House, VII*, 148. On the exporting of metals which
could provide ammunition cf. Sir Walter Raleigh: 'heretofore one Ship of her
Majesties was able to beat ten Spaniards; but now by reason of our own Ordnance we are hardly matcht one to one . . . nothing doth so much threaten
. . . the Kingdom as the transportation of Ordnance'; see P. Bowles (ed.),
*The Journals of all the Parliaments During the Reign of Queen Elizabeth . . .
colected* [sic] *by Sir Simonds D'Ewes* (1682), 671.
    68. *bandy*] shoot, fire; the word was normally associated with the game
of tennis but was frequently used to suggest more violent confrontations; cf.
Nashe's drunken quarrellers who 'bandy balles of Brimstone at one anoth-
ers head' in *Pierce Penilesse* (*Works*, I, 187).
    78–80. *Thou . . . maid*] Shore's terminology is again peculiar to the late
sixteenth century rather than the fifteenth. By 'maid' he means chaste woman
and he is invoking the specifically protestant concept of 'matrimonial
chastity', whereby the monogamous and faithful wife was afforded an untar-
nished status similar to that granted virginity by medieval Catholicism. For
influential theologians sexual activity itself, in its proper marital context,
became a 'holy and undefiled action'; see, for example, William Perkins,
Workes (1631), III, 689.

Thou wast a maid, a maid when thou wast wife;
Thou wast a wife, e'en when thou wast a maid;   80
So good, so modest, and so chaste thou wast.
But now thou art divorced, whiles yet he lives
That was thy husband, while thou wast his wife.
Thy wifehood stained, by thy dishonoured life:
For now thou art nor widow, maid nor wife.   85
Jane. I must confess I yielded up the fort
    Wherein lay all the riches of thy joy.
    But yet, sweet Shore, before I yielded it
    I did endure the long'st and greatest siege
    That ever battered on poor chastity;   90
    And but to him that did assault the same,
    For ever it had been invincible.
    But I will yield it back again to thee.
    He cannot blame me, though it be so done,
    To lose by me what first by me was won.   95
Shore. No, Jane, there is no place allowed for me,
    Where once a king hath ta'en possession.
    Mean men brook not a rival in their love;
    Much less to high unrivalled majesty.
    A concubine to one so great as Edward   100
    Is far too great to be the wife of Shore.
Jane. I will refuse the pleasures of the court.
    Let me go with thee, Shore, though not as a wife,
    Yet as thy slave, since I have lost that name.
    I will redeem the wrong that I have done thee   105
    With my true service, if thou wilt accept it.
Shore. Thou go with me, Jane? O God forbid
    That I should be a traitor to my king.
    Shall I become a felon to his pleasures,
    And fly away as guilty of the theft?   110
    No, my dear Jane, I say it may not be.
    O, what have subjects that is not their king's?
    I'll not examine his prerogative.

---

87. thy] *Q1*; my *Q2*.

87. *thy*] Q2's reading, 'my', is possible, but the insistence on the
importance of chastity is Matthew's, and line 93 renders this a less likely
alternative.
    109. *felon to*] thief of; cf. *The Captives*: 'I saw a theiff comittinge ffellony'
(l. 1962).

Jane. Why then, sweet Mat, let me entreat thee stay.
    What is't with Edward that I cannot do?   115
    I'll make thee wealthier than e'er Richard was,
    That entertained the three great'st kings in Europe,
    And feasted them in London on a day.
    Ask what thou wilt: were it a million
    That may content thee, thou shalt have it, Shore.   120
Shore. Indeed this were some comfort to a man
    That tasted want or worldly misery;
    But I have lost what wealth cannot return.
    All worldly losses are but toys to mine;
    O, all my wealth—the loss of thee was more   125
    Than ever time or fortune can restore.
    Therefore, sweet Jane, farewell. Once thou wast mine:
    Too rich for me, and that, King Edward knew.
    Adieu. O world! He shall deceivèd be
    That puts his trust in women, or in thee.   *Exit.*   130
Jane. Ah Shore, farewell, poor heart! In death I'll tell
    I ever loved thee, Shore; farewell, farewell.
              Exit [JANE, *followed by the other suitors*].

[Scene 23]

      Enter KING EDWARD, LORD MAYOR, HOWARD,
          SELLINGER, *and the train.*

Edward. Having awaked forth of their sleepy dens
    Our drowsy cannons, which ere long shall charm
    The watchful French with death's eternal sleep,
    And all things else in readiness for France,

---

130. *Exit*] *MS annotation to Dyce (1) copy of Q3; not in Qq.*

116–18. *Richard . . . day*] A very muddled reference. By 'Richard' Jane is presumably alluding to Richard Whittington, mayor several times in the reigns of Richard II and Henry IV, about whose wealth, generosity and meteoric rise from humble origins apocryphal stories (including a lost play and a ballad) were beginning to proliferate in the last decades of the sixteenth century. But the lord mayor who really did entertain on this scale was Henry Picard who, according to Stow, held office in 1357, and 'did in one day sumptuously feast *Edward* the third king of England, *Iohn* king of France, *David* king of Scots, the king of Cipres, then all in England . . . and after kept his hall for all commers that were willing to play at dice, and hazard' (*Survey*, I, 106).

Awhile we will give truce unto our care.   5
There is a merry tanner near at hand,
With whom we mean to be a little merry.
Therefore, Lord Mayor, and you, my other friends,
I must entreat you not to knowledge me;
No man stand bare; all as companions.   10
Give me a cloak, that I may be disguised:
Tom Sellinger, go thou, and take another.

> [KING and SELLINGER discard their official
> robes and put on cloaks.]

So, tanner, now come when ye please; we are provided.
And, in good time; see, he is come already.

Enter the TANNER.

Tom Sellinger, go thou and meet him.   15
Sellinger. What, John Hobs? Welcome, i' faith, to court.
Hobs. Grammercies, honest Tom. Where is the hangman,
   Ned? Where is that mad rascal? Shall I not see him?
Sellinger. See where he stands; that same is he.
Hobs. What, Ned? A plague found thee! How dost thou, for   20
   a villain? How dost thou, mad rogue? And how? And
   how?
Edward. In health, John Hobs, and very glad to see thee.
   But say, what wind drove thee to London?
Hobs. Ah, Ned, I was brought hither with a whirlwind, man. 25
   My son, my son! Did I not tell thee I had a knave to my
   son?
Edward. Yes, tanner. What of him?
Hobs. Faith, he's in Capperdochie, Ned; in Stafford Gaol, for
   a robbery, and is like to be hanged, except thou get the   30
   King to be more miserable to him.
Edward. If that be all, tanner, I'll warrant him;

---

9. *knowledge*] recognize, acknowledge, but possibly with the additional
and ironic sense, 'To own as genuine, or of legal force or validity' (*OED* 3).
   10. *bare*] without suitable disguise.
   16. *welcome . . . court*] The location of this scene is fluid, if not confused;
the King's closing speech implies that the action has been taking place in an
official building in which the mayor is host, but up to that point the court
itself must be the imagined setting.
   31. *miserable*] See note to Scene 18, l. 118.
   32. *warrant him*] guarantee his safety.

I will procure his pardon of the King.

Hobs. Wilt thou, Ned? For those good words, see what my
daughter Nell hath sent thee: a handkercher, wrought   35
with as good Coventry silk blue thread as ever thou
sawest.

Edward. And I perhaps may wear it for her sake,
In better presence than thou art aware of.

Hobs. How, Ned? A better present? That canst thou not have,   40
for silk, cloth, and workmanship. Why, Nell made it, man.
But, Ned, is not the King in this company? What's he
in the long beard and the red petticoat? Before God, I
misdoubt, Ned, that is the King. I know it by my Lord
what-ye-call's players.   45

Edward. How by them, tanner?

Hobs. Ever when they play an enterlout or a commodity at
Tamworth, the king always is in a long beard, and a red
gown like him; therefore, I 'spect him to be the King.

Edward. No, trust me, tanner, this is not the King;   50
But thou shalt see the King before thou go'st,
And have a pardon for thy son too, with thee.
This man is the Lord Mayor, Lord Mayor of London;
Here was the Recorder too, but he is gone.

50–4. No . . . gone] *Qq print as prose.*

36. *Coventry . . . thread*] Once a famous commodity, and in the 1590s one
familiar to Londoners if only by imitation; by 1606 Coventry's cloth workers
were complaining that their product was 'counterfeited in London, Manchester, and divers other places . . . and there put off and sold in the name
of Coventrey thridd'; cited in C. Phythian-Adams, *Desolation of a City* (Cambridge, 1979), 42n.

43. *red petticoat*] This is probably a joke about the literal-mindedness of
the tanner but Andrew Borde's *Dyetary of Helth* (1542 but achieving a fourth
edition in 1576) was still referring to a 'petycote of scarlet' as specifically
masculine attire, C3v–C4r.

47. *enterlout . . . commodity*] 'interlude or a comedy'.

48. *Tamworth*] The tanner could, in the fifteenth century, have seen plays
at nearby Coventry, and in the 1590s he could even have witnessed a street
performance there of a play about Edward IV; it is unlikely, however, that
Tamworth itself had much theatrical life, although the Coventry Weavers'
Account Books do show them hiring gowns (including a scarlet one) 'to tan-
vorthe' in 1600; see Ingram (ed.), *REED: Coventry*, 332, 357. See also p. 273
for an account of 'Captin Cox', an amateur performer of the 1570s, one of
whose many turns was 'The King and the Tanner'.

49. *'spect*] suspect.

Hobs. What nicknames these courtnoles have! Mare, and   55
   corder, quotha? We have no such at Lichfield. There is
   the honest bailiff and his brethren; such words 'gree best
   with us.
Edward. My Lord Mayor, I pray ye for my sake
   To bid this honest tanner welcome.   60
Mayor. You are welcome, my honest friend;
   In sign whereof, I pray you see my house,
   And sup with me this night.
Hobs. I thank ye, good goodman Mayor, but I care not for no
   meat. My stomach is like to a sick swine's, that will   65
   neither eat nor drink till she know what shall become of
   her pig. Ned and Tom, you promised me a good turn
   when I came to court: either do it now, or go hang
   yourselves.
Edward. No sooner comes the King, but I will do it.   70
Sellinger. I warrant thee, tanner, fear not thy son's life.
Hobs. Nay, I fear not his life; I fear his death.

   Enter MASTER OF ST KATHERINE'S *and* WIDOW NORTON.

59–60. My . . . welcome] *Qq print as prose.*

---

   56. *corder*] possibly a pun extending the horse ('mare') joke; 'cord' was 'a
disease affecting the sinews of a horse' (*OED* 6).
   57. *bailiff*] Hobs could imply any one of three roles which Elizabethan
usage ascribed to a bailiff: either the chief administrative officer of a district,
or an officer of justice with powers to execute writs or make arrests, or the
agent who supervised a farm on behalf of its owner. The third might be
appropriately rustic but 'honest' would be a typically ironic description of
the second since they were almost proverbially vindictive; Nashe promised
to be his enemy Gabriel Harvey's 'Baily' (*Foure Letters Confuted* (1592), *Works*
I, 333), and cf. Heywood's *The English Traveller* (c.1627), in which 'all the
hellish rabble are broke loose, / Of Seriants, Sheriffes, and Baliffes' (H3r).
   72.01. *MASTER . . . KATHERINE'S*] The district known as St Katherine's
by the Tower. Originally (and in the play's historical time) the Mastership
would refer to the administrator of the Hospital thus named but Elizabethans
would probably think of the quasi-judicial officer, appointed by the Crown,
who was responsible for the 11-acre area. The position was granted in 1582
to Sir Julius Caesar and he held it for the next forty years. Since no such
figure plays even an anecdotal role in any account of Edward's reign, it is
possible that the dramatist was intending a contemporary portrait or caricature, complicating the tone of comic ribaldry in the scene by the ahistorical introduction of a man widely known as the dedicatee of weighty
devotional works by the likes of William Perkins and Arthur Dent. See also
Survey, II, 39.

Master. All health and happiness to my sovereign.

Edward. The Master of St Katherine's hath marred all.

Hobs. Out, alas that ever I was born.   75

> The TANNER *falls in a swoon; they [courtiers] labour to*
> *revive him. Meanwhile, the* KING *puts on his royal robes.*

Edward. Look to the tanner, there, he takes no harm.

I would not have him—for my crown—miscarry.

Widow. Let me come to him, by my King's good leave.

Here's ginger, honest man; bite it.

Hobs. Bite ginger? Bite ginger? Bite a dog's date! I am but a   80

dead man. Ah, my liege, that you should deal so with a

poor, well-meaning man. But it makes no matter. I can

but die.

Edward. But when, tanner? Canst thou tell?

Hobs. Nay, even when you please, for I have so defended ye,   85

by calling ye plain 'Ned', mad rogue and rascal, that I

know you'll have me hanged. Therefore, make no more

ado, but send me down to Stafford, and there, a' God's

name, hang me with my son. And here's another, as

honest as yourself. You made me call him plain 'Tom'; I   90

warrant his name is Thomas, and some man of worship

too. Therefore, let's to it, even when and where ye will.

Edward. Tanner, attend. Not only do we pardon thee,

But in all princely kindness welcome thee.

And thy son's trespass do we pardon too: 95

One go and see that forthwith it be drawn

Under our Seal of England, as it ought.

> [*Exit a courtier.*]

---

73. *ginger*] Ginger was supposed to have restorative properties but its appearance here is undoubtedly part of a joke about the sexual appetites that stereotypical widows were thought to possess; herbalists such as Gerard listed ginger as an aphrodisiac and Henry Buttes wrote drily of its association with old women and how it 'warmes olde mens bellyes', *Dyets Dry Dinner* (1599), O2v.

80. *dog's date*] probably 'dog's turd'.

85. *defended*] offended.

96. *it be drawn*] the pardon is drawn up, issued.

97. *Seal of England*] probably the Great Seal. Royal pardons, even for serious insurgents, were still issued under its auspices in Elizabethan times; see, for example, Hughes and Larkin, *Tudor Royal Proclamations*, II, 159–60.

And forty pounds we give thee, to defray
Thy charges in thy coming up to London.
Now, tanner, what sayst thou to us?   100
Hobs. Marry, you speak like an honest man, if you mean as
    you say.
Edward. We mean it, tanner, on our royal word.
    Now, Master of St Katherine's, what would you?
Master. My gracious lord, the great benevolence—   105
    Though small to that your subjects could afford—
    Of poor St Katherine's do I bring your grace:
    Five hundred pounds here have they sent by me,
    For the easier portage all in angel gold.
    What this good widow, Mistress Norton, will,   110
    She comes herself, and brings her gift with her.
Widow. Pardon me, gracious lord. Presumption,
    Nor overweening in my own conceit
    Makes me thus bold to come before your grace,
    But love and duty to your majesty,   115
    And great desire to see my lord, the King.
    Our Master here spake of benevolence,
    And said my twenty nobles was enough:
    I thought not so, but at your highness' feet,
    A widow's mite, a token of her zeal,   120
    In humble duty gives you twenty pound.
Edward. Now, by my crown, a gallant, lusty girl!

---

113. *conceit*] The context suggests not the customary sixteenth-century
meanings of 'conception', 'understanding', or 'imaginative notion', but rather
the more modern sense of 'over-estimation of one's own qualities, personal
vanity or pride'; this is the definition provided by *OED* (6), and the example
here antedates the dictionary's only pre-nineteenth-century citation by six
years.

120. *mite*] 'In English use mainly as a proverbial expression for an
extremely small unit of money value. In books of commercial arithmetic
in the sixteenth and seventeenth centuries it commonly appears as the
lowest denomination of English money' (*OED* 1, which goes on aptly to
cite Coverdale's 1535 rendering of Mark, 12.43: 'And there came a poore
wyddowe, and put in two mytes, which make a farthinge'; the biblical passage itself was often alluded to as an example of 'an immaterial contribution (insignificant in amount, but the best one can do) to some object or
cause').

Of all the exhibition yet bestowed,
This woman's liberality likes me best.
Is thy name Norton?
Widow.   Ay, my gracious liege.   125
Edward. How long hast thou been a widow?
Widow. It is, my lord,
  Since I did bury Wilkin, my goodman,
  At Shrovetide next, e'en just a dozen years.
Edward. In all which space, couldst thou not find a man   130
  On whom thou mightst bestow thyself again?
Widow. Not any like my Wilkin, whose dear love
  I know is matchless; in respect of whom,
  I think not any worthy of a kiss.
Edward. No, widow? That I'll try. How like you this?   135

                He kisseth her.

Widow. Beshrew my heart, it was a bonny kiss,
  Able to make an agèd woman young;
  And for the same, most sweet and lovely prince,
  See what the widow gives you from her store:
  Forty old angels, but for one kiss more.   140
Edward. Marry, widow, and thou shalt have it. [*Kisses her
  again.*] John Hobs,
  Thou art a widower: lackst thou such a wife?

---

123. *exhibition*] The ostensible meaning is financial allowance or contribution; cf. Nashe's complaint that 'No thanks-worthy exhibition or reasonable pensions will you contribute to maymd Souldiours or poore Schollers, as other Nations doe, but suffer other Nations with your discontented poore to Arme themselues against you' (*Christs Teares Ouer Ierusalem* (1593), *Works*, II, 161). However, it is possible that the word was already beginning to acquire the modern sense of displaying oneself, in this case provocatively; although *OED* classes this as a late seventeenth-century development, I suspect similar connotations are at work in Shakespeare's deployment of the word in *Othello*, 4.3.72–3, and in *Cymbeline*, 1.7.121–3. See also next note.

124. *liberality*] Again, the primary sense is financial generosity, but the word could also indicate the indiscriminate granting of sexual favours; thus Joan la Pucelle's attempt to attribute the paternity of her child to three different men is said to be a 'sign she hath been liberal and free'; *1 Henry VI*, 5.4.82.

136. *Beshrew*] The word means curse but was often used lightly or playfully; cf. Hippolyta's amused response to Bottom/Pyramus's lament, *A Midsummer Night's Dream*, 5.1.279.

Hobs. S' nails, twenty pound for a kiss? Had she as many
    twenty pound bags as I have knobs of bark in my tan-fat,
    she might kiss them away in a quarter of a year. I'll no   145
    St Katherine's widows, if kisses be so dear.
Widow. Clubs and clouted shoes! There's none enamoured
    here.
Edward. Lord Mayor, we thank you and entreat withal
    To recommend us to our citizens;
    We must for France; we bid you all farewell.   150
    Come, tanner, thou shalt with us to court.
    Tomorrow you shall dine with my Lord Mayor,
    And afterward set homeward when ye please.
    God and our right, that only fights with us:
    Adieu; pray that our toil prove prosperous.   155

                                                        Exeunt.

                              FINIS

154. with us:] *Q1*; for vs, *Q2–6*.

---

144. *knobs*] presumably Hobs means lumps, although *OED* does not
record this sense (3) until 1678.
    tan-fat] dialect form of 'tanvat'.
147. *clouted shoes*] Hobnailed boots. Jack Cade will spare no one who
doesn't wear them (*2 HenryVI*, 4.3.178). The phrase came to be synonymous
with boors or country bumpkins; see, for example, Robert Greene's *A Quippe
for an Vpstart Courtier* (1592), B1v, C4v.
148. *withal*] in addition; see commentary to Scene 16, ll. 141–2.
149. *recommend*] The King appears to mean 'pass on our thanks again'
but it is possible to detect an ironic deployment of *OED*'s definition (4b):
'to speak of one as fit or worthy to hold some position', i.e. to justify his
behaviour.
154. *with us:*] It seems fitting to retain the ambiguous and problematic
qualities of Q1's diction at the close of the play, although the later quartos'
comma, which could produce the effect of the King bidding farewell to God
and his right, is very tempting.

THE SECOND PART OF KING EDWARD THE FOURTH

Containing his journey into France, for obtaining of his right there; the treacherous falsehood of the Duke of Burgundy, and the Constable of France used against him, and his return home again. Likewise the prosecution of the history of Master Shore and his fair wife, concluding with the lamentable death of them both.

---

prosecution] the oldest sense recorded in *OED* (1): 'continuing . . . of any action . . . with a view to its accomplishment'.

Characters in the Play (Part Two)

KING EDWARD IV

SIR THOMAS SELLINGER

JOHN, LORD HOWARD

ANTHONY, LORD SCALES

LEWIS, KING OF FRANCE

BOURBON, ADMIRAL OF FRANCE

ST PIERRE

An English HERALD

MUGEROUN

CHARLES, DUKE OF BURGUNDY

COUNT ST POL, the Constable of France

ANTHONY, LORD SCALES] Brother to Queen Elizabeth, and the only member of the Woodville family to receive a favourable press from Tudor historians. He was a cultured man—not only was he a patron of Caxton, but his own translation of the *Moral Proverbs* of Christine de Pisan was amongst the first books to emerge from the new presses—and an earnest one: Mancini observed that he was a 'kind, serious, and just man . . . [w]hatever his prosperity he injured nobody, though benefiting many; and therefore he had entrusted to him the care and direction of the king's eldest son' (67–9).

ST PIERRE] Jean Blosset, Seigneur de St Pierre, the most important of the French diplomats.

MUGEROUN] No such name appears in the historical sources, nor is the word a descriptive one in sixteenth-century French or English (although Mugron is the county town of the Dax district of the Landes region, and 'Mugeroun' might be an inhabitant). A character so named had appeared in Marlowe's *Massacre at Paris* (probably printed and certainly performed before 1600), but Henry III's 'minion' in that play has little in common with the French envoy in this one.

CHARLES, DUKE OF BURGUNDY] Married Margaret, King Edward's sister, in 1468. The court of Charles 'the Bold' was considered the most opulent and sophisticated in Europe; the younger John Paston (in Margaret's retinue) described with awe the splendour of the jousts and pageants, concluding 'I have never heard of none like to it, save King Arthur's court'; J. Warrington (ed.), *The Paston Letters*, 2 vols (London, 1924), II, 50.

COUNT . . . France] Louis de Luxembourg, uncle of Queen Elizabeth. His endless duplicities were finally rewarded when the Duke of Burgundy, to whom he had fled for sanctuary, handed him over to the French king, who in turn had him tried and beheaded for treason.

206

THE LORD OF CONTAY
JANE SHORE
MATTHEW SHORE
JOCKIE, servant to Jane
SIR ROBERT BRACKENBURY, Constable of the Tower
VAUX, Keeper of the Tower
HARRY STRANGUIDGE, a seafarer
MARQUIS DORSET, son to the Queen of England

THE LORD OF CONTAY] A senior diplomat of the Burgundian court. Holinshed notes that on hearing the Constable's envoy impersonate the Duke, he 'was sore displeased to see his master made a iesting stocke' (III, 338); his anger was also revealed during the Anglo-Burgundian wedding celebrations in 1468, when he seriously wounded an opponent in 'joust of peace'; M. G. A. Vale, *War and Chivalry: Warfare and Aristocratic Culture in England, France and Burgundy at the End of the Middle Ages* (London, 1981), 71.

SIR ROBERT BRACKENBURY] The play terms him 'Lieutenant' of the Tower (as does *Richard III*) although all sources describe his title as 'Constable'; the play also implies, especially in Scene 14, ll. 22–30, that his tenure of the post has been of long standing, when in fact he was established in the job—by the new King Richard—in July 1483, and confirmed in it for life as reward for helping to suppress Buckingham's rebellion in the following year. He was a favourite of Richard's: a manuscript Latin poem dedicated to Brackenbury by Pietro Carmeliano (reproduced in A. J. Pollard, *Richard III and the Princes in the Tower* (Stroud, 1991), 184) was probably a bid for the new monarch's patronage. Most chroniclers exempt him from personal blame for the murders—and even Tyrrell calls his reluctance 'kinde hearted' in *True Tragedie*, l. 1207—but he remained loyal to the regime, was killed with Richard at Bosworth, and named in the subsequent Act of Attainder. A tower in Baynard's Castle (see Scene 11, l. 83) still bears his name.

HARRY STRANGUIDGE] No such name appears in any source, Edwardian or Elizabethan. Audiences might, however, have recalled one Henry Strangwyche (also known as Strangways, the Red Rover of the Channel), a man who walked a similarly fine line between piracy and the kind of seafaring for profit which had the nervous sanction of the state. He and his crew of almost eighty were actually sentenced to death at Southwark at the turn of 1559/60, but received a last-minute pardon from Queen Elizabeth (Nichols, I, 75, 79; *CSPD, 1547–80*, 132, 136, 164). He died on a sandbank on the Seine, leading volunteers to an English-backed defence of Rouen in 1563; J. A. Froude, *The Reign of Elizabeth*, 5 vols (London, 1912), II, 188.

MARQUIS DORSET] Thomas Grey, Lord Ferrers, the Queen's eldest son by her first marriage. Despite the lack of enthusiasm amongst the chroniclers for the Woodville family in general, none implies that Dorset was the psychotic of the play. In terms of his violent antagonism to Jane Shore, the historical evidence—to which the playwright would have had no access—would suggest the exact opposite; in 1483 King Richard publicly accused Dorset of holding 'the unshameful and mischievous woman called Shore's

ELIZABETH, QUEEN OF ENGLAND
RICHARD, DUKE OF GLOUCESTER (later King Richard III)
GEORGE, DUKE OF CLARENCE
DOCTOR SHAW
LORD LOVELL
SIR WILLIAM CATESBY
EDWARD, the young Prince of Wales, elder son of King Edward
RICHARD, the young Duke of York, younger son of King Edward
JAMES TYRRELL

wife in adultery' (*Calendar of Patent Rolls, 1476–85*, 371). The major textual
and historical confusion surrounding the appearance of 'Dorset' in the
opening scenes of *Richard III* has been clarified by John Jowett in the Oxford
edition, 375–8.

DOCTOR SHAW] More (and some modern historians) spell his name
'Shaa', but Holinshed's spelling is followed by the playwright; More also
wrongly named him John (instead of Rafe) but his appropriators from
Hardyng onwards rectified the error. The *Great Chronicle*, which has the
fullest account of this episode—Fabyan's printed version in the *Chronicles* is
much abbreviated (669)—says Shaw was held to be the preacher 'moost
ffamous & moost allowyed In the comon peplys meyndys' up to the moment
of his 'illegitimacy' sermon, but that he was haunted by 'obprobrious
Reportys' immediately after it (231–2).

LORD LOVELL] Francis, Viscount Lovell, a close friend to Richard, and
his chamberlain after the fall of Hastings; one of a new breed of courtiers
whose power resided not in a regional power base but in their simply having
the ear of the King (see R. Horrox, *Richard III: A Study of Service* (Cambridge, 1989), 220–2). Shakespeare's play has no place for Lovell, but he
appears twice in *True Tragedie*: first, as a casually misogynistic emissary pressing Richard's suit to the princess Elizabeth (ll. 1582–94), and second as
witness to the King's hallucinations before Bosworth—although the direction suggesting he accompanies the King throughout is probably an error
(see ll. 1873–982), as is the play's report of Lovell's death in the battle.

SIR WILLIAM CATESBY] One of 'the assistant-engineers of [Richard's]
palace revolution'; J. S. Roskell, 'William Catesby, Counsellor to Richard III',
Bulletin of the John Rylands Library, 42 (1959–60), 145. Catesby was formerly
a member of the Hastings clique, and subsequently a conspirator in and
beneficiary of that lord's downfall; Richard made him Chamberlain of the
Exchequer soon after his accession. Captured at Bosworth, he became a rare
exception to Henry Tudor's clemency, and was executed—as was his great-
great-grandson Robert, for his parts in the Essex rebellion and the Gun-
powder Plot.

JAMES TYRRELL] The earliest text to name Tyrrell as the chief murderer
was *The Great Chronicle* (c.1512), just a decade after his execution for treason
(an unrelated offence); Virgil followed suit soon after, but More's account is
the first to mention a confession of guilt (which has never been discovered).

MISTRESS BLAGE
MILES FOREST
JOHN DIGHTON
FRIAR ANSELM, a ghost
MASTER AIRE
MASTER RUFFORD
FOGGE
JEFFREY
THE DUKE OF BUCKINGHAM
Anne of Warwick, Richard's future queen [mute]
Soldiers, Servants, Messengers, Apparitors, Officers
Chorus

Tyrrell was a Yorkist of long standing, whose power base in Wales was crucial to the consolidation of the Ricardian regime; Richard was generous with grants to Tyrrell (see Horrox, *Study of Service*, 259), and so the excuse of doing the King's bidding to recover his fortunes (Scene 14, l. 100–1) is quite without historical authority.

MISTRESS BLAGE] None of the chronicle sources or earlier literary treatments of the Shore episode has suggested this name. Indeed, only Chute's *Beawtie Dishonoured* alludes to any such figure: a false friend, 'a bad seede of base sedition' (sig. D1r), on to whom responsibility for inflaming both the adulteress's lust and the King's is momentarily displaced.

MILES FOREST, JOHN DIGHTON] More names both Forest and Dighton as the murderers of the princes; the former, he claims, 'pecemele rotted away' after the crime, but his suggestion that Dighton was living 'yet' is supplemented in the Hardyng/Hall 'appropriations' by the (unsubstantiated) assertion that he fled to Calais, where he survived 'long after, no lesse disdayned and hated then pointed at, and there dyed in great misery' (pp. 85–7 and textual note). *The True Tragedie* had elevated Forest to the post of 'Keeper' in the Tower, and gave him extended exchanges with both 'Terrell' and Prince Edward; Dighton became 'Jack Denton', and he also acquired an accomplice (possibly lifted from *Arden of Faversham*), called 'Black' Will Slawter.

FOGGE] Sir John Fogge was treasurer of Edward's household during the 1460s, a close associate of the Woodvilles and a persistent thorn in Richard's side. The play's portrayal of him as unscrupulous profiteer may have been suggested by the episode, recounted at length in *The Great Chronicle* (204–8) but also mentioned in Fabyan's *Chronicles* and Stow's *Annals*, in which Fogge's servants (on his instructions) ransacked properties belonging to the Lord Mayor of London, drinking or pouring away all his wine, stealing plate and tapestries, and doing several thousand pounds' worth of damage. The sources suggest that Fogge frequently needed an attorney, but not—see Scene 21, l. 97—that he was one.

The Second Part of King Edward IV

[Scene 1]

Enter KING EDWARD, HOWARD, SELLINGER, *and*
Soldiers marching.

Edward. Is this the aid our cousin Burgundy
      And the great Constable of France assured us?
      Have we marched thus far through the heart of France,
      And with the terror of our English drums
      Roused the poor trembling French, which leave their
          towns,   5
      That now the wolves affrighted from the fields
      Do get their prey, and kennel in their streets?
      Our thund'ring cannons, now this fortnight space,
      Like common bellmen in some market town,
      Have cried the Constable and Burgundy;   10
      But yet I see they come not to our aid.
      We'll bring them in, or by the blessèd light,
      We'll search the groundsills of their city's walls.
      Since you have brought me hither, I will make
      The proudest tower that stands in France to quake.   15
      I marvel Scales returns not, for by him
      I do expect to hear their resolutions.

Enter the Lord SCALES.

Howard. My sovereign, he is happily returned.
Edward. Welcome my lord, welcome good cousin Scales,
      What news from Burgundy? What is his answer?   20
      What, comes he to our succour as he promised?

---

13. city's] *Q2*; Cittie *Q1.*   17. expect] *Q4*; respect *Q1-3.*

---

9. *bellmen*] minor civic officials who prefaced public announcements by
ringing a bell; town-criers.
13. *search*] probe, penetrate.
groundsills] foundations.

Scales. Not by his good will. For aught that I can see
　　He lingers still in his long siege at Neuss.
　　I urged his promise and your expectation,
　　Even to the force and compass of my spirit,　　　　　　25
　　I cheered my firm persuasions with your hopes,
　　And gilded them with my best oratory,
　　I framed my speech still fitly as I found
　　The temper of his humour to be wrought upon;
　　But still I found him earthy, unresolved,　　　　　　　30
　　Muddy, and, me thought, ever through his eyes
　　I saw his wav'ring and unsettled spirit,
　　And, to be short, subtle and treacherous,
　　And one that doth intend no good to you.
　　And, 'he will come, and yet he wanteth power';　　　35
　　'He would fain come, but may not leave the siege';
　　'He hopes he shall, but yet he knows not when';
　　'He purposèd, but some impediments
　　Have hindered his determinèd intent'.
　　Briefly, I think he will not come at all.　　　　　　　40
Edward. But is he like to take the town of Neuss?
Scales. My lord, the town is liker to take him;
　　That, if he chance to come to you at all,
　　'Tis but for succour.
Edward.　　　　　　　　But what says Count St Pol?
Scales. My lord, he lies, and revels at St Quentin,　　45
　　And laughs at Edward's coming into France;

---

30. earthy] *Q1*; earthly *Q2–6.*　unresolved] *Q2*; vnresolute *Q1.*

---

23. *Neuss*] small German town, just north of Cologne, in the Gelderland
territory which came under Burgundian control in 1473. The favoured
spelling in the quartos is 'Nuse'.

25. *force and compass*] utmost extent.

26. *cheered*] animated.

30. *earthy*] Q1's reading is retained, with its connotations of dullness and
pollution; 'earthly', the reading of all subsequent quartos, was invariably
defined in opposition to the celestial.

unresolved] The reading of Qs 2–6 is defensible in terms of metre, sense
and palaeography, although Q1's 'unresolute' conveys a sense of mere hesitation more appropriate than the measured pause implied by 'unresolved'.

45. *St Quentin*] a town in Picardy, recovered as a Burgundian territory in
1465. The reading of the early editions is, variously, 'S. Quintens' or 'S.
Quintins'.

There, domineering with his drunken crew,
Make jigs of us, and in their slav'ring jests
Tell how like rogues we lie here in the field.
Then comes a slave, one of those drunken sots,   50
In with a tavern-reckoning for a supplication,
Disguisèd with a cushion on his head,
A drawer's apron for a herald's coat,
And tells the Count, the King of England craves
One of his worthy honour's dog-kennels   55
To be his lodging for a day or two,
With some such other tavern foolery;
With that, this filthy, rascal, greasy rout
Burst out in laughter at this worthy jest,
Neighing like horses; thus the Count St Pol   60
Regards his promise to your majesty.
Edward. Will no man thrust the slave into a sack-butt?
Sellinger. Now, by this light, were I but near the slave,
With a black-jack I would beat out his brains.
Howard. If it please your highness but to say the word,   65
We'll pluck him out of Quentin by the ears.
Edward. No, cousin Howard, we'll reserve our valour
For better purpose. Since they both refuse us,
Our selves will be unrivalled in our honour.
Now, our first cast, my lord, is at main France,   70
Whilst yet our army is in health, and strong;
And, have we once but broke unto that war,
I will not leave St Pol, nor Burgundy,

---

47. *domineering*] swaggering, aping figures of authority.

48. *jigs*] short, comic, often satirical performances, which were frequently offered in Elizabethan amphitheatres at the end, or in an interval of a play.

slav'ring] literally means allowing saliva to drip; Heywood (?) associated it with deceit in *How a Man May Chuse* (1602), D4r.

51. *supplication*] formal petition.

58. *rout*] gang.

62. *sack-butt*] barrel containing Canary wine.

64. *black-jack*] leather jug.

69. *Our selves . . . honour*] Our glory will be all the greater because we fight unaided; a perfunctory redaction of the theme expansively dramatized in 5.1 of Shakespeare's *Henry V* earlier the same year.

70. *cast*] throw (the term is from gambling with dice).

Not a bare pig's cote to shroud them in.
Herald!   75
Herald. My sovereign.
Edward. Go, herald, and to Lewis, the French king,
Denounce stern war, and tell him I am come
To take possession of my realm of France.
Defy him boldly from us, be thy voice   80
As fierce as thunder, to affright his soul.
Herald, be gone, I say, and be thy breath
Piercing as lightning, and thy words as death.
Herald. I go, my liege, resolved to your high will.
                                               Exit HERALD.
Edward. Sound drum, I say, set forward with our power;   85
And, France, ere long expect a dreadful hour:
I will not take the English standard down
Till thou empale my temples with thy crown.
                                                         [*Exeunt.*]

[Scene 2]

           Enter LEWIS *the French king* [*with attendants*],
              BOURBON, [MUGEROUN] *and* ST PIERRE,
                     with the HERALD *of England.*

Lewis. Herald of England, we are pleased to hear
What message thou hast brought us from thy king;
Prepare thyself, and be advised in speech.
Herald. Right gracious and most Christian king of France,
I come not to thy presence unprepared   5
To do the message of my royal liege.
Edward the Fourth, of England and of France
The lawful king, and lord of Ireland,

---

87. standard] *Q1–2*; standerds *Q4–6*.

74. *pig's cote*] pigsty.
78. *Denounce*] proclaim formally.
88. *empale*] encircle, adorn; but see also commentary to Part One, Scene
1, l. 106.

3. *advised*] judicious, precise.

Whose puissant magnanimous breast incensed,
Through manifest notorious injuries   10
Offered by thee, King Lewis, and thy French,
Against his title to the crown of France,
And right in all these dukedoms following,
Aquitaine, Anjou, Guyenne, Angouleme,
Breathes forth by me, the organ of his speech,   15
Hostile defiance to thy realm and thee:
And trampling now upon the face of France,
With barbèd horse, and valiant armèd foot,
Himself the leader of those martial troops,
Bids thee to battle, where and when thou darst,   20
Except thou make such restitution
And yearly tribute on good hostages
As may content his just conceivèd wrath;
And to this message answer I expect.

Lewis. Right peremptory is this embassage,   25
And were my royal brother of England pleased
To entertain those kind affections
Wherewith we do embrace his amity,
Needless were all these thunder-threat'ning words.
Let heaven, where all our thoughts are registered,   30
Bear record, with what deep desire of peace
We shall subscribe to such conditions
As equity for England shall propound.
If Edward have sustainèd wrong in France,
Lewis was never author of that wrong,   35
Yet, faultless, we will make due recompense.
We are assured that his majestic thoughts
In his mild spirit did never mean these wars,

---

9. *puissant*] powerful.

magnanimous] noble, unmoved by petty injuries; Q1's spelling, 'magnan-imious', was the most common in the period.

14. *Aquitaine*] region in the south-west of France.

Anjou] independent province in north-western France.

Guyenne] swathe of crown territory from the mid-west to the southern reaches of France.

Angouleme] independent province in mid-western France.

15. *organ . . . speech*] speaking instrument, mouthpiece.

21. *Except*] unless.

22. *on*] on the security of.

Till Charles Burgundy, once our fawning friend,
But now our open foe, and Count St Pol,   40
Our subject once and Constable of France,
But now a traitor to our realm and us,
Were motives to incite him unto arms,
Which having done, will leave him, on my life.
Herald. The King, my master, recks not Burgundy,   45
And scorns St Pol, that treacherous Constable.
His puissance is sufficient in itself
To conquer France, like his progenitors.
Lewis. He shall not need to waste by force of war,
Where peace shall yield him more than he can win.   50
We covet peace, and we will purchase it
At any rate that reason can demand,
And it is better England join in league
With us, his strong, old, open enemy,
Than with those weak, and new, dissembling friends.   55
We do secure us from our open foes,
But trust in friends, though faithless, we repose.
My Lord St Pierre, and cousin Bourbon, speak:
What censure you of Burgundy, and St Pol?
St Pierre. Dread lord, it is well known that Burgundy   60
Made show of tender service to your majesty,
Till, by the engine of his flatteries,
He made a breach into your highness' love;
Where entered once, and thereof full possessed,
He so abused that royal excellence,   65
By getting footing into many towns,
Castles and forts belonging to your crown,
That now he holds them 'gainst your realm, and you.
Bourbon. And Count St Pol, the Constable of France,
Ambitious in that high authority,   70
Usurps the lands and signories of those
That are true subjects, noble peers of France.
Your boundless favours did him first suborn,
And now to be your liegeman he thinks scorn.

66. footing] *Q3*; fooiting *Q1–2*.

---

45. *recks*] considers.
59. *censure*] evaluate critically.
71. *signories*] properties of undisputed ownership.

Lewis. By this, conjecture the unsteady course   75
 Thy royal master undertakes in France;
 And Herald, intimate what fervent zeal
 We have to league with Edward and his English.
 Three hundred crowns we give thee for reward,
 And of rich crimson velvet, thirty yards,   80
 In hope thou wilt unto thy sovereign tell,
 We show thee not one discontented look,
 Nor render him one misbeholden word:
 But his defiance, and his dare to war,
 We swallow with the supple oil of peace,   85
 Which, gentle Herald, if thou canst procure,
 A thousand crowns shall justly guerdon thee.
Herald. So please it your most sacred majesty,
 To send unto my gracious sovereign
 Equal conditions for the bonds of peace,   90
 And restitution of his injuries,
 His temper is not of obdurate malice,
 But sweet, relenting, princely clemency.
 Perform your promise of a thousand crowns,
 And second me with some fit messenger,   95
 And I will undertake to work your peace.
Lewis. By the true honour of a Christian king,
 Effect our peace, and thou shalt have our crowns,
 And we will post a herald after thee,
 That shall confirm thy speech, and our designs.   100
 Go, Mugeroun, see to this herald given
 The velvet, and three hundred crowns proposed.
 Farewell, good friend, remember our request,
 And kindly recommend us to King Edward.
    Exeunt ENGLISH HERALD *and* MUGEROUN.
 How think you, lords, is't not more requisite   105
 To make our peace, then war with England's power?
Bourbon. Yes, gracious lord; the wounds are bleeding yet,

---

79. *crowns*] English coins, worth five shillings (one-quarter of £1).
87. *guerdon*] reward.
95. *fit*] appropriate.

That Talbot, Bedford and King Henry made,
Which peace must cure, or France shall languish still.
St Pierre. Besides, my liege, by these intestine foes,   110
The Constable, and treacherous Burgundy,
The state's in danger if the English stir.

Enter MUGEROUN.

Lewis. 'Tis perilous, and full of doubt, my lords;
We must have peace with England, every way.
Who shall be herald in these high affairs?   115
Bourbon. No better man than Monsieur Mugeroun,
Whose wit is sharp, whose eloquence is sound,
His presence gracious, and his courage good,
A gentleman, a scholar, and a soldier,
A complete man for such an embassage.   120
Art thou content to be employed, Mugeroun,
In this negotiation to King Edward?
Mugeroun. If your most sacred majesty command,
Your humble vassal Mugeroun shall go.
Lewis. Grammercies, Mugeroun, but thou must assume   125
A herald's habit, and his office both,
To plead our love, and to procure us peace
With English Edward, for the good of France.
Mugeroun. I know the matter and the form, my lord;
Give me my herald's coat, and I am gone.   130
Lewis. Thou art a man composed for business;
Attend on us for thy instructions,
And other fit supplies for these affairs,
And for thy diligence, expect reward.   *Exeunt.*

---

129. I know] *Q2; Q1 has poorly inked letter* (f?) *after I (thus possibly* 'If now'*).*

---

108. *Talbot*] John, first Earl of Shrewsbury (1388?–1453). The most famous warrior of Henry V's reign, whose exploits had been recently celebrated in Roger Cotton's *An Armor of Proofe* (1596), sigs A3v–A4r, and whose demise had been dramatized in *1 Henry VI* (1592).
Bedford] third son of Henry IV, John of Lancaster (1389–1435), became Duke in 1414, and Regent of France upon the death of Henry V. He was responsible for the capture and burning of Joan of Arc.
Henry] Henry V.
110. *intestine*] internal.

[Scene 3]

Enter several ways BURGUNDY *and* THE CONSTABLE
OF FRANCE.

Constable. Whither away so fast goes Burgundy?
Burgundy. Nay, rather, whither goes the Constable?
Constable. Why, to King Edward, man; is he not come?
    Meanst thou not likewise, to go visit him?
Burgundy. O, excellent. I know that in thy soul   5
    Thou knowst that I do purpose nothing less.
    Nay, I do know, for all thy outward show,
    Thou hast no meaning once to look on him.
    Brother dissembler, leave this colouring,
    With him that means as falsely as thyself.   10
Constable. Ay, but thou knowst that Edward, on our letters,
    And hoping our assistance when he came,
    Did make this purposed voyage into France,
    And with his forces is he here arrived,
    Trusting that we will keep our word with him.   15
    Now, though we mean it not, yet set a face
    Upon the matter, as though we intended
    To keep our word with him effectually.
Burgundy. And for my better countenance in this case,
    My ling'ring siege at Neuss will serve the turn;   20
    There will I spend the time to disappoint
    King Edward's hope of my conjoining with him.
Constable. And I will keep me still here in St Quentin,
    Pretending mighty matters for his aid,
    But not performing any, on my word.   25
    The rather, Burgundy, because I aim   *All*
    At matters which perhaps may cost your head,   *this*
    If all hit right to expectation.   *aside*
    In the mean space, like a good, crafty knave,
    That hugs the man he wisheth hanged in heart,   30
    Keep I fair weather still with Burgundy,

---

8. *meaning*] intention.
9. *colouring*] fraudulent display of integrity.
11. *on*] prompted by.

Till matters fall out for my purpose fit.
Ici, sont mon secrets, beau temps pour moy.
Burgundy. [*Aside*] *Ici, sont mon secrets, beau temps pour moy.*
    Are you so crafty, Constable? Proceed, proceed,   35
    You quick, sharp-sighted man, imagine me
    Blind, witless, and a silly idiot,
    That pries not into all your policies.
    Who, I? No, God doth know my simple wit
    Can never sound a judgement of such reach,   40
    As in our cunning Constable of France:
    Persuade thy self so still, and when time serves,
    And that thou art in most extremity,
    Needing my help, then take thou heed of me;
    In mean while, sir, you are the only man   45
    That hath my heart! Hath? Ay, and great reason too!
    Thus it befits men of deep reach to do—
    Well, Constable, you'll back again to Neuss,
    And not aid English Edward?
Constable.   What else, man?
    And keep thee in St Quentin; so shall we   50
    Smile at King Edward's weak capacity.   *Exeunt.*

[Scene 4]

    Enter KING EDWARD [*at the head of his soldiers*], *with*
    BURGUNDY, HOWARD, SELLINGER, *and* SCALES.

Edward. Tell me not, Burgundy; 'tis I am wronged,
    And you have dealt like a disloyal knight.
Burgundy. Edward of England, these are unkingly words.
Edward. He that will do, my lord, what he should not,

---

41. in] *Q3*; is *Q1-2*.

---

33. Ici . . . moy] Inpenetrable. The phrase 'voila, il y a beau temps que' is
idiomatic, and can be translated as 'it's a long time since'; thus, perhaps,
'Here are my secrets, going back a long way now'. Alternatively, 'beau temps
pour moy' sounds like an exclamation, such as 'bully for me', but this finds
no corroboration in Huguet's massive dictionary of French sixteenth-century
usage. Either way, it's clearly an expression of pantomime smugness.
    40. sound] interpret.
    reach] capacity. The word often carried sinister connotations of concealed
power; see the 'reaching hands' of the Lord Say, *2 Henry VI* (4.7.69).

Must, and shall hear of me what he would not;   5
I say again, you have deluded me.
Burgundy. Am I not come according to my word?
Edward. No, Charles of Burgundy. Thy word was given
To meet with me in April; now 'tis August;
The place appointed Calais, not Lorraine;   10
And thy approach to be with martial troops,
But thou art come not having in thy train
So much as page or lackey to attend thee,
As who should say, thy presence were munition
And strength enough to answer our expect.   15
Summer is almost spent, yet nothing done,
And all by dalliance with uncertain hope.
Burgundy. My forces lay before the city, Neuss,
From which I could not rise but with dishonour,
Unless upon some composition had.   20
Edward. There was no such exception in your letters.
Why smiles Lord Scales?
Scales.   My man reports, my lord,
The composition that the Duke there made
Was mere compulsion; for the citizens
Drove him from thence perforce.
Edward.   I thought so much: 25
We should not yet have seen your Excellence,
But that your heels were better than your hands.
Burgundy. Lord Scales, thou dost me wrong to slander me.
Edward. Letting that pass, it shall be seen, my lord,
That we are able of our self to claim   30
Our right in France, without or your assistance,
Or any others, but the help of heaven.

---

10. *Calais*] The spelling in the quartos—'Calice'—indicates pronunciation.

11–13. *troops . . . thee*] Commines (I, 247) and Holinshed (III, 332) both note that Burgundy arrived with only a small entourage rather than his formidable army, most of which was dispatched to Lorraine; the play anticipates the assessment of modern historians (e.g. R. Vaughan, *Charles the Bold* (London, 1973), 344–5) who see Burgundy's appearance with only his household retinue as an intentional strategy and affront.

15. *expect*] expectations.

20. *composition*] acceptable resolution, deal.

27. *your heels . . . hands*] Proverbial (Dent, H394.11); you were more adept at running away than at fighting.

Burgundy. I make no question of it; yet the Constable,
   Pressed with no such occasion as I was,
   Might have excused us both, if he had pleased.   35
Edward. Accuse him not. Your cities, as we came,
   Were even as much to be condemned as his;
   They gave us leave to lie within the field,
   And scarcely would afford us meat for money.
   This was small friendship, in respect of that   40
   You had engaged your honour to perform.
   But march we forward, as we were determined:
   This is St Quentin, where you say, my lord,
   The Constable is ready to receive us.
Burgundy. So much he signified to me by letter.   45
Edward. Well, we shall see his entertainment. Forward.

> *As they march upon the stage, the* LORD SCALES *is struck*
> *down, and two soldiers slain outright, with*
> *great-shot from the town.*

   Fly to our main battalia; bid them stand.
   There's treason plotted: speak to me, Lord Scales,
   Or if there be no power of life remaining
   To utter thy heart's grievance, make a sign.   50
   Two of our common soldiers slain beside!
   This is hard welcome! But it was not you
   At whom the fatal engineer did aim.
   My breast the level was, though you the mark:
   In which conspiracy, answer me, Duke,   55
   Is not thy soul as guilty as the Earl's?
Burgundy. Perish my soul, King Edward, if I knew
   Of any such intention. [*Aside*] Yet I did,
   And grieve that it hath sped no otherwise.

---

47. battalia] *Q1–2* (battaile); battell *Q3–6*.   58–9. *Qq line:* hath / sped.

36–9. *Your . . . money*] Edward's accusation is corroborated by Commines
(I, 247) and, with indignation, by Holinshed (III, 332).
   46.03. great-shot] cannon balls.
   47. *battalia*] body of the army; cf. *Richard II* (5.3.11). Although Q4–6
'modernize' to 'battell', the line's scansion requires the three syllables implied
by the 'battaile' of Q1–3.
   53. *engineer*] bomb-maker.
   54. *level . . . mark*] The imagery is from archery; 'level' is the target aimed
at, the 'mark' is the part actually struck.

Edward. Howard, and Sellinger,   60
                              BURGUNDY *steals away.*
What, is there hope of life in none of them?
Howard. The soldiers are both slain outright, my lord,
But the Lord Scales a little is recovered.
Edward. Convey his body to our pavilion,
And let our surgeons use all diligence   65
They can devise for safeguard of his life,
    [*Soldiers carry* SCALES *and lay him at one of the doors.*]
Whilst we, with all extremity of war,
Go plague St Quentin. Howard, fetch on our powers.
                              [*Exit* HOWARD.]
We will not stir a foot till we have shown
Just vengeance on the Constable of France.   70
O God! To woo us first to pass the sea,
And at our coming, thus to halt with us!
I think the like was never seen.
But where's the Duke?
Sellinger.   Gone, as it seems, my lord;
Stepped secretly away, as one that knew   75
His conscience would accuse him if he stayed.
Edward. A pair of most dissembling hypocrites
Is he, and this base earl, on whom I vow,
Leaving King Lewis unprejudiced in peace,
To spend the whole measure of my kindled rage!   80
Their streets shall sweat with their effusèd blood,
And this bright sun be darkened with the smoke
Of smould'ring cinders, when their city lies
Buried in ashes of revengeful fire;
On whose pale superficies in the stead   85
Of parchment, with my lance I'll draw these lines:
'Edward of England left this memory,
In just revenge of hateful treachery!'

                    Enter HOWARD *again.*

---

72. *halt*] play false.
79. *unprejudiced*] subject to no condemnation.
81. *effusèd*] shed, spilt.
85. *superficies*] surface layer.

Lord Howard, have you done as I commanded?
Howard. Our battles are disposed, and on the brow   90
Of every inferior servitor, my lord,
You might behold destruction figured,
Greedily thirsting to begin the fight.
But when no longer they might be restrained,
And that the drum and trumpet both began   95
To sound war's cheerful harmony, behold!
A flag of truce upon the walls was hanged,
And forth the gates did issue, meekly paced,
Three men, whereof the Constable is one;
The other two, the gunner and his mate,   100
By whose gross oversight—as they report—
This sudden chance unwittingly befell.
Edward. Bring forth the Constable. [*Soldiers go out.*] The
     other two,
See them safe guarded, till you know our pleasure.

Enter the CONSTABLE [*guarded*].

Now, my Lord Howard, how is't with Scales?   105
Howard. Well, my dread sovereign, now his wound is dressed;
And by the opinion of the surgeons,
It's thought he shall not perish by this hurt.
Edward. I am the gladder. But, unfaithful Earl,
I do not see how yet I can dispense   110
With thy submission. This was not the welcome
Your letters sent to England promised me.
Constable. Right high and mighty Prince, condemn me not,
That am as innocent in this offence
As any soldier in the English army.   115
The fault was in our gunners' ignorance,
Who, taking you for Lewis, King of France,

---

104. SD CONSTABLE] *Constable and Howard Qq.*

90. *battles*] battalions.
91. *servitor*] low-ranking soldier.
104.01. SD] All early editions mark another entrance for Howard here,
but his exit and re-entry after speaking ll. 90–102 is neither necessary nor
plausible; Edward's solicitous question about the welfare of Scales is an effec-
tive opening to his pressurization of the Constable.
110–11. *dispense . . . With*] take a legally flexible stance towards.

That likewise is within the city's ken,
Made that unlucky shot to beat him back,
And not of malice to your majesty;   120
To knowledge which, I brought them with myself,
And thirty thousand crowns within this purse,
Sent by the burghers, to redeem your lack.
Edward. Constable of France, we will not sell a drop
Of English blood for all the gold in France: 125
But in so much two of our men are slain,
To quit their deaths, those two that came with thee
Shall both be crammed into a cannon's mouth,
And so be shot into the town again.
It is not like but that they knew our colours,   130
And of set purpose did this villainy.
Nor can I be persuaded thoroughly
But that our person was the mark they aimed at:
Yet are we well content to hold you excused,
Marry, our soldiers must be satisfied.   135
And, therefore, first shall be distributed
These crowns amongst them. Then, you shall return,
And of your best provision send to us
Thirty wain load, beside twelve tun of wine.
This, if the burghers will subscribe unto,   140
Their peace is made; otherwise, I will proclaim
Free liberty for all to take the spoil.
Constable. Your highness shall be answered presently,
And I will see these articles performed.
Edward. Yet one thing more. I will that you, my lord,   145
Together with the Duke of Burgundy,
Do, ere tomorrow noon, bring all your force
And join with ours; or else we do recant,
And these conditions shall be frustrate.
Constable. Mine are at hand, my lord, and I will write   150

---

118. *ken*] sight-range.
121. *knowledge*] acknowledge.
127–9. *those two . . . again*] There is no record of either this boast or its fulfilment in the chronicle sources.
139. *wain*] wagon.
tun] a huge barrel, containing 252 gallons.
142. *take the spoil*] plunder.
143. *presently*] immediately.

The Duke may likewise be in readiness.
Edward. Let him have safe conduct through our army.
    And 'gainst the morning, every leader see
    His troops be furnished; for no longer time,
    God willing, shall the trial be deferred   155
    'Twixt Lewis, and us.
                    [*A trumpet sounds.*]
                    What echoing sound is this?
Sellinger. A gentleman from the King of France, my lord,
    Craves parlance with your Excellence.
Edward. A gentleman? Bring him in.
    What news, a God's name, from our brother Lewis?   160

                    Enter MUGEROUN.

Mugeroun. Most puissant and most honourable king!
    My royal master, Lewis, the King of France,
    Doth greet your highness with unfeignèd love,
    Wishing you health, prosperity and rule.
    And thus he says by me: when was it seen   165
    That ever Lewis pretended hurt to England,
    Either by close conspirators, sent over
    To undermine your state, or openly,
    By taking arms with purpose to invade?
    Nay, when was it, that Lewis was ever heard   170
    So much as to detract from Edward's name?
    But still hath done him all his due of speech,
    By blazing to the world his high deserts
    Of wisdom, valour and his heroic birth.
    Whence is it, then, that Edward is incensed   175
    To render hate for love, for amity stern war?
    Not of himself, we know, but by the means
    Of some infectious counsel, that, like mud,
    Would soil the pure temper of his noble mind.
    It is the Duke, and that pernicious rebel,   180
    Earl of St Pol, have set abroach these wars,
    Who, of themselves unable to proceed,

179. soil] *Q1*; spoyle *Q2–6.*

---

154. *furnished*] prepared.
158. *parlance*] parley.
167. *close*] secret.

Would make your grace the instrument of wrong.
And when you have done what you can for them,
You shall be sure of nothing, but of this: 185
Still to be doubled and dissembled with.
But, if it might seem gracious in your eye,
To cast off these despised confederates,
Unfit companions for so great a prince,
And join in league with Lewis, my royal master,   190
Him shall you find as willing as of power,
To do your grace all offices of love.
And what commodity may spring thereby
To both the realms, your grace is wise enough,
Without my rude suggestions, to imagine.   195
Besides, much bloodshed for this present time
Will be prevented, when two such personages
Shall meet together to shake hands in peace,
And not with shock of lance and curtle-axe.
That Lewis is willing, I am his substitute;   200
And he himself, in person if you please,
Not far from hence will signify as much.
Edward. Sir, withdraw, and give us leave awhile,
To take advisement of our counsellors.
                                    [*Exit* MUGEROUN.]
What say ye, lords, unto this proffered truce?   205
Howard. In my conceit, let it not be slipped, my lord.
Sellinger. Will't not be dishonour, having landed
So great an army in these parts of France,
And not to fight before we do return?
Howard. How can it, when the enemy submits,   210
And of himself makes tender of allegiance?
Sellinger. Ay, that's the question: whether he will yield,
And do King Edward fealty, or no.
Edward. What, talk ye, lords? He shall subscribe to that,
Or no conditions I'll accept at all.   215
Howard. Let him be bound, my lord, to pay your grace,
Toward your expenses, since your coming over,

206. it] *Q2; omitted in Q1.*

_____

191. *as willing . . . power*] with the will and the means.
193. *commodity*] advantage.
206. *let . . . slipped*] let the opportunity not be missed.

Seventy-five thousand crowns of the sun;
And, yearly after, fifty thousand more,
During your life, with homage therewithal,   220
That he doth hold his royalty from you.
And take his offer; 'twill not be amiss.
Edward. It shall be so. [*To Howard*] Draw you the articles.
And Sellinger, call forth the messenger;
Bring with thee, too, a cup of massy gold,   225
And bid the bearer of our privy purse

[*Enter* MUGEROUN.]

Enclose therein a hundred English royals.
                              [*Exit* SELLINGER.]
[*To Mugeroun*] Friend, we do accept thy master's league,
With no less firm affection than he craves.
If he will meet us here, betwixt our tents,   230
It shall on both sides be confirmed by oath,
On this condition: that he will subscribe
To certain articles shall be proposed.

[*Enter* SELLINGER *with a golden cup.*]

And so thou hast thy answer. To requite
Thy pains herein, we give to thee this cup.   235
Mugeroun. Health, and increase of honour wait on Edward.
Edward. Lord Howard, bring the Frenchman on his way.
                  [*Exit* MUGEROUN, *but the King gestures to*
                              HOWARD *to remain.*]
King Lewis is one that never was precise—
But now, Lord Howard and Tom Sellinger,

---

236. *Mugeroun*] Her. Qq.   238. *Q1–3 have another speech prefix here: 'Ed.'; Q4 (correctly) omits it.*

---

218. *crowns . . . sun*] A French crown was worth four English shillings (i.e. 5 = £1). Of the chroniclers, only Holinshed specifies this unit of currency and this amount; the play ignores entirely the putative marriage settlement that, in all the chronicles, was reported to have accompanied the financial one.

225. *massy*] solid.

227. *royals*] coins, worth ten shillings.

238. *Lewis . . . precise*] The observation comes from Holinshed (III, 332), where it signifies that the French king paid little attention to matters of ceremony.

There is a task remains for you to do,   240
And that is this: you two shall be disguised,
And one of you repair to Burgundy,
The other to the Constable of Fance,
Where you shall learn in secret, if you can,
If they intend to meet us here tomorrow,   245
Or how they take this, our accord with France.
Somewhat, it gives me, you will bring from thence
Worthy the noting. Will you undertake it?
Sellinger. With all my heart, my lord. I am for Burgundy.
Howard. And I am for the Constable of France.   250
                    Exeunt [HOWARD, SELLINGER].
Edward. Make speed again.

                    [*Enter a* MESSENGER.]

                    What news?
Messenger. The King of France, my lord, attended royally,
    Is marching hitherward to meet your grace.
Edward. He shall be welcome. Hast thou drawn the articles?
Messenger. Yes, my dread sovereign.
Edward.   Go, call forth our train;   255
    We may receive him with like majesty.   *Exeunt.*

[Scene 5]

        Enter certain noblemen and soldiers, with a drum; they
        march about the stage. Then enter KING LEWIS *and his*
        train, and meet with KING EDWARD; *the kings embrace.*

Lewis. My princely brother, we are grievèd much
    To think you have been at so great a charge,
    And toiled your royal self so far from home,
    Upon th' unconstant promise of those men
    That both dissemble with your grace, and me.   5
Edward. Brother of France, you might condemn us rightly,
    Not only of great wrong and toil sustained,
    But of exceeding folly, if, incited,

---

7. toil] *Q1–2;* toils *Q3–6.*

    247. *it gives me*] I have a feeling.

We had presumed to enter these dominions,
Upon no other reason than the word   10
And weak assistance of the Earl St Pol,
Or Burgundy's persuasion. 'Tis our right
That wings the body of composèd war;
And though we listened to their flatteries,
Yet so we shaped the course of our affairs,   15
As of our self we might be able found,
Without the trusting to a broken staff.
Lewis. I know your majesty had more discretion;
But this is not th' occasion of our meeting.
If you be pleased to entertain a peace,   20
My kingly brother, in the sight of these,
And of the all-discov'ring eye of heaven,
Let us embrace; for as my life, I swear
I tender England, and your happiness.
Edward. The like do I by you and warlike France.   25
But, princely brother, ere this knot be knit,
There are some few conditions to be signed.
That done, I am as ready as yourself.
Lewis. Fair brother, let us hear them what they be.
Edward. Herald, repeat the articles.   30
Herald. First, it is covenanted that Lewis, King of France,
according to the custom of his predecessors, shall do
homage to King Edward, King of England, as his
sovereign, and true heir to all the dominions of France.
Bourbon. How, as his sovereign? That were to depose,   35
And quite bereave him of his diadem.
Will kingly Lewis stoop to such vassalage?
Edward. Bourbon, and if he will not, let him choose.
Lewis. Brother, have patience; Bourbon seal your lips,
And interrupt not these high consequents.   40
Forward, Herald. What is else demanded?
Herald. Secondly, it is covenanted that Lewis, King of France,

---

16. self] *Q1–2;* selues *Q3–6.*   37. such vassalage] *Q1–3;* such a vassalage
Q4–6.

13. *composèd*] stern, grave.
24. *tender*] care greatly for.
40. *consequents*] matters of consequence.

shall pay unto Edward, King of England, immediately
upon the agreement betwixt their majesties, seventy-five
thousand crowns of the sun, toward the charge King   45
Edward hath been at since his arrival in these parts of
France.
Bourbon. *Mort dieu!* He'll neither leave him crown nor coin!
Lewis. Bourbon, I say be silent. Herald, read on.
Herald. Thirdly, and lastly, it is covenanted that, over and   50
besides these seventy-five thousand crowns of the sun,
now presently to be paid, Lewis, King of France, shall
yearly hereafter, during the life of Edward, King of
England, pay fifty thousand crowns more, without fraud
or guile, to be tendered at his majesty's castle, commonly   55
called the Tower of London.
Bourbon. Nay, bind him that he bring his lordship a couple of
capons too, every year beside!
Here is a peace indeed, far worse than war.
Edward. Brother of France, are you resolved to do,   60
According as you hear the covenants drawn?
Lewis. Brother of England, mount your royal throne.
For subjects' weal, and glory of my God,
And to deal justly with the world beside,
Knowing your title to be lineal   65
From the great Edward, of that name the third,
Your predecessor, thus I do resign,
Giving my crown, and sceptre to your hand,
As an obedient liegeman to your grace.
Edward. The same do I deliver back again,   70
With as large interest as you had before.
Now, for th' other covenants.
Lewis.   Those, my lord,
Shall likewise be performed with expedition,
And ever after, as you have prescribed,
The yearly pension shall be truly paid.   75
Herald. Swear on this book, King Lewis, so help you God,
You mean no otherwise than you have said.
Lewis. So help me God, as I dissemble not.
Edward. And so help he me, as I intend to keep
Unfeignèd league and truce with noble France.   80
And, kingly brother, now to consummate
This happy day, feast in our royal tent.
English and French are one: so it is meant.   *Exeunt.*

[Scene 6]

> *Enter at one door* BURGUNDY, *chafing; with him*
> SELLINGER, *disguised like a soldier. At another,*
> *the* CONSTABLE *of France; with him* HOWARD,
> *in the like disguise.*

Burgundy. A peace concluded, sayst thou? Is't not so?
Sellinger. My lord, I do assure you it is so.
Constable. And thou affirmst the like? Say, dost thou not?
Howard. I do, my lord, and that for certainty.
Burgundy. [*To Sellinger*] I have found it now. The villain
    Constable   5
    Hath secretly with Edward thus compact
    To join our king and him in amity,
    And thereby doubtless got into his hands
    Such lands and dukedoms as I aimed at,
    And leaves me disappointed in my hope.   10
    A plague upon such crafty cozening!
    Now shall I be a mark for them to aim at,
    And that vile slave to triumph in my foil.
Constable. [*To Howard*] 'Tis so, for it can be no otherwise.
    Burgundy hath been privy to this plot,   15
    Conspired with Lewis and the English king
    To save his own stake, and assure himself
    Of all those signories I hoped for;
    And thereupon this close peace is contrived.
    Now must the Constable be as a butt   20
    For all their bullets to be levelled at.
    Hell and hot vengeance light on Burgundy
    For this, his subtle secret villany!
Burgundy. Well, fellow, for thy pains take that.   *To Sellinger.*
    Leave me alone, for I am much displeased.   25
Constable. And get thee gone, my friend. There's for thy pains;
                                     To Howard.
    So, leave me to myself.
Sellinger. Fare ye well, sir. [*Aside to Howard*] I hope I have
    peppered ye!

10–12.] *bracketed stage direction—aside.—in Qq.*   24. SD] *opposite line 25 in
Qq.*   26. SD] *opposite line 27 in Qq.*

28. *peppered*] trounced, comprehensively punished (usually in a jocular
sense).

Howard. [*Aside to Sellinger*] And so I think have I my
    constable.
                      Exeunt SELLINGER *and* HOWARD.
Burgundy. Now, Constable, this peace, this peace;   30
    What think ye of it, man?
Constable. Nay, rather, what thinks Burgundy?
Burgundy. I think that he that did contrive the same
    Was little less than a dissembling villain.
Constable. Dog, bite thyself? Come on, come on,   35
    Have not you played 'John for the King'
    To save yourself, sir?
Burgundy.   Ay, art thou good at that?
    Adieu, sir, I may chance to hit you—pat.   *Exit.*
Constable. You may, sir? I, perhaps, may be before ye,
    And for this cunning, through the nose to bore ye.   40
                               Exit.

[Scene 7]

       Enter KING EDWARD, KING LEWIS, HOWARD,
           SELLINGER *and their train.*

Edward. So, Sellinger, we then perceive by thee
    The Duke is passing angry at our league.
Sellinger. Ay, my dread lord, beyond comparison;
    Like a mad dog, snatching at everyone
    That passeth by. Shall I but show you how,   5
    And act the manner of his tragic fury?

---

33. think that he] *Q1*; think he *Q2–6.*   40. *Exit*] *Exeunt Qq.*

36. *'John for the King'*] A ballad of this title was entered as 'newe' in the
Stationers' Register on 24 October 1603, but its earlier existence is proved
by Nashe's reference to it (as Deloney's) in *Have With You to Saffron Walden*
(1596); he mentions it again in *Lenten Stuffe* of 1599 (*Works*, III, 84, 201). No
text has survived, but C. R. Baskervill (*The Elizabethan Jig* (Chicago, 1929),
295–9) plausibly suggested that the character John fo de King in Marston's
Jack Drum's Entertainment (1600) may have been modelled on the song's
salient features; Marston's caricature lecherous foreigner hires himself out
as a killer, but then decides to keep the money without performing the deed,
and this may also provide the context for the Constable's slur against
Burgundy. Heywood alludes to the song again in *The Rape of Lucrece*
(c.1607), ll. 1240–3.

Edward. No, stay a while. Methought I heard thee say
   They meant to greet us by their messengers.
Sellinger. They did, my lord.
Edward.   What, and the Constable too?
Howard. My sovereign, yes.
Edward.   But how took he the news?   10
Howard. Faith, e'en as discontented as might be,
   But, being a more deep melancholist,
   And sullener of temper than the Duke,
   He chaws his malice, fumes and froths at mouth,
   Uttering but little more than what we gather   15
   By his disturbèd looks and rivelled front;
   Saving that, now and then, his boiling passion,
   Damned up as in a furnace, finding vent,
   Breaks through his severed lips into short puffs,
   And then he mumbles forth a word or two,   20
   As doth a toothless monk when he's at matins.
Edward. O, it was sport alone to note their carriage.
Sellinger. Sport, my lord? Will you but hear me speak,
   And if I do not weary you with laughter,
   Ne'er trust Tom Sellinger more upon his word.   25

          Sound a Trumpet.

Edward. I pray thee, peace. By this, it should appear
   One of their messengers is come; go see.
                  [*Exit* SELLINGER.]
   Upon my life, we shall have some device
   Of new dissimulation.

          [*Enter* SELLINGER.]

          How now, Tom?
Sellinger. 'Tis as your highness did suppose, my lord;   30

---

12. *melancholist*] person of a melancholy disposition. The usage here,
implying affectation, anticipates that detected by *OED* for the later
seventeenth century, where it connotes the posturing of a fanatic.

14. *chaws*] etymologically a variant form of 'chew', but with invariably
pejorative associations. It could mean to mangle without the intent to
swallow (see *Faerie Queene*, I, iv, 30), to brood upon, to make a bullet jagged
by biting, or to speak in a mumbling or grotesque fashion; the comic portrait could comprise any or all of these.

16. *rivelled front*] furrowed look.

Here is a messenger from Burgundy.
Edward. Excellent good, admit him presently.
                                              [*Exit* SELLINGER.]
And brother of France, let me entreat your grace
To stand aside a little, in my tent,
Lest, finding us together, he refrain   35
To tell the message he is sent about;
So sure I am persuaded we shall find
Some notable piece of knavery set afoot.
Lewis. With all my heart. Urge him speak loud enough,
That I, my lord, may understand him too.   40

                    Enter the Lord of CONTAY
                    [*accompanied by* SELLINGER].

Edward. [*To Lewis*] Fear not: I have the method in my mind—
    What, is it you, my lord of Contay? Welcome!
    How doth the valiant Duke? In health, I hope?
Contay. In health, my lord, of body; though in mind
    Somewhat distempered, that your grace hath joined   45
    In league with his professèd enemy.
Edward. How say you that, my lord? Pray you speak out,
    For I, of late, by reason of a cold,
    Am somewhat thick of hearing.
Contay.   Thus, my lord.
    Your grace demanded if the Duke were well: 50
    I answer you, he is in health of body,
    Though inwardly in mind, somewhat perplexed
    That you, without his knowledge, have ta'en truce
    With childish Lewis, that heartless King of France.
Edward. With whom, I pray ye? A little louder, sir!   55
Contay. With childish Lewis, that heartless King of France!
Edward. I now do understand you. Is it that
    He takes unkindly? Why, if he had come
    With his expected forces as he promised,
    I had been still incapable of peace;   60
    But he deceiving me, the fault was his.

---

54. that] *Q1–2; omitted in Q3–6.*

40.01. CONTAY] The quartos spell this name as 'Conte' throughout,
except at l. 197, where they read 'Countie'.

Contay. No, my good lord, the fault was not in him,
    But in that lewd, pernicious counterfeit,
    That crafty fox, the Constable of France,
    Who counselled him to keep him at his siege,   65
    Saying it would be more dishonourable
    To rise from thence, than any way profitable
    To meet your majesty. Beside, my lord,
    It hath been proved since, how much the Constable
    Hates your proceedings, by that wilful shot   70
    Was made against you from St Quentin's walls;
    Which, though he seemed to colour with fair speech,
    The truth is, they did level at your self,
    And grievèd when they heard you were not slain.
Edward. May I be bold to credit your report?   75
Contay. The Duke, upon his honour, bade me say
    That it was true; and therewithal, quoth he,
    Tell noble Edward, if he will recant,
    And fall from Lewis again, knowing it is
    More for his dignity to be sole king,   80
    And conquer France as did his ancestors,
    Than take a fee, and so be satisfied,
    That I am ready with twelve thousand soldiers,
    All well-appointed, and not only will
    Deliver him the Constable of France,   85
    That he may punish him as he sees good,
    But seat him in the throne imperial,
    Which now another basely doth usurp.
Edward. Speak that again; I heard not your last words.
Contay. But seat you in the throne imperial,   90
    Which now another basely doth usurp.
Edward. I thank his honour for his good regard.
    Pleaseth you stay till we have paused upon't,
    And you shall have our answer to the Duke.
    Tom Sellinger, receive him to your tent,   95

---

63. *lewd*] dissolute.
72. *colour*] camouflage.
77. *therewithal*] in the light of all this.
78. *recant*] retract.
79. *fall from*] abandon.

And let him taste a cup of Orleans wine.
                         [*Exeunt* CONTAY, SELLINGER.]
    Now, my kingly brother, have you heard this news?
Lewis. So plainly, my lord, that I scarce held myself
    From stepping forth, hearing my royal name
    So much profaned and slubbered as it was.   100
    But I do weigh the person, like himself
    From whence it came, a sly dissembler,
    And spite my anger, I was forced sometime
    To smile, to think the Duke doth hang his friend
    Behind his back, whom to his face he smooths.   105
Edward. But we shall have far better sport anon:
    Howard tells me that another messenger
    Is come in post-haste from the Constable.
    As you have begun, with patience hear the rest.
Lewis. No more ado; I'll to my place again.   110
    Remember that you still be deaf, my lord.
Edward. I warrant you. Howard, call in the messenger.

                Enter the MESSENGER *from the Constable.*

Messenger. Health to the victorious king of England!
Edward. Tell him he must strain out his voice aloud,
    For I am somewhat deaf, and cannot hear.   115
Howard. His majesty requests you to speak out,
    Because his hearing is of late decayed.
Messenger. The worthy Earl, St Pol—
Edward. Come near me.
Messenger. The worthy Earl, St Pol, greets noble Edward,   120
    And gives your grace to understand by me,
    That whereas Charles, that painted sepulchre,
    And most disloyal Duke of Burgundy,
    Hath but usurped the habit of a friend,
    Being in heart your deadly enemy,   125
    As well appears in his false breach of promise,
    And that, whereas he never meant, himself,

---

    96. *Orleans*] thought in Elizabethan England to be the finest French wine;
see, e.g., George Peele's *The Old Wives' Tale*, ll. 398–402.
    100. *slubbered*] smeared; cf. Scene 23, l. 53.

To send you aid, but likewise was the means
To hinder my lord's well-affected duty,
Alleging you desired his company,   130
But that you might betray him to his king.
Beside, whereas it will be proved, my lord,
That he did hire the gunner of St Quentin
For a large sum of money, to discharge
Three several pieces of great ordinance   135
Upon your coming to that cursèd town,
To slay your majesty; in which regard,
If it will please you to revoke from France,
And think of Burgundy as he deserves,
The Earl, with expedition, bad me say,   140
That he would put the Duke into your hands,
Whereby you might revenge his treach'rous purpose,
And aid you, too, with twice five thousand men,
And seat you like a conqueror in France.
Edward. Can it seem possible that two such friends,   145
So firmly knit together as they were,
Should, on a sudden, now be such great foes?
Messenger. The Earl, my lord, could never abide the Duke,
Since his last treason 'gainst your sacred person,
Before St Quentin came to open light.   150
Edward. Was that the cause of their dissension then?
Messenger. It was, my lord.
Edward.   Well, I will think upon't,
And you shall have our answer by and by.
[*Aside to Howard*] Cousin Howard, take him aside,
But let him be kept from the other's sight.   155
Howard. Sir, will you walk in? My lord will take advice,
And so dispatch you back again unto the Earl.
                        [*Exeunt* HOWARD *and Messenger.*]

---

131. his] *Q1–2*; the *Q3–6*.   140. Earl] Duke *Qq*.   141. Duke] Earle *Qq*.

131. *But that*] Without which. The alteration from 'his King' to 'the king' in Q4–6 compounds the syntactical difficulty of this passage, even if it accentuates the issue of contested sovereignty.

138. *revoke*] withdraw allegeance.

140–1. *Earl . . . Duke*] All six early editions transpose these titles; the emendation is required by both theatrical logic and the evidence provided by the chronicles.

Lewis. Here's vying of villany; who shall have all?
  Fraud with deceit, deceit with fraud outfaced;
  I would the devil were there to cry 'swoop-stake'!   160
  But how intends your grace to deal with them?
Edward. Faith, in their kind. I am the steel, you see,
  Against the which, their envy being struck,
  The sparkles of hypocrisy fly forth.
  'Twere not amiss to quench them in their blood.   165

  Enter another MESSENGER *to the King of France,*
      with letters [*and* HOWARD].

Messenger. My lord, here's letters to your majesty: one from
  the Duke of Burgundy, the other from the Constable.
Lewis. More villany, a thousand crowns to nothing!
Edward. Can there be more than is already broached?
  Methinks they have already done so well,   170
  As this may serve to bring them both to hell.
Lewis. No, no, they are indifferently well laden,
  But yet their freight's not full. See, other ware,
  Other provision to prepare their way. [*He shows letters.*]
  The very same, my lord, which they pretend   175
  In love to you, against my life and crown,
  The same they undertake to do for me
  Against your safety, urging, if I please,
  That they will join their forces both with mine,
  And in your back return to Calais, cut the throats   180
  Of you and all your soldiers.
Edward.   O, damnable!
  But that I see it figured in these lines,
  I would have sworn there had been nothing left
  For their pernicious brains to work upon.

166–7.] *Qq line:* My ... majesty (*verse*) / One ... from / the (*prose*).
184. brains] brain *Qq.*

160. *swoop-stake*] Stakes in a game of gambling, regardless of the winner's
entitlement (cf. *Hamlet*, 4.5.141).
  169. *broached*] set in motion.
  184. *pernicious brains*] Again, emendation is justified; the compositor of
Q1 was struggling in this passage, and turned the 'u' of 'pernicious' too.

Lewis. A traitor's like a bold-faced hypocrite,   185
  That never will be brought unto a *non-plus*,
  So long as he hath liberty to speak.
Edward. The way to cure them is to cut them off.
  Call forth their messengers once more to us.
Howard. Both of them, my lord?
Edward.   Yes, both, together.   190
  We'll see if they have grace to blush, or no,
  At that their masters shame not to attempt.

> *Enter both the* MESSENGERS *[one from Burgundy*
> (CONTAY), *one from the Constable].*

Contay. [*Aside*] What, is his majesty of France so near?
  And Monsieur Rosse, the Earl's secretary?
  I fear some hurt depends upon his presence.   195
Messenger. How comes it that I see the French king here?
  And the lord of Contay too, me thinks.
  Pray God our message be not made a scorn.
Edward. You told me that you came from Earl St Pol.
Messenger. I did, my lord, and therein fabled not.   200
Edward. You told me, too, of many kind endeavours
  Which he intended for our benefit.
Messenger. No more than he is willing to perform.
Edward. Know you his handwriting, if you see it?
Messenger. I do, my lord.
Edward.   Is this his hand, or no?   205
Messenger. I cannot say but that it is his hand.
Edward. How comes it then, that underneath his hand,
  My death is sought, when you that are his mouth
  Tune to our ears a quite contrary tale?
  The like read you, deciphered in this paper,   210

---

185. hypocrite] *Q1–3*; heretick *Q4–6*.   192. not] *Q4–6*; now *Q1–3*.

185. *hypocrite*] The reading of the Jacobean quartos, 'heretick', is intriguing, but has no textual authority.
  186. non-plus] 'A state in which no more can be said' (*OED*, 1).
  194. *Monsieur Rosse*] It's not clear why the dramatist has interpolated this name; Holinshed (III, 337) and Comines (I, 256–7), and all other chronicles which specify the identity of St Pol's envoy agree that he was called Lewis of Creuille.

Concerning treach'rous, wav'ring Burgundy.
Unless you grant they can divide themselves,
And of two shapes become four substances,
How is it I should have their knightly aid,
And yet by them be utterly destroyed?   215
Lewis. And I, to be protected by their means,
And yet they shall conspire against my life?
Edward. What call you this, but vile hypocrisy?
Lewis. Nay, peasant-like, unheard of treachery.
Contay. My lord, upbraid me not with this offence.   220
I do protest, I knew of no such letters,
Nor any other intention of the Duke,
More than before was uttered in my message.
Sellinger. Will you be halting too before a cripple?
Do you not remember what they were,   225
That first did certify the Duke of truce
Betwixt the renowned Edward and the French?
Contay. Yes, they were two soldiers. What of that?
Sellinger. Those soldiers were this gentleman and I,
Where we did hear the foul-mouthed Duke exclaim   230
Against our noble sovereign and this prince,
And roared and bellowed like a parish bull;
And that in hearing, both of you and him.
His words, so please my lord, I can repeat
As he did speak them at that very time.   235
Edward. Well, they are messengers; and for that cause
We are content to bear with their amiss.
But keep them safe, and let them not return
To carry tales unto those counterfeits,
Until you have them both as fast ensnared: 240
To compass which the better, brother of France,
Five thousand of our soldiers here we leave,

---

224. *Will . . . cripple*] Proverbial (Dent, H60) variation on 'it takes one to know one'; halting = limping, and the implication is that Contay is trying to dissemble in front of a consummate dissembler.

232. *parish bull*] proverbially the biggest and loudest animal, kept at the expense of the parish to service all the cows of the locality.

241. *compass*] accomplish; Edward's deployment of a task force to punish the Constable and Burgundy is an invention of the dramatist, without verification in any chronicle account.

To be employed in service to that end;
The rest with us to England shall return.   *Exeunt.*

[Scene 8]

Enter CHORUS.

Chorus. King Edward is returned home to England,
And Lewis, King of France, soon afterward
Surprisèd both his subtle enemies,
Rewarding them with trait'rous recompense.
Now do we draw the curtain of our scene,   5
To speak of Shore and his fair wife again,
With other matters thereupon depending.
You must imagine, since you saw him last
Prepared for travel, he hath been abroad,
And seen the sundry fashions of the world.   10
Ulysses-like, his country's love at length,
Hoping his wife's death, and to see his friends,
Such as did sorrow for his great mishaps,
Come home is he; but so unluckily,
As he is like to lose his life thereby.   15
His, and her fortunes shall we now pursue,
Graced with your gentle sufferance and view.   *Exeunt.*

[Scene 9]

Enter MISTRESS SHORE, *with* JOCKIE, *her man,
and some attendants more, and is met by*
SIR ROBERT BRACKENBURY.

Jane. Have you bestowed our small benevolence
On the poor prisoners in the common gaol

---

244. *Exeunt*] *Exit Qq.*

11–12. *Ulysses-like . . . death*] Sharply ironic juxtaposition: Homer's Ulysses endured decades of trials and travel abroad, and returned home, having declined an offer of deity, because of his love for both his native land and his wife. Ulysses had, in any case, a schizophrenic reputation: to some the pattern of constancy (see, e.g., *Faerie Queene*, I, 3, 21; V, 7, 39), to others—including, recently, the murderously ambitious Richard of Gloucester—the consummate master of deception; see *3 Henry VI*, 3.2.188–93.

Of the White Lion and the King's Bench?
Jockie. Yes, forsuth.
Jane. What prison's this?   5
Jockie. The Marshalsea, forsuth.

Enter SIR ROBERT BRACKENBURY.

Brackenbury. Well met, fair lady, in the happiest time
    And choicest place that my desire could wish.
    Without offence, where have you been this way?
Jane. To take the air, here in St George's Field,   10
    Sir Robert Brackenbury, and to visit some
    Poor patients that cannot visit me.
Brackenbury. Are you a physician?
Jane.   Ay, a simple one.
Brackenbury. What disease cure ye?
Jane.   Faith, none perfectly.
    My physic doth but mitigate the pain   15
    A little while, and then it comes again.
Brackenbury. Sweet Mistress Shore, I understand you not.
Jane. Master Lieutenant, I believe you well.
Jockie. Gude faith, Sir Robert Brokenbelly, my mistress
    speaks deftly and truly, for she hes been till see thore that 20
    cannot come till see her; and they's peatients perforce.
    The prisoners, man, in the twea prisons! And she hes gin
    tham her siller and her gear till buy them fude.
Brackenbury. Grammercies, Jockie, thou resolvst my doubt.
    A comforting, minist'ring, kind physician,   25
    That once a week, in her own person, visits
    The prisoners and the poor in hospitals,
    In London, or near London every way;

4, 6. forsuth] *Q1*; forsooth *Q2–6*.

3–6. *White Lion . . . King's Bench . . . Marshalsea*] Prisons in Southwark;
the first of these was not used as such until after the accession of Elizabeth
(*Survey*, II, 60).
    10. *St George's Field*] Open space stretching from St George's Church in
Southwark towards Lambeth.
    20. *till*] to.
    thore] those.
    23. *siller*] silver.
    gear] possessions.

Whose purse is open to the hungry soul,
Whose piteous heart saves many a tall man's life.   30
Jane. Peace, good Sir Robert. 'Tis not worthy praise,
    Nor yet worth thanks, that is of duty done;
    For you know well, the world doth know too well,
    That all the coals of my poor charity
    Cannot consume the scandal of my name.   35
    What remedy? Well, tell me, gentle knight,
    What meant your kind salute and gentle speech
    At our first meeting, when you seemed to bless
    The time and place of our encounter here?
Brackenbury. Lady, there lies here, prisoned in the
      Marshalsea,   40
    A gentleman of good parents and good descent,
    My dear, near kinsman, Captain Harry Stranguidge,
    As tall a skilful navigator tried
    As e'er set foot in any ship at sea,
    Whose luck it was to take a prize of France,   45
    As he from Rochelle was for London bound;
    For which, except his pardon be obtained
    By some especial favourite of the King,
    He and his crew, a company of proper men,
    Are sure to die, because 'twas since the league.   50
Jane. Let me see him and all his company.
Brackenbury. Keeper, bring forth the captain and his crew.

    Enter [VAUX *the*] *Keeper,* STRANGUIDGE, SHORE
      disguised, and three more fettered.

---

    30. *tall*] valiant.

    42. *Harry Stranguidge*] No such name occurs in printed or MS chronicles of Edward's reign, but see notes on characters. Oddly, Falconbridge himself was accused of the captain's crime in 1472; *Calendar of Patent Rolls, 1467–1477*, 379.

    46. *Rochelle*] La Rochelle; important French port, on the west coast. At the time of the play's composition its merchants were conducting such a volume of trade that a contemporary observed that 'gold and silver were as abundant as stones'; cited in E. Trocmé, M. Delafosse, *La Commerce Rochelais de la fin de XVe siècle au début du XVIIe* (Paris, 1953), 198.

    49. *proper*] upright.

    50. *league*] Here and later reference is made to the peace treaty concluded in Scene 5.

    52.01. *VAUX*] Clearly the same character as the 'Keeper' of Scene 12, although not named until there. 'Vaux' is the spelling of the quartos, and

Jockie. Now, say oth' diell, that silk bonny men sud be
    hampert like plue-jades. Weas me for ye, gude lads.
Brackenbury. Ay, cousin Harry, this is Mistress Shore,   55
    Peerless in court for beauty, bounty, pity.

                              JANE *views them all.*
    And if she cannot save thee, thou must die.
Stranguidge. Will she, if she can?
Brackenbury.   Ay, cousin Stranguidge, ay.
Shore. O torment worse than death to see her face,   *Aside.*
    That caused her shame, and my unjust disgrace.   60
    O, that our mutual eyes were basilisks,
    To kill each other at this interview!
Brackenbury. How like you him, lady? You have viewed him
    well?
Jane. I pity him, and that same proper man
    That turns his back, ashamed of this distress.   65
Shore. [*Aside*] Ashamed of thee, cause of my heaviness!
Jane. And all the rest. O, were the King returned
    There might be hope, but ere his coming home
    They may be tried, condemned, and judged, and dead.
Shore. I am condemned by sentence of defame;   *Aside.*   70
    O, were I dead, I might not see my shame.
Brackenbury. Your credit, lady, may prolong their trial.
    What judge is he that will give you denial?
Jane. I'll rack my credit, and will launch my crowns

---

59. SD] *opposite line 60 in Qq.*   62. this] *his Qq.*

---

also a name which appears in the same form in the Folio text of *2 Henry VI*,
but the spelling in the quarto text of that play, 'Vawse' (*Contention*, ll.
1395–406), indicates probable pronunciation. There is no suggestion that any
Vaux was involved in Tower administration in either the 1480s or the 1590s.
To Elizabethans the best-known Vaux was the Third Lord, who in 1593 was
so poor that he pawned his parliamentary robes and was unable to redeem
them to take his seat in the House of Lords; L. Stone, *The Crisis of the
Aristocracy* (Oxford, 1965), 517.

    54. *plue-jades*] plough horses.
    Weas . . . ye] Would I could take your place.
    61. *basilisks*] mythical serpents whose gaze was said to be deadly.
Heywood is probably remembering the wooing scene from *Richard III*,
1.2.154.
    62. *interview*] literally, a face-to-face exchange.
    74. *rack*] stretch.
    launch] dispense.

To save their lives, if they have done no murder.   75
Shore. O, thou hast cracked thy credit with a crown,   *Aside.*
And murdered me, poor Matthew Shore, alive.
Stranguidge. Fair lady, we did shed no drop of blood,
Nor cast one Frenchman overboard, and yet,
Because the league was made before the fact,   80
Which we poor seamen, God knows, never heard,
We doubt our lives; yea, though we should restore
Treble the value that we took, and more.
'Twas lawful prize when I put out to sea,
And warranted in my commission.   85
The kings are since combined in amity—
Long may it last—and I, unwittingly,
Have took a Frenchman since the truce was ta'en.
And if I die—*via*, one day I must,
And God will pardon all my sins, I trust—   90
My grief will be for these poor harmless men,
Who thought my warrant might suborn the deed;
Chiefly, that gentleman that stands sadly there,
Who, on my soul, was but a passenger.
Jane. Well, Captain Stranguidge, were the King at home, 95
I could say more.
Stranguidge.   Lady, he's come ashore,
Last night, at Dover. My boy came from thence,
And saw his highness land.
Jane.   Then courage, sirs;
I'll use my fairest means to save your lives.
In the mean season, spend that, for my sake.   100
                         [*She*] *casts her purse.*

Enter Lord Marquis DORSET [*with attendants*], *and claps*
                  her on the shoulder.

Dorset. By your leave, Mistress Shore, I have taken pains
To find you out. Come, you must go with me.

---

76. *credit . . . crown*] Where Jane meant 'financial resources' (74),
Matthew's puns invoke moral ones.
   88. *ta'en*] established.
   89. via] come on (an expression of resolution).
   92. *suborn*] sanction. OED does not offer this definition; contemporary usage was always pejorative, so doubt is cast on the moral validity of
Stranguidge's commission.

Jane. Whither, my lord?
Dorset.   Unto the Queen, my mother.
Jane. Good my lord marquess Dorset, wrong me not.
Dorset.   I cannot wrong thee, as thou wrongst my mother.   105
    I'll bring thee to her; let her use her pleasure.
Jane. Against my will I wrong her, good my lord,
    Yet am ashamed to see her majesty.
    Sweet lord, excuse me; say you saw me not.
Dorset. Shall I delude my mother, for a whore?   110
    No, Mistress Shore, you must go to the Queen.
Jane. Must I, my lord? What will she do to me?
    Use violence on me, now the King's away?
    Alas, my lord, behold this shower of tears,
    Which King Edward would compassionate.   115
    Bring me not to her! She will slit my nose,
    Or mark my face, or spurn me unto death.
    Look on me, lord. Can you find in your heart
    To have me spoiled, that never thought you harm?
    O, rather with your rapier run me through,   120
    Than carry me to the displeasèd Queen.
Shore. [*Aside*] O, hadst thou never broke thy vow to me,
    From fear and wrong I had defended thee.
Dorset. I am inexorable. Therefore arise,
    And go with me. What rascal crew is this?   125
    Mistress Shore's suitors? Such slaves make her proud!
    What, Sir Robert Brackenbury? You a Shorist too?
Brackenbury. No Shorist, but to save my cousin's life.
Dorset. Then I'll be hanged if he escape for this,
    The rather for your means to Mistress Shore.   130
    My mother can do nothing, this whore all!
    Come away, minion; you shall prate no more.
Jane. Pray for me, friends, and I will pray for you;
    God send you better hap than I expect.
    Go to my lodging, you, and, if I perish,   135
    Take what is there in lieu of your true service.

---

116. *slit . . . nose*] an actual punishment in early modern England; the authors of *Eastward Ho* (1605) were threatened with it for failing to obtain a licence for the play.

130. *means . . . Shore*] capitalization upon Jane Shore's influence.

Jockie. Na! A may sale ayse ne'er forsake my gude maistress,
  till aye hea seen the worst that spite can du her.
          Exeunt DORSET, *and* JANE, *and theirs* [*attendants*].
Shore. [*Aside*] For all the wrong that thou hast done to me,
  They should not hurt thee yet, if I were free.   140
Brackenbury. See, cousin Stranguidge, how the case is
      changed:
  She that should help thee, cannot help herself.
Stranguidge. What remedy? The God of heaven helps all.
  What say ye, mates? Our hope of life is dashed.
  Now none but God; let's put our trust in him,   145
  And every man repent him of his sin.
  And, as together we have lived like men,
  So, like tall men, together, let us die.
  The best is, if we die for this offence,
  Our ignorance shall plead our innocence.   150
Vaux. Your meat is ready, captain; you must in.
Stranguidge. Must I? I will. Cousin, what will you do?
Brackenbury. Visit you soon; but now I will to court,
  To see what shall become of Mistress Shore.   *Exit.*
Stranguidge. God speed you well.
Vaux.   Come, sir, will you go in?   155
Shore. I'll eat no meat; give me leave to walk here.
          [*Exeunt* VAUX, STRANGUIDGE *and his crew.*]
  Am I now left alone? No; millions
  Of miseries attend me everywhere.
  Ah, Matthew Shore, how doth all-seeing heaven
  Punish some sin from thy blind conscience hid,   160
  Inflicting pain where all thy pleasure was!
  And by my wife came all these woes to pass!
  She falsed her faith, and broke her wedlock's band;
  Her honour fall'n, how could my credit stand?
  Yet will not I, poor Jane, on thee exclaim;   165
  Though guilty, thou, I, guiltless, suffer shame.

137–8.] *Qq print as verse*: maistress / Till.   142. should] *Q1–2*; could *Q3–6*.
151, 155. *Vaux.*] *Keeper. Qq.*

---

  137. *A . . . ayse*] I must say I'll.
  148. *tall*] brave.
  163. *band*] archaic form of 'bond'.
  164. *credit*] See note to l. 76.

I left this land, too little for my grief;
Returning, am accounted as a thief;
Who, in that ship, came but as passenger
To see my friends; hoping the death of her   170
At sight of whom some sparks of former love,
Hid in affection's ashes, pity move,
Kindling compassion in my broken heart,
That bleeds to think on her ensuing smart.
O, see weak women's imperfections,   175
That leave their husbands' safe protections,
Hazarding all on strangers' flatteries,
Whose lust allayed, leaves them to miseries.
See what dishonour breach of wedlock brings,
Which is not safe, even in the arms of kings.   180
Thus do I, Jane, lament thy present state,
Wishing my tears thy torments might abate.   *Exit.*

[Scene 10]

    Enter the QUEEN, *Marquis* DORSET *leading* MISTRESS
    SHORE, *who falls down on her knees before the Queen,*
        fearful and weeping.

Queen. [*Aside*] Now, as I am a queen, a goodly creature!
    Son, how was she attended where you found her?
Dorset. Madam, I found her at the Marshalsea,
    Going to visit the poor prisoners
    As she came by, having been to take the air;   5
    And there, the keeper told me, she oft deals
    Such bounteous alms as seldom hath been seen.
Queen. [*Aside*] Now, before God, she would make a gallant
    queen!
    But, good son Dorset, stand aside awhile.

169. but as] *Q1*; but a *Q2*; for a *Q3–6*.

---

177. *strangers*] Invariably the word signified 'foreigners'; here, remarkably,
it suggests 'outsiders', those beyond the bounds of (and inimical to) a
community.

9. *stand aside*] The violent interventions of Dorset (ll. 36–40, 85–7) clearly
suggest that neither here nor at l. 41 does he respond positively to the
Queen's request for privacy; he certainly does not leave the stage.

God save your majesty, my Lady Shore!   10
My Lady Shore, said I? O, blasphemy,
To wrong your title with a Lady's name!
Queen Shore, nay, rather Empress Shore!
God save your grace, your majesty, your highness—
Lord, I want titles, you must pardon me.   15
What, you kneel there, King Edward's bedfellow,
And I, your subject, sit? Fie, fie, for shame.
Come, take your place, and I'll kneel where you do:
I may take your place; you have taken mine.
Good Lord, that you will so debase yourself!   20
I am sure you are our sister queen at least;
Nay, that you are. Then let us sit together.
Jane. Great queen, yet hear me, if my sin committed
Have not stopped up all passage to your mercy.
To tell the wrongs that I have done your highness   25
Might make revenge exceed extremity.
O, had I words or tongue to utter it:
To plead my woman's weakness, and his strength,
That was the only worker of my fall!
Even innocence herself would blush for shame,   30
Once to be named, or spoken of in this.
Let them expect for mercy whose offence
May but be callèd sin. O, mine is more!
Prostrate as earth, before your highness' feet,
Inflict what torments you shall think most meet.   35
Dorset. Spurn the whore, mother! Tear those enticing eyes,
That robbed you of King Edward's dearest love;
Mangle those locks, the baits to his desires.
Let me come to her: you but stand and talk,
As if revenge consisted but in words.   40
Queen. Son, stand aloof, and do not trouble me.
Aside. Alas, poor soul. As much ado have I
To forbear tears, to keep her company.
Yet once more will I to my former humour.

10–12. *my Lady . . . name!*] With Jane kneeling here, spectators are
reminded of Matthew's kneeling before the King, but refusing the knighthood that would have ennobled Jane as 'Lady Shore'.

36. *Spurn*] Early modern usage comprehended more violence than the
modern one; to kick an unruly dog was to 'spurn' it.

[*To Jane*] Why, as I am, think that thou were a queen,   45
And I, as thou, should wrong thy princely bed,
And win the King, thy husband, as thou mine:
Would it not sting thy soul? Or if that I,
Being a queen, while thou didst love thy husband,
Should but have done as thou hast done to me: 50
Would it not grieve thee? Yes, I warrant thee.
There's not the meanest woman that doth live,
But if she like and love her husband well,
She had rather feel his warm limbs in her bed,
Than see him in the arms of any queen.   55
You are flesh and blood as we, and we as you,
And all alike in our affections,
Though majesty makes us the more ambitious.
What 'tis to fall into so great a hand,
Knowledge might teach thee. There was once a king,   60
Henry the Second, who did keep his leman
Caged up at Woodstock, in a labyrinth;
His queen yet got a trick to find her out,
And how she used her, I am sure thou hast heard.
Thou art not mewed up in some secret place,   65
But kept in court here, underneath my nose.
Now, in the absence of my lord the King,
Have I not time most fitting for revenge?
Fair Rosamond, she a pure virgin was,
Until the king seduced her to his will.   70
She wronged but one bed: only the angry queen's;
But thou hast wronged two: mine, and thy husband's.
Be thine own judge, and now in justice see
What due revenge I ought to take on thee.
Jane. Even what you will, great Queen. Here do I lie,   75

45. were] wert *Qq*.

55. *queen*] a submereged pun on 'quean' = whore.
60–4. *There was . . . heard*] The story of how Queen Elinor tracked down
and caused the destruction of Rosamond, 'leman' (mistress) to Henry II,
was indeed well known; the dramatist would be thinking of, for instance,
Daniel's 'Complaint of Rosamond' (1592), reprinted three times 1594–98),
William Warner's *Albion's England* (fourth and fifth editions issued 1596,
1597) and Drayton's *England's Heroical Epistles*, a source for the Jane and
Edward narrative but which opens with an exchange between Rosamond and
Henry.

Humble and prostrate at your highness' feet.
Inflict on me what may revenge your wrong;
Was never lamb abode more patiently
Than I will do. Call all your griefs to mind,
And do even what you will, or how likes you;   80
I will not stir, I will not shriek or cry,
Be it torture, poison, any punishment.
Was never dove or turtle more submiss,
Than I will be unto your chastisement.
Dorset. Fetched I her for this? Mother, let me come to her,   85
And what compassion will not suffer you
To do to her, refer the same to me.
Queen. Touch her not, son, upon thy life I charge thee,
But keep off still, if thou will have my love.
                                              Exit DORSET.
I am glad to hear you are so well resolved   90
To bear the burden of my just displeasure.

> *She draws forth a knife, and making as though she meant*
> *to spoil her face, runs to her, and falling on her knees,*
> *embraces and kisses her, casting away the knife.*

Thus, then, I'll do. Alas, poor soul!
Shall I weep with thee? In faith, poor heart, I will.
Be of good comfort, thou shall have no harm;
But, if that kisses have the power to kill thee,   95
Thus, thus, and thus, a thousand times I'll stab thee.
Jane, I forgive thee. What fort is so strong
But, with besieging, he will batter it?
Weep not, sweet Jane. Alas, I know thy sex,
Touched with the selfsame weakness that thou are;   100
And if my state had been as mean as thine,
And such a beauty to allure his eye,
Though I may promise much to my own strength,
What might have happ'd to me, I cannot tell.
Nay, fear not, for I speak it with my heart,   105
And in thy sorrow truly bear a part.
Jane. Most high, and mighty Queen, may I believe
There can be found such mercy in a woman—

---

83. *submiss*] archaic form of 'submissive'.
103. *promise . . . to*] profess, have confidence in.

And in a queen, more than in a wife—
So deeply wronged, as I have wrongèd you?   110
In this bright crystal mirror of your mercy,
I see the greatness of my sin the more,
And makes my fault more odious in my eyes.
Your princely pity now doth wound me more
Than all your threat'nings ever did before.   115
Queen. Rise, my sweet Jane, I say thou shall not kneel.
O, God forbid that Edward's queen should hate
Her, whom she knows he doth so dearly love.
My love to her may purchase me his love;
Jane, speak well unto the King of me and mine.   120
Remember not my son's o'er-hasty speech;
Thou art my sister, and I love thee so.
I know thou mayst do much with my dear lord;
Speak well of us to him in any case,
And I and mine will love and cherish thee.   125
Jane. All I can do is all too little, too,
But to requite the least part of this grace.
The dearest thoughts that harbour in this breast,
Shall in your service only be expressed.

     Enter KING EDWARD *angerly, his lords following, and* SIR
                 ROBERT BRACKENBURY.

Edward. What, is my Jane with her? It is too true.   130
See where she hath her down upon her knees!
Why, how now, Bess? What, will you wrong my Jane?
Come hither, love. What hath she done to thee?

       JANE *falls on her knees to the King.*

Jane. O royal Edward, love, love thy beauteous queen:
The only perfect mirror of her kind,   135
For all the choicest virtues can be named!
O, let not my bewitching looks withdraw
Your dear affections from your dearer queen,
But to requite the grace that she hath shown
To me, the worthless creature on this earth,   140

---

109. than in a] *Q2;* then that in *Q1.*   127. But] *Q2;* Tut *Q1.*   128. The]
Q2; Bhe *Q1.*

To banish me the court, immediately.
Great king, let me but beg one boon of thee,
That Shore's wife ne'er do her more injury.

As JANE *kneels on one side of the King, so the* QUEEN
steps and kneels on the other.

Queen. Nay, then, I'll beg against her, royal Edward.
 Love thy Jane still; nay more, if more may be; *kissing* 145
 And this is all the harm that at my hands   *her.*
 She shall endure for it. O, where my Edward loves,
 It ill beseems his queen to grudge thereat.
Edward. Sayst thou me so, Bess? On my kingly word,
 Edward will honour thee in heart for this.   150
 But, trust me, Bess, I greatly was afraid
 I should not find you in so good a tune.
 How now, what would our Constable of the Tower?
Brackenbury. The Queen and Mistress Shore do know my
 suit.
Queen. It is for Stranguidge and his men at sea.   155
 Edward, needs must you pardon them.
Edward. Have I not vowed the contrary already?
 Dishonour me, when I have made a league?
 My word is past, and they shall suffer death;
 Or never more let me see France again.   160
Jane. Why, there is one was but a passenger.
 Shall he die too?
Edward.   Pass me no passage, Jane.
 Were he in company, he dies for company.
Queen. Good Jane, entreat for them.
Jane. Come, Edward, I must not take this answer. 165
 Needs must I have some grace for Stranguidge.
Edward. Why, Jane, have I not denied my queen?

---

149. Sayst] *Q4–6* (saist); Sayest *Q1–3.* 162–3.] *Qq print as prose.*

162. *Pass . . . passage*] The King is blustering, but the fact that the phrase
'pass and repass' was a quasi-technical juggling term might contextualize the
sense: 'don't try to juggle your way past me'.
 163. *company . . . company*] A vicious variation on the proverb 'As a man
is, so is his company', most recently perverted by Falstaff; see *2 Henry IV*,
5.1.75–7.

Yet, what is't, Jane, I would deny to thee?
I prithee, Brackenbury, be not thou displeased.
My word is passed. Not one of them shall live.   170
One go and see them forthwith sent to death.   *Exeunt.*

[Scene 11]

       Enter CLARENCE, GLOUCESTER *and* SHAW.

Gloucester. I cannot see this prophecy you speak of
    Should any way so much displease the King.
    And yet I promise you, good brother Clarence,
    'Tis such a letter as concerns us both.
    [*Reads.*] 'That 'G' should put away King Edward's
      children,   5
    And sit upon his throne'? That 'G' should? Well.
Clarence. God bless the King, and those two sweet young
    princes!
Gloucester. Amen, good brother Clarence.
Doctor Shaw.   Amen.
Gloucester. [*Aside*] And send them all to heaven, shortly, I
    beseech him.
Clarence. The King's much troubled in his sickness with it.   10
Gloucester. I promise you he is, and very much.
    But, Doctor Shaw, who prophesied that 'G'
    Should be so sadly ominous to us?
Doctor Shaw. My Lord of Gloucester, I received the same
    From old Friar Anselm of St Bartholomew's.   15
Gloucester. A great learned man he was, and, as I have heard,
    Hath prophesied of very many things.
    I promise you, it troubles me.
    I hope in me his prophecy is true.   *Aside.*

12–13.] *Qq print as prose.*

    5–6. 'G'... *throne*] The story originates in the Hardyng version of
More's *History*, although it is omitted in both Rastell's English and the Latin
editions. Holinshed mentions it and dismisses it as 'foolish' (346); it features
prominently in *Mirror for Magistrates* (227), and Shakespeare's *Richard III*.
    15. *Anselm* ... *St Bartholomew's*] Stow describes the institution as 'late
dissoulued' (*Survey*, II, 25); just east of Smithfield, it was still an imposing
building in the 1590s. No source mentions such a friar; Heywood (?) used
the same name for a less moralistic friar in *How a Man May Choose* in 1602.

Clarence. And so it does me, I tell you, brother Gloucester.   20
Gloucester. I am sure it does, for look you, brother Clarence,
    We know not how his highness will apply it.
    We are but two: yourself, my lord, and I.
    Should the young princes fail—which God defend—
Clarence. Which God defend!   25
Doctor Shaw. Which God defend!
Gloucester. Aside. But they should be cut off. [*To them*]—
    Amen, amen.
    —You, brother, first, and should your issue fail,
    Poor I am next, the youngest of the three.
    But how far I am from a thought of that,   30
    Heaven witness with me—*Aside.*—that I wish you dead.
Clarence. Brother, I dar'st be sworn.
Gloucester.   God bless you all,
    And take you to him, if it be his will.
    Now, brother, this prophecy of 'G' troubling the King;
    He may as well apply it unto Gloucester,   35
    My dukedom's name, if he be jealous,
    As unto George, your name, good brother Clarence.
    God help, God help! In faith, it troubles me,
    You would not think how—*Aside.*—that any of you live.
Clarence. It cannot choose. How innocent I am,   40
    And how unspotted are my loyal thoughts
    Unto his highness, and those sweet young princes,
    God be my record.
Gloucester. Who, you? Ay, I dar'st answer for you—
    Aside.—That I shall cut you off ere it be long—   45
    [*To them*] But, reverend Doctor, you can only tell,
    Being his highness' confessor, how he takes it.
    Aside to Shaw. Shaw, you know my mind; a villain like
        myself.
Doctor Shaw. My Lord of Clarence, I must tell your lordship,
    His highness is much troubled in his sickness   50
    With this same prophecy of 'G'. 'Who is this 'G'?',
    Oft times he will demand. Then will he sigh,
    And name his brother, George—yourself my lord—
    And then he strikes his breast, I promise you.

32–3. God . . . will] *Qq print as one verse line.* 52. demand. Then] *Q2*;
demaunde, and then *Q1*.

This morning, in th' extremest of his fit,   55
He lay so still, we all thought he had slept;
When, suddenly, 'George is the 'G'!', quoth he,
And gave a groan, and turned his face away.
Clarence. God be my witness, witness with my soul,
My just and upright thoughts to him and his.   60
I stand so guiltless and so innocent
As I could wish my breast to be transparent,
And my thoughts written in great letters there,
The world might read the secrets of my soul.
Gloucester. Ah, brother Clarence, when you are suspected;   65
Well, well, it is a wicked world the while.
But shall I tell you, brother, in plain terms,
I fear yourself and I have enemies
About the king; God pardon them.
The world was never worser to be trusted.   70
Ah, brother George, where is that love that was?
Ah, it is banished, brother, from the world.
Ah, conscience; conscience, and true brotherhood;
'Tis gone, 'tis gone. Brother, I am your friend,
I am your loving brother, your own self,   75
And love you as my soul. Use me in what you please,
And you shall see I'll do a brother's part:
Send you to heaven, I hope, ere it be long—   *Aside.*
I am a true-stamped villain as ever lived.
Clarence. I know you will. Then, brother, I beseech you,   80
Plead you my innocence unto the King;
And in mean time, to tell my loyalty,
I'll keep within my house at Baynard's Castle,
Until I hear how my dread sovereign takes it.
Gloucester. Do so, good brother.
Clarence.   Farewell, good brother Gloucester.   85
Gloucester. My tears will scarcely let me take my leave,
I love you so. Farewell, sweet George.
                                          Exit CLARENCE.

---

55. th' extremest] *Q2*; thextreamest *Q1*.   68. I fear yourself and I] *Q2*; I
feare, I fear, your selfe and I *Q1*.

---

83. *Baynard's Castle*] Between Blackfriars and Paul's Wharf, this impressive house was actually the residence of Cecily, Duchess of York, although
Richard, rather than Clarence, was increasingly using it as a base.

So, is he gone? Now, Shaw, 'tis in thy power
To bind me to thee everlastingly,
And there is not one step that I shall rise,   90
But I will draw thee with me unto greatness;
Thou shalt sit in my bosom, as my soul.
Incense the King, now being, as thou art,
So near about him—and his confessor—
That this 'G' only is George, Duke of Clarence.   95
Doctor, thou needst not my instruction;
Thou hast a searching brain, a nimble spirit
Able to master any man's affections.
Effect it, Shaw, and bring it to pass once:
I'll make thee the greatest Shaw that ever was.   100
Doctor Shaw. My lord, I am going by commandment
Unto the Marshalsea, to Captain Stranguidge,
For piracy of late condemned to die,
There to confess him and his company.
That done, I'll come with speed back to the King,   105
And make no doubt, but I'll effect the thing.
Gloucester. Farewell, gentle Doctor.
Doctor Shaw.   Farewell, my Lord of Gloucester.
                                                          Exit.

Gloucester. Let me awake my sleeping wits awhile.
Ha! The mark thou aimst at, Richard, is a crown,
And many stand betwixt thee and the same.   110
What of all that? Doctor, play thou thy part,
I'll climb up by degrees, through many a heart.   *Exit.*

[Scene 12]

               Enter BRACKENBURY, *with* VAUX *the Keeper.*

Brackenbury. Why, Master Vaux, is there no remedy,
But instantly they must be led to death?
Can it not be deferred till afternoon?
Or but two hours, in hope to get reprieve?
Vaux. Master Lieutenant, 'tis in vain to speak.   5

101. *Doctor Shaw*] Q2; *Glo.* Q1.

5. *Vaux*] *Keeper (throughout scene).*

The King's incensed, and will not pardon them.
The men are patient, and resolved to die;
The captain and that other gentleman
Have cast the dice, whether shall suffer first.
Brackenbury. How fell the lot, to Stranguidge, or to him?   10
Vaux. The guiltless passenger must first go to't.
Brackenbury. They are all guiltless from intent of ill.
Vaux. And yet must die for doing of the deed.
    Besides, the Duke of Exeter, found dead,
    And naked, floating up and down the sea   15
    'Twixt Calais and our coast, is laid to them:
    That they should rob, and cast him overboard.
Brackenbury. My soul be pawn, they never knew of it.
Vaux. Well, bring them forth.
Brackenbury.   Stay them yet but an hour.
Vaux. I dare not do it, Sir Robert Brackenbury.   20
    You are Lieutenant of the Tower yourself,
    And know the peril of protracting time.
    Moreover, here's that pickthank, Doctor Shaw,
    The Duke of Gloucester's spaniel, shriving them.
    Come, bring them forth.
Brackenbury.   Poor Stranguidge, must thou die?   25

    Enter one bearing a silver oar before STRANGUIDGE,
        SHORE [*disguised as* FLOOD], *and two or three more,*
    pinioned, and two or three with bills, [DOCTOR SHAW,]
                and a hangman.

    I dare not say good morrow, but ill day,
    That Harry Stranguidge is thus cast away.

26.] *Qq have new speech prefix: Bra. stil.*

---

    9. *whether*] which.
    14–18. *Duke . . . of it*] Most chroniclers agreed with Brackenbury. Exeter
had been married to Edward's sister, who divorced him to marry Thomas
Sellinger; some accounts implicated him in the Duke's drowning (see commentary to Characters of the Play, Part One), but some accused Edward
himself (*Calendar of Milanese Papers* (London, 1864), I, 220).
    23. *pickthank*] flatterer.
    25.01 silver oar] Since at least 1360 a silver oar had been the symbol of
authority displayed by the High Court of the Admiralty of England when
maritime cases were judged; see S. B. MacKinnon, 'Some Judicial Insignia',
Law Quarterly Review, 59 (1943), 30.

Stranguidge. Good cousin Brackenbury, be as well content
    To see me die, as I to suffer death.
    Be witness that I die an honest man,   30
    Because my fact proves ill through ignorance;
    And for the Duke of Exeter, his death,
    So speed my soul, as I am innocent.
    [*Gestures to Shore.*] Here goes my grief: this guiltless
       gentleman,
    Like Aesop's stork that dies for company,   35
    And came, God knows, but as a passenger.
    Ah, Master Flood, a thousand floods of woe
    O'erflow my soul that thou must perish so.
Shore. Good captain, let no perturbation
    Hinder our passage to a better world.   40
    This last breath's blast will waft our weary souls
    Over death's gulf, to heaven's most happy port.
    There is a little battle to be fought,
            This while the hangman prepares; SHORE *at this*
                       speech mounts up the ladder.
    Wherein by lot the leading must be mine.
    Second me, captain, and this bitter breakfast   45
    Shall bring a sweeter supper with the saints.
Doctor Shaw. This Christian patience at the point of death
    Doth argue he hath led no wicked life,
    However heaven hath laid this cross on him.
    Well, Matthew Flood, for so thou callst thyself,   50
    Finish a good course as thou hast begun,
    And clear thy conscience by confession.
    What knowst thou of the Duke of Exeter's death?
Shore. So God respect the waygate of my soul,
    As I know nothing.
Doctor Shaw.   Then concerning this   55
    For which thou diest: knew Stranguidge of the league

54-7.] *Qq print as prose.*

31. *fact*] action.
35. *Aesop . . . company*] In the *Fables* a stork lands in a trap set for cranes;
to her claim that she is harmless the trapper responds that she deserves punishment just for landing among the wicked. Aesop's 'moral' is that one should
avoid bad company to preclude accusations of guilt by association.
54. *waygate*] departure (in this case, ascension).

Betwixt the kings, before he took that prize?
Shore. No, in my conscience.
Doctor Shaw.   Stranguidge, what say you?
You see there's but a turn betwixt your lives.
You must be next: confess, and save your soul,   60
Concerning that wherein I questioned him.
I am your ghostly father, to absolve
You of your sins, if you confess the truth.
Stranguidge. True, Doctor Shaw, and as I hope for heaven
In that great day when we shall all appear,   65
I neither knew how that good duke came dead,
Nor of the league, till I had ta'en the prize;
Neither was Flood, that innocent, dying man,
Ever with me but as a passenger.
Doctor Shaw. More happy he. Well, Flood, forgive the world,   70
As thou wilt have forgiveness from the heavens.
Shore. O, so I do, and pray the world forgive
What wrong I did whilst I therein did live.
And now, I pray you turn your pains to them,
And leave me private for a little space,   75
To meditate upon my parting hence.
Doctor Shaw. Do, gentle Flood, and we will pray for thee.
Shore. Pray not for Flood, but pray for Matthew Shore;
                                                    Aside.
For Shore, covered with the cloak of Flood.
If I have sinned in changing of my name,   80
Forgive me, God; 'twas done to hide my shame.
And I forgive the world: King Edward, first,
That wracked my state, by winning of my wife;
And though he would not pardon trespass small
In these—in me, God knows, no fault at all—   85
I pardon him, though guilty of my fall.
Perhaps he would, if he had known 'twas I,
But twenty deaths I rather wish to die,
Than live beholding for one minute's breath
To him, that living, wounded me with death: 90
Death of my joy, and hell of my defame,

---

78. SD] *opposite line 79 in Qq.*

59. *turn*] probably punning on the turn of the hangman's noose.

Which now shall die under this borrowed name.
Jane, God forgive thee, even as I forgive,
And pray thou mayst repent while thou dost live.
I am as glad to leave this lothèd light,   95
As to embrace thee on our marriage night.
To die, unknown thus, is my greatest good:
That Matthew Shore's not hanged, but Matthew Flood,
For floods of woe have washed away the shore
That never wife nor kin shall look on more.   100
Now, when you will, I am prepared to go.

Enter JOCKIE *running and crying.*

Jockie. Hawd, hawd! Fay for speed! Untay, untruss, pull
    down, pull off! God seave the King! Off with the helters,
    hence with the prisoners! A pardon, a pardon!
Brackenbury. Good news, unlooked for. Welcome, gentle
        friend;   105
    Who brings the pardon?
Jockie. Stay, first let me blaw! My maistress, maistress Shore,
    she brings tha pardon, tha King's pardon. Off with thore
    bands, bestow them a' tha hangman! Ma maistress made
    me run the nearest way o'er tha fields, she raides apeace   110
    the heeway, she's at hawnd bay this. [*To Shore*] Sirra, yee
    that preach, come down; lat Doctor Shaw hea your place,
    he's tha better scholar. Maistress Shore brings a new
    lesson for you.
Shore. O, I had read my latest lesson well,   115
    Had he been ready to have said 'Amen'.

[*He*] *point[s] to the hangman.*

Now shall I live to see my shame again.

SHORE *comes down.*

O, had I died unwitting to my wife,
Rather than see her, though she bring me life.

Enter JANE *in haste, in her riding cloak and save-guard,*
        with a pardon in her hand.

105–6.] *Qq print as prose.*   110. apeace] *Q1*; a pace *Q2–6*.

119.01. save-guard] an outer skirt for riding.

Jane. Alas, I see that e'en my smallest stay   120
    Had lost my labour, and cast them away.
    God knows, I hasted all that e'er I might.
    Here, Master Vaux, King Edward greets you well:
    His gracious pardon frees this gentleman,
    And all his company, from shameful death.   125
All. God save the King, and God bless Mistress Shore.
Jockie. Amen, and keep these fra coming here any meare.
Jane. You must discharge them paying of their fees,
    Which, for I fear their store is very small,
    I will defray. Hold; here, take purse and all.   130
    Nay, Master Vaux, 'tis gold. If not enough,
    Send to me; I will pay you royally.
Stranguidge. Lady, in the behalf of all the rest,
    With humble thanks I yield myself your slave;
    Command their service, and command my life.   135
Jane. No, Captain Stranguidge, let the King command
    Your lives and service, who hath given you life.
    These, and such offices, conscience bids me do.
Doctor Shaw. Pity that e'er awry she trod her shoe.
Shore. O, had that conscience pricked, when love provoked.   140
Brackenbury. Lady, the last but not the least in debt,
    To your devotion for my cousin's life
    I render thanks; yet thanks is but a breath.
    Command my service, madam, during life.
    Old Brackenbury vows for you to stand   145
    Whilst I have limbs, or any foot of land.
Shore. Thus is her glory builded on the sand.
Jane. Thanks, good Master Lieutenant of the Tower.
    To Jockie. Sirrah, prepare my horse; why stay you here?
                        [*Exit* JOCKIE].
    [*To Brackenbury*] Pray you commend me to my noble
        friend,   150
    The Duke of Clarence, now your prisoner.
    Bid him not doubt the King's displeasure's passed;
    I hope to gain him favour and release.

---

144. Command my service, madam] *Q1*; Command Madame *Q2*;
Command (Madame) *Q3–5*; Command me (Madame) *Q6*.

---

120. *stay*] delay.
128. *fees*] Prisoners were required to pay their own living expenses.

Brackenbury. God grant you may; he's a noble gentleman.
Doctor Shaw. [*Aside*] My patron, Gloucester, will cross it if
  he can.   [*Exit.*]   155

                    Enter a MESSENGER.

Messenger. Where's Mistress Shore? Lady, I come in post.
  The King hath had a very dangerous fit
  Since you came from him; twice his majesty
  Hath swounded, and with much ado revived,
  And still, as breath will give him leave to speak,   160
  He calls for you. The Queen and all the lords
  Have sent to seek you. Haste unto his grace,
  Or else I fear you'll never see his face.
Jane. O God defend. Good friends, pray for the King.
  More bitter are the news which he doth bring,   165
  Than those were sweet I brought to you but late:
  If Edward die, confounded is my state.
  I'll haste unto him, and will spend my blood
  To save his life, or do him any good.
                    Exeunt JANE *and the* MESSENGER.
Shore. [*Aside*] And so would I for thee, hadst thou been true;   170
  But if he die, bid all thy pomp adieu.
Brackenbury. Believe me, but I do not like these news
  Of the King's dangerous sickness.
Vaux.   No, nor I.
  Captain, and Master Flood, and all the rest:
  I do rejoice your pardon was obtained
  Before these news, these inauspicious news.   175
  If the King die, the state will soon be changed.
  Master Lieutenant, you'll go to the Tower;
  I'll take my leave. Gallants, goodbye all.
                    Exeunt VAUX *and his train.*
Stranguidge. Goodbye, Master Vaux; I wis y' have lost good
  guests.   180

---

169. SD JANE] *she Qq.*

180. *Goodbye . . . guests*] The spelling of this line has been modernized and
regularized throughout to make sense of its attribution to Stranguidge; the
dramatist has written it in Jockie's dialect, but the Scot must have left the
stage at l. 149.

Brackenbury. You shall be my guest for a night or two,
　　Cousin, till your own lodging be prepared.
　　But tell me, sir, what means hath Master Flood?
Stranguidge. I cannot tell. I'll ask him, if you will.
Brackenbury. Do so, and if his fortunes be debased,　　185
　　I'll entertain him, if he'll dwell with me
　　On good condition.
Stranguidge.　　　　　　Master Matthew Flood,
　　Hear you my cousin Brackenbury's mind?
　　He hath conceived such liking of your parts,
　　That if your means surmount not his suppose,　　190
　　He'll entertain you gladly at the Tower,
　　To wait on him, and put you in great trust.
Shore. In what I undertake I will be just,
　　And hold me happy, if my diligence
　　May please so worthy a gentleman as he.　　195
　　Whate'er my fortunes have been, they are now
　　Such, as to service make their master bow.
Brackenbury. No, Flood. More like a friend and fellow mate
　　I mean to use thee, than a servitor,
　　And place thee in some credit in the Tower,　　200
　　And give thee means to live in some good sort.
Shore. I thank you, sir. God grant I may deserve it.
Brackenbury. Cousin, and all your crew, come home with me,
　　Where, after sorrow, we may merry be.
　　　　　　　　　　[*Exeunt all but* SHORE.]
Shore. The Tower will be a place of secret rest,　　205
　　Where I may hear good news and bad, and use the best.
　　God bless the King. A worse may wear the crown,
　　And then, Jane Shore, thy credit will come down.
　　For, though I'll never bed nor board with thee,
　　Yet thy destruction wish I not to see,　　210
　　Because I loved thee when thou wast my wife,
　　Not for now saving my disdainèd life,
　　Which lasts too long. God grant us both to mend;
　　Well, I must in, my service to attend.　　*Exit.*

190. *suppose*] estimate.

[Scene 13]

The LORD LOVELL *and* DOCTOR SHAW *meet
on the stage.*

Doctor Shaw. Well met, my good Lord Lovell.
Lovell. Whither away so fast goes Doctor Shaw?
Doctor Shaw. Why, to the Tower, to shrive the Duke of
    Clarence,
    Who, as I hear, is fallen so grievous sick
    As it is thought he can by no means 'scape.   5
Lovell. He neither can, nor shall, I warrant thee.
Doctor Shaw. I hope, my lord, he is not dead already?
Lovell. But I hope, sir, he is. I am sure I saw him dead
    Of a fly's death: drowned in a butt of malmsey.
Doctor Shaw. Drowned in a butt of malmsey? That is strange. 10
    Doubtless, he never would misdo himself?
Lovell. No, that thou knowst right well. He had some helpers.
    Thy hand was in it, with the Duke of Gloucester's,
    As smoothly as thou seekst to cover it.
Doctor Shaw. O, foul words, my lord, no more of that.   15
    The world knows nothing; then what should I fear?
    Doth not your honour seek promotion?
    O give the Doctor, then, a little leave,
    So that he gain preferment with a king,
    Cares not who goes to wrack, whose heart doth wring. 20
Lovell. A king? What king?
Doctor Shaw. Why, Richard, man! Who else? Good Lord, I
    see,
    Wise men sometimes have weak capacity.
Lovell. Why, is not Edward living? And if he were not,
    Hath he not children? What shall become of them?   25
Doctor Shaw. Why, man, lining for beds; a knife or so;
    What, make a boy a king, and a man by,
    Richard, a man for us? Fie, that were a shame.
Lovell. Nay, then, I see, if Edward were deceased,
    Which way the game would go.
Doctor Shaw.   What else, my lord?   30
    That way the current of our fortune runs,

---

26. *lining . . . beds*] like sliced straw, for stuffing mattresses.

By noble Richard, gallant, royal Richard.
He is the man must only do us good;
So I have honour, let me swim through blood.
My lord, be but at Paul's Cross on Sunday next: 35
I hope I have it here shall soundly prove
King Edward's children not legitimate.
Nay, and that for King Edward ruling now,
And George, Duke of Clarence, so late dead,
Their mother happed to tread the shoe awry.   40

Lovell. Why, what is Richard then?

Doctor Shaw. Tut, lawful, man; he says it so himself,
And what he says I'll be so bold to swear,
Though in my soul I know it otherwise.
Beware promotion, while you live, my lord.   45

Enter CATESBY.

Catesby. A staff, a staff, a thousand crowns for a staff!

Lovell. What staff, Sir William Catesby?

Catesby. Why, man, a white staff for my Lord Protector.

Lovell. Why, is King Edward dead?

Catesby. Dead, Lovell, dead. And Richard, our good lord,   50
Is made protector of the sweet young prince.
O, for a staff! Where might I have a staff,
That I might first present it to his hand?

Doctor Shaw. Now do I smell two bishoprics at least.
My sermon shall be peppered sound for this.   55

Enter MISTRESS SHORE, *weeping,* JOCKIE *following.*

Catesby. Why, how now, Mistress Shore? What, put finger
in the eye?
Nay, then I see you have some cause to cry.

38. King] *omitted in Qq.*   41. *Lovell.*] *Q3–6; omitted in Q1–2.*   43. to] *Q2;*
as Q1.

35. *Paul's Cross*] a location for public preaching since the thirteenth
century, and still the most important—and controversial—of such sites in
Elizabethan London.

48. *white staff*] symbol of the headship of a (in this case royal) household,
of particular significance during the rituals which transferred authority upon
the death of a nobleman.

55. *peppered . . . this*] really spiced up in the light of this news.

56. *finger in the eye*] See commentary to Part One, Scene 1, l. 66.

Lovell. I blame her not. Her chiefest stay is gone,
    The only staff she had to lean upon.
    I see, by her, these tidings are too true.   60
Jane. Ay, my Lord Lovell, they are too true indeed.
    Royal King Edward now hath breathed his last,
    The Queen turned out, and every friend put by;
    None now admitted, but whom Richard please.
Lovell. Why, doubtless Richard will be kind to you.   65
Jane. Ah, my Lord Lovell, God bless me from his kindness.
    No sooner was the white staff in his hand,
    But finding me and the right woeful Queen,
    Sadly bemoaning such a mighty loss,
    'Here is no place', quoth he. 'You must be gone,   70
    We have other matters now to think upon.
    For you', quoth he to me, and bit his lip,
    And struck me with his staff, but said no more;
    Whereby I know he meaneth me no good.
Catesby. Well, Mistress Shore, it's like to be a busy time;   75
    Shift for yourself. Come, lads, let us be gone:
    Royal King Richard must be wait upon.
Doctor Shaw. Well, Mistress Shore, if you have need of me,
    You shall command me to the uttermost.
           Exeunt [DOCTOR SHAW, CATESBY, LOVELL].
Jane. First let me die, ere I do put my trust   80
    In any fleering spaniel of you all.
    Go, Jockie, take down all my hangings,
    And quickly see my trunks be conveyed forth
    To Mistress Blage's, an inn in Lombard Street,
    The Flower-de-Luce. Good Jockie, make some speed;   85
    She, she must be my refuge in this need.
    See it done quickly, Jockie.   *Exit.*
Jockie. Whickly, quotha? Marry, here's a whick change;
    indeed sic whick change did I ne'er see before. Now,
    dream I that I's be a very puir fellow, an' hardly ha' any   90

---

81. *fleering*] sneering.
82. *hangings*] tapestries.
85. *Flower-de-Luce*] A very common name for London taverns; at least
three others so-called were within half a mile, but this is the only known reference to one on the corner of Gracechurch Street (see below, Scene 16, l.
52) and Lombard Street.

siller to drink with a gude fellow. But what stand I tatling
here? I must go do my maistress' bidding, carry all her
stuff and gear to Maistress Blage's, at the Flower-de-Luce
in Lombard Street. Whick then, dispatch.   *Exit.*

[Scene 14]

    Enter BRACKENBURY *and* [SHORE *disguised as*] FLOOD.

Brackenbury. Come hither, Flood. Let me hear thy opinion;
    Thou knowst I build upon thy confidence,
    And honest dealing in my greatest affairs.
    I have received letters from the Duke—
    Gloucester, I mean, Protector of the land—   5
    Who gives in charge the Tower be prepared
    This night, to entertain the two young princes.
    It is my duty to obey, I know,
    But manifold suspicion troubles me.
Shore. He is their uncle, sir, and in that sense,   10
    Nature should warrant their security.
    Next, his deceasèd brother, at his death,
    To Richard's care committed both the realm
    And their protection; where humanity
    Stands, as an orator, to plead against   15
    All wrong suggestion of uncivil thoughts.
    Beside, you are Lieutenant of the Tower:
    Say there should be any hurt pretended,
    The privilege of your authority
    Pries into every corner of this house;   20
    And what can then be done without your knowledge?
Brackenbury. Thou sayst true, Flood. Though Richard be
       Protector,
    When once they are within the Tower limits,
    The charge of them—unless he derogate

0.1.] *Qq add 'to them the two young princes, Edward and Richard, Gloster, Cates.
Louell, and Tirill.'*   10. Shore.] *Qq have Flo. throughout the scene.*   24-6.
unless . . . time] *Q6 (in parenthesis); (unless . . . derogate) Q1-5.*

    0.1.] Qq mark an entrance for Lovell here, but he does not speak in the
scene and his presence is neither necessary nor desirable dramatically.
    24-5. *derogate . . . this*] quasi-legal term, meaning to diminish the author-
ity of a post or its holder.

From this, my office, which was never seen   25
   In any king's time—doth belong to me;
   And ere that Brackenbury will consent,
   Or suffer wrong be done unto these babes,
   His sword, and all the strength within the Tower,
   Shall be opposed against the proudest comer.   30
   Be it to my soul, as I intend to them.
Shore. And faith in me unto this commonwealth,
   And truth to men, hath hitherto been seen
   The pilot that hath guided my life's course,
   Though 'twas my fortune to be wronged in both;   35
   And therefore, sir, neither the mighty's frown,
   Nor any bribes shall win me otherwise.
Brackenbury. 'Tis well resolved. Still, methinks they should
   Be safe enough with us, and yet I fear.
   But now no more; it seems they are at hand.   40

     Enter [GLOUCESTER, PRINCE EDWARD, PRINCE
       RICHARD, TYRRELL and CATESBY].

P. Edward. Uncle, what gentleman is that?
Gloucester. It is, sweet prince, Lieutenant of the Tower.
P. Edward. Sir, we are come to be your guests tonight.
   I pray you tell me, did you ever know
   Our father Edward lodged within this place?   45
Brackenbury. Never to lodge, my liege, but oftentimes
   On other occasions I have seen him here.
P. Richard. Brother, last night when you did send for me,
   My mother told me, hearing we should lodge
   Within the Tower, that it was a prison;   50
   And therefore marvelled that my uncle Gloucester,
   Of all the houses for a king's receipt
   Within this city, had appointed none
   Where you might keep your court, but only here.

---

34. life's] *liues Qq.*   40. SD] *Qq have only 'enter' opposite line 41.*

40.01. SD] All six quartos have the perfunctory *enter* here; it is improbable that the compositor missed so many character names, and more likely, particularly given the marginal position of the word, that the playwright felt his opening SD had been sufficiently expansive, and only a 'reminder' was necessary.

52. *receipt*] reception.

Gloucester. [*Aside*] Vile brats, how they do descant on the
    Tower!   55
My gentle nephew, they were ill-advised
To tutor you with such unfitting terms—
Whoe'er they were—against this royal mansion:
What if some part of it hath been reserved
To be a prison for nobility?   60
Follows it, therefore, that it cannot serve
To any other use? Caesar himself,
That built the same, within it kept his court,
And many kings since him. The rooms are large,
The building stately, and for strength beside,   65
It is the safest and the surest hold you have.
P. Richard. Uncle of Gloucester, if you think it so,
'Tis not for me to contradict your will.
We must allow it, and are well content.
Gloucester. On, then, a' God's name.   [*Exit.*]
P. Edward.   Yet, before we go,   70
One question more, with you, Master Lieutenant.
We like you well, and but we do perceive
More comfort in your looks than in these walls—
For all our uncle Gloucester's friendly speech—
Our hearts would be as heavy still as lead.   75
I pray you tell me, at which door or gate
Was it my uncle Clarence did go in,
When he was sent a prisoner to this place?
Brackenbury. At this, my liege. Why sighs your majesty?
P. Edward. He went in here that ne'er came back again.   80
But, as God hath decreed, so let it be.
Come, brother, shall we go?
P. Richard. Yes, brother, anywhere with you.
        Exeunt [BRACKENBURY, SHORE *and the princes*].

---

83. *P. Richard*] *Q2 (Ric.); Fish. Q1.*

  55. *descant on*] Improvise on the theme of; the musical term implies a limitless resourcefulness, and the dramatist is probably recalling the same character's endless capacity to 'descant on mine own deformity' in the opening
soliloquy (1.1.27) of *Richard III*.
  62–3. *Caesar . . . court*] Again the dramatist is probably recalling the parallel scene in *Richard III*, 3.1.68–89. Stow insists on the lack of evidence for
these claims in the *Survey* (I, 44–5).

[Coming forward,] TYRRELL *pulls* CATESBY
by the sleeve.

Tyrrell. Sir, were it best I did attend the Duke,
    Or stay his leisure till his back return?   85
Catesby. I pray you, Master Tyrrell, stay without.
    It is not good you should be seen by day
    Within the Tower, especially at this time.
    I'll tell his honour of your being here,
    And you shall know his pleasure presently.   90
Tyrrell. Even so, sir. Men would be glad by any means
    To raise themselves, that have been overthrown
    By fortune's scorn, and I am one of them.

Enter DUKE *of* GLOUCESTER.

    Here comes the Duke.
Gloucester.   Catesby, is this the man?
Catesby. It is, if't like your Excellence.   *[Exit.]*
Gloucester.   Come near.   95
    Thy name, I hear, is Tyrrell, is it not?
Tyrrell. James Tyrrell is my name, my gracious lord.
Gloucester. Welcome. It should appear that thou hast been
    In better state than now it seems thou art.
Tyrrell. I have been, by my fay, my lord, though now
        depressed,   100
    And clouded over with adversity.
Gloucester. Be ruled by me, and thou shalt rise again,
    And prove more happy than thou ever wast.
    There is but only two degrees, by which
    It shall be needful for thee to ascend,   105
    And that is faith, and taciturnity.
Tyrrell. If ever I prove false unto your grace,
    Convert your favour to afflictions.
Gloucester. But, canst thou, too, be secret?
Tyrrell.   Try me, my lord;
    This tongue was never known to be a blab.   110
Gloucester. Thy countenance hath, like a silver key,
    Opened the closet of my heart. Read there:
    If, scholar-like, thou canst expound those lines,

95. if't] *Q2* (ift); if *Q1*.   102. and thou] *Q4–6*; and then thou *Q1–3*.

Thou art the man ordained to serve my turn.
Tyrrell. So far as my capacity will reach,   115
    The sense, my lord, is this: this night, you say,
    The two young princes both must suffer death.
Gloucester. Thou hast my meaning. Wilt thou do it? Speak.
Tyrrell. It shall be done.
Gloucester.   Enough. Come, follow me,
    For thy direction, and for gold to see,   120
    Such as must aid thee in their tragedy.   [*Exeunt.*]

[Scene 15]

       Enter MISTRESS BLAGE, *and* JOCKIE, *laden.*

M. Blage. Welcome, good Jockie. What good news bring you?
Jockie. Marry, maistress, my gude maistress greets ye,
    maistress, and prays ye, maistress, til dight up her
    chamber, for she'll lig wi' ye tonight, maistress. And here's
    her cat-skin, 'till she come.   5

              Enter JANE.

Jane. Why, how now, loiterer? Make you no more haste?
    When will my trunks and all my stuff be brought,
    If you thus loiter? Go, make haste withal.
Jockie. Marry, sall I, gin ye'll be bud petient awhile.   *Exit.*
Jane. Now, gentle Mistress Blage, the only friend   10
    That fortune leaves me to rely upon,
    My counsel's closet, and my tower of strength,
    To whom for safety I retire myself
    To be secure in these tempestuous times,
    O smile on me, and give me gentle looks.   15
    If I be welcome, then with cheerful heart
    And willing hand, show me true signs thereof.
M. Blage. Doubt you of welcome, lady, to your friend?
    Nay, to your servant, to your bedeswoman,
    To speak but truth, your bounty's bondwoman.   20

0.1. *laden*] *loden Qq.*

3. *dight*] archaic word meaning 'prepare'.
5. *cat-skin*] probably a bag; *OED*'s only citation.
9. *gin*] if.

Use me, command me, call my house your own,
And all I have, sweet lady, at your will.
Jane. Away with titles; lay by courtly terms.
The case is altered now the King is dead;
And with his life, my favouring friends are fled.   25
No 'madam' now, but, as I was before:
Your faithful, kind companion, poor Jane Shore.
M. Blage. I loved you then, and since, and ever shall;
You are the woman, though your fortunes fall.
You, when my husband's lewd transgression   30
Of all our wealth had lost possession
By forfeiture into his hghness' hands,
Got restitution of our goods and lands.
He fled, and died in France. To heal that harm,
You helped me to three manors in fee farm,   35
The worst of which clears three score pound a year.
Have I not reason, then, to hold you dear?
Yes, hap what will until my life do end,
You are, and shall be my best lovèd friend.
Jane. How if misfortune my folly do succeed?   40
M. Blage. Trust me. True friends bide touch in time of need.
Jane. If want consume the wealth I had before?
M. Blage. My wealth is yours, and you shall spend my store.
Jane. But the Protector prosecutes his hate.
M. Blage. With me live secret from the world's debate.   45
Jane. You will be weary of so bad a guest.
M. Blage. Then let me never on the earth be blessed.
Jane. Ah, Mistress Blage, you tender me such love,
As all my sorrows from my soul remove;
And though my portion be not very large,   50
Yet come I not to you to be a charge.
Coin, plate and jewels prized at lowest rate,
I bring with me to maintain my estate,
Worth twenty thousand pound; and my array,

---

25. *favouring*] unusual usage, in that Jane implies that these 'friends' have
been receiving rather than extending favours.
35. *in fee farm*] at a fixed (and therefore affordable) rent.
41. *bide touch*] prove true (from testing the purity of gold).
45. *debate*] See commentary to Part One, Scene 19, l. 54.

If you survive to see my dying day,   55
From you no penny will I give away.
M. Blage. And I thank you, that so my wealth increased,
Am worth, I trow, ten thousand pounds at least.
I think like two warm widows we may live,
Until good fortune two good husbands give;   60
For surely, Mistress Shore, your husband's dead.
When heard you of him?
Jane.   Never, since he fled.
O, Mistress Blage, now put you in my head
That kills my heart. Why should I breathe this air,
Whose lost good name no treasure can repair?   65
O, were he here with me to lead this life,
Although he never used me as a wife,
But as a drudge, to spurn me with his feet,
Yet should I think, with him that life were sweet.
M. Blage. How can you once conceit so base a thing,   70
That have been kissed and cockered by a king?
Weep not. You hurt yourself, by God's blessed mother;
Your husband's dead, woman: think upon another.
Let us in to supper. Drink wine, cheer your heart;
And, whilst I live, be sure I'll take your part.   *Exeunt.*   75

[Scene 16]

> *Enter* BRACKENBURY, SHORE [*disguised as* FLOOD],
> DIGHTON, FOREST, TYRRELL.

Tyrrell. Sir, I assure you, 'tis my Lord Protector's warrant.
Brackenbury. My friend, I have conferred it with his letters,
And 'tis his hand indeed, I'll not deny.
But blame me not, although I be precise
In matters that so nearly do concern me.   5
Dighton. My Lord Protector, sir, I make no doubt,
Dare justify his warrant, though perhaps

---

75. *Exeunt*] *Q6; Exit Q1–5.*

71. *cockered*] indulged, coddled.

2. *conferred*] soon to be obsolete but original meaning: 'brought together
for examination', 'compared'.

He doth not now acquaint you why he doth it.
Brackenbury. I think, sir, there's no subject now in England
    Will urge his grace to show what he dare do,   10
    Nor will I ask him why he does it.
    I would I might, to rid me of my doubt.   *Aside.*
Forest. Why, sir, I think he needs no precedent
    For what he does; I think his power is absolute enough.
Brackenbury. I have no power, sir, to examine it,   15
    Nor will; I do obey your warrant,
    Which I will keep for my security.
Tyrrell. You shall do well in that, sir.
Brackenbury.   Here's the keys.
Shore. Aside [*to Brackenbury*] And yet, I could wish my
    Lord Protector
    Had sent his warrant thither by some other;   20
    I do not like their looks, I tell you true.
Brackenbury. Nor I, Flood, I assure thee.
Forest. What does that slave mutter to his master?
Dighton. I hear him say he does not like our looks.
Tyrrell. Why not our looks, sir?
Forest.   Sirrah, we hear you.   25
Shore. I am glad you do, sir. All is one for that.
    But if you did not, hearken better now:
    I never saw three faces in whose looks
    Did ever sit more terror, or more death.
    God bless the princes, if it be his will.   30
    I do not like these villains.
Dighton. Zounds, stab the villain! Sirra, do you brave us?
                   [*He draws a knife.*]
Shore. Ay, that's your coming; for you come to stab.
Forest. Stab him.
Shore. Nay, then, I'll stab with thee!   35
       [*He draws a knife and fights with* DIGHTON.]
Tyrrell. S' blood, cut his throat!
Brackenbury. Hold, gentlemen, I pray you!
Shore. Sir, I am hurt, stabbed in the arm.

---

16. will; I do obey] *Q2*; will I do: I doe obey *Q1*.   20. thither] *Q1–3*; hither
Q4–6.

---

15. *examine*] question.
32. *brave*] challenge.

Brackenbury. This is not to be justified, my friends,
    To draw your weapons here within the Tower,   40
    And by the law, it is no less than death.
    I cannot think the Duke will like of this.
    Pray you, be content; too much is done.
Tyrrell. He might have held his peace, then, and been quiet.
    Farewell, farewell.   45
                [*Exeunt* TYRRELL, FOREST, DIGHTON.]
Shore. Hell and damnation follow murderers!
Brackenbury. Go, Flood; get thee some surgeon to look to
    thy wound.
    Hast no acquaintance with some skilful surgeon?
    Keep thy wound close, and let it not take air.
    And, for my own part, I will not stay here.   50
    Whither wilt thou go, that I may send to thee?
Shore. To one Mistress Blage's, an inn in Gracechurch Street.
    There you shall find me, or shall hear of me.
Brackenbury. Sweet, princely babes, farewell. I fear you sore;
    I doubt these eyes shall never see you more.   [*Exeunt.*]   55

[Scene 17]

    Enter the two young princes, EDWARD *and* RICHARD, *in*
       their gowns and caps, unbuttoned, and untrussed.

P. Richard. How does your lordship?
P. Edward.   Well, good brother Richard.
    How does yourself? You told me your head ached.
P. Richard. Indeed it does. My lord, feel with your hand
    How hot it is.

    He [EDWARD] *lays his hand on his brother's head.*

P. Edward.   Indeed, you have caught cold
    With sitting yesternight to hear me read.   5

1–2. Well . . . ached] *Qq line:* Well . . . yourself / You . . . ached.   4. How]
how *Qq.*

---

54. *fear you*] fear for you.
55. *I doubt . . . more*] This double negative is for emphasis and, as frequently in the period, is not to be understood literally.

I pray thee go to bed, sweet Dick, poor little heart.
P. Richard. You'll give me leave to wait upon your lordship?
P. Edward. I had more need, brother, to wait on you,
    For you are sick, and so am not I.
P. Richard. O Lord, methinks this going to our bed,   10
    How like it is to going to our grave.
P. Edward. I pray thee, do not speak of graves, sweetheart;
    Indeed, thou frightest me.
P. Richard. Why, my lord brother, did not our tutor teach us
    That when at night we went unto our bed,   15
    We still should think we went unto our grave.
P. Edward. Yes, that's true:
    That we should do as every Christian ought,
    To be prepared to die at every hour.
    But, I am heavy.
P. Richard.   Indeed, and so am I.   20
P. Edward. Then let us say our prayers, and go to bed.
        They kneel, and solemn music the while within;
                the music ceaseth, and they rise.
P. Richard. What, bleeds your grace?
P. Edward.   Ay, two drops, and no more.
P. Richard. God bless us both, and I desire no more.
P. Edward. Brother, see here what David says, and so say I:
    'Lord, in thee will I trust, although I die'.   25

    As the young princes go out, enter TYRRELL.

Tyrrell. Go, lay you down, but never more to rise.
    I have put my hand into the foulest murder
    That ever was committed since the world.
    The very senseless stones, here in the walls,
    Break out in tears but to behold the fact.   30
    Methinks the bodies lying dead in graves

---

13. frightest] *Q2*; frightst *Q1*. 17–20. Yes . . . heavy] *Qq line:* Yes . . .
ought / To bee . . . heauie.

24–5. *David . . . die*] The Psalmist does not says this. The close of 55 is
similar but, typically, the speaker seems to be imagining the death of his
enemies not himself. Job, however, does (albeit in a textually contentious
line at 13.15), and it is also the promise offered by Christ in John, 11.25.

Should rise and cry against us. O, hark, hark!
                                            A noise within.
The mandrakes' shrieks are music to their cries.
The very night is frighted, and the stars
Do drop like torches to behold this deed.   35
The very centre of the earth doth shake.
Methinks the Tower should rent down from the top,
To let the heaven look on this monstrous deed.

>   *Enter at one door* DIGHTON, *with* EDWARD *under his*
>   *arm; at the other door* FOREST, *with* RICHARD.

Dighton. Stand further, damnèd rogue, and come not near
      me.
Forest. Nay, stand thou further, villain; stand aside.   40
Dighton. Are we not both damned for this cursèd deed?
Forest. Thou art the witness, that thou bearst the king.
Dighton. And what bearst thou?
Forest. It is too true. O, I am damned indeed.
                        He looks down on the boy under his arm.
Tyrrell. I am as deep as you, although my hand   45
      Did not the deed.
Dighton.   O, villain, art thou there?
Forest. A plague light on thee.
Tyrrell.   Curse not;
      A thousand plagues will light upon us all.
                                    They lay them down.
The priest here in the Tower will bury them;
Let us away.   [*Exeunt.*]   50

[Scene 18]

>   *Enter* MISTRESS BLAGE *and her two men, bringing in*
>   SHORE, *alias* FLOOD, *in a chair, his arm bleeding apace.*

M. Blage. So, set him here awhile, where is more air.
      How cheer you, sir? Alack, he doth begin

47–8. Curse . . . all] *One line in Qq.*

---

33. *mandrakes*] It was believed that when plants of the genus *mandragora*
were pulled from the earth they uttered shrieks which caused madness or
death to the hearer.

To change his colour. Where is Mistress Shore?
[*Servant.*] Gone to her closet for a precious balm;
   The same, she said, King Edward used himself.   5
M. Blage. Alack, I fear he'll die before she come.
   Run quickly for some rosa-solis.   [*Exit Servant.*]
                                   Faint not, sir,
   Be of good comfort.

          [*Servant enters again, followed by* JANE.]

                    Come, good Mistress Shore,
   What have you there?
Jane.   Stand by, and give me leave.
M. Blage. Unhappy me, to lodge him in my house.   10
Jane. I warrant you, woman, be not so afraid.
   If not this blood-stone, hanged about his neck,
   This balm will staunch it, by the help of God.
   Lift up his arm, whilst I do bathe his wound.
   The sign, belike, was here when he was hurt,   15
   Or else some principal and chief vein is pierced.
M. Blage. However, sure the surgeon was a knave,
   That looked no better to him at the first.
Jane. Blame him not, Mistress Blage. The best of them,
   In such a case as this, may be to seek.   20
M. Blage. Now, God be blessed! See, the crimson blood
   That was precipitate, and falling down
   Into his arm, retires into his face.
   How fare you, sir? How do you feel yourself?
Shore. O, wherefore have you waked me from my sleep,   25
   And broke the quiet slumber I was in?

4–9. Gone . . . there?] *Q2–6 print lines 1–9 as one continuous speech by M.*
Blage. Q1's 'redundant' speech prefix (M. Blage) at line 6 proves the need to real-
locate lines 4–5 to an interlocutor (one of the 'two men' specified in the scene's
opening SD).

7. *rosa-solis*] restorative cordial, made from the sundew plant.
12. *blood-stone*] any precious stone with vivid red markings might be used
as a talisman to staunch bleeding.
15. *sign*] Not a medical term; Jane infers that the wound is larger than
might be expected from a stabbing, but the text may clumsily suggest what
an actor could convey with subtlety: that Matthew's physical wound is exacerbated by an emotional one beyond the cure of surgeons.

Methought I sat in such a pleasant place,
So full of all delight as never eye
Beheld, nor heart of man could comprehend.
If you had let me go, I felt no pain;   30
But being now revoked, my grief renews.
Jane. Give him some rosa-solis, Mistress Blage,
And that will likewise animate the spirits
And send alacrity unto the heart
That hath been struggling with the pangs of death.   35
M. Blage. Here, sir, drink this. You need not fear it, sir,
It is no hurt; see, I will be your taster.
Then drink, I pray you.
Jane. Now, fellows, raise his body from the chair,
And gently let him walk a turn or two.   40
M. Blage. Good sooth, Mistress Shore, I did not think till now
You had been such a cunning, skilled physician.
Shore. O, Mistress Blage, though I must needs confess
It would have been more welcome to my soul
If I had died, and been removed at last   45
From the confusèd troubles of this world,
Whereof I have sustainèd no mean weight,
Than lingering here, be made a packhorse still
Of torments, in comparison of which
Death is but the pricking of a thorn,   50
Yet I do thank you for your taken pains,
And would to God I could requite your love.
M. Blage. Sir, I did you little good. What was done,
Ascribe the benefit and praise thereof
Unto this gentlewoman: kind Mistress Shore,   55
Who, next to God, preserved your feeble life.
Shore. How? Mistress Shore? Good friends, let go your hold;
My strength is now sufficient of itself.
[*Aside*] O, is it she, that still prolongs my woe?
Was it ordained not only at the first   60
She should be my destruction, but now twice?
When gracious destinies had brought about
To end this weary pilgrimage of mine,

---

31. *revoked*] the usual meaning—called back—unlike the usage in Part
One, Scene 15, l. 98.
42. *cunning*] knowledgeable.

Must she, and none but she, prevent that good,
And stop my entrance to eternal bliss?   65
O lasting plague! O endless corrosive!
It now repents me double that I 'scaped,
Since life's made death, and life's author, hate.
Jane. Sir, take my counsel, and sit down again.
It is not good to be so bold of foot   70
Upon the sudden, till you have more strength.
Shore. Mistress, I thank you. And I care not much
If I be ruled by you.   [*He*] *sits down.*
[*Aside*] O God, that she should pity me unknown,
That, knowing me, by her was overthrown;   75
Or ignorantly she should regard this smart,

Enter BRACKENBURY.

That heretofore spared not to stab my heart.
Brackenbury. By your leave, Mistress Blage, I am
    somewhat bold;
Is there not a gentleman within your house
Called Master Flood, came hither, hurt, last night?   80
M. Blage. Is his name Flood? I knew it not till now;
But here he is, and well recovered,
Thanks to this gentlewoman, Mistress Shore.
Brackenbury. Pardon me, Mistress Shore, I saw you not;
And trust me, I am sorry at the heart   85
So good a creature as your self hath been,
Should be so vilely dealt with as you are;
I promise you, the world laments your case.
Jane. How mean you, sir? I understand you not.
Lament my case? For what? For Edward's death?   90
I know that I have lost a gracious friend,
But that is not to be remedied now.
Brackenbury. No, Mistress Shore, it is for Richard's hate,
That too much envies your prosperity.
Jane. I know he loves me not, and for that cause   95
I have withdrawn me wholly from the court.
Brackenbury. You have not seen the proclamation, then?

---

66. *corrosive*] The spelling common to all the quartos—'corasive'—is misleading; Shore clearly means 'irreversible destruction', and not the very rare
word meaning 'scraping together'.

Jane. The proclamation? No, what proclamation?
Brackenbury. O, Mistress Shore, the King in every street
    Of London, and in every borough town,   100
    Throughout this land hath publicly proclaimed,
    On pain of death, that none shall harbour you,
    Or give you food, or clothes to keep you warm;
    But, having first done shameful penance here,
    You shall be then thrust forth the city gates,   105
    Into the naked, cold, forsaken field.
    I fable not; I would to God I did.
    See, here's the manner of it, put in print;
    'Tis to be sold in every stationer's shop,
    Besides a number of them clapped on posts;   110
    Where people crowding, as they read your fall
    Some murmur, and some sigh, but most of them
    Have their relenting eyes e'en big with tears.
Jane. God's will be done. I know my sin is great,
    And he that is omnipotent and just   115
    Cannot but must reward me heavily.
Brackenbury. It grieves me, Mistress Shore, it was my chance
    To be the first reporter of this news.
Jane. Let it not grieve. I must have heard of it,
    And now as good as at another time.   120
Brackenbury. I pray you, Mistress Blage, have care of Flood,
    And what his charge is, I will see you paid.   *Exit.*
Jane. 'Farewell to All': that still shall be my song,
    Let men impose upon me ne'er such wrong;
    And this extremity shall seem the less,   125
    In that I have a friend to lean unto.
    Sweet Mistress Blage, there were upon the earth
    No comfort left for miserable Jane,
    But that I do presume upon your love.
    I know, though tyrant Richard had set down   130

108–13. *print . . . tears*] Purposefully anachronistic; not only was the dissemination of printed proclamations an innovation of the later Tudors, but in the 1590s such widespread 'publication' of women as whores was invariably performed by the communities—especially apprentices—that pity Jane here.

123. *'Farewell to all'*] Possibly the title of a lost ballad; I can find no reference to it.

A greater penalty than is proclaimed
—Which cannot well be thought—yet in your house
I should have succour, and relief beside.

M. Blage. What? And so I should be a traitor, should I?
Is that the care you have of me and mine?   135
I thank you, truly. No, there's no such matter.
I love you well, but love myself better.
As long as you were held a true subject,
I made account of you accordingly;
But being otherwise, I do reject you,   140
And will not cherish my King's enemy.
You know the danger of the proclamation:
I would to God you would depart my house.

Jane. When was it ever seen Jane Shore was false,
Either unto her country, or her King?   145
And, therefore, 'tis not well, good Mistress Blage,
That you upbraid me with a traitor's name.

M. Blage. Ay, but you have been a wicked liver;
And now you see what 'tis to be unchaste.
You should have kept you with your honest husband.   150
'Twas never other like, but that such filthiness
Would have a foul and detestable end.

Jane. Time was that you did tell me otherwise,
And studied how to set a gloss on that,
Which now you say is ugly and deformed.   155

M. Blage. I told you then, as then the time did serve,
And more, indeed, to try your disposition,
Than any way to encourage you to sin;
But when I saw you were ambitious,
And faintly stood on terms of modesty,   160
I left you to your own arbitrement.
Can you deny it was not so? How say you?

Jane. We will not, Mistress Blage, dispute of that;
But now, in charity and womanhood,
Let me find favour, if it be but this: 165
That in some barn or stable I may shroud,
Till otherwise I be provided for.

---

160. *faintly . . . of*] half-heartedly went through the motions of appearing
publicly to profess.

M. Blage. I pray you, do not urge me, Mistress Shore.
    I will not have my house endangered so.
Jane. O, you did promise I should never want,   170
    And that your house was mine, and swore the same;
    To keep your oath, be then compassionate.
M. Blage. So you did swear you would be true to Shore,
    But you were not so good as your word.
    My oath's dispensed with by the King's command.   175
Jane. Yet let me have those jewels and that money
    Which is within my trunks.
M. Blage.   I know of none.
    If there be any, I'll be so bold
    As keep it for your diet, and your man's.
    It is no little charge I have been at,   180
    To feed your dainty tooth since you came hither;
    Beside, house-room, I am sure, is somewhat worth.
Shore. [*Aside*] Ah, Jane, I cannot choose but pity thee.
    Here's the first step to thy deep misery.
Jane. O, that my grave had then been made my house,   185
    When either first I went unto the court,
    Or from the court returned unto this place.

                    Enter two APPARITORS.

Servant. How now, what are you? It had been manners,
    You should have knocked before you had come in.
1 Apparitor. We are the bishop's 'parritors, my friend;   190
    And, Mistress Shore, our errand is to you.
    This day it is commanded by the King,
    You must be stripped out of your rich attire,
    And in a white sheet go from Temple Bar
    Until you come to Aldgate, bare-footed,   195

---

170. *Jane*] Q2; *omitted in text of Q1, but is the catchword at the foot of sig. T4v.*
175. dispensed with by] *Q1*; disherit which by *Q2–3*; dischargde now by
Q4–6.   176. let me] *Q2*; me let *Q1.*

---

175. *dispensed . . . command*] An ironic reworking of her pseudo-legalistic
sophistry in Part One, Scene 19, l. 31.
    187.01. *APPARITORS*] officers of an ecclesiastical court (see l. 190).
    190. *bishop*] of London.
    194–5. *Temple . . . Aldgate*] None of the chronicles or earlier treatments of
Jane's downfall specifies the route of her public penance. The playwright

Your hair about your ears, and in your hand
A burning taper. Therefore, go with us.
Jane. Even when, and whither you will. And would to God
The King as soon could rid my soul of sin,
As he may strip my body of these rags.   200
2 Apparitor. That would be soon enough; but come away.
And Mistress Blage: you'll hardly answer it,
When it is known we found her in your house.
                                    [*Exit* 2 APPARITOR *with* JANE.]
1 Apparitor. It seems you do not fear to harbour her.
M. Blage. I harbour her? Out on her, strumpet quean!   205
She pressed upon me, where I would or no:
I'll see her hanged ere I will harbour her.
                                        [*Exit* 1 APPARITOR.]
So, now her jewels and her gold is mine,
And I am made at least four thousand pound
Wealthier by this match than I was before.   210
And what can be objected for the same?
That once I loved her? Well, perhaps I did.
But now I am of another humour;
And women all are governed by the moon,
Which is, you know, a planet that will change.   215

                    [*Enter* CATESBY, *with a Sheriff.*]

Catesby. Now, Master Sheriff of London, do your office.
Attach this rebel to his majesty,
And having stripped her to her petticoat,
Turn her out o' doors, with this condition:
That no man harbour her, that darst presume   220
To harbour that lewd courtesan, Shore's wife,
Against the straight commandment of the King.

---

199. could] *Q1–2;* would *Q3–6.*   213–14.] *thus Q6; lines transposed in Q1–5.*

wishes to convey that it traversed the entire breadth of the city; Heywood's
friend Shackerley Marmion would describe a couple's hopeless separation
as 'as far asunder as Temple Bar and Aldgate' in his *A Fine Companion* (1633),
in J. Maidment, W. H. Logan (eds) *The Dramatic Works* (Edinburgh, 1875),
191.
    202. *hardly*] with difficulty.
    206. *where*] whether.
    217. *Attach . . . to*] arrest on behalf of.

M. Blage. I beseech you, sir.
Catesby.   Away with her, I say.
                    [*Exeunt the Sheriff with* MISTRESS BLAGE.]
    The while I'll seize upon her house and goods,
    Which wholly are confiscate to the King.   *Exit.*   225
Shore. O, what have I beheld? Were I as young
    As when I came to London to be 'prentice,
    This pageant were sufficient to instruct,
    And teach me ever after to be wise.
    First have I seen desert of wantonness,   230
    And breach of wedlock; then, of flattery;
    Next, of dissembling love; and last of all,
    The ruin of base, catching avarice.
    But poor Jane Shore, in that I loved thee once,
    And was thy husband, I must pity thee.   235
    The sparks of old affection long ago,
    Raked up in ashes of displeasure, kindle;
    And in this furnace of adversity,
    The world shall see a husband's loyalty.   *Exit.*

[Scene 19]

        Enter DOCTOR SHAW, *pensively reading on his book;*
        after him follows the ghost of FRIAR ANSELM, *with a*
                        lighted torch.

    Doctor Shaw. Spuria vitulamina non agent radices altas:
    Bastardly slips have always slender growth.
    Ah, Shaw, this was the cursèd theme
    That at Paul's Cross thou mad'st thy sermon of:
    To prove the lawful issue of thy king,   5
    Got out of wedlock, illegitimate.

---

230. *desert*] the reward.

1. Spuria . . . altas] This slight misquotation from the Vulgate text of The
Wisdom of Solomon (3.4)—from the Apocrypha, and therefore omitted in
both the Geneva and King James bibles—appears in More (66/ 27–8), whose
translation is close to Shaw's: 'bastard slippes shal neuer take depe roote'.
Thomas Middleton had recently provided a more expansive (and more free)
verse translation in his *The Wisdom of Solomon Paraphrased* (1597); see *Works*,
VIII, 166.

Ah, Duke of Gloucester, this didst thou procure.
Did Richard? Villain, no; it was thy fault
Thou wouldst be won to such a damnèd deed,
Which now to think on makes my soul to bleed.   10
Ah, Friar Anselm, sleep among the blessed;
Thy prophecy thus falsely did I wrest.

Enter ANSELM.

Anselm. Thou didst, and be thou damnèd therefore;
    Ne'er come thy soul where blessedness abides.
    Didst thou not know the letter 'G' was 'Gloucester'?   15
Doctor Shaw. Anselm, I did.
Anselm.   Why, then, didst thou affirm
    That it was meant by George, the Duke of Clarence?
    That honourable, harmless gentleman,
    Whose thoughts all innocent as any child,
    Yet came, through thee, to such a luckless death.   20
Doctor Shaw. I was enforcèd by the Duke of Gloucester.
Anselm. Enforced, sayst thou? Wouldst thou then be enforced,
    Being a man of thy profession,
    To sin so vilely, and with thine own mouth
    To damn thy soul? No. Thou wast not enforced,   25
    But gain, and hope of high promotion
    Hired thee thereto. Say, was it so, or no?
Doctor Shaw. It did, it did.
Anselm. Why then, record in thy black, hellish thoughts,
    How many mischiefs hath ensued thereon!   30
    First, wrongèd Clarence, drownèd in the Tower.
    Next, Edward's children, murdered in the Tower.
    This day, at Pomfret, noble gentlemen
    Three, the Queen's kindred, lose their harmless heads.
    Thinkst thou that here this flood of mischief stays?   35
    No, villain. Many are markèd to the block,

---

17. *was . . . by*] signified.
33–4. *Pomfret . . . heads*] The dramatist follows Holinshed's spelling of
Pontefract (in Yorkshire) here. The sources are bewilderingly imprecise about
the executions; More's Latin text specifies Rivers and Grey, but the English—
followed by Holinshed—mentions only 'fore remembred lordes & knightes'
(57/ 18–19). As *Richard III* had shown, Sir Thomas Vaughan, although not
of 'the Queen's kindred', made a third eminent victim.

And they the nearest, think them furthest off.
Even Buckingham, creator of that king,
Shall he to woe and wretched ending bring.
All this, accursèd man, hath come by thee,   40
And thy false wresting of my prophecy,
For England's good, disclosèd to thy trust;
And so it had been, hadst thou provèd just.
But thou, and every one that had a hand
In that most woeful murder of the princes,   45
To fatal ends you are appointed all.
Here, in thy study, shalt thou starve thyself,
And from this hour not taste one bit of food;
The rest shall after follow, on a row,
To all their deaths. Vengeance will not be slow.   50

Enter a MESSENGER *to* SHAW.

Messenger. Where is Master Doctor Shaw?
Doctor Shaw. Here, friend. What is thy will with me?
Messenger. King Richard prays you to come to him straight,
     For he would be confessed.
Doctor Shaw. I cannot come. I pray thee, take that friar,   55
     For he can do it better far than I.
Messenger. A friar, Master Doctor? I see none.
Doctor Shaw. Dost thou not? No, thy untainted soul
     Cannot discern the horrors that I do.
Anselm. Shaw, go with him, and tell that tyrant, Richard,   60
     He hath but three years limited for life;
     And then a shameful death takes hold on him.
     That done, return, and in thy study, end
     Thy loathèd life, that didst us all offend.
Doctor Shaw. With all my heart. Would it were ended now.   65
     So it were done, I care not where, nor how.   *Exeunt.*

---

37. *furthest off*] furthest from safety.
47–8. *starve . . . food*] The playwright's invention. More and his appropriators suggest a death brought about by shame; the 1587 Holinshed version
bizarrely illustates Shaw's death with a (mis)quotation from Ovid's *Metamorphoses* (3, l. 396), which describes Echo pining away in unrequited love
for Narcissus.

[Scene 20]

Enter the two APPARITORS, *with* MISTRESS SHORE *in a*
white sheet, bare-footed, with her hair about her ears, and
in her hand a wax taper.

1 Apparitor. Now, Mistress Shore, here our commission ends.
Put off your robe of shame, for this is Aldgate,
Whither it was appointed we should bring you.
Jane. My robe of shame? O, that so foul a name
Should be applied unto so fair a garment;   5
Which is no more to be condemned of shame,
Than snow of putrefaction is deserved,
To cover an infectious heap of dung.
My robe of shame, but not my shame, put off,
For that sits branded on my forehead still;   10
And therefore, in derision, was I wrapped
In this white sheet; and, in derision, bore
This burning taper to express my folly,
That, having light of reason to direct me,
Delighted yet in byways of dark error.   15
2 Apparitor. Well, Mistress Shore, I hope you grudge not us;
We showed you all the favour poor men could.
Jane. O, God forbid. I know the King's edict
Set you a' work, and not your own desires.
1 Apparitor. Ay, truly, mistress; and, for our parts,   20
We could be well content 'twere otherwise,
But that the law's severe. And so we leave you.
                                    Exeunt [APPARITORS].
Jane. Farewell unto you both. And London too.
Farewell to thee, where first I was enticed,

---

22. *Exeunt*] *Exit Qq.*

0.2. white . . . ears] Jane enters in the costume of the publicly shamed
whore. Having her 'hair about her ears' is a further visual signal; although
more usually a sign of madness (as in Q1 *Hamlet*'s Ophelia), it appears as
an indicator of sexual disgrace in, for example, Massinger's *The Emperor of*
the East (1632), 5.3.0.1.
7-8. *snow . . . dung*] Jane argues that, like her white sheet, snow should
not be deemed the source of the corruption it covers.
10. *branded . . . forehead*] Malefactors, and especially prostitutes, were literally branded thus, with a red-hot iron: neither the play nor the sources
suggest that Jane suffered this punishment herself.

That scandalized thy dignity with shame.   25
But now thou hast returned me treble blame:
My tongue, that gave consent, enjoined to beg;
Mine eyes adjudged to hourly laments;
Mine arms, for their embracings, catch the air;
And these quick, nimble feet, that were so ready   30
To step into a king's forbidden bed?
London, thy flints have punished for their pride,
And thou hast drunk their blood for thy revenge.
What now avails to think what I have been?
Then welcome, nakedness and poverty.   35
Welcome, contempt. Welcome, you barren fields.
Welcome, the lack of meat, and lack of friends.
And, wretched Jane, according to thy state,
Sit here, sit here, and lower, if might be.
All things that breathe, in their extremity   40
Have some recourse of succour; thou hast none.
The child, offended, flies unto the mother.
The soldier, struck, retires unto his captain.
The fish, distressèd, slides into the river.
Birds of the air do fly unto their dams,   45
And underneath their wings are quickly shrouded.
Nay, beat the spaniel, and his master moans him,
But I have neither where to shroud myself,
Nor anyone to make my moan unto.
Come, patience, then; and though my body pine,   50
Make then a banquet to refresh my soul.
Let heart's deep-throbbing sighs be all my bread;
My drink, salt tears; my guests, repentant thoughts;
That whoso knew me, and doth see me now,
May shun, by me, the breach of wedlock's vow.   55

Enter BRACKENBURY *with a prayer book, and some relief
in a cloth for Mistress Shore.*

Brackenbury. O God, how full of dangers grows these times,
And no assurance seen in any state.
No man can say that he is master, now,
Of anything is his, such is the tide

---

47. *moans him*] bemoans, is sympathetic in retrospect.

Of sharp disturbance running through the land.   60
I have given over my office in the Tower,
Because I cannot brook their vile complots,
Nor smother such outrageous villanies.
But Mistress Shore to be so basely wronged,
And vilely used, that hath so well deserved!   65
It doth afflict me in the very soul.
She saved my kinsman, Harry Stranguidge, life;
Therefore, in duty I am bound to her,
To do what good I may, though law forbid.
See where she sits.—God comfort thee, good soul.   70
First, take that, to relieve thy body with.

                                       [*He gives food.*]

And next, receive this book, wherein is food,
Manna of heaven, to refresh thy soul.
These holy meditations, Mistress Shore,
Will yield much comfort in this misery;   75
Whereon, contemplate still, and never lin,
That God may be unmindful of thy sin.
Jane. Master Lieutenant, in my heart I thank you
For this kind comfort to a wretched soul.
Welcome, sweet prayer book, food of my life,   80
The sovereign balm for my sick conscience;
Thou shalt be my soul's pleasure and delight,
To wipe my sins out of Jehovah's sight.
Brackenbury. Do so, good Mistress Shore. Now I must
       leave you,
Because some other business calls me hence;   85
And God, I pray, regard your penitence.   *Exit.*
Jane. Farewell, Sir Robert; and for this good to me,
The God of heaven be mindful still of thee.

       As she sits weeping and praying, enters at one door young
            Master AIRE, *and old* RUFFORD *at another.*

Aire. This way she went, and cannot be far off,
For but even now I met the officers   90

---

82. soul's] *Q2–6* (soules); soule *Q1.*

62. *complots*] plots; the archaic word was probably suggested by its double
use at the parallel stage in Gloucester's scheming in *Richard III*, 3.1.189–197.
   76. *lin*] desist, give up; another archaic form.

That were attendant on her in her penance.
Yonder she sits. Now then, Aire, show thyself
Thankful to her, that sometime saved thy life,
When law had made thee subject to base death.
Give her thy purse, for here comes somebody.   95
Stand by a while, for fear thou be discovered.
                                        [*He withdraws.*]
Rufford. What, Mistress Shore, King Edward's concubine,
Set on a mole-hill? O, disparagement!
A throne were fitter for your ladyship.
Fie, will you slubber these fair cheeks with tears?   100
Or sit so solitary? Where's all your servants?
Where is your gown of silk, your periwigs,
Your fine rebatoes, and your costly jewels?
What, not so much as a shoe upon your foot?
Nay, then, I see the world goes hard with whores.   105
Aire. The villain slave jibes at her misery.
Rufford. Now, whether is it better to be in court,
And there to beg a licence of the King
For transportation of commodities,
Than here to sit forsaken, as thou dost?   110
I think upon condition Edward lived,
And thou were still in favour as before,
Thou wouldst not say that Rufford had deserved
To have his ears rent for a worser suit
Than licence to ship over corn and lead.   115
What, not a word? Faith, wench, I'll tell thee what:
If thou dost think thy old trade out of date,
Go learn to play the bawd another while.
Aire. [*Coming forward*] Inhuman wretch! Why dost thou
        scorn her so,
And vex her grievèd soul with bitter taunts?   120
Rufford. Because I will. She is a courtesan,
And one abhorrèd of the world for lust.

---

95. somebody] some Ladie *Qq.*

100. *slubber*] obscure, disfigure.
103. *rebatoes*] a stiff, tall collar supporting a ruff.
114. *rent*] torn. Could be figurative, meaning he had been shouted at, or
literal; the most famous victim of such judicial violence was the anti-the-
atrical polemicist, William Prynne.

Aire. If all thy faults were in thy forehead writ,
　　Perhaps thou wouldst thyself appear no less,
　　But much more horrible than she doth now.　　　　　125
Rufford. You are no judge of mine, sir.
Aire.　　　　　　　　　　　　Why, nor thou of her.
Rufford. The world hath judged, and found her guilty,
　　And 'tis the King's command she be held odious.
Aire. The king of heaven commandeth otherwise.
　　And if thou be not willing to relieve her,　　　　　130
　　Let it suffice thou see'st her miserable,
　　And study not to amplify her grief.

　　　　　Enter MISTRESS BLAGE, *very poorly, a-begging with
　　　　　　her basket and clap-dish.*

　　What other woeful spectacle comes here?
　　　　　　　When RUFFORD *looks away,* AIRE *throws
　　　　　　　　his purse to* MISTRESS SHORE.
　　Mistress, take that, and spend it for my sake.
M. Blage. O, I am pinched with more than common want.　135
　　Where shall I find relief? Good gentlemen,
　　Pity a wretched woman, like to starve,
　　And I will pray for you. One half penny,
　　For Christ's sake, to comfort me withal.
Rufford. What, Mistress Blage, is't you? No marvel, sure,　140
　　But you should be relieved. A halfpenny, quotha?
　　Ay, marry, sir; and so be hanged myself.
　　Not I; this gentleman may, if he please.
　　Get you to your companion, Mistress Shore,
　　And then there is a pair of queans well met.　　　　145
　　Now, I bethink me, I'll go to the King,
　　And tell him that some will relieve Shore's wife,
　　Except some officer there be appointed,
　　That carefully regards it be not so.
　　Thereof myself will I make offer to him,　　　　　150
　　Which questionless, he cannot but accept;
　　So shall I still pursue Shore's wife with hate,
　　That scorned me in her high, whore's estate.　　*Exit.*

133.01.] *SD after line 134 in Qq.*　136. gentlemen] *Q1*; Gentleman *Q2–6.*

132.02. clap-dish] wooden dish, normally carried by lepers, with a lid
which was 'clapped' to attract attention.

M. Blage. Good gentleman, bestow your charity;
    One single halfpenny, to help my need. 155
Aire. Not one, were I the master of a mint.
    What, succour thee, that didst betray thy friend?
    See where she sits, whom thou didst scorn indeed;
    And therefore, rightly art thou scorned again.
    Thou thoughtst to be enrichèd with her goods, 160
    But thou hast now lost both thy own and hers;
    And, for my part, knew I 'twould save thy life,
    Thou shouldst not get so much as a crumb of bread.
    Pack, counterfeit! Pack away, dissembling drab! [*Exit.*]
M. Blage. O, misery! But shall I stay to look 165
    Her in the face, whom I so much have wronged?
Jane. Yes, Mistress Blage, I freely pardon you.
    You have done me no wrong. Come, sit by me;
    'Twas so in wealth, why not in poverty?
M. Blage. O, willingly, if you can brook her presence, 170
    Whom you have greater reason to despise.
Jane. Why, woman, Richard that hath banished me,
    And seeks my ruin, causeless though it be,
    Do I, in heart, pray for; and will do still.
    Come thou, and share with me what God hath sent. 175
    A stranger gave it me, and part thereof
    I do as freely now bestow on you.
M. Blage. I thank you, Mistress Shore. This courtesy
    Renews the grief of my inconstancy.

        Enter MASTER SHORE *with relief for his wife.*

Shore. Yonder she sits. How like a withered tree, 180
    That is in winter leafless, and bereft
    Of lively sap, sits the poor, abject soul.
    How much unlike the woman is she now,
    She was but yesterday; so short and brittle
    Is this world's happiness. But who is that? 185
    False Mistress Blage? How canst thou brook her, Jane?
    Ay, thou wast always mild, and pitiful.
    O, hadst thou been as chaste, we had been blessed!

---

160. to be enrichèd] *Q4–6*; beene riched *Q1–3*. 182. the] *Q2–6*; shee *Q1*.

But now no more of that. She shall not starve,
So long as this, and such as this, may serve.   190
                    [*He unwraps food and drink.*]
—Here, Mistress Shore. Feed on these homely cates,
And there is wine to drive them down withal.
Jane. Good sir, your name, that pities Jane Shore?
That in my prayers I may remember you?
Shore. No matter for my name. I am a friend   195
That loves you well. So, farewell, Mistress Shore.
When that is spent, I vow to bring you more.   [*Exit.*]
Jane. God's blessing be your guide, where e'er you go.
Thus, Mistress Blage, you see, amidst our woe,
For all the world can do, God sends relief,   200
And we will not yet perish in our grief.
Come, let us step into some secret place,
Where, undisturbed, we may partake this grace
M. Blage. 'Tis not amiss, if you be so content,
For here the field's too open, and frequent.   *Exeunt.* 205

                    MASTER SHORE *enters again.*

Shore. What, is she gone so soon? Alack, poor Jane,
How I compassionate thy woeful case!
Whereas we lived together, man and wife,
Oft on an humble stool by the fireside
Sat she contented, whenas my high heat   210
Would chide her for it. But what would she say?
'Husband, we both must lower sit one day.'
When, I dare swear, she never dreamed of this;
But see, good God, what prophesying is.

        Enter RUFFORD *and* FOGGE, *with the counterfeit letters
                patent;* SHORE *stands aside.*

---

192. drive] *Q1*; drinke *Q2–6*.   203. Where . . . grace] *Qq place this line
at the end of M. Blage's next speech.*   214.01–2. letters patent] *Letters Pattents
Qq.*

---

192. *drive*] Q 2–6 'correct' to 'drinke', but Q1's reading is plausible; cf.
Part One, Scene 14, l. 89 and commentary.
205. *frequent*] busy.
208. *Whereas*] archaic form of 'where'.
210. *whenas*] at which time.

Rufford. This is King Richard's hand! I know it well,   215
    And this of thine is justly counterfeit,
    As he himself would swear it were his own.
Shore. [*Aside*] The King's hand counterfeit? List more of that.
Rufford. Why, every letter, every little dash
    In all respects alike! Now may I use   220
    My transportation of my corn and hides,
    Without the danger of forbidding law.
    And so I would have done in Edward's days,
    But that good Mistress Shore did please to cross me;
    But mark how now I will requite her for it.   225
    I moved my suit, and plainly told the King
    Some would relieve her, if no man had charge
    To see severely to the contrary.
    Forthwith, his grace appointed me the man,
    And gave me officers to wait upon me,   230
    Which will so countenance thy cunning work,
    As I shall no way be suspected in it.
    How sayst thou, Fogge?
Fogge.   It will do well, indeed.
    But, good sir, have a care in any case,
    For else you know what harm may come thereon.   235
Rufford. A care, sayst thou? Why, man, I will not trust
    My house, my strongest locks, nor any place
    But mine own bosom. There will I keep it, still;
    If I miscarry, so doth it with me.
Shore. [*Aside*] Are you so cunning, sir? I say no more.   240
    Jane Shore, or I, may quittance you for this.   *Exit.*
Rufford. Well, Fogge, I have contented thee.
    Thou mayst be gone; I must about my charge,
    To see that none relieve Shore's wife with aught.
                               Exit FOGGE.

Enter the Officers, with bills.

Come on, good fellows, you that must attend   245
King Richard's service, under my command:
Your charge is to be very vigilant

232-3. As . . . Fogge?] *One line in Qq.*

___

216. *justly*] exactly.

Over that strumpet whom they call Shore's wife.
If any traitor give her but a mite,
A draught of water, or a crust of bread,   250
Or any other food, whate'er it be,
Lay hold on him; for it is present death,
By good King Richard's proclamation.
This is her haunt; here stand I sentinel.
Keep you unseen, and aid me when I call.   255

Enter JOCKIE *and* JEFFREY, *with a bottle of ale, cheese,*
and halfpenny loaves, to play at bowls. MISTRESS SHORE
enters, and sits where she was wont.

Jockie. Now must I, under colour of playing at bowls, help til
relieve my gude maistress, maistress Shore. Come,
Jeffrey, we will play five-up for this bootle of ale, and
yonder gude, puir woman shall keep the stakes, and this
cheese shall be the maister.   260

They play still toward her, and JOCKIE *often breaks bread*
and cheese, and gives her; till JEFFREY *being called away,*
then he gives her all, and is apprehended.

Rufford. Here is a villain, that will not relieve her,
But yet he'll loose his bowls that way, to help her.
Apprehend him, fellows, when I bid ye.
Although his mate be gone, he shall pay for it.
Take him, and let the beadles whip him well.   265
Jockie. Hear ye, sir. Shall they be whipped and hanged that

---

259. stakes, and this] *Q2*; stakes, this *Q1*.   262. loose his bowls that way,
to] *This ed.*; loose his bowls, that way to *Q1*; loose he bowls, that way to
Q2–5; loose; he bowls that way to *Q6 and Field.*

---

252. *present*] immediate.
258. *five-up*] a game of bowls in which each player has five shots at the
target ball.
260. *maister*] a term for the 'jack', the smaller ball at which the other balls
are aimed; 'mistress' was used similarly, as in Pandarus's sexual metaphor in
Troilus and Cressida, 3.2.50.
261–85. *Here . . . Aire*] Perhaps to characterise his sadism and boorish-
ness, the lines allotted to Rufford in this sequence are sometimes metrical
and sometimes clearly not so. Q1 reveals no hesitation in its deployment of
prose for Jockie's speeches, and its lineation of his antagonist's words (as
irregular verse) is retained here.

give to the puir? Then they shall be damn that take fro'
the puir!

They lead him away.
Enter [at one door] young AIRE *again, and* SHORE *[who,*
entering at the other door, then] stands aloof off.

Aire. O, yonder sits the sweet, forsaken soul,
    To whom for ever I stand deeply bound.   270
    She saved my life; then, Aire, help to save hers.
Rufford. Whither go you, sir?
    You come to give this strumpet some relief.
Aire. She did more good than ever thou canst do;
    And if thou wilt not pity her thyself,   275
    Give others leave, by duty bound thereto.
    Here, Mistress Shore, take this; and would to God
    It were so much as my poor heart could wish.
                           He gives her his purse.
Shore. [*Aside*] Who is it that pities my poor wife?
    'Tis Master Aire. God's blessing on him for it.   280
Rufford. Darest thou do so, Aire?
Aire. Rufford, I dare do more.
    Here is my ring, it weighs an ounce of gold;
    And take my cloak to keep you from the cold.
Rufford. Thou art a traitor, Aire.   285
Aire. Rufford, thou art a villain so to call me.
Rufford. Lay hold on him. Attach him, officers.
Aire. Rufford, I'll answer thine arrest, with this!

    He draws his rapier, but is apprehended.

Rufford. All this contending, sir, will not avail.
    This treason will be rated at thy life.   290
Shore. [*Coming forward*] Is he a traitor, sir, for doing good?
    God save the King, a true heart means no ill.
    I trust he hath reclaimed his sharp edict,
    And will not that his poorest subject perish;
    And so persuaded, I myself will do   295
    That which both love and nature binds me to.
    I cannot give her as she well deserves,

---

290. *rated at*] deemed to have earned (the sacrifice of).
293. *reclaimed*] recalled, withdrawn.

For she hath lost a greater benefit.
Poor woman, take that purse.
Rufford.   I'll take't away.
Shore. You shall not, sir; for I will answer it   300
    Before the King, if you enforce it so.
Rufford. It must be so. You shall unto the King.
Shore. You will be he, will first repent the thing.
    Come, Master Aire, I'll bear you company,
    Which wise men say doth ease calamity.   305
            Exeunt [SHORE *and* AIRE, *guarded, and* RUFFORD].
Jane. If grief to speech free passage could afford,
    Or for each woe I had a fitting word,
    I might complain. Or if my floods of tears
    Could move remorse of minds, or pierce dull ears,
    Or wash away my cares, or cleanse my crime,   310
    With words and tears I would bewail the time.
    But it is bootless. Why live I to see
    All those despisèd that do pity me?
    Despised? Alas, destroyed, and led to death,
    That gave me alms, here to prolong my breath.   315
    Fair dames, behold: let my example prove,
    There is no love like to a husband's love.   *Exit.*

[Scene 21]

        Enter KING RICHARD, LOVELL, CATESBY, RUFFORD;
        SHORE *and* AIRE *pinioned, and led betwixt two Officers.*

Richard. Now, tell us, Rufford, which of these it is,
    That in the heat of his upheavèd spleen,
    Condemns our crown, disdains our dignity,
    And arms himself against authority.
Rufford. Both have offended, my dread sovereign,   5
    Though not alike; yet both faults capital.
    These lines declare what, when, and where it was.
                    [*Gives document to the King.*]
Richard. Which is that Aire?
Rufford.   This young man, my liege.
Richard. I thought it was some hot, distempered blood,

---

1. *Richard.*] *Qq have speech prefix Glo. throughout the scene.*

That fired his giddy brain with business.   10
   Is thy name Aire?
Aire.   It is.
Richard.   This paper says so.
Aire. Perish may he, that made that paper speak.
Richard. Ha! Dost thou wish confusion unto us?
   This paper is the organ of our power,
   And shall pronounce thy condemnation: 15
   We make it speak thy treasons to thy face,
   And thy malicious tongue speaks treason still.
   Relievst thou Shore's wife, in contempt of us?
Aire. No; but her just desert.
   She saved my life, which I had forfeited,   20
   Whereby my goods and life she merited.
Richard. And thou shalt pay it, in the self-same place
   Where thou this man, our officer, didst outface,
   And scorned us; saying, if we stood by,
   Thou wouldst relieve her.
Aire.   I do it not deny.   25
   For want of food, her breath was near expired;
   I gave her means to buy it, undesired;
   And rather choose to die for charity,
   Than live condemnèd of ingratitude.
Richard. Your good devotion brings you to the gallows.   30
   He hath his sentence. Rufford, see him hanged.
                They [Officers] lead out AIRE.
   Now, sir, your name?
Shore.   Is it not written there?
Richard. Here's 'Matthew Flood'.
Rufford.   That is his name, my lord.
Richard. Is thy name Flood?
Shore.   So Master Rufford says.
Richard. Flood and Aire? The elements conspire   35
   In air and water, to confound our power.
   Didst thou relieve that hateful wretch, Shore's wife?
Shore. I did relieve that woeful wretch, Shore's wife.
Richard. Thou seemst a man well staid, and temperate;
   Darst thou infringe our proclamation?   40
Shore. I did not break it.
Rufford.   Yes, and added more:
   That you would answer it before the King.

Shore. And added more: you would repent the thing.
Rufford. Who, I? His highness knows my innocence
   And ready service, with my goods and life.   45
   Answer thy treasons to his majesty.
Richard. What canst thou say, Flood, why thou shouldst
   not die?
Shore. Nothing; for I am mortal, and must die
   When my time comes. But that, I think's, not yet;
   Although, God knows, each hour I wish it were,   50
   So full of dolour is my weary life.
   Now say I this: that I do know the man
   Which doth abet that traiterous libeller,
   Who did compose and spread that slanderous rhyme
   Which scandals you, and doth abuse the time.   55
Richard. What libeller? Another Collingbourne,
   That wrote: *The Cat, the Rat, and Lovell, our Dog,*
   Do rule all England, under a Hog?
   Canst thou repeat it, Flood?
Shore. I think I can, if you command me so.   60
Richard. We do command thee.
Shore.   In this sort it goes:
   The crook-backed Boar the way hath found
   To root our Roses from our ground.
   Both flower and bud will he confound,
   Till king of beasts the swine be crowned.   65
   And then the Dog, the Cat, and Rat,
   Shall in his trough feed and be fat.
   'Finis', quoth Master Fogge, chief secretary and
   counsellor to Master Rufford.
Richard. How sayst thou, Flood? Doth Rufford foster this?
Shore. He is a traitor if he do, my lord.   70

56–8. *Collingbourne . . .* Hog] Holinshed (lll. 422) records the first two
lines of this verse, together with some disparaging remarks about how the
metrical demands of the libel required the versifier to substitute 'hog' for the
'boare' which should have represented Richard. The chronicler goes on to
suggest that the efforts of this 'poeticall schoolemaster' caused Collingbourne, a 'poore' but rebellious 'esquier' from Wiltshire, 'to be abbreuiated
shorter by the head, and to be diuided into foure quarters'; Collingbourne
was actually executed for treasons more serious than the penning of satirical squibs.

Rufford. I foster it? Dread lord, I ask no grace
    If I be guilty of this libelling.
    Vouchsafe me justice, as you are my prince,
    Against this traitor that accuseth me.
Shore. What justice cravst thou? I will combat thee;   75
    In sign whereof I do unbutton me,
    And in my shirt my challenge will maintain.
    Thou callst me traitor; I will prove thee one.
    Open thy bosom, like me, if thou darst.
Rufford. I will not be so rude before his grace.   80
Shore. Thou wilt not ope the pack of thy disgrace,
    Because thy doublet's stuffed with trait'rous libels.
Richard. Catesby, tear off the buttons from his breast.
    What findst thou there?
Catesby.   Your highness' hand and seal,
    For transportation of hides, corn and lead.   85
Richard. Traitor, did I sign that commission?
Rufford. O pardon me, most royal King.
Richard. Pardon? To counterfeit my hand and seal?
    Have I bestowed such love, such countenance,
    Such trust on thee, and such authority,   90
    To have my hand and signet counterfeit?
    To carry corn, the food of all the land,
    And lead, which after might annoy the land,
    And hides, whose leather must relieve the land,
    To strangers, enemies unto the land?   95
    Didst thou so nearly counterfeit my hand?
Rufford. Not I, my liege, but Fogge, the attorney.
Richard. Away with him! Lovell and Catesby, go:
    Command the sheriffs of London presently
    To see him drawn, and hanged, and quartered.   100
    Let them not drink before they see him dead.
    Haste you again.
                  LOVELL *and* CATESBY *lead out* RUFFORD.
Rufford.   Well, Flood, thou art my death.
    I might have lived t' have seen thee lose thy head.
Shore. Thou hast but justice for thy cruelty
    Against the guiltless souls in misery.   105
    I ask no favour, if I merit death.
Richard. Cravst thou no favour? Then I tell thee, Flood,
    Thou art a traitor, breaking our edict,

By succouring that trait'rous quean, Shore's wife;
And thou shalt die.
Shore.   If I have broke the law.   110
Richard. If, traitor? Didst thou not give her thy purse?
And dost thou not maintain the deed?

Enter LOVELL *and* CATESBY *again.*

Shore.   I do,
If it be death, to the relenting heart
Of a kind husband, wrongèd by a king,
To pity his poor, weak, seducèd wife,   115
Whom all the world must suffer, by command,
To pine and perish for the want of food.
If it be treason for her husband, then,
In the dear bowels of his former love,
To bury his own wrong and her misdeed,   120
And give her meat whom he was wont to feed,
Then Shore must die; for Flood is not my name,
Though once I took it to conceal my shame.
Pity permits not injured Shore pass by,
And see his once loved wife with famine die.   125
Richard. Lovell, and Catesby, this is Shore, indeed!
Shore, we confess that thou hast privilege,
And art excepted in our proclamation,
Because thou art her husband, whom it concerns;
And thou mayst lawfully relieve thy wife,   130
Upon condition thou forgive her fault,
Take her again, and use her as before.
Hazard new horns! How sayst thou? Wilt thou, Shore?
Shore. If any but your grace should so upbraid,
Such rude reproach should roughly be repaid.   135
Suppose, for treason that she lay condemned:
Might I not feed her till her hour of death,
And yet myself no traitor for it?
Richard.   Thou mightst.
Shore. And why not now? O, pardon me, dread lord:
When she hath had both punishment and shame   140
Sufficient, since a king did cause her blame,

112–3. I do . . . heart] *One line in Qq.*

May I not give her food to save her life,
Yet never take and use her as my wife?
Richard. Except thou take her home again to thee,
    Thou art a stranger, and it shall not be;   145
    For, if thou do, expect what doth belong.
Shore. I never can forget so great a wrong.
Richard. Then never feed her, whom thou canst not love.
Shore. My charity doth that compassion move.
Richard. Move us no more. Lovell, let Aire be hanged,   150
    Just in the place where he relieved Shore's wife.
    Shore hath his pardon for this first offence:
    The name of husband pleads his innocence.
    Away with them. Catesby, come you with us.
                        Exeunt [several ways].

[Scene 22]

> JOCKIE *is led to whipping over the stage, speaking some*
> *words, but of no importance. Then is young* AIRE *brought*
> *forth to execution, with the* SHERIFF *and Officers;*
> MISTRESS SHORE *weeping, and* MASTER SHORE
> *standing by.*

Aire. Good Mistress Shore, grieve me not with your tears,
    But let me go in quiet to mine end.
Jane. Alas, poor soul!
    Was never innocent thus put to death.
Aire. The more's my joy, that I am innocent;   5
    My death is the less grievous, I am so.
Jane. Ah, Master Aire, the time hath been ere now,
    When I have kneeled to Edward on my knees,
    And begged for him that now doth make me beg.
    I have given him, when he hath begged of me,   10
    Though he forbids to give me, when I beg.
    I have, ere now, relieved him, and his,
    Though he and his deny relief to me.
    Had I been envious then, as Richard now,
    I had not starved; nor Edward's sons been murdered;   15
    Nor Richard lived to put you now to death.

7–12. *time . . . his*] No chronicle accounts offer evidence to support Jane's
claim that she had interceded with Edward on Richard's behalf.

Aire. The more, Jane, is thy virtue, and his sin.
Sheriff. Come, sir, dispatch.
Aire. Dispatch, say you? Dispatch you may it call:
    He cannot stay, when death dispatcheth all.   20
Jane. Lord, is my sin so horrible and grievous,
    That I should now become a murderer?
    I have saved the life of many a man condemned,
    But never was the death of man before.
    That any man thus, for my sake, should die,   25
    Afflicts me more than all my misery.
Aire. Jane, be content.
    I am as much indebted unto thee
    As unto nature. I owed thee a life,
    When it was forfeit unto death by law: 30
    Thou beggedst it of the King, and gavst it me.
    This house of flesh, wherein the soul doth dwell,
    Is thine, and thou art landlady of it;
    And this poor life a tenant, but at pleasure.
    It never came to pay the rent till now,   35
    But hath run in arrearage all this while,
    And now, for very shame, comes to discharge it,
    When death distrains for what is but thy due.
    I had not owed thee so much as I do,
    But by thy only mercy to preserve it,   40
    Until I lose it for my charity.
    Thou givst me more than ever I can pay.
    Then, do thy pleasure, executioner.
    And now farewell, kind, virtuous Mistress Shore;
    In heaven we'll meet again, in earth no more.   45

             Here he is executed.

Jane. Farewell, farewell! Thou for thy alms dost die,
    And I must end here, starved in misery.
    In life my friend, in death I'll not forsake thee;
    Thou go'st to heav'n, I hope to overtake thee.
Shore. O world, what art thou? Man, even from his birth,   50
    Finds nothing else but misery on earth.

---

36. *arrearage*] arrears.
38. *distrains*] seizes by legal process.
48. *In*] as in.

Thou never, world, scorndst me so much before,
But I, vain world, do hate thee ten times more.
I am glad I feel approaching death so nigh;
World, thou hatest me; I thee, vain world, defy.   55
I pray you yet, good master officers,
Do but this kindness to poor wretched souls,
As let us have the burial of our friend;
It is but so much labour saved for you.
Sheriff. There, take his body. Bury it where you will,   60
So it be quickly done, out of the way.
                                        Exit SHERIFF *and Officers.*
Jane. What's he that begs the burial of my friend,
And hath so oftentimes relievèd me?
Ah, gentle sir, to comfort my sad woe,
Let me that good, kind man of mercy know.   65
Shore. Ah, Jane, now there is none but thou and I.
Look on me well. Knowest thou thy Matthew Shore?
Jane. My husband? Then break heart, and live no more.

        She swoons, and he supports her in his arms.

Shore. Ah, my dear Jane, comfort thy heavy soul.
Go not away so soon, a little stay,   70
A little, little while, that thou and I
Like man and wife may here together die.
Jane. How can I look upon my husband's face,
That shamed myself, and wrought his deep disgrace?
Shore. Jane, be content. Our woes are now alike: 75
With one self rod thou see'st God doth us strike.
If for thy sin, I'll pray to heaven for thee,
And if for mine, do thou as much for me.
Jane. Ah, Shore, is't possible thou canst forgive me?
Shore. Yes, Jane, I do.
Jane.   I cannot hope thou wilt: 80
My fault's so great that I cannot expect it.
Shore. I' faith, I do, as freely from my soul
As at God's hands I hope to be forgiven.

---

68. heart] *Q4–6; omitted in Q1–3.*

76. *self*] same.

Jane. Then God reward thee, for we now must part:
    I feel cold death doth seize upon my heart.   85
Shore. And he is come to me. Lo, here he lies;
    I feel him ready to close up mine eyes.
    Lend me thy hand, to bury this, our friend,
    And then we both will hasten to our end.

Here they put the body of young AIRE *into a coffin,*
and then he sits down on the one side of it, and she
on the other.

    Jane, sit thou there, here I my place will have.   90
    Give me thy hand. Thus we embrace our grave.
    Ah, Jane, he that the depth of woe will see,
    Let him but now behold our misery.
    But be content. This is the best of all:
    Lower than now we are, we cannot fall.   95
Jane. Ah, I am faint. How happy, Aire, art thou,
    Not feeling that, which doth afflict us now.
Shore. O happy grave, to us this comfort giving!
    Here lies two living dead, here one dead, living.
    Here, for his sake, lo, this we do for thee: 100
    Thou lookst for one, and art possessed of three.
Jane. O, dying marriage! O, sweet married death!
    Thou grave, which only shouldst part faithful friends,
    Bringst us together, and dost join our hands.
    O, living death! Even in this dying life,   105
    Yet, ere I go, once, Matthew, kiss thy wife.

He kisses her, and she dies.

Shore. Ah, my sweet Jane, farewell, farewell, poor soul.
    Now, tyrant Richard, do the worst thou canst:
    She doth defy thee! O, unconstant world,
    Here lies a true anatomy of thee: 110
    A king had all my joy, that her enjoyed,
    And by a king again she was destroyed.
    All ages of my kingly woes shall tell;
    Once more, inconstant world, farewell, farewell.
                                He dies.

86. Lo] *Q4–6; omitted in Q1–3.*

Enter SIR ROBERT BRACKENBURY, *with two or three of*
his servants.

Brackenbury. Sirs, if the King, or else the Duke of
    Buckingham   115
    Do send for me, I will attend them straight.
    But what are these, here openly lie dead?
    O God! The one is Mistress Shore! And this is Flood,
    That was my man. The third is Master Aire,
    Who suffered death for his relieving her.   120
    They shall not thus lie in the open way.
    Lend me your hands, and heavy hearts withal;
    At mine own charge, I'll give them burial.
                            They bear them hence [*Exeunt*].

[Scene 23]

    Enter KING RICHARD *crowned,* BUCKINGHAM, ANNE *of*
    Warwick, LOVELL, CATESBY, FOGGE *and attendants.*

Richard. Most noble lords, since it hath pleasèd you,
    Beyond our expectation on your bounties,
    T'empale my temples with the diadem,
    How far my quiet thoughts have ever been
    From this great and majestic sovereignty,   5
    Heaven best can witness. Now, I am your king;
    Long may I be so, to deserve your love.
    But, I will be a servant to you all;
    Pray God my broken sleeps may give you rest.
    But only that my blood doth challenge it,   10
    Being your lawful prince by true succession,
    I could have wished—with all my heart I could—
    This majesty had sitten on the brow
    Of any other!
    So much do I affect a private life,   15
    To spend my days in contemplation.
    But since that heaven, and you, will have it so,
    I take the crown as meekly at your hands,
    As free and pure from an ambitious thought,
    As any new born babe. [*Aside*] Thus must thou, Richard,   20

0.1. ANNE] *Q5; Aire Q1–4.* 5. this great] *Q1–3;* this so great *Q4–6.* 6.
Now] *Q4–6; omitted Q1–3.* 14–15. Of . . . life] *One line in Qq.*

Seem as a saint to men, in outward show,
Being a very devil in thy heart.
Thus must thou cover all thy villanies,
And keep them close from overlookers' eyes.
Buckingham. My sovereign, by the general consent   25
Of all the lords and commons of the land,
I tender to your royal majesty
This princely lady, the lady Anne of Warwick,
Judged the only worthiest of your love,
To be your highness' bride, fair England's queen.   30
Richard. My royal, princely cousin Buckingham,
I see you strive to bless me more and more.
Your bounty is so large and ample to me,
You overflow my spirits with your great love.
I willingly accept this virtuous princess,   35
And crown her angel beauty with my love.
Lovell. Then, as the hand of your high parliament,
I give her here unto your majesty.
Richard. Lord Lovell, I as heartily receive her.
Welcome, fair queen.   40
Catesby. And from the lords and commons of your land,
I give the free and voluntary oath
Of their allegiance to your majesty,
As to their sovereign and liege lord and lady,
Richard the Third, and beauteous Anne, his queen,   45
The true and lawful King and Queen of England.
Richard. I do accept it, Catesby, and return
Exchange of mutual and party love.
Now, Fogge too; that in your traitorous libels,
Besides the counterfeiting of our hand and seal   50
For Rufford, though so great a fault deserved
To suffer death, as he already hath,
Going about to slubber our renown,

---

48. *party*] Apparently means 'equal' but *OED* records neither this or any
similar adjectival use of the word; all examples are not only obsolete by 1600
but imply division or separation.

49–57. *Fogge . . . thee*] More (81/31–82/2) records the ostentatious hand-
shake with which the King forgave Fogge, and notes that 'wise men tooke it
for a vanitye'.

53. *slubber*] disfigure; cf. Scene 20, l. 100.

And wound us with reproach and infamy,
Yet, Fogge, that thou thyself mayst plainly see   55
How far I am from seeking sharp revenge,
Fogge, I forgive thee. And, withal, we do
Repeal our heavy sentence 'gainst Shore's wife,
Restoring all her goods; for we intend
With all the world now to be perfect friends.   60
Catesby. Why, my good lord, you know she's dead already.
Richard. True, Catesby, else I ne'er had spoke such words.
                                        Aside.
Alas, I see our kindness comes too late,
For Catesby tells me she is dead already.
Catesby. Ay, my good lord, so is her husband too.   65
Richard. Would they had lived to see our friendly change.
But, Catesby, say: where died Shore and his wife?
Catesby. Where Aire was hanged for giving her relief.
There both of them, round circling his cold grave
And arm in arm, departed from this life.   70
The people, for the love they bear to her
And her kind husband, pitying his wrongs,
For ever after mean to call the ditch
Shores' Ditch, as in the memory of them.
Their bodies, in the Friars' Minories   75
Are in one grave interred all together.
But Mistress Blage, for her ingratitude
To Mistress Shore, lies dead, unburied,
And no one will afford her burial.
Richard. But Mistress Blage, she shall have burial too.   80
What, now? We must be friends, indeed we must!
And now, my lords, I give you all to know,
In memory of our eternal love,

---

77. her] *Q4–6; omitted Q1–3.*

71–4. *people . . . them*] The playwright departs from both More—in whose
account Mistress Shore is said to have lived on in poverty into the early
sixteenth century—and from Stow; he has a testy marginal note insisting
(correctly) that 'Soerditch so called more then 400. yeares since, as I can
prove by record', *Survey*, II, 74. See Introduction, p. 57.

75. *Friars' Minories*] Former site of a convent. In the time of the play the
Minories was the name of a street about a mile south of Shoreditch, con-
necting Houndsditch and the Tower—and a two-minute walk from the Boar's
Head playhouse; see Introduction, pp. 3, 21.

I do ordain an Order of the Bath;
Twelve knights, in number of that royal sort,   85
Which order, with all princely ceremonies,
Shall be observed in all royal pomp,
  As Edward's, our forefather, of the Garter;
Which feast, our self, and our beloved queen,
Will presently solemnize in our person.   90
Buckingham. Now am I bold to put your grace in mind
Of my long suit, and partly your own promise:
The Earl of Hereford's lands.
Richard.   Cousin,
  We'll better think on that hereafter.
Buckingham. My pains, my lord, hath not deserved delay.   95
Richard. Will you appoint our time? Then ye shall stay;
For this hot hastiness, sir, you shall stay.
Move us no more, you were best.
Buckingham. Ay, Richard, is it come to this?
In my first suit of all, dost thou deny me,   100
Break thine own word, and turn me off so slightly?
[*Aside*] Richard, thou hadst as good have damned thy soul,
As basely thus to deal with Buckingham.
Richard, I'll sit upon thy crumped shoulder;
I' faith, I will, if heaven will give me leave.   105
And, Harry Richmond, this hand alone
Shall fetch thee home, and seat thee in his throne.
                                        Exit.
Richard. What? Is he gone? In heat? Why, farewell, he.
He is displeased. Let him be pleased again;
We have no time to think on angry men.   110
Come, my sweet queen, let us go solemnize
Our Knighthhood's Order, in most royal wise.
                                        Exeunt.

FINIS

93. lands] *Q1–2*; land *Q3–6*.

84–5. *Order . . . Twelve*] As the chronicles report, Richard invested eighteen (not twelve) knights into the Order just before his coronation, but he
did not 'ordain' it; the Order took on its name and procedure at the coronation of Henry IV. The most expansive account of its ceremonies is in
Middleton's *Civitatis Amor* (1616), in *Works*, VII, 282ff.
  112. *wise*] fashion, manner.

Index

Note: Part, scene and line citations refer to the playtext and the commentary; other citations are to the Introduction.

ghostly father, *One* 11.92
gibbet, *One* 10.13
giff, *One* 22.45
gin, *Two* 15.9
ginger, *One* 23.79
God's blue bodkin, *One*
    11.134
good sadness, *One* 3.32, 17.142
gorgets, *One* 3.0.2
Great Chronicle, 13–14, 25
great-shot, *Two* 4.46.03
groundsills, *Two* 1.13
guerdon, *Two* 2.87
Guildhall, *One* 7.16
Guyenne, *Two* 2.14

ha and ree, *One* 13.9
halidom, *One* 13.36, 18.77
halt, *Two* 4.72
halting, *One* 11.64
Ham, *One* 3.41
hangings, *Two* 13.82
hap, *One* 17.60
hardly, *Two* 18.202
hauds, *One* 22.46
Hayward, Sir John, 18–19
Helgerson, Richard, 15, 55
Henslowe, Philip, 1–6, 8–11
Hippocras, *One* 2.70
holidame, *One* 11.111
Holinshed, Raphael, 12, 25, 53
Hood, Robin, 32–5, 37, 40
Houndsditch, *One* 6.4
humour, *One* 1.61, 9.39, 13.17,
    16.181

immovèd, *One* 19.95
impeach, *One* 6.19
in fee farm, *Two* 15.34
infuse, *One* 5.16
interview, *Two* 9.62

intestine, *One* 18.11; *Two* 2.110
it gives me, *Two* 4.247

jade, *One* 1.64
jerk, *One* 10.20
jobbed faces, *One* 11.34
justly, *Two* 20.216

ken, *Two* 4.118
Kirkman, Francis, 9
kiss the post, *One* 13.96
knobs, *One* 23.144
knowledge, *One* 23.9; *Two* 4.121

Langley, Francis, 3–4
launch, *Two* 9.74
Leadenhall, *One* 2.53
Leather industry, 28–30, 35–6
let, *One* 9.172
let the world slide, *One* 11.78
lewd, *Two* 7.63
liberality, *One* 23.124
light, *One* 4.54
lin, *Two* 20.76
Lion Quay, *One* 17.24
liquorish, *One* 14.70
Lombard Street, *One* 9.20; *Two*
    13.84
loser, *One* 17.113
lottest, *One* 10.81
loun, *One* 22.46
Lownes, Humfrey, ix, 5, 61–2,
    64

magnanimous, *Two* 2.9
maintain, *One* 16.123
maister, *Two* 20.260
malt pies, *One* 2.86
mandrakes, *Two* 17.33
marks, *One* 10.139, 18.37
mask, *One* 11.19.02, 22.2.02

Printed in the USA
CPSIA information can be obtained
at www.ICGtesting.com
JSHW011452261124
74350JS00003B/213

9 780719 080647